THE ROAD TO THE DAYTON ACCORDS

THE ROAD TO THE DAYTON ACCORDS

A STUDY OF AMERICAN STATECRAFT

Derek Chollet

First published in hardcover in 2005 by PALGRAVE MACMILLAN® in the United States—a division of St. Martin's Press LLC, 175 Fifth Avenue, New York, NY 10010.

Where this book is distributed in the UK, Europe and the rest of the world, this is by Palgrave Macmillan, a division of Macmillan Publishers Limited, registered in England, company number 785998, of Houndmills, Basingstoke, Hampshire RG21 6XS.

Palgrave Macmillan is the global academic imprint of the above companies and has companies and representatives throughout the world.

Palgrave® and Macmillan® are registered trademarks in the United States, the United Kingdom, Europe and other countries.

ISBN: 978–1–137–34805–0

The Library of Congress has cataloged the hardcover edition as follows:

Chollet, Derek H.
    The road to Dayton : a study in statecraft / by Derek Chollet.
        p. cm.
    Includes bibliographical references (p.) and index.
    ISBN 978-1-4039-6500-4
    1. United States—Foreign relations—Bosnia and Hercegovina. 2. Bosnia and Hercegovina—Foreign relations—United States. 3. Dayton Peace Accords (1995). 4. Yugoslav War, 1991–1995—Bosnia and Hercegovina. 5. Yugoslav War, 1991–1995—Peace. 6. Yugoslav War, 1991–1995—Diplomatic history. 7. United States—Foreign relations—1993–2001. 8. Diplomacy—Case studies. I. Title.

E183.8.B67C58 2005
949.703—dc22   2005047209

A catalogue record for this book is available from the British Library.

Design by Newgen Imaging Systems (P) Ltd., Chennai, India.

First PALGRAVE MACMILLAN paperback edition: August 2013

10 9 8 7 6 5 4 3 2 1

In memory of Andrew Carpendale

CONTENTS

FOREWORD

By

Richard Holbrooke

There were over 30 ceasefires and agreements in Bosnia prior to the Dayton Peace Accords. All of them collapsed. Yet what was agreed upon at Dayton not only survived, it established the basis for a country that, with all its problems, is moving forward, however painfully, towards becoming a peaceful participant in twenty-first-century Europe.

In the ten years since Dayton—the name of the city has become not only a simple shorthand for the entire Bosnian peace process, but an internationally understood metaphor for taking an aggressive, engaged approach to conflict resolution—there have been numerous negotiations in conflict areas around the world which have not been successful, most notably of course, in the Middle East. Dayton, therefore, has contemporary relevance not because of the inherent drama in the negotiation—although there was plenty of that—but because it succeeded; in short, it ended a war.

By the time negotiations began behind a high barbed-wire fence at the Wright-Patterson Air Force Base on November 1, 1995, the Bosnian war had become the worst in Europe since 1945, posing a real and present threat to the stability of post–Cold War Europe. Parts of Bosnia were becoming a sanctuary for Islamic terrorists, some of whom belonged to an organization whose name was still unknown in the West, Al-Qaeda. Criminal gangs ran much of the country, sometimes pretending to be nationalist movements. The Bosnian Serbs were openly seeking the destruction of Europe's largest Muslim community in an ancient homeland—a clear case of genocide. And most Bosnian Croats would not have objected if the Serbs had succeeded. A "war within a war" between Croats and Muslims had destroyed most of the once beautiful medieval city of Mostar and its historic bridge. Refugees by the hundreds of thousands had fled to Western Europe, overburdening the resources of countries such as Germany, Switzerland, and Austria.

Yet, for the four preceding years, the European Union and the United States had done little to stop the war. Their mediation efforts were puny and poorly coordinated; NATO was involved only as an accessory to a pathetic UN effort, which the UN's own Secretary General, Boutros Boutros-Ghali, did everything he could to hamper and undermine. Both Washington and Brussels refused to even threaten, let alone use, decisive force against Bosnian Serb aggression. In 1993, when President Clinton briefly considered a more aggressive policy (as he had called for as a candidate the previous year), a majority of Congress, as well as most of the American military, led by a towering Washington figure, the Chairman of the Joint Chiefs of Staff, General Colin Powell, arrayed themselves in opposition. Even after the Dayton Accords ended the fighting almost three years later, an overwhelming majority of the American public still opposed using U.S. troops to help enforce the peace and there were predictions, many from leaders of the foreign policy elite, that Dayton would fail, and that in any case it was not worth its risks and costs.

My generation had been taught in school that Munich and the Holocaust were the benchmark horrors of the 1930s. Leaders of the Atlantic alliance had repeatedly pledged it would never happen again. Yet between 1991 and 1995 it *did* happen again—not only in the Balkans, but also in Rwanda, where an even greater number of people—an estimated 800,000—were killed for purely ethnic reasons in an even shorter period of time.

Bosnia was, as I wrote at the time, "the greatest collective security failure of the West [in Europe] since the 1930s." Rwanda was even worse. How could all this have happened at the end of the twentieth century, in the middle of Europe—and could it happen again?

BOSNIA CANNOT BE UNDERSTOOD except in its precise historical context: the pre–September 11, 2001, world. In the decade before 9/11, Americans had turned away from the outside world after 60 years of continuous and expensive international involvement, from Pearl Harbor to the disintegration of the Soviet Union at the end of 1991. Americans were proud, of course, that their sacrifices had succeeded in defeating both fascism and communism during that long period, but they were exhausted and ready to turn inward.

Of course, we will never know what America would have done if Bosnia had occurred after September 11, 2001—9/11 made Americans far more willing to support American military interventions in faraway lands, not only in a situation as clear-cut as Afghanistan, but even in Iraq, which had no involvement in the terrorist attacks on New York and Washington. But, as Derek Chollet reminds us in this book, we are dealing here with pre–9/11 realities. It was not a coincidence that the three greatest disasters of international peacekeeping, disasters that almost brought the United Nations down—Somalia, Rwanda, and Bosnia—all occurred in the decade between the end of the Cold War and 9/11; call it, if you will, "the interwar years."

Sometimes, however, a horrific event can force even the most reluctant people to action. In the summer of 1995, over 7,000 Muslims, including some women and children, were butchered in an isolated town in eastern Bosnia called Srebrenica, while UN peacekeepers from The Netherlands stood by helplessly and NATO refused to intervene. I argued then, and still believe today, that NATO airstrikes would have stopped the Bosnian Serbs, who preferred long-range artillery and short-range murder to anything resembling a real military operation. But London, Paris, and The Hague were fearful for the safety of their own troops, and refused suggestions for military actions until their forces had left the three "safe areas" they had pledged to protect.

President Clinton recognized immediately that, although the American people still would not like it, the United States could no longer avoid involvement. His choice boiled down to this: either assist the UN peace-keeping force in a humiliating withdrawal, or else make an all out American effort to end the war on terms that protected the beleaguered Muslim community.

So in August 1995, President Clinton launched the diplomatic effort described in vivid detail in this book. It must be stressed that, at the time we began our shuttle diplomacy, no one in Washington imagined that the diplomatic effort would be accompanied by a NATO bombing campaign. That was a result of two events that occurred in the first few days of our travels: the death on Mount Igman on August 19 of three of the five members of my original negotiating team—Bob Frasure, Joe Kruzel, and Nelson Drew—and the Sarajevo marketplace shelling nine days later. These two events rocked the administration (the men who died were extremely popular in Washington, and we paid them emotional farewells at Arlington Cemetery), and changed, in intangible ways, Washington's sense of personal involvement in the war. After the funerals, President Clinton immediately sent me back to the Balkans with a new team, including then Lt. General Wesley Clark, my military advisor and original team member who represented the Joint Chiefs of Staff; Chris Hill, a State Department colleague then on the cusp of a brilliant diplomatic career; Jim Pardew, a tough former Army officer representing the civilian side of the Pentagon; then Brigadier General Donald Kerrick, representing the White House; and Roberts Owen, our wise legal advisor whom we affectionately called "mad dog."

WHAT IS REMARKABLE, especially in hindsight, is that strong political opposition to putting American resources, especially troops, into Bosnia continued even after a combination of American airpower and American leadership brought the war to a negotiated conclusion at Dayton. Despite this agreement, which achieved all of the primary objectives of the United States and Europe, there were questions from almost every quarter of the American body politic about President Clinton's decision to send 20,000 American troops to Bosnia as part of the 60,000-strong NATO implementing force. In a national poll taken right after Dayton, only 36 percent of the American public supported sending troops; it was by far the lowest support that President Clinton had on any issue at that time.

Opposition to the deployment was fueled by widespread predictions that Dayton would fail, and that, after the disastrous and bloody experience of the UN peacekeeping force in Bosnia, American casualties would be similarly heavy. "It's not going to work," said America's most respected senior statesman, Henry Kissinger, summarizing a widely held view just after the agreement had been signed. "When you're asking Americans to die, you have to be able to explain it in terms of the national interest. I see no vital United States interest to support a combat mission there." A month later, Kissinger changed his position, but only slightly. "The only valid purpose for American troops in there," he said, "is to move into a demilitarized zone between the warring parties. . . . We should not risk American lives in nation-building, peacemaking, creating political institutions." His comments were echoed by many on both the liberal and conservative sides of the political spectrum.[1]

The opposition did not let up. In a stunning repudiation of the Administration, the House of Representatives—Newt Gingrich's House, with its Contract for America calling for a strong American national security policy—approved by a lopsided vote of 287 to 141 a bizarre resolution opposing the President's Bosnia policy but "supporting the troops."[2] During the debate, members of Congress waved copies of *Time* Magazine, its cover story captioned, "Is Bosnia worth dying for?" In a comment typical of the hostility among most Republicans,[3] Senator Phil Gramm from Texas attacked the Dayton agreement almost as soon as it was signed. "Adding American names to the casualty lists cannot save Bosnia," he said.

There was also trouble in the Pentagon. Secretary of Defense Bill Perry publicly predicted casualties on roughly the same scale as the 1991 war against Iraq, or the failed UN peacekeeping mission in Bosnia. The American military feared Bosnia would be another quagmire. For the older officers, including the Joint Chiefs of Staff themselves, Vietnam was a distant but ever present ghost. (My own three years there, as a Foreign Service Officer working on the pacification effort in the Mekong Delta and Saigon, had marked me deeply, but I felt that the differences between Vietnam and Bosnia were fundamental.) The most notable exceptions were Wesley Clark, who had very close ties to Powell's successor as the Chairman of the Joint Chiefs, General John Shalikashvili, and Donald Kerrick, then on the NSC staff. Clark and Kerrick understood the issues well, and argued courageously with officers senior in rank over the need for very strong "rules of engagement" for NATO.

It therefore took real political courage for President Clinton to send American troops to Bosnia. This was the most important decision in regard to Europe of his presidency; opposed, incidentally, by most of his political advisors. Bill Clinton has not received as much credit as he deserves for this classic Commander-in-Chief decision, which he made alone, without Congressional support, and only reluctant backing from the Pentagon. But it worked; without those 20,000 troops, Bosnia would not have survived, several million refugees would still be wandering the face of Western Europe today, a criminal state would be in power in parts of Bosnia itself—and we would probably have fought Operation Enduring Freedom not only in Afghanistan but also in the deep ravines and dangerous hills of central Bosnia.

LARGE NUMBERS OF BODY BAGS—as always, the exact number was a closely guarded military secret—had been prepared for the casualties that the Pentagon believed were certain to come. But in the end, *none* of the body bags were ever used for combat related deaths; not one NATO soldier was killed from hostile action in Bosnia. This was due, in large part, to the authority given to NATO in the Dayton agreement: to shoot first and ask questions later—the exact opposite of the sorry rules of engagement under which the UN peacekeeping mission had operated and suffered so many casualties.

NATO was thus respected from the very beginning—a vital lesson, I hope, for any future operations involving international peacekeepers.

SEVEN YEARS AGO, I wrote, "On paper, Dayton was a good agreement; it ended the war and established a single multiethnic country. But countless peace agreements have survived only in history books as case studies in failed expectations. The results of the international effort to implement Dayton would determine its true place in history."

Events since support this view. *Vigorous implementation is the key to the success of any ceasefire or peace agreement.* One cannot depend on the voluntary compliance or goodwill of recently warring parties. Force must be used, if necessary (and better early than late) to demonstrate that the agreement must be respected and will be enforced. And while Bosnia is at peace today and moving slowly forward, it would be in much better shape if the initial implementation effort had been more aggressive. "The start," as I wrote at the time, "was rocky."

The international community, including, I regret to say, NATO, did not use its authority enough in the crucial initial phase, the months right after Dayton. NATO was fine in force protection—that is, protecting itself—an important and necessary goal, particularly if compared to the substantial American casualties suffered in Afghanistan and Iraq. But several failures of the NATO command left a permanent mark on the land, inhibiting more rapid progress even today. The first and most important was the failure not to seek the immediate arrest of the two leading Bosnian Serb war criminals, Radovan Karadzic and General Ratko Mladic. These two men, who were still at large ten years later, were most vulnerable right after Dayton, but the opportunity was essentially lost after the NATO commander in Bosnia, U.S. Admiral Leighton Smith, told Bosnian Serb television, "I don't have the authority to arrest anybody." This statement, which was a deliberately incorrect reading of his authority under Dayton, constituted a devastating invitation to Karadzic to resume his political activities, which he did with a vengeance until a subsequent agreement, which I negotiated in the summer of 1996, finally drove him underground. Incredibly, as of the summer of 2005, Karadzic was still moving secretly across the Balkans, supported and hidden by a network of Serb sympathizers that undoubtedly included core members of his political party, the SDS as well as hard-core monks in the Serb church. His continued freedom, no matter how constrained, was a daily challenge to progress in Bosnia. (After President Clinton left office, he told me that he considered Smith's behavior to have verged on "insubordination.")

The lesson is, I hope, clear: once the United States is committed in such a perilous project, it cannot afford halfway, tentative measures—"in for a dime, in for a dollar," sums it up accurately. To this day, this lesson has not been applied adequately in the Balkans.

IN HINDSIGHT, there were many other things we could have done better before, during, and after Dayton. I still regret, for example, agreeing to let the Bosnian Serbs keep the name "Republika Srpska" for their entity. Bosnian President Alija Izetbegovic was right when he told me it was a "Nazi name"; we should have tried harder to change it, for practical and symbolic reasons. On the other hand, I should not have acceded to a strange Izetbegovic request, nine months after Dayton, to allow the SDS (Karadzic's party) to remain a legal party. Instead, we should have disenfranchised it before the first Bosnian elections in September 1996, despite Izetbegovic's statement to me that, while he hated the SDS, he "could work with them." Two weeks before he died, lying in a hospital bed in Sarajevo in October 2003, he told me that he thought I was "joking [in 1996] about dismantling the SDS." If that was the real reason for his position against shutting down that criminal party, it was a costly misunderstanding. The SDS has been the main promoter of divisive ethnic politics in Bosnia, while providing the core of the network that has protected Karadzic. If we had banned it and forced it underground, things would be better today, even if parts of it resurfaced under a different name.

A serious mistake was permitting one country to have three armies. It is obvious that such a situation cannot be allowed in a single country. But in 1995, NATO refused to accept responsibility for dismantling the three ethnic armies and creating a single, integrated force, something General Clark and I thought was eminently possible. Yet the NATO high command inaccurately thought it would be dangerous work and refused to allow it in the Dayton agreement. In recent years, NATO belatedly recognized the necessity of dealing with this problem, and has begun slowly to integrate the army, creating a single defense ministry and an integrated senior staff and command. But under the 2005 reorganization, units are still organized on an ethnic basis at the battalion level. This is not a true solution to the problem. The military—and the police, whose reform has been even more difficult—must eventually be organized without regard to ethnicity down to the lowest levels if Bosnia is ever to function without an international security force.

At the end of 2004 that international security presence was transformed from a NATO force (SFOR) into a European Union force (EUFOR). This received almost no attention in the United States, and not much in Europe. But it represented a major evolution, not only in Bosnia but in regard to the NATO–EU relationship. I felt at the time that NATO's departure (except for a small NATO "office") should not have taken place until Karadzic and Mladic were in custody. Yet the pressure of deployments in Iraq and Afghanistan far larger and longer than anticipated was taking its toll on the American military, and Secretary of Defense Donald Rumsfeld insisted on the change, despite quiet misgivings expressed by Bosnians. Ironically, the change also suited the long-term French goal of reducing the EU's dependency on NATO, and thus made Rumsfeld and French President Jacques Chirac unlikely bedfellows on this issue. EUFOR deserves close study to see if it works, but its initial affect was clearly unfortunate: it left the impression that the United States, the only power universally respected in the Balkans, was starting to depart, thus giving encouragement to the obstructionists in Srpska and weakening moderates everywhere.

In the spring of 2005, the new Secretary of State, Condoleezza Rice, placed Balkan policy (including Kosovo) in the hands of her Undersecretary of State, Nicholas Burns, a highly capable professional diplomat who had been at Dayton. This upgrading of the importance of the region—which Rice and Burns confirmed to me in private meetings—was welcome news in a region that respects the United States above all other nations, because without a revitalized American policy, Bosnia and Kosovo will drift aimlessly.

I HOPE STUDENTS of conflict resolution will examine the Dayton negotiations carefully, not because they were successful, but to learn what might be applied to other problems. Of course, few other negotiators will have the added leverage that comes with bombing one of the parties, and not all negotiators will be able to lock up the leaders of the contending sides on an American military base. But much can be accomplished without such unusual incentives. To me, the key ingredient is leadership—determined leadership from the world's leading nation, with the clear backing of its allies. Assembling and holding together a coalition of friends is sometimes harder than fighting an enemy, as the current U.S. Administration learned in Iraq. It is often forgotten that it was not easy in Bosnia either; as this book shows, frictions within the Contact Group and the NATO alliance were at times almost unbearable. But the effort has to be made, for the returns are enormous, especially when there is an expectation that other countries will foot the larger part of the reconstruction or nonmilitary bill. This was, of course, the case in Bosnia, as it is in most other parts of the world today, notably including Africa.

It was a huge honor to be part of the team that ended the war in Bosnia—and to have a role in the dramatic events that Derek Chollet skillfully chronicles in the pages to follow. Like the band of brothers Henry V spoke to before the battle of Agincourt, whatever else we do, each of us will remember those amazing days for the rest of our lives.

TEN YEARS AFTER SREBRENICA, on July 11, 2005, I found myself back in that valley of evil, as part of the official American delegation appointed by President George W. Bush to represent the nation. It was a moving moment; I walked through muddy hills under a leaden sky as widows and mothers buried almost 700 recently identified remains, their grief undiminished by a decade.

But there had definitely been progress. When I had last visited Srebrenica five years before, ten brave—one might say, recklessly brave—Muslim families had returned, living among 12,000 Serbs who had taken over old Muslim houses. By July 2005, however, over 4,000 Muslims had returned and an equal number of Serbs had left. This was astonishing, and more of the same seemed certain if the international community stayed involved.

It was also a day filled with irony and high drama. From Belgrade and Banja Luka came senior Serb leaders who laid wreaths at the memorial, an appropriate silent acknowledgment of a great war crime. Our route into

Srebrenica, and the security itself, was the responsibility of the entity we were in, which happened to be the Republika Srpska. The police—presumably including some who had been involved in the murderous events of 1995— were respectful, if not exactly enthusiastic; they saluted as we passed and, more importantly, treated the endless line of victim families with correct politeness. An event that could have exploded into violence was incident-free (although a large bomb had been found at the site a few days earlier).

Unfortunately, it was also a day for hypocrisy. Senior European, American, and international officials spoke, some apologizing for the past failures, all pledging, as usual, that it must never ever happen again—and that the hunt for Karadzic and Mladic would be pursued with implacable determination. Then they got into their sedans and helicopters and went home.

AUTHOR'S NOTE

This is the story of how the United States led the effort to end the Bosnian war and forge the Dayton Peace Accords in 1995. It is an account of high-stakes international diplomacy, the pressure-cooker of complex negotiations, and the pushing and pulling of Washington's intense bureaucratic struggles. It is also a tale of many extraordinary American public servants who reversed years of disappointment and frustration by working tirelessly to bring peace to Bosnia. Their efforts restored pride and confidence in American leadership. But most important, they gave millions of people in Bosnia reason to hope for a better life and an opportunity to build a peaceful future.

This book originated as an internal study written under the auspices of the U.S. Department of State during 1996–1997, as part of a special historical effort directed by the Bureau of Public Affairs and the Office of the Historian. This unique initiative collected and organized thousands of documents and conducted numerous interviews with American officials to create a government archive of materials concerning the Bosnia peace process. After assisting with creating a documentary collection of materials from the State Department, National Security Council, Defense Department, CIA, and other agencies, I wrote an original manuscript based on its contents, which aimed to shed light on the bureaucratic and diplomatic process behind a difficult policy problem and, eventually, a major success. The draft study was completed in May 1997, declassified and released by the Department of State in 2003, and is now available to researchers through the nonprofit National Security Archive in Washington, DC.

Based on these original sources, this book is a shorter, substantially revised version of the key decisions and events that led to the 1995 Dayton peace agreement. It includes many new insights and information from recent memoirs and studies, as well as follow-up interviews with several of the key participants—it is therefore a far more comprehensive account. The endnotes cite hundreds of documents that, unfortunately, still remain classified, and are therefore unavailable for other scholars to review at the moment (the citations themselves reveal no secrets). Although it is uncommon for a book to be based on still-classified records—and to provide specific citations of such records as sources—it is not unprecedented. Two other histories of major American diplomatic efforts, Philip Zelikow and Condoleezza Rice's account of Germany's unification, *Germany Unified and Europe Transformed*, and Ronald Asmus's book on NATO enlargement, *Opening NATO's Door*, are also based on government records that remain classified but available to cite.

Like them, I have tried wherever possible to reference public materials along with the official documents—and the vast majority of information presented here can be cross-checked with these open sources.

THIS BOOK WOULD NOT HAVE BEEN possible without extraordinarily generous assistance from many others. That begins with thanks to an institution, the U.S. Department of State, which launched the effort to create a documentary archive and oral history of the Bosnian peace process. This initiative serves as but one example of the State Department's commitment to understanding the past to draw lessons that, hopefully, can be applied to today's challenges. I am deeply indebted to my former colleagues who helped create the archive of materials upon which much of this book is based and who proved indispensable to the drafting of the original study. First and foremost Bennett Freeman, who began as my boss and editor, became my valued career advisor and colleague, and remains as all of these—but is most importantly my friend. Also, I thank Chris Hoh, David Goldman, Pat Attkisson, William Slany, Paul Claussen, Scott Zeiss, and Steven Engel for all of their help.

Several American participants in the negotiations read all or parts of the original draft manuscript, and their thoughtful recommendations and insights proved essential. Richard Holbrooke, Chris Hill, Chris Hoh, Rosemarie Pauli, Phil Goldberg, William Burns, John Kornblum, and Miriam Sapiro all read my work with considerable care. I am similarly indebted to Robert Jervis, Jim Goldgeier, and Melvyn Leffler, three scholars who generously provided their comments and suggestions during two lively day-long seminars to discuss the draft study.

During the long process of transforming the internal study into this book, I incurred even greater debts. The greatest are those owed to three remarkable American diplomats and public servants, Warren Christopher, Richard Holbrooke, and Strobe Talbott. They are central players in this story, and I am deeply grateful for all their support. Each read and commented on this book with their customary insight, wisdom, and sound judgment. By giving me the opportunity to work with them in government, and to assist them with their own books, I learned a great deal not only about many of the events described here, but the history and practice of American statecraft and the importance of public service. I am especially grateful to Richard Holbrooke, who has added his own important perspective by writing the foreword to this book.

Jim O'Brien's advice and wise counsel have guided me throughout the writing of this manuscript, and together with Mark Ramee, he helped shepherd the original study through the declassification process. I appreciate Bennett Freeman for once again deploying his editing pen with skill and candor, Debbie Isser and Laurel Miller for walking me through the thickets of post–Dayton Bosnia, and Jim Goldgeier for his return to service by reading some of the new chapters, and especially for his continuing friendship. Jason Forrester provided many helpful comments on several sections of the book, and Warren Bass helped me think about the triage of Dayton. Ivo Daalder's own work on this subject has helped clarify my thinking about many parts of this story, and his comments on a draft of this book were greatly appreciated. My many conversations over the years with Ivo and other friends like Tom Donilon, Jim Steinberg, John Bass, John Norris, Phil Goldberg, and Ron Asmus improved my understanding of these events. I appreciate the support and encouragement from my colleagues at CSIS, especially Kurt Campbell and Julie Smith, who helped push this project across the finish line. Ashley Bommer and Loretta Graham were indispensable to moving things forward, doing so with good cheer. And my thanks go to David Pervin and the team at Palgrave Macmillan for their talents and, most important, their patience.

This book is far better because of this help from others, but its shortcomings are mine. And while based on thousands of the State Department documents and interviews with current and former government officials, the views, opinions, and especially mistakes expressed here are my own and do not necessarily reflect the official views of the Department of State or the U.S. government.

I would not have survived this process if not for the warm support, good humor, strong shoulders, (and technical assistance!) of friends like John Norris, Jason Forrester, and Adam Hostetter; my parents, Ray Chollet and B.J. Brittenham; and most important my wife, Heather Hostetter, who is my best friend and greatest love. She suffered through my distractions and helped in many essential ways, from editorial to emotional. Without her this book would not have been possible.

Finally, this book is dedicated to the memory of my friend Andrew Carpendale. We all miss him.

D.C.
Washington, DC
August 2005

PROLOGUE: AMERICA AND THE BOSNIA NIGHTMARE

From 1991 to 1995, the crisis in Bosnia cast a dark shadow over American foreign policy. All other accomplishments abroad during those years were diminished by Bosnia's bleeding. This shattered the world's confidence in American leadership and power. It also spoiled the hopes of many for a new Europe and a transformed U.S.-European relationship. When the war erupted in 1992, the European powers saw an opportunity to test their mettle, and to increase the influence of their fledgling political bloc then known as the European Community (EC). As Luxembourg's Foreign Minister and EC President Jacques Poos famously said at the time, "the hour of Europe has dawned." Yet as time went on, Europe's response proved feckless, and the introduction of European troops under a United Nations mandate did little to stop the horrendous bloodshed. By the spring of 1995, as the crisis threatened to spin out of control, nearly 300,000 people had been killed, and 1.2 million were refugees.

The United States had initially encouraged the Europeans to take the lead in Bosnia—in former Secretary of State James A. Baker III's equally famous phrase, the United States did not think it "had a dog" in the Bosnian fight. American leaders were focused on other challenges like the end of the Soviet empire, the 1991 Persian Gulf war, the unification of Germany, and the Middle East peace process. They also failed to foresee how bad the conflict could get.

But in early 1993, the Clinton Administration took office, and it came with a new resolve—and the baggage of bold campaign promises—to end the war in Bosnia. President Bill Clinton described Bosnia as a measure not just of his foreign policy, but of what role the United States would play in the post–Cold War era. As his first Secretary of State, Warren Christopher, put it in February 1993, Bosnia "tests our ability to adopt new approaches to our foreign policy in a world that has fundamentally changed. It tests our commitment to nurturing democracy . . . it tests our willingness to help our institutions of collective security, such as NATO, evolve in ways that can meet the demands of the new age. . . . We cannot afford to miss any further opportunities to help pursue a resolution to this conflict."[1]

Unfortunately, for the next two-and-a-half years, the United States did not live up to this lofty rhetoric. It missed many opportunities to end the conflict. Indeed, the American view of Bosnia during this period is best summed up by another quotation from Christopher: it was the "problem from hell." The Clinton Administration made several attempts to jump-start the diplomatic process. It pushed for NATO airstrikes to enforce UN Security Council Resolutions. It tightened the economic noose around the perpetrators. It worked with its European allies to help negotiate a settlement. But every effort, no matter how well intentioned, ran into the ceiling of political will. The United States did not want to engage in Bosnia if it meant accepting significant costs, whether measured by money, political capital, or especially American lives.

THIS DEPRESSING HISTORY makes the 1995 transformation of American policy—in which the Clinton Administration turned away from disengagement to use America's military might, political prestige and diplomatic skill to forge the Dayton peace accords and a lasting peace in Bosnia—truly remarkable. A decade later, in the wake of the September 11 attacks, the wars in Iraq and Afghanistan, and the global fight against terrorism, it is indeed difficult to recall how wrenching Bosnia was, and how important Dayton would be not just for the future of Europe, but for America's leadership in the world.

From 1991 to 1995, Bosnia was the defining issue for the United States in the post–Cold War era. For nearly three years, the Clinton Administration's struggles with the crisis illustrated its own deep uncertainties, and degree of ambivalence, about America as a global power. Yet in the course of six months between June and November 1995, President Clinton and his team dramatically reversed months of indecision by setting a bold course, defying expectations both in the risks they undertook and the success they achieved. It is important to remember how and why they found this resolve, how they implemented it, and how difficult their effort proved to be. Because while many challenges now seem far different, the lessons from this story—whether concerning the use of force, managing the Transatlantic alliance, asserting American leadership to solve conflicts, or conducting complex international negotiations—still influence the history that is being made today.

YUGOSLAVIA FALLS APART

The Bosnia crisis began with the 1991 breakup of Yugoslavia, a country of six republics—Bosnia-Herzegovina, Croatia, Serbia, Macedonia, Slovenia, and Montenegro—that had been cobbled together in the wake of World War I.[2] The small country sat at the intersection of three imperial expansions: Orthodox Christianity, the Muslim Ottoman Empire, and the Catholic Holy Roman Empire. For more than seven decades, Yugoslavia's rich ethnic and religious diversity remained stable, led for most of that time by a single leader, Josef Broz Tito. Although a communist autocrat, Tito had broken with the Soviet Union in 1948 and enjoyed special status in the West. Half Slovene and half Croat, Tito himself embodied the complex unity of his country—it was often said that Yugoslavia had six republics, five nations, four languages, three religions, two alphabets, and one Tito.

Yugoslavia's troubles began after it lost its "one Tito." Following his death in 1980, the country stayed together by a fragile consensus of shared power among its six republics. Yet as economic hardship set in, its leaders turned to nationalism and accentuated ethnic and religious differences, and as a wave of independence movements swept across Europe after the fall of the Berlin Wall in 1989, pressures increased within each republic to break away from Yugoslavia. The first two republics to go were Slovenia and Croatia, which declared independence in June 1991. Fighting broke out immediately to bring these breakaway republics back in to the fold. In Slovenia, light battles between the Yugoslav national army and Slovene troops lasted for ten days, in what became known as a "phony war." As a Catholic country with very few Serbs (the dominant ethnic group in Yugoslavia), Slovenia had traditionally been the most "Western" republic and the most remote from the central government in Belgrade, so it was in many ways the easiest to let go.

Croatia was a different story. Unlike Slovenia, Croatia had thousands of Serbs that lived within its borders—Serbs who not only feared living as a minority under an independent regime based in Croatia's capital, Zagreb, but who aspired to live apart from Croatia as a unified "Greater Serbia." Intense fighting broke out between Croatian nationalists and the Serb-dominated Yugoslav national army, backed by Serbian leader Slobodan Milosevic, which aligned with local Serb insurgents within Croatia. The fighting was especially brutal as the Serbs worked to "liberate" their lands from Croatia. By November 1991, Croatia had lost two key areas to Serb forces—the Krajina region and Eastern Slavonia—in what to that point was the bloodiest fighting Europe had witnessed since the end of World War II.

Led by the Europeans, the international community launched a diplomatic effort to end the fighting or at least prevent it from spreading. The EC dispatched envoys to negotiate a cease-fire, which began at the end of 1991. By early 1992, the Europeans recognized the independence of Croatia and Slovenia. Also by that time, the international community had made two major decisions in response to the bloodshed: to impose a United Nations mandated arms embargo on the entire region, and to deploy 12,000 troops as part of a UN protection force (in what became known as UNPROFOR) to provide humanitarian relief and keep the peace in Serb-controlled areas of Croatia—nearly 30 percent of the country's territory.

U.S. PRESIDENT GEORGE H.W. BUSH and his Administration were happy for the Europeans to assume the lead in this effort, limiting America's own actions to little more than supportive votes in the UN Security Council. "During the summer and fall of 1991, it has been fair enough to give the European Community a chance to what it called a 'European problem,' " the last U.S. Ambassador to Yugoslavia, Warren Zimmermann, later wrote.[3] But as tensions simmered and finally boiled over in a third Yugoslav republic—Bosnia—the United States began to take notice. Bosnia was the most diverse republic of the former Yugoslavia (roughly 44 percent Muslim, 31 percent Serb, and 18 percent Croat), and many feared the consequences of its explosion.

In March 1992, the Muslim-led Bosnian government in Sarajevo declared independence, which both the United States and Europeans quickly recognized. Soon fighting raged between the Bosnian government forces and Bosnia's Serbs, headquartered in Pale, an alpine village that had been the venue for the 1984 Olympic skiing competition. Sarajevo came under ruthless Serb attack. Backed again by Milosevic, the Bosnian Serbs fought not to keep Bosnia together, but to carve out their own state (which they called Republika Srpska). They killed and brutalized thousands of Muslims, driving them from their homes in an effort to achieve "ethnic cleansing."

By the summer of 1992, images of Bosnian Muslim men in concentration camps shocked the world, finally forcing the Bush Administration to act. Bosnia had become, in Secretary of State Baker's words, a "humanitarian nightmare." Washington joined with the European governments to impose comprehensive economic sanctions on Milosevic's Serbia, cut off diplomatic ties, and organize a humanitarian relief effort to get supplies into Sarajevo. But they stopped short of any greater commitment—they considered threatening airstrikes against the Serbs, but decided that it posed too great a risk. Despite Bosnia's horrors, the Bush Administration did not believe that the United States should take military action. As Baker later wrote, "President Bush's decision that our national interests did not require the United States of America to fight its fourth war in Europe this century . . . was absolutely the right one."[4]

President Bush's opponent in the 1992 presidential election, the young Arkansas Governor, Bill Clinton, disagreed. For both policy and political reasons, he wanted to outflank Bush on Bosnia. During the campaign, he hammered Bush on his inaction, arguing that the President was "turning his back" on human rights and needed to show "real leadership." Clinton supported airstrikes against the Serbs and lifting the arms embargo to help the Bosnia Muslims, who were hurt most by the embargo because the Bosnian Serbs were supported by Milosevic. He promised that if elected, he would make the United States a "catalyst for a collective stand against aggression." After his victory in November, Clinton had an opportunity to put these words into action.[5]

A ROUGH START

Forging a tougher Bosnia policy as President turned out to be much harder than candidate-Clinton had imagined. The proposals he promoted met stiff resistance from the Europeans, who had troops on the ground as part of the UN force and were pursuing their own diplomatic approaches to solve the problem. After months of what Clinton's first UN Ambassador, Madeleine Albright, remembered as "rambling and inconclusive meetings about the crisis we had inherited," in May 1993 Clinton decided to pursue a policy of "lift and strike"—lifting the UN arms embargo against the Bosnians and threatening NATO airstrikes against the Serbs. He dispatched Secretary of State Christopher to Europe to consult with the allies to get them on board.

But Christopher's trip was a failure. The Europeans had no stomach for lift and strike, and the Clinton Administration had no stomach to implement the policy alone or risk rupturing Transatlantic relations. As Clinton put it, "we have bigger fish to fry with the Europeans."[6]

After this episode of what one historian describes as "blunderbuss diplomacy," the best the United States could do was to get the Europeans to agree to protect six UN-declared "safe areas" in Bosnia—Muslim enclaves threatened by the Serbs—with NATO airstrikes.[7] UNPROFOR forces composed mostly of European troops would be deployed in these enclaves to ensure that humanitarian supplies could be delivered. Yet to extract European agreement, the Clinton Administration had to accept a complex arrangement for authorizing airstrikes, with the decision shared by both the UN civilian leadership and NATO. Under this "dual key," both organizations would have to agree—and therefore they both would have a veto—over whether, when, and where airstrikes could be launched. Under these convoluted rules, swift and sustained actions would be very difficult, and some feared that these "safe areas" would become little more than shooting galleries.

These new policies were tough to negotiate, but they did little to end the bloodshed. The war raged on, leaving American policymakers frustrated. Warren Christopher remembered that these early efforts to deal with the crisis "affected the course and content of our diplomacy there over the next two years . . . we kept coming back to the core questions about acceptable risk and political will." They might have wanted to do more, but did not want to do it alone for fear of undermining larger interests, such as the cohesion of the NATO alliance or the future of the UN. And they were unwilling to put America's own military forces on the ground. As President Clinton wrote in his memoirs, "I was reluctant [to unilaterally lift] the arms embargo, for fear of weakening the United Nations. I also didn't want to divide the NATO alliance by unilaterally bombing Serb military positions . . . And I didn't want to send American troops there, putting them in harm's way under a UN mandate I thought was bound to fail." With all these options off the table, Clinton admitted that after a year in office, "we were still a long way from a solution."[8]

PROGRESS AND SETBACKS

Throughout 1994, American officials struggled to solve these dilemmas, but still could not find the will or the way to do so. With such self-imposed constraints, they ended up just trying to make it through one crisis before bracing for the next. As Albright recalled, "we employed a combination of half-measures and bluster that didn't work." However, at times events forced them to take action, and they did have some modest successes. For example, in February 1994, the Bosnian Serbs shelled an outdoor Sarajevo marketplace, killing 68 people. During the previous two years, the fighting in the Bosnian capital had already killed 10,000 people, but this slaughter of innocent men, women, and children—the aftermath of which had been filmed by television cameras and beamed around the world—could not be ignored. The Clinton Administration responded to this outrage by demanding that the Serbs withdraw from their positions in the mountains around the city or face NATO airstrikes. After intense negotiations with the Europeans, NATO delivered its ultimatum. The Serbs began withdrawing, temporarily lifting the siege of Sarajevo.[9]

No longer satisfied to leave the negotiating to the Europeans, the Clinton Administration also became more active diplomatically. This started with brokering an agreement to create an alliance between Bosnia's Muslims and Croats. While the Bosnian Serbs had successfully captured 70 percent of Bosnia's territory, the Muslims and Croats were fighting over what remained. The Sarajevo leadership deeply distrusted the Bosnian Croats, who were supported by Croatia's government in Zagreb. This had led to significant bloodshed itself, and it also further fueled Serb aggression. With a divided adversary, the Bosnian Serbs had little incentive to negotiate, and they pressed their military advantage.

The Clinton Administration believed that for peace to have any chance, the Muslims and Croats had to cooperate politically, economically, and most important, militarily. "From our perspective," Secretary of State Christopher later wrote, "the two sides needed to turn their energies against the stronger and more threatening adversary, the Bosnian Serbs." During early 1994, the United States worked intensely to bring both sides together, concluding an agreement in March to create a Muslim–Croat Federation. This Federation (which would have economic links with Croatia) would control about half of Bosnian territory and exist alongside a Bosnian Serb entity in a unified Bosnian state. Although criticized by some observers as a "shotgun wedding" amounting to "nothing more than a glorified cease-fire," the Americans believed that the Muslim–Croat alliance was the only chance for the Muslims in Bosnia to develop the resources to balance Serb power. While many questions remained about how the Federation would work in practice, especially with such deep suspicions between both sides, the administration considered this partnership a significant step forward.[10]

PRESIDENT CLINTON and his team also worked to forge greater international unity to solve the crisis. That spring, the United States joined with Germany, France, the United Kingdom, and Russia to create a five-nation "Contact Group" to coordinate strategies and create a common policy. By July 1994, the Contact Group had come up with a peace plan and a detailed map that placed 51 percent of Bosnia under Federation control, leaving 49 percent for the Bosnian Serbs. Many of the specifics were left for direct negotiations by the parties, which the Contact Group would mediate. The Croats and Muslims immediately accepted the plan (seeing that they would get back nearly 20 percent of the territory they had lost), while the Bosnian Serbs refused to sign on without adding conditions that would render it meaningless. For the remainder of the year, the Contact Group struggled to get these negotiations on track, pressuring Milosevic to convince his Bosnian Serb patrons to agree. But they had little success.

MEANWHILE, the fighting intensified on the ground, and in November 1994 a UN "safe area" in western Bosnia named Bihac came under a vicious Bosnian Serb assault. Concerned that this might lead to a major escalation of the war—and further humiliation of the international community—the United States again pressed for NATO airstrikes against the Serbs. In late November, NATO launched limited air attacks against Serb positions in Bosnia and an airfield across the border in a Serb-controlled part of Croatia. While these "pin-prick" airstrikes were hardly decisive, the Europeans feared retaliation against their troops in the UN force on the ground, and refused to agree to further attacks. The French (who had about 7,000 troops in UNPROFOR) and the British (who had 4,000) were the most resistant. Worried that the issue could destroy the veneer of Contact Group unity—or worse, rupture the NATO alliance—the Clinton Administration pulled back from its demand for military force. The Bosnians ended up hanging on to Bihac, but the damage was done.

Despite success in brokering the Muslim–Croat Federation and helping create the Contact Group and its plan, the Clinton Administration's Bosnia policy ended the year basically where it had begun: without a diplomatic initiative, without the threat of military action, and without much credibility to deliver on either. In fact, at the end of 1994 the Administration and its European allies were at such a deadlock that it took former United States President Jimmy Carter, an outsider acting on his own, to negotiate a four-month cease-fire agreement between the parties. As Ivo Daalder, a National Security Council official at the time, later wrote, President Clinton's "policy toward Bosnia had reached a virtual dead end."[11]

THE CONFLICT RESUMES . . . AND AMERICA'S POLICY CRATERS

After this winter of frustration, the Clinton Administration entered the spring of 1995 with an approach toward the conflict criticized as unfocused, uninspired, and unprincipled. Newspaper editorials declared that Bosnia was in a "freefall," and the Administration seemed to be unable to define a coherent policy, let alone pursue one.[12] Led by the United States, the international community appeared only capable of carrying out policies to contain and limit the Bosnian tragedy, not end it.

Hoping to find a way forward, the Clinton Administration focused its efforts on negotiating with the parties on the basis of the Contact Group plan. Tired of the Bosnian Serbs' unwillingness to come to the table, they turned to Serbian President Milosevic to force them to do so. Robert Frasure, the Principal Deputy Assistant Secretary of State for European Affairs and the American envoy to the Contact Group, met with Milosevic numerous times in Belgrade throughout the spring. Instead of the sticks of airstikes, Frasure carried only carrots. He offered Milosevic partial relief from economic sanctions in return for recognition of a single Bosnian state and pressure on his rebel Serb clients to begin serious negotiations. But Frasure's talks had stalled over the mechanism for reimposing the sanctions should Milosevic not live up to his end of the deal.[13]

As FRASURE'S EFFORTS inched along, the Clinton Administration's policy, pungently described by Director of Central Intelligence John Deutch as "muddle through," appeared increasingly untenable. The month of May brought what Madeleine Albright later called the "return to hell." On April 30, the four-month "Carter cease-fire" ended, and fighting broke out throughout Croatia and Bosnia. A week later, Bosnian Serbs began to shell Sarajevo. Acting with UN authority, NATO planes responded to the Bosnian Serb attacks with another limited air campaign against Serb ammunition dumps and weapons.[14]

But having stared down the international community before, the Bosnian Serbs had become increasingly bold in their defiance of the United Nations peacekeeping forces. To retaliate against the NATO strikes, the Bosnian Serbs took hundreds of UNPROFOR troops hostage, chaining them to ammunition dumps and bridges that were the targets of NATO attacks. By late May, over 350 UN peacekeepers, including French and Canadian soldiers, were detained at gunpoint by the Bosnian Serbs. These "human shields" were prominently displayed before television cameras. Horrified and humiliated, European leaders and UN officials refused to turn their "keys" and allow further airstrikes. The UN issued new guidelines for airstrikes: "the security of the United Nations personnel took priority over UNPROFOR's mandate in Bosnia," essentially giving the Bosnian Serbs an invitation to thwart the UN's peacekeeping mission further. The Europeans also began to discuss openly the withdrawal of their troops. They had become increasingly weary of the hostage-taking, potential casualties, the sharp criticisms by the Western press, and the perception that the UN mission was only delaying the inevitable victory of the Bosnian Serbs. If there was no hope to solve the conflict, the Europeans wanted out.[15]

THE HOSTAGE CRISIS summoned the end of America's brief diplomatic effort, leaving Milosevic emboldened. Frasure informed Washington that "Milosevic's position in this complicated game has been immensely strengthened, and he is well aware of that fact." Concerning future negotiations, Frasure explained, "we face a stark choice: either we back off from these talks—and run the risk that either the Russians/British/French fill the vacuum—or we agree to pay the Balkan political hit man the price he now demands for his promise to resolve our Bosnia problem."[16] Christopher solicited the views of his Contact Group counterparts about next steps, explaining that "Milosevic might interpret Frasure's continued presence in Belgrade as a sign of our urgent need to conclude the talks on terms increasingly acceptable to Serbia."[17] Given the Serb leader's unrelenting intransigence, the Clinton Administration decided to call it quits and bring Frasure home. Although Frasure's talks were officially characterized as "at a standstill," in fact, the Americans let the Europeans, led by their new EU-appointed negotiator, former Swedish Prime Minister Carl Bildt, assume primary responsibility for the negotiations. Few expected any breakthroughs.[18]

WITH THE SITUATION on the ground deteriorating, military power stifled by the "dual key," and the diplomatic track on life-support, the Clinton Administration grew increasingly worried that it might soon have to send in ground forces to help its European allies withdraw. The reason was a decision it had made months earlier—a decision that had more to do with salvaging the Transatlantic alliance than bringing peace to Bosnia. In December 1994, right after the crisis in Bihac, President Clinton decided that should the situation on the ground prevent UN peacekeepers from carrying out their mission, American troops should be part of a NATO force to help UNPROFOR leave Bosnia. The reason for this remarkable decision, as a senior Administration official explained at the time, was to demonstrate "that the United States will assist our allies if their forces are in danger."[19]

By the spring of 1995, NATO's military planners in Brussels had created a detailed, 1,300 page operational plan to facilitate UNPROFOR's withdrawal. NATO's plan—called Op-plan 40104—called for as many as 20,000 American troops to participate as part of a 60,000-soldier withdrawal force. Wesley Clark, then an Army Lieutenant General and a senior planner on the Joint Chiefs of Staff, described this as a "major effort . . . with a real possibility of conflict during and after the withdrawal. It was the equivalent of a major war plan." For years, the Americans resisted putting troops on the ground in Bosnia. Now, because of a decision whose implications were still not widely understood throughout the highest levels of the Administration, they had made exactly the kind of commitment they had long sought to avoid. As Carl Bildt described it: "This was the perfect military plan for a major political disaster."[20]

American officials realized that they were in a dangerous bind. As President Clinton's National Security Advisor, Anthony Lake, recalled, "We all agreed that [UN] collapse would mean that American troops would have to go into Bosnia in order to rescue UNPROFOR, which meant that we were going in the context of a defeat. And nobody wanted that."[21]

But how could they prevent this? Perhaps they could convince their European partners to keep their troops on the ground, hoping that the situation stabilized. Or maybe they should simply throw in the towel and push for the UN mission's collapse, lifting the arms embargo and leaving the Balkan parties to fight it out on their own. Or possibly they could pursue the option that seemed the most remote: try to forestall the UN's withdrawal by pushing the parties toward peace—preferable to Op-plan 40104, but would require a major political and diplomatic commitment and likely still demand American troops to enforce a settlement. None of these choices were particularly appealing, and none would be easy to implement. All carried significant costs and risks. As spring turned to summer, the Clinton Administration knew that it faced a moment of decision. Few imagined the transformation of America's approach that lay ahead.

1

OVER THE WATERFALL:
MAY–JULY 1995

As the Clinton Administration's frustration with its Bosnia policy grew, the process to change that policy ground to a halt. Tough choices are often the enemy of quick decision-making—and concerning Bosnia, the options during the spring of 1995 could hardly have been less appealing. In meeting after meeting, senior Administration officials debated every angle of the crisis, but since they could not even agree on what they wanted to achieve, these discussions always ended up where they started.

For weeks, the National Security Council's top European experts, Alexander (Sandy) Vershbow and his deputy, Nelson Drew, an Air Force Colonel who had just joined the NSC staff, had been looking for ways to maneuver out of this dead end.[1] "Now is the time to review the fundamental principles guiding our policy and to determine the steps necessary to shape events before strategic choices are completely dictated by the situation on the ground," Drew wrote in an internal paper designed to probe the Administration's policy options and frame the basic choices it faced. With UN's military mission badly crippled, Drew argued that it remained in America's interest to try to save it: "U.S. interests are best served by finding a way to restore credibility to the UNPROFOR mission in a manner that permits existing troop contributors to sustain their continued presence and the Bosnian government to agree to retain that presence."[2]

President Clinton's senior foreign policy advisers discussed many of the points Drew outlined at a May 23 White House meeting of the Principals Committee—or as it was known throughout the bureaucracy, the "PC."[3] They confronted the particulars of a post-UNPROFOR withdrawal strategy: what to do about the arms embargo, possible arming and training of Bosnian forces, and future NATO airstrikes. Although the bureaucratic wheels began turning on these issues, the Principals still could not come up with more than "muddle through." They only agreed on what they wanted to prevent: U.S. troops going into Bosnia. To avoid this, they needed to make a concerted effort to press the Europeans to keep their forces in the game.[4]

ACROSS THE ATLANTIC, the newly elected French President, Jacques Chirac, had already begun maneuvering to do just that. Often called the "bulldozer" for his unsubtle style, he used his first day on the job to make his presence felt, responding angrily to published pictures of French UNPROFOR soldiers being held hostage and chained to ammunition dumps by Bosnian Serb troops. "I will not accept this," he screamed at his aides. "You can kill French soldiers! You can wound them! But you cannot humiliate them! That will end today . . . we will change the rules of the game!"[5]

The new French Foreign Minister, Herve de Charette, began laying the groundwork to change these rules in a series of phone calls with Secretary of State Christopher in late May. Chirac, de Charette told Christopher, was anxious to make specific recommendations "to prevent the further humiliation of UNPROFOR forces."[6] President Chirac followed up with a May 27 phone call with President Clinton, explaining that the UN forces had to be leaner and meaner: "we need to change its mission, give it more weapons, consolidate the forces in less vulnerable positions, and let them defend themselves."[7]

Only minutes after he hung up with Chirac, Clinton called British Prime Minister John Major, who expressed his support for the French view in principle. But the two leaders shared concerns about Chirac's plan: Clinton worried that if UNPROFOR consolidated forces (as the UN Commanders on the ground in fact wanted to do), the Bosnian Serbs may perceive a "green light" to take the areas it left vulnerable; Major wanted more on Chirac's specifics. "What does he mean by UNPROFOR being beefed up?" Major asked Clinton. "Is this putting people in place to withdraw? [My agreement] depends on what Chirac means by beefing up."[8]

These discussions concluded with a British and French proposal to create a "Rapid Reaction Force" (RRF) of up to 10,000 heavily armed troops that could be deployed to defend the 24,000 UN peacekeepers from Serb attacks. Some American officials were skeptical that this new muscle would be enough either to help the UN militarily or bolster the resolve of its civilian leaders to stand up to the Serbs. Yet they hoped that it would at least deter the Serbs from further humiliating UNPROFOR. But if these forces failed to invigorate the UN mission, few doubted that the Europeans would withdraw their troops before the next Balkan winter.[9]

THE AIR FORCE ACADEMY SPEECH

In the meantime, the Americans and their European allies still faced an immediate crisis. The RRF was only an idea, and they had to decide how—if at all—they would help protect UN troops currently in harm's way. And they did not know how long they could continue to push for NATO airstrikes. Despite NSC meetings and memos, the Clinton Administration still didn't have any answers. At the end of May, Christopher planned to attend a NATO ministerial meeting in The Netherlands, and at the very least, he needed a unified American position to present to the Europeans. On Sunday, May 28, he went to the White House to get one.

Christopher wore the strains of Bosnia more visibly than most of his colleagues, perhaps because of the pummeling he had taken on the issue as the nation's top diplomat, especially after his difficult May 1993 mission to

Europe. Having served as Deputy Attorney General under President Lyndon Johnson and Deputy Secretary of State under President Jimmy Carter, he was in many ways the elder statesman of Clinton's Cabinet. While not in government, he had been a prominent lawyer practicing in Los Angeles. Yet other than his exquisitely tailored suits, Christopher hardly had any of southern California's indulgent flashiness; his personality and style were more reminiscent of his native North Dakota—modestly savvy, quietly confident, and cautiously pragmatic. He doubted whether the American people were prepared for the sacrifices required to end a war that presented no direct threat to U.S. security. Yet he worried about the impact the crisis was having on the Clinton presidency, and was deeply frustrated by the administration's lurching and disorderly policymaking process.

AT THIS SUNDAY MEETING of the Principals Committee in the White House Situation Room, chaired by Deputy National Security Advisor Sandy Berger in Tony Lake's absence, Christopher joined Secretary of Defense William Perry and Army General John Shalikashvili, the Chairman of the Joint Chiefs of Staff, in agreeing to what amounted to a retreat. Since UN peacekeepers remained vulnerable to Serb retaliation, they decided to abandon "quietly" their demands for NATO airstrikes. Chirac and Major had recommended this to the President on the phone and in a written proposal sent to the White House. On the question of what to do about UNPROFOR withdrawal, the Principals simply decided to reaffirm their pledge to Op-plan 40104.

Yet as a way to delay full UNPROFOR's collapse from happening, they tried to solve the problem by enlarging it. Perry and Shalikashvili argued that the American commitment to provide troops for the UN's withdrawal should be extended "to apply to assistance and relocation" of UN forces from the isolated eastern Bosnian "safe area" enclaves of Srebrenica, Zepa, and Gorazde. In effect, this actually meant a possible *expansion* of the U.S. military commitment to protect the UN troops—an idea that Christopher warned would not have the support of the Congress or the American people.

But Perry, Shalikashvili, and Lake argued that helping the UN troops relocate to defensible positions might actually prolong the UN's mission, thus delaying a massive U.S. intervention under Op-plan 40104. In a memorandum to President Clinton drafted by the NSC staff, Lake explained that "we don't want to see UN withdrawal from the Eastern enclaves, but if it comes to that, U.S. credibility among NATO Allies would be seriously damaged" if they refused to assist UN forces evacuate from an untenable position and relocate elsewhere in Bosnia. "This would support our main goal," Lake wrote, "of maintaining UNPROFOR presence and making that presence more robust."[10]

PRESIDENT CLINTON AGREED with this controversial decision, taking Lake's advice to announce it publicly in a May 31 speech before the graduating cadets at the Air Force Academy in Colorado. Lake told the President that this was a unanimous recommendation of his advisors, although in fact at least two key players—Christopher and Berger—did not agree, and were not given a chance to tell the President so.

In the speech, Clinton said that the United States should be prepared to "assist NATO if it decides to meet a request from the United Nations troops for help in a withdrawal or a reconfiguration and a strengthening of its forces." He explained that "we have obligations with our NATO allies . . . and I do not believe we can leave them in the lurch." The President qualified this, however, by adding that he would "carefully review" any requests for American ground troops and that any deployment would only be "temporary."[11]

Despite these finely tuned caveats, his statement was widely interpreted as a major change in strategy. It triggered an intense barrage of criticism about the possible introduction of American troops into the region, and the apparent shift in rationale from using troops only to facilitate complete UN withdrawal or monitor a peace settlement. Senate Republican Leader Robert Dole from Kansas, Clinton's likely opponent in the 1996 presidential election, called the statement a "significant policy shift," which was "nothing more than a policy of reinforcing failure."

Although Lake and his staff argued that this supposed "shift" was being blown out of proportion, Christopher complained that this decision had been made behind his back. The President's political advisors were also livid. One of his closest aides, George Stephanopoulos, believed that "the prospect that we'd get drawn into a Balkan ground war looked more likely than ever." The President's top political consultant, Dick Morris, also argued that he had to retract the pledge. "No groundwork had been laid for this hurried statement," he recalled, "and the nation was not prepared for a military involvement reminiscent of Vietnam." He warned the President that "eighty percent of the country is against sending ground troops to Bosnia . . . you don't want to be Lyndon Johnson." At Morris's urging, Clinton scrambled to clarify what he had promised. On June 3, in his weekly Saturday radio address to the nation, Clinton explained that U.S. troops would only be used in one of three ways: to implement a peace settlement, to help withdraw UNPROFOR, or in an emergency extraction operation if UN troops were trapped under siege. This clarification helped resolve the confusion and quiet the political firestorm, but it also reminded everyone on Clinton's senior team of the difficulty of their situation: one way or another, American troops were committed to be on the ground in Bosnia, presenting a great threat to the President's political standing.[12]

THE BULLDOZER COMES TO WASHINGTON

By this point, Clinton was worrying more and more about Bosnia. For years, he had hoped that by some combination of European actions and American diplomatic prodding, "muddling through" would end the war. Yet it was only getting worse. Clinton had entered office as the first post–Cold War president, and he thought that foreign policy would take a back seat to domestic priorities. But here he was, a year before his reelection campaign, and a war in small country in the middle of Europe threatened to consume his Presidency.

The issue was spilling over into the political arena: the flap over the Air Force Academy Speech, the UN hostage crisis, and the recent downing of American F-16 pilot Scott O'Grady by the Bosnian Serbs had focused public attention on the President's much-maligned policy, and criticism from Republican members of Congress had intensified. Recent polls showed that public approval for the President's foreign policy had dropped to 39 percent.[13] Capitol Hill opposition to funding the RRF prevented Clinton from supporting it formally with a UN Security Council vote (under the plan, the United States would have to fund 30 percent of the force, and congressional authorization would be required for such an expenditure).

Clinton was also furious with how decisions about Bosnia were being made. With good reason, he did not feel well served by his senior advisors, believing that their differences and bitter backbiting led to the worst possible outcome: bad decisions badly executed. After the Air Force Academy speech, he called Christopher to complain about the "bad advice" he was getting and to apologize to him for being cut out of the final deliberations that went into the speech. The President implored his team to "figure out how to fix this," complaining mostly to Lake, who he held responsible for such breakdowns.

On June 14, French President Chirac arrived at the White House for his first official meeting with President Clinton. As the President's advisors gathered in the Oval Office to prepare him for the meeting, the usually routine briefing devolved into a tense discussion of Bosnia, reflecting their collective frustration about the policy drift. Chirac's powerful advocacy for a tougher line had "put the Administration in a tight bind," Assistant Secretary of State for Europe Richard Holbrooke recalls, "but one that was important in forcing us to start dealing with the reality . . . that the U.S. could no longer stay uninvolved." Clinton understood this, venting to his aides that "we need to get the policy straight." Vice President Al Gore said that "it's the issue from hell . . . the need for us to protect and preserve the [NATO] alliance is driving our policy." Without action soon, Clinton argued, "we're just going to be kicking the can down the road again." With the situation in Bosnia festering, the West was directionless: "we've got no clear mission, no one's in control of events."[14]

BOSNIA DOMINATED Clinton's discussion with the French leader. Explaining that he had secured the support of Russian President Boris Yeltsin (which the Americans doubted), Chirac pushed for a full American commitment to the RRF. Clinton expressed concern that if they pushed a UN Security Council vote too soon, it would enflame tensions with Congress. Snapping his fingers, he told Chirac that "I would vote like this if I didn't have to get the money [from Congress]. If we voted tomorrow, it could undermine our ability to keep the word of the United States on funding of the RRF, and it could cause more trouble. That is the only issue."

Chirac wanted to take the risk and push for a vote. "There are two problems, political and financial," he said. "Politically, everyone including the Russians is ready to vote for the resolution. The situation in Bosnia being what it is, I think we should approve the resolution tomorrow—that is, before the G-7 summit [scheduled to begin the next day in Halifax, Nova Scotia]." Chirac warned that if the pace slowed at the UN, leaders such as Yeltsin would get more "oxygen" to oppose the RRF. Chirac and Clinton agreed to pursue impromptu negotiations with congressional leaders, particularly Speaker of the House Newt Gingrich and Dole, to "tell them that their behavior is helping the Serbs and not the Bosnians."[15]

THE NEXT DAY, the G-7 leaders met in Halifax for their annual economic summit. Though Bosnia found its way onto the agenda, the summit itself broke little new ground. American officials described the talks as little more than a "hand-wringing session," more pomp and circumstance that would do nothing to change the reality in Bosnia.[16] Along with Russian President Yeltsin (whose country was not yet a G-7 member, but attended as a guest) the leaders called for a moratorium on fighting in the region, recommended a UN Security Council resolution authorizing the RRF, and requested the parties' support for the Contact Group plan. Clinton, for his part, publicly stated that he remained committed to lifting the arms embargo should the UN withdraw. While united in sentiment, the leaders were far from an agreement over how to translate these hopes into reality.[17]

More important was the symbolism of Halifax—and the message this sent to Washington. Participating in his first G-7 summit, Jacques Chirac towered over his counterparts, especially on Bosnia. Chirac's performance personified the contrast between bold French activism and American indecision. During the joint press conference, Chirac seized the center of attention by reading aloud portions of a French intelligence document about the current situation in Bosnia while his fellow leaders strained to look over his shoulder, looking like a supporting cast. Some U.S. officials mused (off the record) that Chirac's grand-standing may have helped to dramatize the converging continental consensus that if the United States wasn't willing to lead on Bosnia, others nations like France would. Chirac himself was amazed by such American disarray and indecision, later saying that the position of leader of the free world was "vacant."[18]

CHOOSING "WATERFALLS" AND SEARCHING FOR A NEW STRATEGY

Throughout Washington, senior officials understood that they had to get control of the situation. Sandy Berger recalled that they had spent weeks "chasing our tails." Deputy Secretary of State Strobe Talbott described the policy process in a way that many of his colleagues—including the President—clearly shared: a "pattern of ad-hockery, of letting tactics, even logistics, totally eclipse strategy." In a June 16 personal note to Christopher, Talbott wrote that "we simply don't have a clear answer in our own minds on what we think we can do in Bosnia . . . the absence of an overarching strategy deserving of the name magnifies the damage we sustain with every tactical shift or setback. We've seen that in spades in the last three weeks; that's the real lesson of the screw-ups over the Air Force speech and Chirac's visit to DC."[19]

Across the government, officials began to meet in small groups—or in some cases act alone—to brainstorm and try to hammer out a new approach. These efforts were kept quiet and conducted outside the formal NSC interagency policymaking process—reflecting the fact that over the previous few months, that process had been unable to produce a viable overall strategy—leaving everyone, from the President on down, anxious to find a way forward.

STROBE TALBOTT ORGANIZED one of these groups. As the Deputy Secretary of State, Talbott was one of the most influential members of Clinton's national security team. While his main identity was as the Administration's "Russia guy" because of his deep experience with the country as a student, writer, and journalist for *Time* Magazine, he also played a prominent role in many other areas, such as NATO enlargement, Haiti, and Bosnia (and later, Kosovo). An extremely effective bureaucratic player and one of the administration's deepest thinkers, he often communicated to his colleagues—especially his boss Christopher and closest NSC ally, Sandy Berger—through detailed, private memos (which came to be called "Strobegrams") that he usually wrote in the wee hours of the morning. Unlike most of his senior colleagues—such as Lake, Christopher, and Defense Secretary Perry—Talbott had a long-standing friendship with Bill Clinton, starting with their student days together at Oxford in the late 1960s. While he was careful about how he used his unique standing, Talbott understood the president's moods and mind as well as anyone. And he had heard directly from Clinton about his frustrations with their approach toward Bosnia.

Over the course of the spring and summer, Talbott hosted several meetings at his home in Washington's Woodley Park neighborhood. Held in the late afternoon, these quiet sessions usually included Berger, Christopher's Chief of Staff Tom Donilon, State's Director of Policy Planning James Steinberg, CIA Director John Deutch, Undersecretary of State Peter Tarnoff, and Leon Fuerth, Vice President Gore's National Security Advisor. Before these "non-meetings," Talbott would seek Christopher's advice on the questions to raise, and then provide Christopher with what he called a "non-record" report afterward.[20]

The most important of these meetings took place on June 20, when Berger, Deutch, Donilon, Fuerth, and Steinberg sat down in Talbott's spacious backyard and discussed Bosnia over bagel chips and bottled water. After consulting with Christopher, Talbott had written a series of questions to guide the discussion. These went to the heart of the problem they faced. What does the United States do if UNPROFOR does become untenable? Should the United States prepare to push for a lift of the arms embargo, and if so, how hard? Should the West relax its demands that any talks with the Bosnian Serbs be conditional on their acceptance of the 1994 Contact Group map—and the division of Bosnia as 51 percent for the Bosnians and 49 percent for the Serbs—as the basis for negotiations? Should the United States even be working to forestall the withdrawal of UNPROFOR, or should it try to promote it?

The group focused mainly on three basic options: (1) an American-led application of "all necessary means" to force the Serbs to behave, (2) "muddle through," or (3) "accelerated withdrawal." They unanimously rejected the first option, debated the merits of the third, but in the end, spent most of the evening talking about option two, maintaining UNPROFOR while continuing to seek a political settlement. As Talbott later explained to Christopher, "as always on this dreadful subject, it was much easier to identify the problems than the virtues associated with each course of action." They all saw "muddle through" for what it was: a lowest common denominator policy. As John Deutch put it, "we can't just flap around as a government without an end point." But they also agreed that in a universe of bad choices, it might be the best they could do.[21]

MADELEINE ALBRIGHT, the UN Ambassador, wasn't at the Talbott meeting, and she had come to a different conclusion: they had to stop muddling through. From the beginning of the Administration, Albright had been one of the most vocal and persistent advocates for strong action in Bosnia. Born in Czechoslovakia, her family fled to escape the Nazis, and she often talked about the influence of the lessons of Munich. She also had deep ties to and affection for Yugoslavia: her brother had been born there, her father had served as a diplomat in Belgrade, and she had lived in the country and studied it as an academic. Now, as the U.S. Ambassador to the United Nations, Albright used her Cabinet rank and place among the President's senior advisers to push for an aggressive approach to end the war. She had long believed that for political, strategic, and moral reasons, the United States could not stand aside while Serb aggression went unchecked.

Albright also knew the damage Bosnia was doing to America's role in the world. From her perspective at the United Nations, she saw how Bosnia weakened America's diplomatic leverage. "It didn't matter what the subject was we were talking about in New York," she recalled, "the U.S. position on Bosnia affected it." She believed that the Administration's unwillingness to take the lead on Bosnia was crippling its foreign policy generally. "When U.S. leadership is being questioned in one area, it affects our leadership in others . . . it was important for the President to understand how this subject affected so many other subjects we were dealing with." Sensing that events on the ground in Bosnia—especially the possible withdrawal of UNPROFOR—would force the Administration to take some action, the UN Ambassador had begun "agitating" among her senior colleagues about the need for a new policy.[22]

At a June 21 meeting in the Oval Office, Albright made her move. Gathered to discuss funding for the RRF, the President and his top advisers again veered into a broader discussion of their lack of an overall strategy.

President Clinton complained that the UN was "paralyzing our actions and weakening the arguments for our current policies."[23]

Seizing this opening, Albright surprised the group with a written proposal, entitled "Elements of a New Strategy," recommending that the Administration start planning immediately for a Bosnia without UNPROFOR. "Bosnia is destroying our foreign policy domestically and internationally," she wrote. The present strategy "makes the President appear weak." Albright argued that her proposal "recognizes reality," calling on the President to get ahead of the game and take steps to lead the alliance, rather than being reluctantly "sucked [into] much of the same policy decisions."[24]

Albright advised a bold move: The Americans should press the Europeans to withdraw from Bosnia and end the UN mission. This was the one issue that Talbott's colleagues had unanimously ruled out during their backyard discussion the previous afternoon. But in Albright's view, if the United States did this, the international community would lift the arms embargo against the Bosnian government, and NATO would follow up with airstrikes to protect Muslim-held territory. This was basically the "lift and strike" proposal the Europeans had rejected two years earlier. If UNPROFOR withdrew, Albright believed that the Europeans could no longer block the Administration's policy. Then, the United States would demand that Milosevic accept the sanctions relief proposal or else face the consequences of a Bosnia without UNPROFOR: "Either Milosevic agrees to existing sanctions relief for recognition package or he will face a new dilemma this coming winter; namely, no UNPROFOR, a more powerful army threatening the Bosnian Serbs and a decision by him whether to intervene on behalf of Pale."

The President seemed intrigued by her presentation, although he admitted that he didn't agree with everything she said. Not elaborating any further, he said that he "liked the thrust of it and . . . that it was the right direction to go."[25]

ALBRIGHT'S MEMO BECAME must-reading inside the Administration. She earned respect for daring to challenge the prevailing caution. Her effort—perhaps combined with the knowledge of Talbott's backyard discussions—prompted Tony Lake and his staff to begin developing their own proposal.

The National Security Advisor, who was supposed to be managing the interagency deliberations of policy, had lost control of the process. By virtue of his job, Lake spent more time with Clinton than any other senior foreign policy official. Yet the two were not especially close, maintaining a distant and occasionally awkward relationship (in fact, Lake's deputy and eventual successor at the NSC, Sandy Berger, had known the president much longer and was far closer to him personally). Lake's style was quiet and professorial, and when compared to the usual senior Washington policymaker, he had the rarest of traits: he did not like to draw attention to himself. But many of his colleagues believed that he was in fact secretive and territorial. They complained, at times directly to Clinton, that Lake was not an honest broker and failed to communicate their views—the way Air Force Academy speech had been handled was seen as the most recent, and damaging, example. To a certain extent, their claims were true: Lake was a hawk on Bosnia, and when frustrated by his colleagues' indecision, he sometimes went around them. But Lake was also in a difficult situation with the President, who frequently blamed him—whether fair or not—for the poor choices they faced and the way that Bosnia policy was being handled generally.

So on Saturday morning, June 24, Lake called Sandy Berger, Sandy Vershbow, Nelson Drew, and his assistant Peter Bass into his West Wing office for a brainstorming session. All had Albright's ideas on their minds, and Berger, at least, knew what had been discussed at Talbott's house four days earlier.

"We cannot go on like this," Lake said. "We need to think about carrots and sticks and gaining leverage; we need to get this [Bosnia] thing off the table." Rather than focus on dealing with the immediate problems at hand, Lake suggested that the group consider what kind of Bosnia they hoped to find at the end of a peace process, and to work back from there. The Administration had to "start thinking about the unthinkable"—UNPROFOR withdrawal. If that occurred, what would the next steps be? They needed to look at the conflict comprehensively, figuring out not only how to get things started, but get them to the finish line. By formulating a Balkan "endgame," Lake hoped they would be able to figure out how to get there. Lake asked Vershbow, his senior advisor on Europe, to draft a strategy.[26]

Lake also knew that he needed to get President Clinton more involved. The President's anger about Bosnia was boiling over with more frequency, and he worried aloud about how it would impact his other priorities, both at home and abroad. "Everything in foreign policy is seen through the prism of Bosnia," Clinton fumed. He did not like his Administration's policy drift, complaining that "I don't look strong here or have a clear position." But at the same time, he didn't know what to do. Considering the range of unappealing options, he worried that whichever one he chose, the issue would "bite me in the butt."[27]

Knowing this, Lake gauged the President's willingness to take a chance on a new initiative to end the conflict. Failure might damage the Administration even further, he warned, and success still meant sending American soldiers into Bosnia during an election year. The status quo was untenable, replied the President. He was willing to risk new ideas, because they were not getting anywhere with the old ones. After this discussion, Lake continued to brief the President periodically on the status of what his colleagues began to call the "endgame" paper. These briefings served several purposes: they reassured the President that Lake was working to solve the problem; and they helped ensure that the President remain informed on current NSC thinking, allowing Lake to prime him against the views of others that might run counter to the emerging strategy.[28]

MEANWHILE, STATE DEPARTMENT officials continued their own deliberations, moving the discussion from Talbott's backyard to Foggy Bottom's bureaucratic corridors. This effort was led by Robert Frasure, the career Foreign

Service Officer who had negotiated with Milosevic that spring and who understood the Balkans better than anyone in the government, and Jim Steinberg, State's Policy Planning Director, who was one of the Administration's brightest minds and one of Christopher's closest confidantes.

Frasure doubted that the Administration had the guts to risk what would be necessary for peace. Weeks of negotiating with Milosevic had led him to believe that the Serbian President's asking price was far higher than they were willing to pay. As he put it to John Shattuck, the Assistant Secretary of State for Human Rights, "there's no gas in our negotiating tank." On June 23, Frasure circulated his thoughts to his State Department colleagues, suggesting grimly that the most prudent course for the Administration would be to "write off the Bosnia policy."[29]

Frasure was not one to pull punches. He argued that "over the last three years, we have handled this extraordinarily difficult issue ineptly. Within the Administration there have been competing policies on Bosnia . . . we have not imposed upon ourselves discipline, choice or prioritizing." Since events on the ground flowed "increasingly out of our control," the United States "unfortunately no longer can muddle through." The UN's top political leadership, the French and British were signaling that unless things got better fast, they wanted UNPROFOR out—once they did so, the Op-plan 40104 "doomsday machine" would start. They were heading over a waterfall, Frasure wrote, and the only choice to make was about which part it wanted to go over.

Observing that "a lingering death" of Bosnia was not in America's interests, Frasure recommended that the Administration's main priority should be the "avoidance of a substantial U.S. military presence in Bosnia, in particular in the extraction of UNPROFOR, which could lead to casualties and would highlight the reality that we're at the end of a failed adventure." He suggested a policy of containment: extracting UNPROFOR as quickly and painlessly as possible; forestalling any other American diplomatic missions; maintaining the arms embargo; and pursuing a modest covert program to arm the Bosnians.

The President could gain little by this approach, but it would minimize the disaster that would follow if the Administration went over another part of the waterfall—and was sucked into the Balkan whirlpool via Op-plan 40104. "There will be no credit for any of us in this one," Frasure gloomily concluded. "[The policy] is beyond redemption now and should be brought to an end before the 1996 presidential campaign commences. Otherwise we will be handing a sharp sword to this Administration's political opponents next year. And we can expect they will use it."

As Frasure circulated his memorandum, Jim Steinberg worked on his own, decidedly more hopeful approach. He believed that there was still a chance to salvage American policy. Steinberg's proposal combined negotiations based on the Contact Group plan with the sanctions relief-mutual recognition package Frasure had discussed with Milosevic earlier that year. The core of the strategy would be a presidential summit where the presidents of Croatia,

Serbia, and Bosnia would recognize each other and agree on a set of principles to govern negotiations among the Pale and Sarajevo leaders. In return for Milosevic recognizing his neighbors and bringing the Bosnian Serbs to the negotiating table, he would receive some sanctions relief. By combining intra-Bosnian negotiations with a broader regional settlement, Steinberg hoped to create greater incentives for the parties to reach agreement.[30]

THE FRASURE AND STEINBERG PROPOSALS came together after the Department's top officials met in Christopher's back office on June 30, and the next day, Frasure drafted a new memorandum proposing an amended version of Steinberg's paper.[31] Writing with more (and perhaps forced) optimism, Frasure explained that "we probably have one more roll of the diplomatic dice." He sought to simplify the Steinberg proposal by installing Milosevic as the negotiator for the Bosnian Serbs. Frasure suggested that in return for Milosevic's assistance, the Contact Group should be more flexible on sanctions relief, willing to lift the sanctions if necessary, rather than simply suspend them. As a final note, Frasure reiterated his strong view that the Administration had to stay firm—"If we decide that the crisis has now come and at all cost we must avoid UNPROFOR departure/40104 and we need a diplomatic solution, then we must make that choice, impose discipline and stay the course."

The Secretary of State outlined this proposal in a memorandum to the President sent on July 6. As the culmination of the State Department's policymaking process over the previous few weeks, Christopher's memo urged that the Administration restart negotiations, increasing the pressure on the Bosnian Serbs and providing "a plausible basis for urging that UNPRO-FOR should stay the course."[32]

The State Department's bottom-line was that the Administration's main priority should be to avoid a significant military ground presence in Bosnia. As Frasure's references to the 1996 elections suggest, Christopher was not convinced that the American people would support such a move. From the perspective of many officials outside the State Department, particularly Albright and those at the NSC, Christopher and his top advisors were too cautious.[33]

OP-PLAN 40104: "EVERYTHING BUT THE KITCHEN SINK"

The key part of Christopher's message to President Clinton—and one of the reasons for his caution—was what he described as the "failure scenario" of UNPROFOR withdrawal and the American commitment to help it do so. For the past month, Christopher and his senior team (as well as NSC officials such as Sandy Berger) had worried that Op-plan 40104 entailed a massive military commitment with little flexibility to adjust to specific circumstances. Strobe Talbott described it as an "everything but the kitchen sink" plan. The military planners were "building a machine with a single off-on toggle switch. Once the President throws the switch . . . the machine will go from zero to sixty in 5 seconds flat; it will pour 25,000 or so U.S. troops into Bosnia on the theory that more is better, most is best." Such an introduction of massive American force could, Talbott believed, "bog us down and guarantee fairly large numbers of U.S. casualties. We could, in short, get the worst of both worlds: cut-and-run and quagmire, all wrapped up in one fiasco."[34]

Christopher, Talbott, and others like Richard Holbrooke had already tried to make these risks clear to President Clinton and their colleagues. All of them had been briefed on the details of the military planning (including the President himself, in a June 2 Oval Office briefing), but they still believed that the President deserved a broader range of choices than the "terrible set" that he faced—and told him so directly.

STANDING ON THE WHITE HOUSE'S North Portico after a private dinner with Jacques Chirac on June 14, Christopher and Holbrooke found themselves alone with President Clinton and Sandy Berger. The President asked about Bosnia. They explained to him just how constrained they believed the United States really was. Referring to Op-plan 40104, Holbrooke told Clinton that "under existing NATO plans, the United States is already committed to sending troops to Bosnia if the UN decides to withdraw. I'm afraid that we may not have as much flexibility and options left."

Both Christopher and Holbrooke thought that Clinton seemed surprised—which worried them more. Perhaps the President did not appreciate the extent to which Op-plan 40104 limited his options to either do nothing or conduct a massive intervention; perhaps he understood this but simply did not want to hear what Holbrooke had to say (those who know Clinton well claim that he often responds to news he does not like with feigned shock and anger). Whatever the reason, that night President Clinton pushed back. "I'll decide the troops issue when the time comes," he snapped. Christopher told Clinton that under current circumstances, he did not have that luxury. Given that the plan contained a "large degree of automaticity," and that the consequences of reneging on such a pledge would severely damage U.S. leadership in Europe, the Secretary of State said that at that point no other "practical options existed." As he described the situation several years later, "I felt that this would be an embarrassing as well as perilous use of American forces, but, on the other hand, failure to keep our commitment would undermine our credibility as the leader of the [Atlantic] Alliance." Or, as he noted to the President in his typically understated way as they stood on the Portico that June evening: "We have a problem."[35]

THIS IMPROMPTU MEETING ended abruptly and without any resolution. Christopher and Holbrooke had made their point, but there was no sign that the President was getting any new military options—or, for that matter, whether he or anyone had even asked for different options. Yet if there was any question about what Clinton knew or didn't know that evening, there was now no doubt that he understood the position he was in—and that he was not happy about it. After this discussion, he claimed that he was "locked into a decision I didn't know I was making," once again letting his advisors know that he held them responsible. "The way this thing was presented to me was about helping with withdrawal if the allies get in trouble," he said. "But now its looking like a *fait accompli* . . . I was asked to agree to a contingency plan. Now I'm being presented with what looks like a dead-bang loser."[36]

Knowing the President's frustrations, Christopher used his July 6 memorandum to make another push for more modest military options. "I think you need a wider variety of options than now provided by NATO Operation Plan 40104, with its heavy reliance on large numbers of U.S. ground troops," the Secretary wrote. "With all respect for the NATO planners, the 'all or nothing' character of 40104 does not seem to me to take into account the wide variety of circumstances in which withdrawal may actually take place—or the strength of public and congressional opinion against the commitment of U.S. ground troops." Christopher repeated that the military's planning was not "sufficiently nuanced; that it was an all-or-nothing approach." Whereas the Secretary of State understood that the United States was committed to 40104, he felt that it "was the worst of all possible choices," as they "would have to put troops on the ground to crown a failure and not to achieve a success."[37]

President Clinton saw merit in Christopher's suggestion for more options, as he scribbled "agree" in the margins next to this suggestion and passed the memorandum to his National Security Advisor to take action. Lake apparently talked the President out of this recommendation or just ignored it—the President never received more military options from the Pentagon. That left him with only one.[38]

THE FALL OF SREBRENICA

While Washington officials struggled to reformulate America's diplomacy and tailor its military commitment, Bosnia slipped deeper into chaos. And as is often the case, events outpaced planning—forcing the Administration's hand.

On July 6, the Bosnian Serb Army began a brutal assault on Srebrenica. The tiny enclave, located in eastern Bosnia just miles away from the Serbian border, was home to 40,000 Bosnian Muslims, many of them refugees. As a UN "safe area," Srebrenica had a tiny garrison of Dutch peacekeepers stationed there for protection. But as the Bosnian Serbs began to close in on the town, it soon became clear that there was little the Dutch could or would do. The UN soldiers quickly abandoned their posts and fled to their base at nearby Potocari. At the last moment, the UN called in NATO air support, but by this point there was little that could be done. While NATO planes destroyed two Serb tanks, on July 11 the Serb forces overtook the town, driving out tens of thousands of refugees and taking many more captive. By July 16, they had murdered over 7,000 Muslim boys and men in what was the greatest single massacre in Europe since World War II.[39]

THIS CRISIS HAMMERED the final nail in the coffin of America's—and Europe's—Bosnia policy. Soon after Srebrenica fell, another safe area, Zepa, appeared next, and a third, Gorazde, was vulnerable. The UN guarantees to protect the enclaves had proved meaningless. Humiliated once again, the UN and the Europeans began to talk about pulling out. Writing in his memoirs, President Clinton admitted that the "Bosnian Serbs had made a mockery of the UN and, by extension, of the commitments of NATO and the United States."[40]

As if to underscore Washington's paralysis, French President Chirac responded first to the crisis, offering a typically bold but unrealistic proposal to lead the Americans and other Western allies in a massive military intervention to retake the safe area. In a July 13 phone call to Clinton, Chirac said that "the fall of Srebrenica, the probable fall of Zepa tomorrow and the threat to Gorazde represent a major failure of the UN, NATO and all democracies." Chirac's proposal amounted to an all-or- nothing approach—either they throw "all of their forces in the effort" to liberate Srebrenica or they pull-out entirely. The initiative made little military sense; even if the costs of such an operation were worth it, it was far from clear what the next step would be. "Can you believe he proposed that?" Clinton said to his aides after he hung up. "Then what do we do? Do we go out and then they take it back? Or should we take over the whole country?"[41]

A MAJOR PROPOSAL

Clinton immediately called British Prime Minister Major and German Chancellor Helmut Kohl, and they wondered aloud whether Chirac was serious or whether he was bluffing to capture the moral high ground. Whatever Chirac's intention, the three leaders recognized they had to do something. On July 14, Major announced that the Contact Group, NATO, and other UN contributors should meet in London the next week to discuss the way forward.[42]

Some in the State Department had mixed feelings about going to London. Although Christopher saw this as a "bolder step than [Major] had ever taken," he was skeptical, believing that such large, multilateral gatherings produced more rhetoric than substance. Holbrooke recalled that the conference was "an initially unpromising idea. The British did not have a clear goal for the conference, nor did the United States."

But the Administration had little choice other than to accept Major's offer—as Clinton later described it, the idea was "an almost desperate attempt to regain the initiative"—so they set out aggressively to shape what the allies should rally around. Chirac had backed down from his proposal of retaking Srebrenica (even French military leaders saw this as posturing, and never started planning for it), but was now arguing for reinforcing UNPROFOR troops in Gorazde. He thought the United States could use its helicopters to transport 1,000 French peacekeepers into the area. This idea did not have a lot going for it: it would likely bring American casualties, force NATO to bomb Serb air defenses in a preemptive strike, and would not dramatically improve the ability of the enclave to hold out against Serb armor and artillery. From

Chirac's perspective, the military significance of the act was not as important as the political gesture to demonstrate the West's determination to stand firm.[43]

American officials agreed that they needed to draw a line and hold it against further Serb attacks to have any chance of maintaining the UN mission—and salvaging the President's political standing. Clinton worried that he looked indecisive and weak, and that the United States was taking a backseat to countries such as France. "Why aren't you giving me more options? Chirac at least has some new ideas," the President complained to his aides. Sandy Berger saw such outbursts as a "primal scream" from the President, "and a kick in the butt for everyone." Even those political consultants who had once cautioned against military action, like Dick Morris, now took a more hawkish line. Morris had opinion polls showing support for using force against the Serbs, and started agitating that the President launch a bold military action, asking "why can't Clinton just bomb Bosnia on his own?"[44]

Although no one supported Morris's call to act alone, all agreed that the overrunning of Srebrenica presented the United States and Europe with an unappealing choice. "We reached a point where you either have to declare the UN mission a failure and pull it out of there," Secretary of Defense Perry recalled, "or you have to be prepared to take strong military action." Perry and General Shalikashvili determined that the only way to stop the Bosnian Serbs was to threaten them with overwhelming air power. The President concurred. "The only time we've ever been effective is when the NATO air threat has been credible," he said.

Perry suggested that the goal of the London meeting should be to present an ultimatum to the Bosnian Serbs: "don't even think about going into Gorazde or any other safe areas. If you do, you will be met by a massive air campaign. Not a bomb or two, not a pinprick, but a massive air campaign." That would mean changing the rules of engagement, empowering NATO to conduct air operations without the UN "dual-key."[45]

Bill Perry's argument carried a lot of weight within the President's inner circle. Since the beginning of the Administration, the Pentagon's military and civilian leaders had been among the most skeptical about U.S. military involvement in Bosnia, believing that it would require an intervention too massive and dangerous to justify to the American people. They were always quick to remind the President about the high degree of risk—and likely costs—of a military campaign. But now the Defense Secretary—a soft-spoken, career defense intellectual who had earned tremendous respect throughout Washington, especially among military officers—was calling for decisive action. His support gave the Clinton Administration's more hawkish civilians, who had rarely been eager to confront the Pentagon on this issue, the critical backing they needed.

WHILE THE MAIN PRIORITY was to defend the remaining safe areas, Lake and his NSC staff continued to develop a strategy to find a way out of the Balkan morass altogether. Taking advantage of his proximity to the Oval Office, Lake briefed Clinton on the details of the "endgame" strategy paper that they had been quietly developing since late June. Desperately trying to stay ahead of events—and struggling to respond to the President's impatience with the lack of a policy—Lake showed Clinton a draft of the proposal he planned to present at a July 17 breakfast with the President's other senior advisers. To illustrate the seriousness of this effort, Lake asked Clinton to drop by the meeting.[46]

Lake's proposal called for a major American initiative to end the war. But it also focused on what the United States should do if a new effort failed. If UNPROFOR withdrew, the Americans should insist on lifting the arms embargo or assist the Bosnians through a covert arms program, supplying military advisors to train them. The aim would be to level the playing field in Bosnia, to help the Sarajevo government gain by force of arms what it had sought at the negotiating table. The United States would be prepared to support NATO air strikes against the Serbs, but for a limited time. Once the playing field was leveled, the Bosnians would stand alone. The proposal called for Milosevic to put up or shut up—any relief from sanctions would be predicated on his recognition of Bosnia as a single state and curbing military support for the Bosnian Serbs. Lake's idea entailed a level of commitment from the White House—and a degree of risk—that the State Department's proposal did not.[47]

THE MORNING OF JULY 17, Christopher, Perry, Shalikashvili, Albright, and Berger gathered in Lake's West Wing office for their weekly breakfast meeting. Lake's presentation surprised most of his colleagues, whose minds were focused on the immediate problems of the Srebrenica crisis and upcoming London conference. Albright expressed her support, while Christopher, Perry, and Shalikashvili were skeptical. It was one thing to defend the safe areas. But Lake's proposal risked drawing the United States further into the conflict, and its plan to assist the Bosnians militarily might further strain relations among the allies.[48]

As Lake had arranged, President Clinton entered the room unannounced as his advisers discussed the proposal. He spoke briefly, saying that the present course was not sustainable, although he was not sure what to do. He repeated his earlier thought that to regain leverage, the United States had to restore the credibility of NATO's airpower.

Everyone got the message. After Clinton left, Lake asked the others to prepare their own thoughts on the direction of Bosnia policy. In a few weeks, he said, they should submit a series of strategy papers to the President in order to develop those ideas into a new diplomatic effort.[49]

PREPARING FOR LONDON

But before the Administration could launch any new initiatives, it first had to decide how to respond to Chirac's proposal to reinforce Gorazde with 1,000 ground troops supported by American helicopters and NATO airstrikes.[50] At another White House breakfast meeting on July 18, Vice President Al Gore made an impassioned appeal to urge the President not to "acquiesce to genocide." They could not ignore Srebrenica, Gore argued. Although there was little the Americans could do to protect the tiny enclave of Zepa, which was under Serb assault, they could not write off the 65,000 Bosnians in Gorazde. Yet the French proposal was too risky. Instead, Clinton decided to accept Secretary of Defense Perry's recommendation and push for defending Gorazde with a decisive, broad air campaign, unrestrained by the UN's "dual-key." With the Pentagon's indispensable support, Clinton chose to use airpower to achieve political aims. This decision set the stage for the robust new position that was adopted three days later in London.[51]

President Clinton and his advisors understood that such a decision had implications beyond Bosnia—it would shape America's relationship with Europe, the United Nations, and NATO. For three years, the Clinton Administration felt constrained by fears that decisive action would damage relations with Europe; now it believed that the relationship would be hurt *without* decisive action. It believed that nothing less than the credibility and solidarity of the entire Transatlantic Alliance was at stake. If Europe and the United States couldn't bring peace to a conflict in their own backyard, what could they do? "The issue was not taking some [UN] peacekeepers hostage," Perry recalled, "the issue is taking the whole policy of the international community hostage." Albright said that they had to be firm with the Europeans. "We need to tell them this is it," she said. Agreeing, the President told his advisers that they would "need to press the UK and French to go our way. The U.S. can't be a punching bag anymore."[52]

The Americans had made a decision; now they needed to get their allies on board. In a conference call that day with his counterparts from Spain and Germany, Christopher shared his concern about the "potentially disastrous outcome" of deadlock in London.[53] The next morning, July 19, Clinton spoke with Chirac. "We propose issuing a clear warning to Bosnian Serbs that any attack on Gorazde or Sarajevo will be met by a sustained air campaign that will actually cripple their military capability," the President said. Chirac worried that the peacekeepers already on the ground were too vulnerable. "The minute we attack . . . they [Bosnian Serbs] will retaliate by taking hostages or attacking with massive artillery." Clinton responded that this fact undermined Chirac's own proposal to insert 1,000 troops—any French reinforcements would be just as vulnerable as the troops already there. Although they could not reach an agreement, the two presidents agreed to consult with their military advisors and talk the next day.[54]

THE AMERICANS FARED better with the British, perhaps because Downing Street officials feared the French proposal more than the American one. After talking with Chirac, Clinton called British Prime Minister Major, who agreed that the American plan was the best one on the table. Clinton said he knew the risks, but believed they were worth taking. "It is better to go out with a bang than with a whimper," he told Major, "otherwise we go out with our tail between our legs." The British leader insisted that they not go down the military route "one-legged," without a plan for a political settlement. With Tony Lake's policy review likely in mind, the President agreed that "if we make a bold military thrust, we should accompany it with a bold diplomatic initiative."[55]

By July 20, the Europeans began coalescing around the American plan. That morning, the British announced their support. That afternoon, Chirac called Clinton and told him that "I am still against airstrikes . . . but I will not oppose them. What is essential is to draw a red line around Gorazde and then make sure it is respected." Chirac recognized that Clinton's proposal represented the only hope for a unified position at the London conference. "If everyone agrees with your solution and they all agree to reject my solution, then obviously I won't oppose it because I don't want to take the responsibility of having tomorrow's conference fail," Chirac said.[56]

A TURNING POINT AT LANCASTER HOUSE

Although the French and British leaders pledged their support to President Clinton, their subordinates restated their lingering doubts to Christopher, Perry, and Shalikashvili when the conference opened in London. UN Secretary General Boutros Boutros-Ghali arrived and "found no two views alike." In the sweltering summer heat of London's Lancaster House, once used as grand reception hall during the 19th century reign of Queen Victoria, the Americans worked intensely to prevent the deal from unraveling. "The closer the Europeans get to bombing, the more nervous they get," Secretary Christopher later told the President.[57]

Surprisingly, the Russians, who had always opposed airstrikes against the Serbs, were not part of the problem. "The Russians were not as distant from our position as I feared," Secretary Perry reported to the President. Russian Defense Minister Pavel Grachev did argue against airstrikes on military grounds—asserting that they would not deter the Bosnian Serbs—but he agreed on the basic consensus at London. Perry recalled that "I had a long discussion with Grachev, and got some very positive statements from him [that] we could not let the Bosnian Serbs continue to attack, to violate safe havens; and the alternative, which was pulling the UN forces out, was unacceptable to them."[58] The Russians did, however, block the conference from producing a signed statement (as was standard diplomatic practice) from the talks. Instead, the results from London were announced publicly by John Major in a "Chairman's Statement."[59]

After a day of American arm-twisting, the international community agreed to Clinton's proposal on Gorazde: any attack on the safe area would be met with a "substantial and decisive" air campaign. Unlike past NATO strikes, they would not respond with limited "pin-prick" attacks on small targets; they would respond overwhelmingly against the Serbs with a broad campaign throughout Bosnia. Although not announced specifically, all agreed that the "dual-key" would be modified to remove UN civilian officials—Secretary General Boutros Boutros-Ghali and his special civilian representative for Bosnia,

Yasusi Akashi—from vetoing the strikes. Finally, they decided to defer the Americans' idea to extend this ultimatum, now known as the "Gorazde rules," to the remaining safe areas of Sarajevo, Bihac, and Tuzla (Clinton had already mentioned this to Chirac). The North Atlantic Council, NATO's political decision-making forum, would consider expanding the rules as they hammered out the details of the agreement in the coming days. To emphasize the seriousness of these decisions, American, French, and British military commanders would travel to the Balkans to deliver the ultimatum directly to Bosnian Serb General Ratko Mladic.

THE AMERICANS considered the London conference a critical achievement—perhaps their first real success concerning Bosnia. Perry, Christopher, and Shalikashvili all referred to London as the "turning point." As Perry saw it, the Bosnian Serbs had "overplayed their hand" with the Srebrenica attack; "their strategic judgment that the international community did not have the will to use military force led them to an action that [was] so egregious it actually stiffened the backbone of the international community." No one knew whether their ultimatum would deter the Serbs, and they realized that any military action would be risky. But, Perry says, "we just believed that the potential negative consequences of [military action] could not be as serious as the consequences of sending NATO forces to pull out the UN forces in disgrace."

"The conference was a turning point," the Defense Secretary reflected. "At that stage, the whole international community said yes . . . either we pull out the UN force or we reinforce it with strong military action." As Christopher described it, "we finally decided to put some real muscle behind our rhetoric."[60]

Possibly this new resolve would translate into progress at the negotiating table. But more fundamental problems remained. "I fear we are sailing a course between Scylla and Charybdis," Perry wrote to the President after London. Even if they succeeded in deterring an attack on Gorazde, the London decisions guaranteed neither the survival of UNPROFOR nor a peaceful resolution to the Bosnian conflict. "We have avoided disaster for the moment, but we are lurching toward another," he continued. "Our hope is that the momentum from this course change will carry us into a period of calm where we can bring diplomatic efforts to play."[61]

2

Through the Window of Opportunity: The Endgame Strategy

The Americans left London with an agreement—one that would finally confront the Bosnian Serbs with the full force of NATO's airpower. Now the North Atlantic Council (NAC) had to implement formally the new "Gorazde rules," determining precisely what would trigger bombing, what the targets could be, how long any campaign would last, and how to extend these new rules to protect the other safe areas. Despite the fact that U.S. officials believed London had achieved a strong consensus, indeed had been a "turning point," they soon found themselves at odds with their British and French allies on the details.

Specifically, they disagreed about when UN Secretary General Boutros Boutros-Ghali had to give up his half of the "dual-key." The British and French strongly supported maintaining this cumbersome decision-making process, as it was the safety of their troops that the rules protected. But the fecklessness of the UN civilian leaders, specifically the Secretary General, testified to UNPROFOR's impotence, and Washington officials believed the removal of the UN key from their civilian leaders a critical step toward making any threat against the Bosnian Serbs meaningful.

Fighting over the Keys

The Americans thought that they had made very clear that under certain circumstances they expected the UN key to be turned on automatically. Bill Perry had reported to the President that a "key feature [of London] is that we have agreed to remove the UN civilian authorities from the decision process on airstrikes," and, in a press conference, Secretary Christopher stated that the "existing command-and-control arrangements for the use of NATO air power will be significantly adjusted to ensure that responsiveness and unity—our purposes—are achieved. The new [decision-making] system is a much improved system."[1] Since this understanding seemed obvious, U.S. officials saw no need to address it formally or explicitly in the Chairman's concluding statement.

Yet others—notably the UN Secretary General—had different views. Boutros-Ghali was genuinely conflicted about his role in the dual-key system. "I could see that the British and the French [were] saying one thing in the Contact Group, another in NATO, and blowing another in Boutros' ear," Albright recalled. UN military commanders on the ground in Bosnia "were preoccupied with the protection of their troops and thus [against] an air campaign" and were telling Boutros-Ghali to hold firm. Notwithstanding this, the bottom-line seemed to be, as Albright later explained, that the UN Secretary General was playing games. "I don't think we'll ever know the absolute truth as to whether Boutros-Ghali was telling the British and French that he was reluctant to [give up his key] . . . Boutros-Ghali blamed it on the British and French to me."[2]

ON THE MORNING OF JULY 24, Boutros-Ghali called his counterpart, NATO Secretary General Willy Claes. In a tense conversation, he told Claes that he opposed the London decision on broad airstrikes, which he claimed violated UN Security Council resolutions. Boutros-Ghali protested that the Americans were rushing the international community's deliberations in an effort to "force the play before a Senate vote on lift," referring to an upcoming vote in the U.S. Senate on unilaterally lifting the arms embargo against Bosnia. Boutros-Ghali told Claes that he would not agree to relinquish his key until "he heard personally" from each head of state, noting that "a decision of your sixteen NATO ambassadors would not be enough." Alarmed, Claes asked the "Quad" NATO representatives—United States, United Kingdom, France, and Germany—to get their leaders to begin lobbying the UN Secretary General.[3]

In Washington, the White House worked to clear up this confusion—but in fact got drawn into more haggling. President Clinton called Chirac to argue that the authority for requesting airstrikes should go to the British Lt. General Rupert Smith, the commander of UN ground forces in Bosnia.[4] He believed that placing the key in the hands of the military would make the UN civilians less of an obstacle. Chirac agreed, but he wanted to assign the key to Smith's superior, General Bernard Janvier, who was the overall UNPROFOR commander. The fact that Janvier was a French General was no coincidence, and would no doubt enable Paris to retain a strong influence over the course of the airstrikes.

Chirac also believed that the UN's authority over airstrikes should be divided into three phases of bombing. These options had been created by NATO military planners to organize bombing targets into three rungs of escalation. *Option One* airstrikes would target specific military positions involved in attacking a safe area. This first option offered little more than the "pin-prick" targeting that had defined past NATO air operations. Chirac argued that authority to conduct these could rest with the local commander; Janvier could subdelegate such authority to those on the ground as necessary.

The next level, *Option Two* airstrikes, were the "substantial and decisive" airstrikes promised by the London Conference. This second option expanded the target list to include weapons not directly involved in an attack, like command and control facilities, radars, and ammunition depots. Chirac felt that authority for this option should remain in Janvier's hands.

Option Three was the broadest level of strategic bombing, including attacks on Serb troop concentrations and equipment throughout Bosnia, including civilian infrastructure like power grids. In essence, this option outlined a full-throttled bombing campaign, not unlike that directed against Iraqi targets during the 1991 Gulf War or in 1999 against Milosevic's forces in Kosovo. Chirac stressed that the power to authorize this must remain in the hands of the UN Secretary General. Requiring a green light from the UN, he argued, would allow other nations with forces on the ground to have a voice in a decision to pursue Option Three.[5]

Although the Americans accepted Chirac's conditions on Options One and Two, they could not agree to his recommendations for Option Three. They wanted Boutros-Ghali completely eliminated from the chain of command. In a phone call after the Clinton–Chirac conversation, French Foreign Minister de Charette tried to reassure Christopher that Boutros-Ghali would not be an impediment to airstrikes, but Christopher responded that this was "directly contrary to what we agreed to in London . . . under your proposal, [Boutros-Ghali] would have veto power."[6]

The UN Secretary General played on these divisions. He refused to meet with the American, French, or British UN ambassadors until they presented him with a proposal outlining the details of the agreement between NATO and the UN.[7] In a July 25 conversation with Christopher, Boutros-Ghali said he could not give a "blank-check" to the Americans. Christopher noted that "things seem to have fallen back" since the London Conference, demanding that the Secretary General to get this resolved in 24 hours.[8]

THE LONG NIGHT AT THE NAC

On July 25, the 16 NATO ambassadors met in Brussels to hammer out an agreement. Going into the meeting, the prospects for success did not look good. The U.S. Ambassador to NATO, Robert Hunter, called Washington to tell Assistant Secretary of State Holbrooke that it was "fifteen-to-one against the U.S." Hunter recommended that they cut a deal with the Europeans, and called Perry to lobby his case. Outraged, Holbrooke told Hunter to keep the NAC up all night if necessary, and to accept no less than the conclusions reached at the London Conference. "Otherwise," he said, "the West's decision would be revealed as a charade."

There were three key issues that the NAC had to settle: (1) whether to attack massing Serb troops; (2) how to delegate authority for the Option Three airstrikes; and (3) how to retaliate against Serb hostage-taking.[9] On the first issue, the British were concerned by the American demand that NATO could attack concentrations of Serb troops preemptively, before they attacked a safe area. U.S. officials argued that if the Serbs were massing forces for an attack, NATO needed the flexibility to preempt the assault, rather than waiting until it had already begun. With French support, the Americans finally prevailed on the British to agree that military commanders on the ground would decide when to initiate an attack on Serb troop concentrations.[10]

Concerning Option Three airstrikes, the French still believed that authorization must require a UN political decision from Boutros-Ghali. None of the ambassadors argued against delegating Options One and Two authority to the local UN military commanders, thus taking Boutros-Ghali's civilian key away. However, the nations with troops on the ground believed that an escalation to Option Three, which would in effect be an all-out air war against the Serbs (and therefore leave UN troops throughout Bosnia vulnerable to Bosnian Serb reprisal), was a crucial political decision that could not be made by the theater commanders alone. In order to avoid scuttling the entire agreement, the Americans agreed that this point could be deferred for further discussions.[11]

The final and most contentious issue was how to respond to hostage-taking. The Americans wanted to avoid the embarrassment of May and send the Serbs a strong message that even if they retaliated, NATO airstrikes would continue. But again, those nations with troops on the ground remained deeply concerned. Several of them, especially France and Britain, argued that since no U.S. troops were there, the Americans had no standing to tell the Europeans what to do. The NAC worked out a deal that did more to obscure these differences rather than resolve them: there would be an understanding that while UNPROFOR troops needed to take risks, local commanders could suspend air operations if they determined that the safety of their troops was at stake. The key reason this compromise was possible, Ambassador Hunter later noted, was that by then the hostage-taking issue was moot. With the fall of Srebrenica and Zepa, the withdrawal of UNPROFOR troops from the most vulnerable areas had already begun.[12]

EARLY THE MORNING OF JULY 26, after an agonizing 13 straight hours of debate, the NAC finally approved the "Gorazde rules": NATO airpower would protect any threat to Gorazde and the UN civilians would relinquish their "key." The NAC also asked NATO's military planners to decide how to extend those rules to the other safe-areas—like Tuzla, Bihac, and Sarajevo—which they did successfully on August 1.[13]

But even after this breakthrough in Brussels, the UN Secretary General remained reluctant to delegate his authority. The morning of July 26, Christopher complained to his top aide Tom Donilon and Holbrooke that Boutros-Ghali was still "dragging his feet." He called Boutros-Ghali to stress that the Administration expected his support. "I told him that the London Conference represented the leading participants in the UN as far as Europe was concerned, and [that] he shouldn't stand in the way of NATO taking action if there were another safe area attacked," Christopher recalled. Boutros-Ghali told Christopher that he would give his consent, but he needed time to work out the details with his UN staff. When Boutros-Ghali had taken no action by midday, Christopher called him again. Boutros-Ghali's wavering was wearing the Secretary of State's patience; Holbrooke later described these two conversations as "hammer calls," while Christopher more diplomatically characterized them as "not unfriendly, but firm." Finally, at 2 P.M. that afternoon, the UN Secretary General finally announced that he would delegate his "key" to General Janvier.[14]

THE CROATIAN OFFENSIVE

Once again, events on the ground outpaced the diplomats' deliberations. On July 22, the presidents of Bosnia and Croatia met in Split, Croatia to discuss ways to improve their military cooperation. The Bosnian Muslim government needed help. In June it had launched unsuccessfully a major offensive near Sarajevo. Srebrenica and Zepa were gone. Now Bihac in northwest Bosnia was again under assault from several fronts. There, Bosnian troops were besieged from all sides—by the Bosnian Serb forces, by a Muslim separatist army, and the Croatian Serb Army, operating out of the neighboring Krajina territory.[15]

The United States hoped that this meeting between Bosnian President Alija Izetbegovic and Croatian President Franjo Tudjman would help strengthen the Muslim–Croat Federation it had helped create in March 1994. But the Americans knew that this meeting meant more than strengthening diplomatic ties. The Croats had told the U.S. Ambassador in Zagreb, Peter Galbraith, that they were planning on sending their forces into Bosnia in order to relieve pressure on Bihac. At their meeting in Split, the two presidents reached an agreement on military cooperation that would invite the Croats to reenter the war.[16]

Croatia had its own reasons for defending Bihac from the Serbs. The enclave's fall would connect Serb territories in Croatia and Bosnia, strengthening the Krajina Serb position and potentially leading to the region's unification with Bosnian Serb territory. Croatia could not allow the Krajina, which it had lost in 1991 and accounted for nearly 30 percent of its land, to remain in Serb hands much longer. President Tudjman wanted it back, but first he had to ensure that the Serb rebels did not capture Bihac.

IN WASHINGTON, the Deputies Committee met on July 24 to discuss how to respond to the Bosnian–Croat agreement. Since the international community was not willing to take strong action to protect Bihac, they agreed that the United States could not stop the Croats from doing so. However, they also agreed that Croatia should be warned against taking this opportunity to launch an attack against the Krajina.[17] The Deputies' worried that, even if the Croats might win, the conflict would be protracted and costly. They instructed Galbraith to ask the Croatian government to limit any military action with Bihac. The Croats agreed, reassuring him that they had no intention of expanding their operations into the Krajina. In a phone call with Russian President Boris Yeltsin, President Clinton said that both he and German Chancellor Helmut Kohl had cautioned the Croats "to exercise restraint and avoid a wider war." Clinton urged Yeltsin to reiterate this message to the Serbs.[18]

Croat forces launched their defense of Bihac on July 25. In the two years since Croatia had been largely removed from the Bosnia war, its military had been rebuilt and modernized, despite the international arms embargo on the region, which Croatia easily skirted.[19] Part of its rearming included the now notorious flow of weapons from Iran into Bosnia which Croatia skimmed off of. Despite this blatant violation of the UN arms embargo, U.S. officials took a "don't ask, don't tell" position toward Croatia's rearming—they understood that restoring a military balance of power among the three Balkan parties may help bring a settlement. From the moment Croat forces entered Bosnia, the rearming effort proved successful. Croatia easily overran the Serb military, sending an estimated 8,000 Serb troops and civilians fleeing.[20]

With this success, the Croatian army turned toward Knin, a small town in the middle of Krajina. It had been a trigger for the disintegration of Yugoslavia beginning in 1991, when local Serbs declared the region autonomous from Croatia. On July 29, Croatian forces mobilized around Krajina and began to shell Knin. President Tudjman threatened to retake all of Krajina if the Bosnian Serbs did not end their siege of Bihac. Although the two sides opened talks to solve the dispute, it appeared clear that Tudjman had no intention of coming to any deal—he wanted Krajina back.[21]

Croatian troops attacked Krajina on August 4. The State Department had again instructed Galbraith to advise the Croats against attacking Krajina, but stopped short of threatening any penalty if Zagreb did so. In a matter of days, the military strike aptly called "Operation Storm" had run Serb troops and civilians out of Krajina, sending another massive stream of refugees toward Serbia. On August 6, a victorious Tudjman raised the Croatian flag over Knin. For the first time in the four-year Balkan conflict, the Serbs had suffered a significant military defeat.[22]

An Opening for Diplomacy . . . and a Push from Congress

Despite American pleas for restraint, Croatia's offensive changed the situation dramatically in Bosnia. "In hindsight, one can see that there were some useful results accomplished by these offensives in the Krajina," Christopher recalled. In late July, the Bosnian Muslims had appeared only weeks from defeat, with Bihac under assault, Gorazde vulnerable, and UNPROFOR withdrawal probable. Then, the London Conference had produced an umbrella of air defense above Gorazde, and the Croatian victory had helped liberate Bihac, resupplying its civilians and its Bosnian defenders. Now the Croat military appeared poised to advance deeper into western Bosnia.[23]

The Croat offensive created the ideal opportunity for the Administration to push for a negotiated settlement. Secretary of Defense Perry explained that "it must have been evidently clear to the [Serbs]—with the threat of bombing being real now and with the loss to the Croats on the ground—that they had already passed their high-water mark and were better off by making peace. So it seemed to me it was an opportunity to go in with a diplomatic initiative." Writing in his memoirs, President Clinton recalled that "I was rooting for the Croatians . . . [I knew] that diplomacy could not succeed until the Serbs sustained some serious losses on the ground."[24]

Surprisingly, Serbian leader Slobodan Milosevic stood by as the Croatian forces rolled into Knin, producing more than 100,000 Serb refugees. While Milosevic's military had mobilized near Eastern Slavonia—the remaining Serb-held territory in Croatia—the Serb leader's inaction signaled that he did not wish to expand the war further. As the U.S. Embassy in Belgrade reported to Washington, the Serb setbacks could evolve into a more realistic attitude toward negotiations, but could "also develop into a martyr complex and resentment of the outside world that will lead to thousands of more victims before the conflict ends." If anything, it would be vital for the Americans to move as quickly as possible "to show the Serbs the right direction to take."[25]

EVENTS ON THE GROUND in Bosnia were not the only factor pushing the Clinton Administration toward a new diplomatic initiative. It also had come under heavy pressure from the Congress. For the past several months, congressional hawks—led by Senate Republican leader Robert Dole—had been pushing an effort to arm the Bosnians by lifting unilaterally the arms embargo the UN had imposed in 1991 against all the states of former Yugoslavia. "Clinton had a lot of sympathy for the Senators on this," Sandy Berger remembered. His boss Tony Lake agreed. "This was a painful issue for us . . . the President rightly felt very strongly that the embargo was a mistake . . . penaliz[ing] the victim as much as the aggressor." But since lifting the embargo would likely endanger UN troops on the ground, "our allies were somewhere between strongly opposed and apoplectic about our violating" it. Moreover, lifting the embargo unilaterally without any clear diplomatic direction would almost certainly prompt the withdrawal of UNPROFOR— forcing the United States to get involved in a way that the Administration (and most of Congress) was actually trying to prevent.[26]

Presidents hate nothing more than getting squeezed by Congress— especially when it comes to "commander-in-chief" issues—and Clinton railed against the Hill in private conversations with his counterparts. He had told Chirac that he faced "the most isolationist Congress since the 1930s." They had been able to hold off congressional action for months, but after Srebrenica, the pressure became overwhelming. Many of those who had opposed lifting the embargo were outraged by the massacres, and Senator Dole, along with Democrats like Connecticut Senator Joseph Lieberman, turned up the heat and worked to push the arms embargo bill to a vote—and appeared to have enough support to override the President's veto. "This issue has me in a fun-house," President Clinton complained to British Prime Minister Major on July 14. "Our citizens have good motives. Compassion and neo-isolationism are leading to support for lifting the arms embargo. They don't want our soldiers there, but they badmouth the UN and want to give them [the Bosnians] arms."[27]

Clinton had prevailed upon Dole to delay any action until after the London Conference, but the Senator was less than impressed with London's results, and moved ahead with a vote. After an emotional Senate floor debate—in which many Democrats labored to explain why they would break with their President on a major foreign policy issue—the Senate voted on July 26 to lift the embargo, and six days later, the Republican-controlled House of Representatives did the same.

Dole argued that rather than undermining the Administration's position, he had actually strengthened it. He told Christopher that now they had leverage to press the Europeans. They could claim that since Congress would force them to lift the embargo unilaterally, they needed to take bold diplomatic action. Perhaps true, but Clinton promised to veto the measure—even though both bills passed with enough votes to override. With Congress adjourned for the summer and not returning until after September's Labor Day holiday, the Administration had time. Senior officials figured that combined with the successful Croatian offensive, the month-long congressional recess created a small window through which a new diplomatic effort could be launched.

This was just not an opportunity; the President's political advisors saw this as a political necessity—especially because the congressional pressure was being applied by Clinton's likely opponent in the 1996 election. As George Stephanopoulos recalled, "Clinton could sustain a veto and avoid a political defeat only by forcing a peace in Bosnia now."[28]

DECIDING THE ENDGAME

If "forcing a peace" was what the Administration needed to do, what would such a peace look like, and how would they do it? For the past few weeks, officials in the State Department, Defense Department, the Joint Chiefs of Staff, the NSC Staff, and the office of the UN Ambassador had been working on their own versions of an "endgame" paper that Lake had requested on July 17. Representatives from each of these agencies worked in an informal group to refine the differences between the four proposals so that in the end the President would be presented with distinct options, not just finely nuanced choices. These talks began in late July, as Berger and Vershbow at the NSC worked with Steinberg, Frasure and under Secretary Peter Tarnoff from State, and from the Pentagon, under Secretary of Defense Walter Slocombe, and Deputy Assistant Secretary of Defense Joe Kruzel. The product of their work was the package of "endgame" papers that Lake submitted to the President on August 5. These papers were to be discussed by the President and his top advisors at a meeting scheduled for August 7.[29]

As Lake explained in the cover memo he wrote to frame the 31-page package, the four papers concluded that the United States should pursue a diplomatic initiative in the coming weeks. On the future of UNPROFOR, all agencies agreed that if a settlement could not be reached or if UNPROFOR's credibility continued to stagger, the United States should fulfill its commitment to help it withdraw, lift the arms embargo, and move to a "post-withdrawal" strategy—for example, providing arms, training, and economic assistance to the Bosnians along with NATO air support.

THE PROPOSALS differed on what the goals of a diplomatic initiative should be. The State and Defense Departments tended to be more cautious and argued for a limited commitment: the United States should help the Bosnians consolidate the territory they had, but not support any efforts to recover lost territory. Both agencies worried that if the United States were to go that route, it would ruffle relations with the Europeans and Russia, and at worst, become militarily entangled in the Bosnian conflict.

The NSC and Albright papers, in contrast, outlined more ambitious goals. They supported the view that any initiative should seek to preserve Bosnia along lines broadly consistent with the Contact Group Plan—as a single state with roughly 51–49 percent territorial breakdown in favor of the Muslims. "Anything less," Lake wrote to the President, "would be tantamount to ratifying aggression and would, in any case, be rejected by Sarajevo."[30] Such support could be provided by creating an "arm and train" initiative along with NATO airstrikes against Bosnian Serb positions.

THE MAJOR CONCEPTUAL GULF between the NSC/Albright position and State/Defense was the risks the United States should run to achieve a settlement. Albright felt that the stakes were so high that the Americans had no choice but to be daring. She believed, as she had forcefully articulated back in June, that the failure to end the conflict in Bosnia undermined the Clinton Administration's leadership both at home and abroad. If the President could not bring a solution to Bosnia, then his political opponents would seize on the issue. The problem had become bigger than America's more limited strategic interests in Bosnia—or even broader interests in Europe. As Albright argued in her memorandum, the West's approach toward Bosnia has "caused serious erosion of the credibility of the NATO alliance and the United Nations. Worse, our continued reluctance to lead an effort to resolve a military crisis in the heart of Europe has placed at risk our leadership of the post-Cold War world."

Moreover, on the eve of the 1996 presidential campaign, Bosnia threatened to engulf all other areas of the Clinton Administration's foreign policy. "We should recognize that," Albright continued, "notwithstanding our successes in trade, Russia, and the Middle East and despite general agreement regarding Bosnia's complexity—our Administration's stewardship of foreign policy will be measured—fairly or unfairly—by our response to this issue. That is why we must take the lead in devising a diplomatic and military plan to achieve a durable peace. If we agree that American troops will be in Bosnia sooner or later, why not do it on our terms and our timetable?"[31]

While both State and Defense recognized the possibility that a renewed diplomatic initiative could reinvigorate U.S. leadership abroad, they feared a long and costly entanglement. Consistent with the argument Bob Frasure had articulated in late June, the State Department's main objective was to avoid carrying the United States over the wrong part of "the waterfall." The State paper advocated a "limited approach"—working to end the conflict, yet doing so without risking fundamental U.S. strategic and political interests. The Pentagon concurred, explaining that "the Administration's central problem is to find a policy that will meet American goals and get the support of the American public, not that of the Bosnians." Defense officials likewise agreed that the top priority was to avoid a sustained military presence in Bosnia. They saw too many echoes of Vietnam in the arm-and-train and airstrike proposals—and feared that the Bosnians would come to expect U.S. support to win back lost territory. This was too close to a quagmire scenario for Pentagon policy-makers.[32]

The Secretary of State, in particular, worried that the NSC and Albright proposals were far too risky.[33] Christopher was away from Washington at the time of this debate, meeting with the Vietnamese in Hanoi to establish American ties for the first time in 20 years. Yet he had made clear to his advisors that he feared that the Lake plan might promise more than the United States could deliver. Christopher believed that the while the Administration should work to solve Bosnia, this should not be done by shifting attention from its other foreign policy objectives, such as in Asia or Latin America. Pursuing more modest goals would "not only lessen our exposure, but are more likely to enjoy the support of others," the Secretary argued. He later told the President that "while we urgently need to get Bosnia behind us, we must not neglect the main themes [or] accomplishments of your foreign policy."[34]

ON AUGUST 7, President Clinton met with his senior advisers—Lake, Albright, Perry, Shalikashvili, and Peter Tarnoff (in the place of the traveling Christopher and Talbott) in the White House Cabinet Room to discuss the strategy papers.[35] Lake set out the choices before them: Should they take the risks advocated by the NSC and Albright, or should they hedge their bets and pursue the more limited objectives proposed by State and Defense?

Considering President Clinton's frustration with Bosnia, and his determination to take control of the issue, his choice was clear. "We should bust our ass to get a settlement within the next few months," he said. "We've got to exhaust every alternative, roll every die, take risks . . . We must commit to a unified Bosnia. And if we can't get that at the bargaining table, we have to help the Bosnians on the battlefield." The London Conference, Croatian offensive and congressional recess had created a window of opportunity that might soon close. "If we let this moment slip away," he said, "we are history."[36]

Clinton decided to make a big bet, the equivalent of pushing all his chips into the middle of the table: the mission should encompass the bold goals set forth in the NSC and Albright papers. The United States would commit itself to a unified Bosnia, and if that were not attainable through negotiations, it would be willing to assist the Bosnians militarily. The President also agreed that if this diplomatic effort failed or if UNPROFOR continued to founder, the United States would "pull the plug" on the UN mission and unilaterally lift the arms embargo.[37]

But they still needed to sort out the specifics. Both the NSC and State proposals detailed the parameters of a possible diplomatic mission. The NSC advocated launching the initiative by visiting the key European allies, getting them on board first to present the plan with a unified front. But the proposal remained vague on how to approach the Balkan leaders. It suggested only that the United States should broaden negotiations with Milosevic—either through the Europeans or with an American representative—to encourage him to bring his Bosnian Serb clients to the negotiating table, and to begin a bilateral dialogue with the Sarajevo government, pressing it to be more flexible.

The State paper presented a modified version of the earlier Steinberg/Frasure proposal to reach a three-party conference by combining the Milosevic track with Sarajevo–Pale talks and broadening the negotiations to include Croatia. They would offer Milosevic the carrot of sanctions relief in exchange for cooperation toward a negotiated settlement. After this, talks would begin between Izetbegovic and Milosevic, and would be broadened to include Tudjman as well.

CLINTON DECIDED TO COMBINE elements from both proposals in developing the mission's strategic and logistical form. The initiative would begin, as the NSC had suggested, with an American team traveling to at least London, Bonn, and Paris. This would not be like Warren Christopher's mission to Europe in May 1993, where he was sent to consult with the Europeans about "lift and strike" and came home unsuccessful (as Christopher admitted later, that trip "was not consistent with global leadership"). The Americans would go to explain what they were doing, not ask for permission. The message would be "part invitation, part ultimatum." To give the mission a presidential imprimatur, Lake would lead it, but he would be accompanied by an inter-agency team, representing the unity of the entire Administration. After the visit to Europe, the American mission would continue on to the region, conducting shuttle diplomacy between the three Balkan capitals. Eventually, they envisioned bringing the parties together for a peace conference—although at the time, that seemed like a distant possibility.[38]

They also agreed that it would be impractical for the President's National Security Advisor to spend his time conducting the protracted negotiations that would hopefully follow his European trip. He would bow out after briefing the Europeans, and Richard Holbrooke would lead the team to negotiate in the Balkans.

CHOOSING HOLBROOKE TO LEAD THE MISSION was not an easy one for some of the President's senior advisors. As the Assistant Secretary of State for Europe and Clinton's first Ambassador to Germany, Holbrooke was the obvious choice—in fact, fixing Bosnia, along with managing the enlargement of

NATO, was what he had been brought back from Germany to Washington to do. But he had a well-deserved reputation as a maverick, and while he undoubtedly was a rare diplomatic talent who could get results, his bull-in-a-china-shop style made more understated officials, especially Lake and Christopher, uneasy. He had consistently pushed for a tougher policy in Bosnia, and in 1993 had volunteered to be a special envoy but had been rebuffed. Holbrooke had not hidden his disdain with the direction of the Administration's approach—earlier that year he had written in the influential journal *Foreign Affairs* that Bosnia represented "the greatest collective security failure of the West since the 1930's."[39] In an attempt to influence the President to take stronger action, earlier that summer he had even reached out privately one of Clinton's closest friends, Vernon Jordan, and to the First Lady, Hillary Rodham Clinton, warning her that Bosnia was a "cancer on the presidency."

Yet he considered Lake's policy process to be, as he put it, "wheel-spinning," and only worth the paper it was written on. He doubted whether the Administration had the will to implement any tough choices. Nor was it a secret that Holbrooke wished to return to the private sector in New York City, where his family lived. Newly married, Holbrooke had spent the latter part of July and early August—a time of intense political deliberation—on a long-scheduled vacation. He had opted out of most of the policy debates on Bosnia that summer, deferring to two of his most trusted colleagues, Frasure and Talbott. Holbrooke later explained that he had "deliberately remained at a distance, not only because of my family commitments, but also because my participating might have reduced my negotiating flexibility later."[40]

Lake professed concern as to whether or not Holbrooke's "head was in the game." He advocated giving the lead to Tarnoff, Frasure, or even Charles Redman, the former American envoy to the Contact Group who had replaced Holbrooke as the American Ambassador to Germany. But Holbrooke clearly wanted the job, and had long said that he would leave the Administration if he did not get it, as he had been promised. Christopher, with the critical backing of Talbott and Tom Donilon (close Holbrooke allies who had always assumed most of the responsibility for handling their friend), supported Holbrooke and told President Clinton that he had full confidence in him.

"I concluded that he was perfect for the task," Christopher recalls. "The very qualities for which he was sometimes criticized—aggressiveness, impolitic interaction with adversaries, a penchant for cultivating the media—were exactly what the situation required. I could imagine no better match for the likes of Milosevic, Izetbegovic, and Tudjman, and I knew many who would have paid money from their own pockets for ringside seats." In the end, the President agreed.[41]

WITH THE DECISION MADE on the plan and the way to carry it forward, Clinton immediately called his three key European partners—Chirac, Major, and Kohl—to tell them that Lake would be coming. The President did not discuss specifics, since they were still being worked out. But all three leaders expressed enthusiasm for Washington's new resolve.[42]

THE SCRIPT

Over the course of the next day, August 8, the NSC's Sandy Vershbow and his staff worked with other officials, including Jim Steinberg and Bob Frasure, to draft the talking points for Lake. The points were carefully crafted, as they were intended to be read verbatim as a script at each stop. Clinton personally edited the document, going through the details line-by-line, and they finalized it only minutes before Lake departed for Europe the morning of August 9.[43]

Lake's nine-page, single-spaced script began with the broad themes under which the United States approached the crisis.[44] American policy, it read, "is still guided by several enduring principles and interests: maintaining our relationships with allies and credibility of NATO; avoiding conflict with Russia that could undermine reform and international cooperation; and preventing the spread of the Bosnian conflict into a wider Balkan war." Croatia's recent military offensive, although "not endorsed by any of us," created a unique strategic opportunity by mitigating Bosnian Serb strengths and reducing their territorial holdings. Lake would tell the Europeans that this opening provided a chance to pursue a bold initiative: "We don't have the time to think in terms of partial solutions or muddling through. We should think boldly and make an all-out effort to reach a settlement."

THE SCRIPT OUTLINED the terms for peace in Bosnia, as well as a solution to the tensions between Croatia and Serbia. In the days following the August 7 meeting, these terms had been reduced to seven points:

1. The settlement would be comprehensive, based on the Contact Group plan (and a 51–49 territorial split).
2. It would include three-way mutual recognition among Croatia, Serbia, and Bosnia, with an end to offensive military operations.
3. The Americans would push the parties to negotiate "more viable borders" reflecting the recent changes on the ground in Bosnia, such as pressing the Bosnians to trade vulnerable areas like Gorazde for Serb-held territory.
4. Bosnia would remain one state with one constitution, but would be composed of two highly autonomous entities (one majority-Serb and another majority-Muslim/Croat).
5. The United States would take a "bold approach" to sanctions relief, accepting a "suspension" of economic sanctions against Serbia once an agreement was signed, with complete lifting of sanctions when an agreement was implemented.
6. The settlement would include a Croat-Serb agreement on Eastern Slavonia, the resource-rich land between Croatia and Serbia that the two countries fought over in 1991 and the Serbs now occupied. This would, of course, be a prerequisite for winning mutual recognition between Serbia and Croatia.
7. The settlement would include a comprehensive program for regional economic reconstruction. This last point was particularly significant to

the diplomatic initiative, because although the United States would lead the negotiations, European contributions to the reconstruction program would be a substantial incentive for agreement.

The keys to this new initiative were the incentives and disincentives—or "carrots" and "sticks"—that would be used with both sides. In addition to economic reconstruction, the "carrots" were: for the Bosnians, enforcement of the peace terms by NATO and military assistance; for the Croats, movement toward integration into European institutions; for the Serbs, sanctions relief; and for the Bosnian Serbs, legal territorial rights within a unified Bosnia.

But the proposed "sticks" were what made this plan unique. The United States would outline to the Balkan leaders the consequences of the "failure scenario"—not reaching a settlement and UNPROFOR withdrawal. The sticks would be calibrated to the particular failure scenario. If the Bosnians negotiated in good faith, but the Serbs stood in the way, the Bosnians would get "lift and strike" and "equip and train," that is, NATO air strikes against the Serbs during UNPROFOR withdrawal, a lifting of the arms embargo, and American military training. But if the Bosnians were the cause of failure, they would be faced with "lift and leave"; that is, the United States would lift the arms embargo, but provide no airstrikes, arms, or training. This latter "stick" was crucial, because the Americans feared the Bosnians would otherwise find the former failure scenario—leading to "lift-and-strike"—more attractive than agreeing to a settlement. The United States would have to make it clear to Sarajevo that American support would not be unconditional.

AT HIS FINAL MEETING with the President before he left for Europe, Lake restated the goals of the mission: to inform the Europeans of what had been decided and invite them to come on board. While the Americans would listen to suggestions, they were committed to go ahead—with or without their allies' help. Christopher, who had just returned from Asia, expressed his support, although he remained guarded about the difficulties the United States would face should it have to implement a failure scenario. As for the President, he remained convinced that the United States had to take advantage of this opportunity. If they did not act now, they would not have the chance later. Lake left for the airport with his interagency delegation—Peter Tarnoff and Bob Frasure from State; Sandy Vershbow and Peter Bass of the NSC; Lt. General Wesley Clark of the Joint Chiefs of Staff; and Joseph Kruzel, the Deputy Assistant Secretary of Defense for Europe and NATO Affairs—and the U.S. mission to bring peace to Bosnia got underway.[45]

THE MISSION BEGINS

At first, Lake and his team only planned to stop in London, Bonn, and Paris. Uncertain about the reception they would receive, particularly in the

United Kingdom and France, they wanted to test the waters before moving further. But after the London stop on August 10, they had confidence. "As we got out there," Tarnoff recalled, "the idea seemed to gain favor. Tony in particular felt that the time had come to touch as many bases as possible." Soon they added stops in Rome, Madrid (Spain then held the chair of the EU presidency), Ankara, and Sochi, Crimea, where they would consult with the vacationing Russian Foreign Minister, Andrei Kozyrev.

The Europeans' enthusiasm did not diminish along the way—as one American participant put it, the meetings were "a piece of cake." The Germans were very supportive, although were worried that the diplomatic sticks would be used too forcefully to compel the Bosnians to accept an "unreasonable" agreement. Even the French—who the Americans expected to raise objections given Chirac's efforts to assert his own leadership earlier that summer—expressed "one-hundred percent support" for the initiative, welcoming the "new U.S. determination." And the Russians were less grumpy about the plan than even the French. Kozyrev recommended that the United States deal directly with Milosevic in order to "deliver" the Bosnian Serbs, and urged that they push for an early cease-fire between the parties.[46] But overall, Kozyrev told Lake, "we don't want to argue about ideas, we just want to engage with you to search for solutions."[47]

WITH THE ALLIES ON BOARD, Lake and his team returned to London on August 14 to rendezvous with Holbrooke and NSC aide Nelson Drew, who along with Frasure, Clark, and Kruzel, would conduct the regional shuttle. The talks with the European partners had been a huge success. They seemed relieved that—finally—the Americans were leading. Now the diplomatic initiative could be presented to the Balkan parties with the full weight of the international community behind it.

Things had gone so well, in fact, that some members of Lake's team urged him to assume the lead from Holbrooke. This was fueled, at least in part, by a New York Times article about Holbrooke that had appeared while the Lake delegation was in Rome, in which Holbrooke was quoted as criticizing Lake's policy process as a "gigantic stalemate machine" that produced a "watered down policy." The story might have accurately reflected Holbrooke's views, but the timing wasn't deliberate—in fact, Holbrooke had been interviewed weeks before he had even been asked to lead the mission, and was already making his way to Europe when the story appeared. While the article turned out to be little more than fuel for the insider gossip that was so common for August in Washington (outraging many officials, especially Christopher, who had insisted that he be the negotiator), it added an additional layer of drama to the private hand off meeting between Lake and Holbrooke.[48]

Sitting down alone in the American Embassy in London, Lake and Holbrooke talked for an hour about the next phase of the mission. Holbrooke recalls telling Lake that the United States needed to prepare for failure: "We should not let expectations outrun reality. We [will] give it our best, but it [will] be a very difficult process." he said.[49] Lake handed

Holbrooke his own script for the parties, which had been finalized by the delegation the night before. The points reviewed the seven terms of the settlement and outlined the "carrots" and "sticks."[50] Lake urged Holbrooke to stick to the script—but Holbrooke said that he would not push the Bosnians to abandon Gorazde, as the NSC and Pentagon had been recommending.

Their discussion—which Holbrooke remembered as "quietly emotional"— turned to their shared history and the opportunity before them. Lake later recalled that he wanted to "fire Holbrooke up." The two had been linked for over 30 years personally and professionally; they had entered the Foreign Service in 1962, served together in Vietnam during the 1960s, and held high-level State Department posts in the Carter Administration. They were both genuine friends and fierce rivals. After the events of the summer and the unkept secret that Holbrooke was unhappy with both the process and the policy, Lake wanted to be sure his old friend understood the stakes. This was what Holbrooke had been preparing for his whole life, Lake told him. This was his moment. "If the effort failed, we in Washington would stand by him and take the blame," Lake recalls saying. If it went well, Holbrooke would garner the glory.[51]

3

TRAGEDY AS TURNING POINT: THE FIRST SHUTTLE, MT. IGMAN, AND OPERATION DELIBERATE FORCE

The new American envoy and his team—Bob Frasure from State, Army Lt. General Wesley Clark from the Joint Chiefs of Staff, Joe Kruzel from the Defense Department, the NSC's Nelson Drew, and Holbrooke's indispensable assistant, Rosemarie Pauli—left London the afternoon of August 14 to fly to Split, Croatia. With a credible threat of NATO airstrikes, Croatia's military success, and now a unified diplomatic front with Europe, the Americans had considerable momentum behind them—perhaps more than any previous attempt to end the Bosnia war. But the Balkans were littered with failed diplomatic initiatives far less ambitious than the one they carried. Depending on how this mission went, the American effort could end quickly. Holbrooke's team knew that they wouldn't end the war with one trip. What they needed was a strong start.

All diplomatic negotiations are complex, but the challenge ahead seemed uniquely so. Success required difficult concessions from all three parties within Bosnia—Muslims, Croats, and Serbs—as well as their allies and leaders in Croatia and Serbia. Each of these groups had their own sense of entitlement, their own interpretations of history, and their own sets of expectations. What the Americans needed from each side sounded deceivingly simple—as a detailed "gameplan" paper prepared by the State Department's European Bureau for Holbrooke's team summarized, "the Bosnians will have to adjust their thinking on the map. Croatia will have to accept something short of immediate return of Sector East (Eastern Slavonia), [and] Milosevic will have to adjust his stance on sanctions relief to fit the new situation." Easier said than done.[1]

THE BOSNIANS: ARE THE STICKS ACTUALLY CARROTS?

The first hurdle would be to get the Bosnian Muslim leadership—the main victims of the war—to support the basic outlines of the initiative. Holbrooke's delegation knew that this would be tough. They were informed by intelligence reports that many Bosnians were already suspicious of the U.S. proposal, believing that it simply amounted to a "carve-up" of Bosnia. The Sarajevo government was angry that they had not been consulted during the formation of the American plan, and felt that it was "an effort to obtain peace at any price." It had also gained confidence. Invigorated by the Croatia's successes in the Krajina and around Bihac, they were optimistic about their own military possibilities.

This fact became clear during the American team's first meeting with Bosnian Foreign Minister Mohamed Sacirbey on August 15. A U.S. citizen who had played football at Tulane University in New Orleans, Sacirbey was well-known to the Americans, and his many television appearances had made him the Sarajevo government's public face. Sitting in the back of the U.S. delegation's Air Force plane on the tarmac in Split, Holbrooke described to Sacirbey Lake's seven points, explaining, with emphasis, that everything had President Clinton's full support. As he outlined the carrots and sticks, Sacirbey paid particular attention to UNPROFOR withdrawal and lift-and-strike, indicating that this "might be more interesting for the Bosnians than reaching a peace accord." He also complained about what he called the "red light" from Washington on Bosnian military advances.

These hints that the Bosnians might actually prefer the so-called failure scenario were troubling. Did the Bosnians really want to be left on their own without an arms embargo to fight the Serbs? Already, Holbrooke and his team feared that there could be a devastating weakness in the plan they carried—the Bosnians might see the intended "stick" of lift-and-leave as a "carrot." The Sarajevo government had faith in its ability to mobilize support within the United States, particularly on Capitol Hill, and believed that the Clinton Administration would never simply lift the arms embargo and walk away.

Aside from this insight into Bosnian expectations, this three-hour meeting included the first departure from Lake's seven points. The script had outlined that the Americans would "steer" the Bosnians to trade Gorazde for Serb concessions. Sacirbey insisted that they keep the enclave. Without argument, Holbrooke agreed—as he had told Lake he would—and told Sacirbey to deny publicly that the United States had pressured them to give it up. Although many American officials, particularly those in the Pentagon, felt that Bosnia's territory needed to be more compact and therefore less difficult to defend, Holbrooke rejected this. With Sacirbey's public statement, Holbrooke hoped that trading Gorazde would now be off the table for good.[2]

TUDJMAN: DIZZY WITH SUCCESS

The next morning, the American delegation went to Zagreb to meet with Croatian President Franjo Tudjman. As a former General in the Yugoslav Army and strident nationalist, Tudjman was energized by his military's gains in Krajina. Frasure observed that the Croat President was "flush with victory."

U.S. Ambassador to Croatia Peter Galbraith, who joined Holbrooke for this meeting, remarked that he had not seen Tudjman so ebullient in 18 months. The Croatian President responded positively to the American plan, explaining that his military's recent victories on the battlefield offered "favorable conditions" for a peaceful solution. Unsurprisingly, he stressed that his highest priority was to reintegrate Eastern Slavonia into Croatia. Tudjman also complained that the Bosnian–Croat Federation—the shaky alliance the Americans had helped create in 1994—was "a heavy cross to bear" because of considerable resistance from Bosnian Croats to cooperate with Bosnian Muslims.

Tudjman argued that three-way territorial partition would be the only lasting solution for Bosnia. Holbrooke rejected this, asserting that "no involuntary dismemberment [of Bosnia] was acceptable." Joseph Kruzel added that the purpose of the American plan was to provide Bosnia a chance to decide its own future. Backtracking a bit, Tudjman said that he supported that idea "for the time being," but said that they must keep in mind the "strategic realities" in drawing the boundaries between the "eastern" and "western" worlds.[3]

Frustrated by Tudjman's comments, the Americans wanted to make clear to the Croats that they would not get a slice of Bosnia. Frasure and Kruzel delivered this message in an afternoon meeting with Croatia's Foreign Minister, Mate Granic. Frasure told Granic that Tudjman's "historically deterministic" approach toward Bosnia was unacceptable. "Croatia must decide if it wishes to be viewed as a Western nation, with Western values and respectful of democratic processes," Kruzel said, "or Croatia can forego such Western political, military and economic support should it decide to take advantage of short-term gains and carve up Bosnia based on fears of an Islamic state in Europe."[4]

As the American diplomats left Zagreb for Belgrade, they were worried. Tudjman's boastful performance, clearly inspired by his recent military victories, could be a big problem. Did it foreshadow a renewed Croat–Serb, and possibly Croat–Muslim conflict? Dizzy with success, the Croat President might push things too far. To Ambassador Galbraith, "the success of Krajina and [Tudjman's] belief that the U.S. is Croatia's best friend favoring it over all other Balkan parties, the old Tudjman has reemerged with even greater vigor." While the Americans considered it unlikely that he would act to capture a piece of Bosnia in the near future, Tudjman's behavior could bring down the fledgling Muslim–Croat Federation. This potential Tudjman problem, Galbraith cabled Washington, "needs to be nipped in the bud."[5] Despite these very real concerns, the Holbrooke team had to deal with the more immediate problem challenge: Slobodan Milosevic.

To the Table with "The Gambler"

Milosevic, the leader most responsible for the Balkans' nightmare, would be the linchpin in any peace agreement. The Serb president was the Balkan version of Syria's longtime president, Hafez al-Assad—a keen, relentless negotiator and ruthless dictator averse to compromise, but critical to comprehensive peace in the region. The top American diplomat in Belgrade, Rudolph Perina, aptly characterized Milosevic as a "gambler"—someone who desperately wanted to "transform his hand into real winnings," but willing to up the ante and wait if the deal proved unacceptable. "Milosevic the gambler is also Milosevic the wily rug merchant," Perina explained in a cable to Holbrooke. "If [Milosevic] does not get his bottom price, he will pass on the deal and move to limit his political damage." Milosevic was prone to behavior described by the Serb word "*inat*"—a word that Serbs use to refer to their proud, stubborn, all-or-nothing attitude. Perina noted that while "Milosevic is more cunning and realistic than most Serb leaders in coping with pressure, he is not immune to the '*inat*' syndrome . . . after all he has gambled over the past year, [he] will be looking for a deal that he can portray as a win, not just an easing of punishment."[6]

This would be a pivotal meeting for Holbrooke. He had never met the Serb leader—Frasure and Perina were the two American officials who knew Milosevic best—and this first encounter would allow him to show that there had been a new departure in U.S. diplomacy. Milosevic had been described by former Secretary of State James Baker as a "tough," a person who only understood the language of power. Holbrooke, himself a formidable negotiator, also knew this idiom, and was ready to use it.

Perina suggested that Holbrooke play hardball with Milosevic, exploiting his "inherent prejudices, fears, and emotions." Chief among these were his hatred of Tudjman and the Bosnian Serb leader, Radovan Karadzic, two men "he considers far inferior to himself and yet perceived as successful in defying and upstaging him. His personification of this conflict is key to his mindset and tactics." Perina advised Holbrooke to warn Milosevic that any delay on his part would prolong circumstances "that allow Tudjman to circumvent the arms embargo," and leave open the threat that Karadzic could be rehabilitated if he proved more forthcoming than Milosevic. While the United States didn't want to deal with the Bosnian Serb leader, leaving this option open would cause Milosevic to worry about being sidelined. "Milosevic should be aware that he is not out of the woods on becoming another Saddam Hussein or Colonel Qadhafi if he fails to deliver when needed."[7]

THE SIX-HOUR MEETING ON AUGUST 17 at the Presidency building in Belgrade was little more than a "get to know you session" between Holbrooke and Milosevic. Talking over dinner, they bantered about New York City and the banking world (Milosevic had once had a brief experience in the New York banking community, where Holbrooke had worked for many years). As Bob Frasure observed, "the two egos danced all night."

Milosevic said that he could not recognize Croatia after what had happened in Krajina, and routinely demanded a full lifting of sanctions against Serbia. Milosevic also argued that any agreement should be put to a referendum of all Serbs (both in Serbia and Bosnia) as a way to convince Pale to accept it. He tried to distance himself from the Bosnian Serbs, belittling them as unsophisticated rubes, agreeing with a military assessment provided by Wes Clark on the deteriorating situation of their army, and repeatedly railing against Karadzic as a "crazy, dumb maniac." Holbrooke baited Milosevic by playing to his machismo, saying that he had to show he could handle Karadzic by overtaking him—proving that he alone would speak for the Bosnian Serbs. "We will not talk to you until you make a deal with the Bosnian Serbs," Holbrooke said. He also warned Milosevic that if the negotiating effort failed, the United States would implement certain "sticks," such as lift-and-strike.[8]

MILOSEVIC HAD SAID nothing new, instead focusing on his referendum proposal, which was a way for him to dodge responsibility. And his tirade against the Bosnian Serbs was a classic piece of empty showmanship well known to those with experience dealing with him. That night, Holbrooke and Frasure stayed at the Ambassador's residence with Perina, where they talked about how nothing had changed since Frasure had last met the Serbian leader in June.

Holbrooke was discouraged. "Milosevic was playing word games devoid of substance—and he knew it," he recalled. "Without budging, he focused on inconsequential changes in draft documents over which he and Frasure has been arguing since the beginning of the year." After stewing about this overnight, Holbrooke awoke the morning of August 18 angry and determined. He wanted to "make clear that we would not continue the cat-and-mouse game [Milosevic] had played with previous negotiators."

"Listen you guys," Holbrooke said to Perina and Frasure, "I'm going back to see Slobo and I'm going to throw a Goddamned fit this morning." Holbrooke wanted to lay down a marker with Milosevic, to "scare the hell out of him, to tell him that what he was doing was totally unacceptable." Feeling that the large group meeting had been too unwieldy, and wanting "to create an impression of greater intensity and intimacy," Holbrooke asked only Frasure and the NSC's Drew (representing the White House) to accompany him.[9]

The three-hour meeting went according to plan. After Milosevic recited his usual positions, Holbrooke lit into him with his choreographed but intense tirade. He told Milosevic that there was no time for endless bargaining, and that the Americans needed something more than his tired demands. The Serb leader seemed unmoved; he just stared back at Holbrooke. To the rest of the delegation waiting in the anteroom, only shouts could be heard from behind the closed doors.[10]

Holbrooke demanded that Milosevic secure a route through which the American team could safely travel to Sarajevo. He said that "it was disgraceful, as well as time-consuming and dangerous, to continue to travel from Belgrade to Sarajevo by the current method—flying on a plane to Split, negotiating with the UN and French for helicopters, taking the choppers over tough terrain in uncertain weather to ever-changing drop-off points, and then driving in armored personnel carriers over Mt. Igman." Holbrooke believed that if Milosevic could secure such a route, it would also be seen as a confidence-building measure and create "a public sense of progress" toward peace. Milosevic had said that he was willing to work for peace, and Holbrooke wanted him to prove it.

Milosevic immediately ordered an aide to contact Bosnian Serb General Ratko Mladic to find out if this was possible. Despite his claims that he had no control over the Bosnian Serbs, this proved that Milosevic at least had the credibility to try. As Holbrooke reflected, "it was the first time we had seen what was later to become a recurring pattern in our negotiations—a direct line between Milosevic . . . and Mladic. Sometimes it produced results, sometimes not." This day it failed. Mladic replied that he could not guarantee their security, but that he could ensure safety on a shorter route over the Bosnian Serb-protected Kisiljak road. EU envoy Carl Bildt had recently used this route, as had Holbrooke during a trip to Sarajevo as a private citizen in 1992. But he now felt that an official American delegation could not be subjected to the numerous Bosnian Serb checkpoints along Kisiljak. Holbrooke demanded that Milosevic provide his own personal guarantee (not Mladic's) that the delegation would not be stopped en route to Sarajevo. Milosevic refused, and the Americans decided that they had to take the Mt. Igman route. They would return to Zagreb that night to brief the Croats, and set out for Sarajevo on Saturday, August 19. They told Milosevic they would be back to see him on August 20.[11]

ALTHOUGH FAR FROM delivering any diplomatic breakthroughs, the team left Belgrade feeling that they had been given enough to work with. Their talks so far did reveal trouble ahead, as all three parties presented special challenges. Yet each side had now been briefed on the initiative's points, and none had rejected them outright. They seemed to understand that American's patience had run out. Most important, perhaps, Holbrooke and his colleagues believed they had sent an unmistakable message that the United States finally meant business and was willing to use the full range of "sticks"—economic, political, and military—if the parties refused to cooperate.

THE MT. IGMAN TRAGEDY

Holbrooke's team flew to Zagreb to review the Milosevic talks with the Croats. They told Tudjman that Milosevic's remained unwilling to recognize Croatia in the aftermath of Krajina, and reiterated the need for Croatia's military restraint in Eastern Slavonia. They also pressed Tudjman again to support the territorial integrity of Bosnia. Tudjman repeated that partition was not his strategy, it was simply a fact, even quoting a view attributed to Henry Kissinger to make his point: "If you couldn't hold together Yugoslavia, you can't hold together Bosnia."[12]

IN MANY WAYS, the Croats were responsible for creating the environment that made the American initiative possible—their successful lightning strike against Krajina provided the final push that convinced President Clinton to move forth with the mission. In his memoirs, Clinton writes that Croatia's actions "changed both the balance of power on the ground and the psychology of all the parties." To Holbrooke, the offensive was "a complete success," delivering a defeat for the Serbs for the first time in four years. "[The] success of the Croatian offensive was a classic illustration of the fact that the shape of the diplomatic landscape will usually reflect the balance of forces on the ground . . . The abandonment of the Bosnian Serbs by Milosevic eliminated one of our greatest fears—that Begrade would re-enter the war."[13]

But Croatia's gains had left its leadership excessively confident, and Holbrooke's team worried that their hubris could destroy this rare diplomatic opportunity. In a written report to Secretary of Defense Perry, Joe Kruzel elaborated on these concerns. During the talks in Zagreb, Kruzel had had a long discussion with Croatian Defense Minister Gojko Susak as they walked around the grounds of Tudjman's villa. The military gains in western Bosnia, Kruzel reported, would allow the Muslim–Croat Federation to hold just over half of Bosnia. "The good news is that the Federation is finally at 51% [the Contact Group plan's goal]," Kruzel wrote. "The bad news is that the territory held by the Federation will be overwhelmingly Bosnian Croat land. The Muslims are severely shortchanged." Susak had implied that the "Croats were not about to swap 'their' territory within the 51% for increases in Muslim territory." Kruzel saw that "the Croats are now, or will soon be, a status quo power in the region, delighted with what they have and willing to fight to hold onto it."

Kruzel was convinced that Croatia's posture meant big problems for the "lift-and-leave" option if talks failed. If the idea would be to provide weapons and training to the Federation to balance the Serbs, "that's not possible, because the Croats won't fight the Serbs over the Muslims, [nor] will they let the Muslims acquire enough weapons to be in a position to pose any sort of challenge to Zagreb." Kruzel saw that the potential for infighting within the Federation was a "fundamental conceptual flaw" of the U.S. proposal. In the year-and-a-half since the Americans helped create the Federation, little progress had been made to reduce the deep distrust between the Croats and Bosnian Muslims. Given that a strong Federation with some semblance of unity was one of the basic premises of the American plan, they knew they had a problem. Tragically, Kruzel's memorandum, dated August 18, would be his last. By the time Pentagon officials found it on their desks the morning of August 19, all of Washington was focused on reports of an accident on Mt. Igman.[14]

AFTER AN OVERNIGHT STOP IN SPLIT, Holbrooke, Clark, Frasure, Kruzel, Drew, and Clark's aide Lt. Colonel Daniel Gerstein set off via helicopter for the Mt. Igman road, which would lead them into Sarajevo (Rosemarie Pauli stayed behind). They began to travel up Mt. Igman at 10 A.M. Sarajevo time (4 A.M. in Washington) in two French military vehicles: Holbrooke and Clark in a Humvee, and Frasure, Kruzel, Drew, Gerstein, and U.S. Diplomatic Security Agent Peter Hargreaves in an Armored Personnel Carrier (APC).

At 6:15 A.M. Washington time the morning of August 19, John Menzies, the U.S. Ambassador-designate in Sarajevo, telephoned the State Department Operations Center to convey reports he had received about an accident involving Holbrooke's convoy on Mt. Igman. In trying to maneuver around a French truck on a narrow mountain bend, the APC with Frasure, Kruzel, Drew, Gerstein, and Hargreaves slipped off a cliff and rolled several hundred yards down the Igman slope. Frasure, Kruzel, and Drew were killed.

ONLY MINUTES AFTER MENZIES'S PHONE CALL, officials at the State Department scrambled to get information. Christopher Hill, Frasure's deputy in the European Bureau, called Sarajevo to get a full read-out of the situation, and then called Strobe Talbott and Sandy Berger (both Christopher and Perry were on vacation). Holbrooke first talked to the officials in Washington almost two hours later in a call with Talbott, Lake, Berger, and General Shalikashvili. He then spoke with President Clinton. "We must suspend the mission long enough to bring our fallen comrades home," Holbrooke said. "You sent us here as a team. We'll come back as a team, and then we're anxious to resume our mission."

"That's fine," the President said. "Come home as soon as you can, but make it clear that our commitment to the peace effort will continue and that you will lead it."

After a short and somber meeting with Bosnian President Izetbegovic in Sarajevo, the delegation departed for Ramstein Air Force Base in Germany. On August 21, the Holbrooke team returned to Washington to bury the bodies of their colleagues, and the U.S. government began to regroup.[15]

PUTTING THE PIECES BACK TOGETHER

The accident left American officials reeling. But the tragedy forced the Clinton administration to consider more deeply the fundamental goals of and prospects for its initiative. In this way, the process of regrouping emotionally also provided an opportunity to assess the status and sharpen the focus of the mission. Had the Holbrooke trip accomplished enough to warrant continuing the diplomatic effort? If so, what should the next U.S. move be?

The U.S. government had lost three officials whose efforts had been integral to its policy and diplomacy throughout 1995. Bob Frasure had been a key player in the State Department's policy toward the Balkans, serving throughout 1995 as the top envoy to the region. More important, he had had an established negotiating rapport with Milosevic, and had tremendous institutional knowledge about the players and issues involved. Joe Kruzel had been Secretary of Defense Perry's own point man for the region. He had developed a good relationship with Croat Defense Minister Susak and understood acutely the brewing problems with the Bosnia–Croat Federation. Nelson Drew, who had worked closely with Lake, Berger, and Vershbow in managing the process to create the "endgame strategy," was the NSC's only link to the initiative it had launched. Although negotiators such as Frasure, Kruzel, and Drew could never be replaced, new people would have to be found to fill their roles.

There was no debate that the United States should continue its diplomatic effort. In a phone call with French Foreign Minister de Charette only hours after the Mt. Igman accident, Secretary Christopher said that the tragedy "would cause us to redouble our efforts and sharpen our resolve to see peace in the region."[16] President Clinton himself reiterated publicly what he had already told Christopher and Holbrooke privately: "I think the thing that they [Frasure, Kruzel and Drew] would want us to do is press ahead, and that's what we intend to do."[17] Although this first shuttle mission had revealed some problems—a Bosnian leadership perhaps willing to pursue a military solution, Croatia's desire for partition, and Milosevic's recalcitrance—these were not reasons to give up, especially when compared to how other diplomatic efforts had fared.

THE ACCIDENT ALSO MUFFLED criticism that had been building against the Administration from Capitol Hill. On August 11, President Clinton—in only the second veto of his Presidency—blocked passage of the Dole-Lieberman bill to lift the American arms embargo against Bosnia unilaterally. On August 18, the day before the Mt. Igman tragedy, Senator Dole wrote to Clinton to express his concerns about the U.S. initiative, particularly regarding the sanctions "carrots" being offered to Milosevic. In an August 28 reply, Clinton wrote that in the aftermath of Mt. Igman, "we intend to persevere in our efforts to achieve a just and lasting peace in the Balkans and are exploring with the parties ideas that include both carrots and sticks." On sanctions, the President reassured the Kansas Republican that "we are proposing suspension of a broad range of sanctions—not full lifting as your letter states—only if there is agreement on a political settlement in Bosnia." Clinton wrote that while he disagreed with Dole's position toward the arms embargo, he understood that the ultimate purpose was to restore a balance of power that would hopefully bring peace. Yet, President Clinton concluded, "I believe we must seize this moment to see if we can achieve a fair and durable settlement *now* (underlined in letter), without another year of fighting. I hope that you will give that effort a full and unencumbered opportunity to be tested and your strong support if it is successful."[18] Congress did step aside to let the Administration's diplomacy unfold; yet getting its strong support for the policy proved far more difficult.

ALONG WITH THE IMMEDIATE CONCERNS that the next shuttle would have to address—which would be left largely to Holbrooke and his team—officials in Washington began to think about what the shape of a future agreement might look like. Lake's seven-point script envisioned an outcome consistent with the principles the Contact Group endorsed the previous year: Bosnia would remain a single state, divided into two autonomous entities, with a special relationship between the Bosnian Serbs and Serbia and the Muslim–Croat Federation and Croatia, respectively. But these were the just general parameters, and the negotiators had to figure out a way to get from here to there.

The effort to flesh out these basic principles began with the decision to make the Washington lawyer Roberts Owen part of the reconstituted shuttle team. Many officials, most notably Christopher, believed that if they were going to try to help create a new Bosnian state and constitution, an experienced attorney had to be part of the negotiating delegation. "It seemed to me," Christopher recalled, "that we lacked anyone who had had significant experience in drafting international documents, anyone who was basically an international lawyer." He knew that "the things that [would be] put to paper on the shuttles were going to have a profound affect on the governing structures of Bosnia." So on August 20, the day after the Mt. Igman accident, Christopher asked Owen to join Holbrooke's team. Christopher and Owen were longtime professional associates and personal friends; they had worked together in the State Department under President Carter (Christopher as Deputy Secretary, Owen as Legal Advisor), and Owen had played a key role under Christopher in negotiating the release of the American hostages in Iran during 1979–1980. Christopher believed that Owen's experience with Iran uniquely suited him for what promised to be a long and arduous negotiating process. A highly respected partner at Dean Acheson's old law firm, Covington & Burling, Owen had also been the lead American arbitrator to help create the Muslim–Croat Federation, so he already understood many of the key issues (although some of the Europeans grumbled that he was not a constitutional lawyer).[19]

MEETING AT FORT MYER

On August 23, over 300 people gathered at the yellow-brick chapel of Fort Myer, an Army base in Virginia across the Potomac River from Washington, to pay tribute to their three fallen comrades. President Clinton, who had interrupted a vacation in Wyoming to preside over the memorial, eulogized the three fallen officials as "quiet American heroes who gave their lives so that others might know a future of hope and a land at peace." Following the 25-minute ceremony, the President introduced the new team of envoys Holbrooke would lead to the region—Clark; Owen; Brigadier General Don Kerrick, an Army intelligence specialist at the NSC; James Pardew, a retired Army colonel who was director of the Pentagon's Balkan Task Force; and Christopher Hill, Frasure's deputy at State who headed the office of South Central European Affairs.

After the memorial service, the President and his top foreign policy advisors—Christopher, Perry, Lake, Albright, Shalikashvili, Talbott, Berger, CIA Director John Deutch, and Vice President Gore's advisor Leon Fuerth—joined Holbrooke and his new negotiating team in a backroom of the chapel. With his senior leadership all in one place, the President wanted to discuss the future of the initiative. Holbrooke provided a status report on each of Tony Lake's seven points. While the National Security Advisor had led the effort that summer to bring the bureaucracy together and forge a peace initiative, this was now Holbrooke's show.[20]

Holbrooke reported that everyone in the region understood that "this effort would be different, an all-out attempt to reach this ambitious goal." He said that three-way mutual recognition and a cease-fire would be unlikely until the end of the negotiating process, and that, in his view, pushing the parties toward a cease-fire would be premature as long as the trend on the battlefield remained helpful to the Bosnians. He also reiterated that it would be "politically and morally unjustifiable" to press the Bosnians to give up remaining enclaves like Gorazde, and that he had told the Bosnians that.

HOLBROOKE'S PRESENTATION provoked little discussion until he turned to the last of Lake's seven points, regarding the economic reconstruction for Bosnia. He thought—and argued forcefully to the group—that a major American economic assistance package for Bosnia would be critical both for achieving and implementing any settlement. Bosnia had been destroyed by three years of war, and now stood alone after years of dependence on Yugoslavia. Eighty percent of its population relied on international assistance for food. Holbrooke believed that the United States would have to shoulder a substantial part of the burden in this aid effort.

The problem was the political atmosphere in Washington created by the new Republican majority on Capitol Hill. Congress was traditionally hostile to foreign aid, but in those budget-cutting times, the issue had become politically lethal. Because of these domestic political implications, neither Lake nor Holbrooke had been authorized to discuss specific financial numbers with the Europeans or Balkan parties. Yet since this instrument would be a crucial carrot, Holbrooke wanted to get the Administration to pledge some assistance soon.

They discussed creating an assistance package as high as $1 billion a year, which the President initially seemed to agree too. "If we get peace, we should be prepared to put up a billion dollars," Holbrooke recalls him saying. But with a budget crisis looming, Clinton was in no position to request additional expenditures, such domestic advisors as Chief of Staff (and former Budget Director) Leon Panetta explained. As the meeting ended, Holbrooke saw that "it was clear that the amount of American assistance would be far less than desirable."

LAYING THE GROUNDWORK FOR PEACE

The new envoys only had four days until they entered the Balkan maelstrom. Roberts Owen immediately joined discussions to prepare basic points to negotiate with the parties, meeting on August 23 with Holbrooke, his deputy John Kornblum, the legendary Washington attorney and former White House Counsel to Presidents Carter and Clinton, Lloyd Cutler, and Miriam Sapiro, a young lawyer on the State Department's Policy Planning Staff.[21] Holbrooke and Kornblum had decided that they needed a working group of legal experts in Washington to serve as a backstop for the shuttle team as they negotiated the political and legal details of a future Bosnian state, and enlisted Cutler to help. In the early stages, this group supported Owen as he negotiated with the parties on broad principles; later, they began to translate these agreements into a draft settlement. Kornblum led the group, which, to avoid bureaucratic haggling and turf wars, operated in secret, conducting business outside regular State Department channels and the interagency process.[22]

Following these meetings—a few of which included Bosnian Foreign Minister Sacirbey, who had flown to Washington to attend the memorial services—Owen sketched a proposal for the constitutional structure of a Bosnian state. This first draft outlined an agreement in which the Muslim–Croat Federation and Bosnian Serb entities would be joined at the top by a Federal Government "superstructure," composed of a three-person Presidency (Muslim, Croat, and Serb) and temporary Governing Council to conduct foreign affairs and defense. The members of the Presidency would be elected, as would local representatives to each "Federation Assembly." Owen viewed the draft as a way "of getting something started . . . to get ideas organized on paper and get people talking."[23]

ON AUGUST 24, senior Washington officials made another somber trip out to Fort Myer for the funerals of Nelson Drew and Joe Kruzel. After the ceremonies, Holbrooke asked the reconstituted shuttle team to have lunch together at the Officers Club. They were joined by Leon Fuerth, Vice President Gore's National Security Advisor and informal "sanctions czar" of the Administration, who briefed them on the status of economic sanctions against Serbia.

Sanctions were the key tool of U.S. bargaining leverage over Milosevic. These sanctions—comprised of an international trade embargo and freezing of assets—had been in place since May 1992, when the UN imposed them in retaliation for Serbia's role in the outbreak of the Bosnian war. They were crippling. Serbia's economic output had plummeted by nearly half, with hyperinflation peaking at 313 percent a month.

Despite such devastating impact, the future of the sanctions regime remained uncertain. The Europeans—particularly the Russians—had tired of sanctions. Holbrooke believed that the Europeans wanted to lift "all or most of the sanctions in return for almost nothing." The Americans, led by Fuerth and Madeline Albright, remained opposed to lifting sanctions absent meaningful concessions by Milosevic. To Albright, sanctions provided "one of the few times we managed to get the upper-hand and it was a lever I felt was important . . . [I tried] to maintain them so that we would get the most out of them."[24]

The problem with the sanctions wasn't their effectiveness in inflicting pain on Milosevic but with maintaining them. It had become increasingly difficult for the Administration to deflect European opposition. Fuerth explained that there was probably a small window of time— possibly closing as soon as the end of the year—during which sanctions could stay in place. He had the "sense that sanctions were becoming a wasted asset." To Holbrooke, the issue threatened to open a wide fissure between the U.S. and the Europeans, as few issues had "caused greater tensions with our major European allies and Russia."[25]

Holbrooke believed that while sanctions were important, "we must not lose sight that sanctions are a means to the end of a negotiated settlement, not an end in their own right." Fuerth argued that the United States should hold tight and maximize the time it had left before the sanctions regime became too difficult to maintain. Holbrooke later acknowledged that while he had "tactical differences" with Fuerth, he agreed not to stray from the Administration's hard-line.[26]

THE MILOSEVIC STRATEGY

Less than a week after the Mt. Igman tragedy, the Clinton Administration had reconstituted its team and sustained the momentum created by the Lake and Holbrooke missions. Officials had begun to consider the specifics of a possible settlement, from basic political and legal relationships to the future of economic sanctions. The first shuttle had probed each side's interests and intentions. The next shuttle would need to dive deeply into the specifics, hopefully producing some tangible result to signify progress.

Perhaps the key issue on the upcoming shuttle would be procedural: how to deal with the Bosnian Serbs. Since the spring of 1995, the Americans had worked to isolate the Bosnian Serbs out of the negotiating process, forcing Milosevic to "deliver" them to agreement.

This approach, referred to as the "Milosevic strategy," had been devised and championed by Bob Frasure, who had first pursued it during his negotiations that spring. After seeing how Milosevic and the Bosnian Serb leaders would exploit their differences to undermine an agreement, Frasure had concluded that the best strategy would be to force the two sides together—linking cooperation by the Bosnian Serbs with sanctions relief for Milosevic. Moreover, on July 25, the two most powerful Bosnian Serb leaders, Radovan Karadzic and General Ratko Mladic (the mastermind of the Srebrenica massacre), had been indicted by the International War Crimes Tribunal—and Washington would not negotiate with indicted war criminals. So they would focus on Milosevic.

Holbrooke fully embraced Frasure's approach, but others, especially the Secretary of State, were concerned about relying solely on Milosevic. As a party to the conflict, the Bosnian Serbs somehow had to be brought into the negotiations. If the Milosevic strategy proved ineffective over the long term, the United States would have to consider other ways to include the Bosnian Serbs, possibly by establishing a second channel. In the short term, though, Holbrooke would press the Milosevic strategy, forcing the Serb leader to demonstrate he could deliver.[27]

OPENING THE SECOND SHUTTLE:
TERROR BRINGS ACTION

As the Holbrooke team flew to Paris early the morning of August 28 to begin the second shuttle, another horrific tragedy unfolded on the streets of Sarajevo. Since July, the renewed threat of NATO military action had curbed the constant shelling and sniper fire that had driven Sarajevo's citizens underground for the better part of three years. Many had begun returning to the shops and coffee houses that had made the city famous before the war. On that sunny Monday morning, the outdoor Markale market was particularly crowded.

Shortly after 11 A.M. five mortar shells from the hills above rained on the bustling marketplace, wounding 85 and killing 37. It was the same spot where 68 people had been murdered in the February 1994 attack. A year-and-a-half later, this nightmarish encore symbolized the emptiness of Western threats against the Serbs—as one press report characterized it, the carnage of August 28 "demonstrated how Western attempts to end the war have gone around in circles, drifting from threats to new peace proposals as the killing has continued."[28]

The American negotiators learned of the shelling shortly after arriving in Paris and believed that there was no question that NATO should strike. "You couldn't let [the bombing go by]," General Wesley Clark recalled. NATO's guidelines for how to respond were clear. The August 1 NAC decision to extend the "Gorazde rules" authorized the use of force.

"All that mattered," Holbrooke reflected, "was whether the U.S. would take a decisive leadership role and persuade its NATO Allies to join in a meaningful military response—the sort of massive air campaign that we had so often talked about but never come close to conducting." The attack immediately became a test of Western resolve—if the allies allowed such terror against civilians to go unanswered, the commitments agreed to at London would prove meaningless. Holbrooke immediately called his friend Strobe Talbott to press for airstrikes. He stressed that it "was better to risk negotiating failure with bombing rather than try for progress without it . . . simple justice required such a response." Secretary of Defense Perry felt that "we [had to] act immediately. We [had to] carry out the threat we made." President Clinton, who had returned to his vacation in Wyoming, had several long phone conversations with Tony Lake and Perry in which he ordered them to demand that the UN and NATO act. The President gave a clear command: "We have to hit 'em hard."[29]

WHILE WASHINGTON PUSHED FOR AIRSTRIKES, Holbrooke's delegation "sleepwalked" through a busy schedule in Paris, meeting first with Carl Bildt, the former Prime Minister of Sweden and the EU's top envoy to Bosnia. For the previous several weeks Bildt had been conducting his own talks to negotiate a settlement, but he had had little success. The Croatians refused to meet with him because he had strongly criticized their attack on Krajina (and raised the question of whether war crimes had been committed—which as the world later discovered, they had). Unlike U.S. negotiators, Bildt talked to Bosnian Serbs leaders (although he did not meet with Karadzic), discussing with them his own constitutional and map proposals. Although he had open channels to Pale, Bildt also understood that a major problem for any peace process was that there was no credible figure who could agree to and implement a solution on behalf of the Bosnian Serbs. Even though Bildt was a very articulate advocate, American officials were somewhat skeptical of him, likely reflecting their own frustrations with the Europeans' inability to handle such negotiations and their suspicions about how much authority he actually had. Nevertheless, Holbrooke had agreed to meet with him to coordinate approaches and discuss their respective proposals.[30]

LATER THAT DAY, Holbrooke's team met with Bosnian President Alija Izetbegovic, who had traveled to Paris at Jacques Chirac's invitation.[31] A quiet and frail man, Izetbegovic was uneasy with public leadership and almost monastic in lifestyle. Informally referred to by the Americans as "Izzy," the Bosnian leader has been best described by former U.S. Ambassador Warren Zimmermann as a man who "seemed diminished, rather than inflated" by the trappings of presidential power. A devout Muslim who had been jailed twice by the Yugoslav Communist regime, Izetbegovic was a reluctant nego-tiator. He reminded Holbrooke of "Mao Zedong and other radical Chinese communist leaders—good at revolution, poor at governance." The Bosnian President was reportedly intrigued by the American plan, but was less anxious to move toward a settlement than some of his top advisors.[32]

Joined by Sacirbey (who was often at Izetbegovic's side during important meetings), this session lasted for almost three hours. The Bosnians were very upset about the marketplace shelling; Sacirbey had even threatened not to meet until the bombing started. Izetbegovic demanded that NATO act. "I don't want to negotiate further unless you start bombing," he told Holbrooke. "It's quite possible that this was deliberately done to disrupt the talks." The Americans agreed, but told Izetbegovic that they could not guarantee when—or even if—the bombing would begin. They were worried that the Europeans were getting cold feet.[33]

Mindful of the possibility that the Bosnians might be more interested in the fruits of failure—lift-and-strike—rather than a settlement in which they would have to compromise, the team worked hard to persuade Izetbegovic that Bosnia would be better off with an agreement. Holbrooke emphasized the economic carrots that would be available if they cooperated. There were costs as well: they could not stall, blame the Serbs, fail to get an agreement, and still expect unconditional U.S. support. Holbrooke had wanted to make these carrots more appealing with specific numbers of U.S. assistance, but was told not to. Nevertheless, Strobe Talbott said he could be "expansive and assertive . . . emphasizing to the Bosnians that we are absolutely committed and serious on the issue." These points seemed to register with the Bosnian President.[34]

DESPITE IZETBEGOVIC'S THREAT to stall any talks until the bombs were away, the Paris meetings were quite productive. Izetbegovic reacted positively to the comprehensive nature of the American plan. On constitutional issues, the Bosnians surprised Owen and others with their own proposal, which went much further than anyone expected in granting autonomy to the Bosnian Serbs—indicating that while the Sarajevo government did not want a divided state, it was equally unenthusiastic about sharing governmental powers with its Serb enemies.

They did not deal with territorial issues extensively in these early meetings, although they discussed enough to convince the Americans that territory would be among the most contentious parts of the negotiations. Izetbegovic himself predicted to Holbrooke—as it turned out, prophetically—that "the map" would be far more difficult to resolve than constitutional issues. Izetbegovic and Sacirbey also said that they wanted to strengthen the Muslim–Croat Federation. And on the crucial question of how to deal with the Bosnian Serb leaders, Izetbegovic supported with the "Milosevic Strategy," agreeing that the United States only meet with Karadzic or Mladic if they were part of a Milosevic-led delegation in Belgrade.[35]

WHILE THESE MEETINGS WERE UNDERWAY in Paris, UN and NATO military leaders had been conferring—and were being pushed hard by Washington— to respond to the Sarajevo massacre. The night of August 28, UNPROFOR's ground commander, British Lt. General Rupert Smith, worked with American and NATO military officials to draw up specific operational and targeting plans. Determined to prevent another hostage drama, they worked to withdraw the 92 UN troops stationed in Gorazde.[36] By the next day, the troops were out of danger, removing the last hurdle to airstrikes. At 5:45 that afternoon in Paris (11:45 A.M. in Washington), UN Under Secretary General Kofi Annan, who was filling in for a suspiciously absent Boutros-Ghali, informed Washington that the UN's military commanders had "turned their key" to authorize NATO airstrikes. The military plan, known as "Operation Deliberate Force," was underway. The airstrikes, Annan assured, would be more than pinpricks. American officials would later point to Annan's willingness to take responsibility at this critical moment as pivotal for their decision less than a year later to support Annan to replace Boutros-Ghali as UN Secretary General.[37]

When Holbrooke's team finally departed Paris for Belgrade the morning of August 30, NATO planes were eight hours into their bombing campaign against the Bosnian Serbs.[38] Following 40 months of inconsistent resolve, NATO had stepped squarely into the Bosnian conflict with what was then the largest military action in the Alliance's history.

The talks with the Bosnians had gone surprisingly well, and members of the U.S. team were now optimistic that "some sort of realistic deal" was achievable.[39] But most important, the Holbrooke delegation knew they would now arrive on Milosevic's doorstep with a key asset that previous diplomats had lacked: bargaining leverage backed by massive and sustained military force.

4

THE WAY TO GENEVA: THE PATRIARCH LETTER AND NATO BOMBING

When Holbrooke and his team landed in Belgrade on August 30, they braced themselves for a bitter greeting. But to their surprise, Milosevic did not angrily rebuke them for the fact that NATO bombs were pounding his allies—in fact, his reaction was quite the opposite. The Serb leader acted as though he didn't really care about either the marketplace massacre or NATO's response. Instead, he began the meeting with some kind words for the three fallen American diplomats, speaking with particular sincerity about Bob Frasure.

He then made an unexpected announcement. "I've been busy man while you were away," he said triumphantly. Handing Holbrooke a letter dated August 29 and signed by seven members of the Bosnian Serb leadership and the Patriarch of the Serbian Orthodox Church, Milosevic explained that Karadzic, Mladic and Serbian Parliament President Momcilo Krajisnik had agreed to join a negotiating delegation in which he would have the final and deciding vote.[1]

By forging this so-called Patriarch letter, Milosevic solved how to deal with the Bosnian Serbs, and handed the Americans the first breakthrough of their brief diplomatic effort. Throughout the war, Milosevic had always tried to distance himself from the Pale leadership, claiming that he had no control over them. Now, Milosevic alone would speak for the Bosnian Serbs—tying his destiny directly to them. "For a moment," Holbrooke recalled, "I did not dare to believe it."[2]

Why did Milosevic do this? One can only speculate. The Holbrooke team believed that this was a direct result of the pressure they had put on him at their first meeting to speak for the Bosnian Serbs. During this early phase of the negotiations, Milosevic had tried to portray himself as a man of peace. "And in response to our challenge about his influence," Wes Clark later observed, "he reached into his pocket and pulled out [the] Patriarch letter." Outside observers report that Milosevic acted on his own volition, sensing that NATO bombing would begin and wanting to grab "the opportunity to win his war against the Bosnian Serb leaders." According to Montenegrin

President Momir Bulatovic (who was present when the Patriarch letter was signed), Milosevic forced the Bosnian Serbs to sign. "They were conscious of all the mistakes they'd made and that everything could be destroyed: Republika Srpska could disappear," Bulatovic reportedly said. "[Yet], it was difficult for them to sign. This was their political suicide." There are also reports that the Serb leaders negotiated secret annexes to the Patriarch letter, with Milosevic agreeing to protect certain territories for the Bosnian Serbs (such as Bosnian Serb control of the town of Brcko).[3]

WHATEVER THE REASON, it was a major step forward. Milosevic had shown little willingness to engage in substance during the Americans' first shuttle; now, emboldened by his diplomatic coup, he poured forth with commitments and proposals. He repeated that the 51–49 percent territorial division would be the basis for negotiations, even suggesting that the Bosnian state should be a "union" within its current boundaries with a Muslim-controlled Sarajevo as its capital. Outlining specific ideas about how Bosnia's territory should be divided between the Muslims and Serbs, Milosevic lit a cigar and pushed for convening a "3-by-5" international conference (Milosevic, Izetbegovic, and Tudjman joined by the Contact Group) to ratify an agreement. Holbrooke hinted that he might explore such an idea with the three Balkan foreign ministers. But he did not want to get the three Presidents together yet.[4]

It took two hours for Milosevic to mention NATO's airstrikes. Yet it seemed perfunctory, leaving the impression that he actually welcomed the air campaign against his Bosnian Serb clients. With a conspicuous lack of emotion, he asked that the bombing be stopped to help the negotiations. Holbrooke explained that while he had no direct authority to demand a bombing halt, he would work with NATO to implement a "suspension" of the campaign, as long as Mladic ended the Serb shelling of Sarajevo. As he had done when discussing the possibilities for safe travel into Sarajevo during Holbrooke's first shuttle, Milosevic immediately contacted the Bosnian Serb general to secure his agreement. Holbrooke believed that a temporary pause might help negotiations by providing the Bosnian Serbs a chance to withdraw. Once they had retreated, the United States could use the resumption of bombing as leverage to negotiate a cease-fire.[5]

DURING THIS EIGHT HOUR meeting, Milosevic the "gambler" was at the top of his game. Jim Pardew, the Defense Department's representative on the shuttle team, described Milosevic's performance as "commanding, charming, a convincing debater, obstinate and enthusiastically agreeable—all in five minutes." By unveiling the Patriarch letter, the Serb leader had completely changed the dynamic of the negotiations. This accomplished, in effect, what the Americans had been insisting that the Bosnian Serbs do for over a year—accept the Contact Group plan and the 51–49 split in Bosnia as a starting point for negotiations. Shrewdly, Milosevic had done so while allowing the Bosnian Serbs to save face. They did not have to concede anything publicly yet, only announce that Milosevic would negotiate on their behalf. Although

Holbrooke deliberately played down the development publicly as a "procedural" victory so as not to raise expectations, Milosevic's move opened the
door for real negotiations to begin. "I've put down the hammer I was using
to beat down my optimism," Pardew reported back to his Pentagon colleagues. "This may work."[6]

A WATERSHED DAY: SEPTEMBER 1

After stopping in Zagreb to brief Tudjman and Sacirbey on the Milosevic
talks, the American team returned to Belgrade on September 1. They awoke
that morning to the news that NATO's bombing would be halted for at
least a day.

The Bosnians were outraged about the bombing pause. In a call to Strobe
Talbott, Sacirbey said that fighting in and around Sarajevo was continuing,
and demanded that the airstrikes resume immediately. At first, Talbott
explained that the cessation was called for technical military reasons. But as
Sacirbey pressed him further, Talbott admitted that the pause had certain
diplomatic benefits, although the United States wanted to keep this secret.
He reassured the Bosnian Foreign Minister that it was "not, repeat not
a rolling suspension . . . it is a limited one designed to offer Mladic the
opportunity to comply with all demands" to lift the siege of Sarajevo.[7]

IN BELGRADE, Holbrooke's team welcomed the halt and hoped to use it
to their advantage. Along with the Patriarch breakthrough, they believed
the pause provided an opportunity to push the three sides to agree publicly to
a set of political principles.

Holbrooke had set out on this second shuttle with the goal of getting the
parties to endorse a general legal and political framework for Bosnia. He and
Bob Owen thought that it would be a useful step forward, and officials in
Washington anxiously sought a public symbol of progress. They planned to
arrange a conference in Geneva where the Bosnian, Croatian, and Serbian
foreign ministers could bless an interim agreement. "Our theory," Holbrooke
explained later, "which was central to our operating strategy as we went
along, was to use Geneva to create a public and private sense of momentum . . . I wanted to use Geneva only for the announcement of those forward
steps [previously] agreed, and then adjourn without getting into unproductive
arguments."[8]

During the short flight between Zagreb and Belgrade, Owen began
sketching out political principles based on his initial work with the legal
team in Washington as well as the discussions with Izetbegovic in Paris.
He outlined that Bosnia would remain a single state composed of two
"constituent entities," the Muslim–Croat Federation and the Bosnian Serb
entity. The draft also described a three-person Bosnian Presidency, which
would be empowered to conduct foreign relations, appoint and supervise
a Commission for Displaced Persons, and an arbitration system to resolve
disputes.[9]

A MACEDONIAN SIDEBAR

While the rest of the delegation prepared to meet with Milosevic, Chris Hill and Jim Pardew secretly traveled to Skopje, Macedonia to meet with Macedonian officials on a possible agreement to solve tensions with neighboring Greece. Since February 1994, Greece had imposed an economic embargo on Macedonia out of anger that the tiny, landlocked former Yugoslav republic had assumed the name of a Greek region (Republic of Macedonia) and had used a traditional Greek symbol on its flag. The Greeks feared that this was not only a threat to Hellenic culture, but might also lead to an attempt by Macedonia to annex part of northern Greece.

Although some thought the dispute was a distraction, it had proven one of the more intractable in the region, and the Americans were concerned that it could escalate into bloodshed. Holbrooke and his team believed that these tensions added to the region's instability, indirectly making their efforts in Bosnia more difficult. The problem was very tricky: while Macedonia was seen as a likely flashpoint for violence, Greece was a NATO ally and the Clinton Administration was under heavy pressure from vocal Greek–American groups not to press the weak Greek government. Nearly 550 U.S. soldiers had been deployed in Macedonia for two years as part of a larger UN "tripwire" force trying to prevent hostilities from spilling over from Bosnia.

Over the past few months, the two sides had made some progress in talks mediated by two UN envoys, former U.S. Secretary of State Cyrus Vance and Special Envoy Matthew Nimetz (Christopher, Holbrooke, Lake, and many others had worked for Vance at State during the Carter Administration). However, the remaining issues were the most troubling, and Holbrooke, Hill, and Marshall Adair, another Holbrooke deputy, decided that the United States had to engage at a higher level to try to bring the talks to closure. Holbrooke sensed that "a deal was ready," and that a final high-level push would do the job. He saw the negotiations over Bosnia and Macedonia as mutually reinforcing: the momentum from the Bosnia shuttle could help close the deal over Macedonia, which in turn would show the Balkan parties that this was an American negotiating team that could get results.[10]

Hill and Pardew's two-hour meeting with Macedonian President Kiro Gligorov went smoothly. Gligorov was indeed eager for a deal, telling Pardew and Hill that "when I learned you were coming today, I decided that now is the right moment for agreement." Pardew showed him the Patriarch letter, which impressed Gligorov. The three discussed a draft agreement that Greek and Macedonian negotiators had been working on at the UN, outlining mutual recognition, with Macedonia allowed to keep its name given certain conditions. Gligorov seemed satisfied with the draft, and after two hours of talks, Hill and Pardew returned to Belgrade with optimism. The remaining step would be for Holbrooke to convince the Greek leadership, which he would try to do during a previously scheduled visit on September 4.[11]

BONDING WITH THE GODFATHER

Hill and Pardew rejoined the team that afternoon at Dobanovci, one of Tito's old military compounds outside Belgrade that Milosevic used as his retreat. There they found their colleagues already hours into what Pardew later described as a "day of bonding with the Godfather." With the Patriarch letter under his belt, Milosevic acted as the Don Corleone of all Serbs. Over the course of 12 hours, the delegation saw a Milosevic at once "drunk and sober, spouting Shakespeare and Latin, overbearing and raging, patronizing and joking. He covered topics from the future of Russia in the post–Cold War world to the sexual preferences of [Bosnian Prime Minister] Haris Siladjzic." He took Holbrooke and Clark on a long walk around the compound's grounds, where they talked about everything from international banking and Balkan personalities to duck hunting. The informality created a sense of possibility—Milosevic had loosened up, and seemed ready to make a deal. "More than anything else," Pardew reported to Perry, "Slobodan and his buddies remind you of a mafia boss who has decided to make a deal with you. This has all the air of a predetermined agreement. We just don't know the bounds yet."[12]

ROBERTS OWEN PRESENTED Milosevic with the draft political and legal principles. Fueled by cigars and wine, Milosevic agreed to all the main points. The Serb leader expressed most interest in the "special ties" the principles would permit between Serbia and the Bosnian Serb entity, seeing in them a precursor to the Bosnian Serb republic's eventual incorporation into Serbia proper. He wanted these "special ties" specifically described in these principles.[13]

Milosevic also asked that one of the "outstanding issues" outlined in the draft—concerning possible disqualification from the joint Presidency persons indicted as war criminals—be deferred for later consideration. Bringing this up would push his Bosnian Serb colleagues too far, too fast. "In a house of [a] man just hanged, don't talk about rope," the Serb leader told Owen. Holbrooke confronted him on this question, saying that Karadzic and Mladic would not be able to participate in any international peace conference. Milosevic complained that no matter how odious these two might be, they were needed to make peace. But Holbrooke had none of it. "You have just shown us a piece of paper giving you the power to negotiate for them. It's your problem."[14]

The Americans asked Milosevic about the idea of convening a foreign ministers meeting to ratify the principles, and the Serb leader didn't seem to care. "It's up to you," he said, "You decide."[15] Milosevic only insisted that the United States be in charge—he did not want the Europeans to control the agenda. Holbrooke immediately called Washington. Neither his colleagues nor the Contact Group had any idea that such a meeting was in the works, and they would have to act quickly to set one up. Speaking with Strobe Talbott, Holbrooke requested that senior Washington officials start to inform the other Contact Group ministers that the United States was convening a meeting in Geneva on September 8. The Contact Group partners quickly agreed, and later that day officials in Washington made the announcement.[16]

Although the team had Milosevic's agreement on their draft paper for Geneva, they still had not discussed the draft with the Bosnians or Croats. They were less worried about Tudjman—he showed little interest in anything other than Eastern Slavonia—but the Sarajevo government would be a different story. The Americans now had a major public meeting on the calendar, and only a week to create something that all sides could agree to.

SEPTEMBER 1 ENDED as the most significant day yet in the negotiations. Over the course of the previous 12 hours, Holbrooke's delegation had seen the Serbian leader in a way that was entirely unexpected, dramatic, and at times bizarre. With the bombing suspended, the United States could now test if the Bosnian Serbs were ready to deal. The Hill–Pardew visit to Skopje seemed to be just enough to pocket a solution to the Greek–Macedonian dispute. Finally, with the Geneva meeting scheduled, the negotiating team established a goal for all the parties to work toward.

THE CONTACT GROUP AND NAC

The next day, the American team flew to Bonn, Germany, where they met with their colleagues in the Contact Group. Gathering in Petersberg, the magnificent national guest house atop a mountain overlooking the Rhine, Holbrooke's delegation briefed their German, French, British, and Russian colleagues on their discussions in Zagreb and Belgrade. As the primary forum for negotiations during the past two years, the Contact Group had failed to bring the parties any closer to agreement. With this in mind, Holbrooke and his colleagues were deeply skeptical of the Contact Group's ability to be a constructive partner. This meeting made them even more so.

The Europeans understood that their role had become, in Carl Bildt's words, "supportive and complementary." Yet they did not believe that they were irrelevant. They complained about the lack of consultation, and were upset at Holbrooke's decision to hold the upcoming foreign ministers meeting in the American mission in Geneva rather than a neutral UN site. All this grousing accomplished nothing. As Holbrooke reflected later, "Such arguments over the location and 'hosting' of meetings may seem comical, but they were a constant and time-consuming subplot of the negotiations. In fact, disagreements over substance were rarely as intense as those concerning procedure and protocol."[17]

Although the Contact Group was essential as a mechanism to exchange views and present a united front to the parties, Holbrooke and his team really saw it as more of a nuisance. "They had long called for greater American involvement," Holbrooke later wrote, "but at the same time, they feared that they would be publicly humiliated if the United States took the lead." The Contact Group's 1994 plan was indeed the basis for the current negotiations, but the endless bickering at its meetings was at best time-consuming, and at worst counterproductive. Given the complexity and fast-pace of the talks, Holbrooke felt that the Contact Group wasn't able to function effectively. "Our colleagues in the Contact Group were disturbed that we planned to negotiate first, and consult with the Contact Group second, reversing the previous procedure in which we tried to work out the Contact Group position internally among the five nations *before* taking it to the parties—a system that had proved to be cumbersome, unworkable, and unproductive."[18]

Nevertheless, the American diplomats realized that they had to feed Europe's desire to feel involved—and need to be seen to be involved. Holbrooke and his colleagues knew that the Contact Group served the purpose of providing the facade of Russian and European unity. And they also know that if they got an agreement, they would need the Contact Group countries and others to help implement it.

In late August, Holbrooke summed up the Contact Group dilemma in a memorandum to Secretary Christopher. "We can't live without the [Contact Group]," Holbrooke explained, but "we can't live with it. If we don't meet with them and tell them what we are doing, they complain publicly. If we tell them, they disagree and leak—and worse. In the end, we must keep [the Contact Group] together for public reasons, especially since we may need it later to endorse and legitimize any agreement—but we must also reduce significantly the amount of material we share with them."

When Tony Lake had initially framed the initiative for the Europeans as a "Contact Group effort," he was simply building the public symbol of unity that Holbrooke described. The Americans believed in a strong U.S.–European partnership—but they also believed in results. They hoped that by paying occasional homage to the Contact Group, such as holding the Geneva meeting under its auspices, they could garner the support of its respective governments and lend legitimacy to their efforts. This was rarely easy and never much fun, but the Americans knew they had to do it. Europe would ultimately play a critical role in implementing any settlement, from supplying troops to providing economic assistance to the Bosnians. "We must never forget that we will need them all if there is ever a settlement—the EU for economic assistance, our NATO Allies for the new post-UN peacekeeping force, the UN for legitimizing resolutions, the Islamic Conference for additional aid, and the Russians and Greeks for their influence (however limited) on Belgrade," Holbrooke explained. Accordingly, the United States had to seek the Contact Group's assistance, but in a way that kept it sufficiently distant to prevent it from wrecking the negotiating process.[19]

The Americans had a straight forward strategy: limit the information the Contact Group received. In his August memorandum to Christopher, Holbrooke suggested that they only provide the Europeans a "rough outline of where we are, issue by issue, without revealing anything not already known or agreed by each of the parties. With respect to our future plans, we intend to keep the focus on the process, and while we will be eager to hear from them their ideas for initiatives, we don't intend to share ours to the group."

Overall, Holbrooke explained, the "dilemma now is how to keep the actual negotiations in our hands alone."[20]

As THE HOLBROOKE DELEGATION haggled with the Contact Group in Germany, they learned about several meetings between French General Bernard Janvier and Mladic, who were discussing terms for a cease-fire and lifting the siege of Sarajevo. The Bosnian Serbs were taking advantage of the bombing pause to circumvent their obligations—moving their weapons around rather than withdrawing them from the hills above Sarajevo, as NATO demanded.

In a September 2 call with President Clinton, NATO Secretary General Claes reported that the Janvier-Mladic talks were "very difficult." This wasn't surprising, Claes said, because "we are working with former communists and their negotiating techniques." The two agreed that if Mladic did not accept the Alliance's "very reasonable" terms, bombing would resume. NATO, Claes noted, would be ready "within two hours."[21]

Holbrooke and his team had supported the bombing pause in order to gauge the impact of the air campaign and secure allied unity (the Europeans remained skittish about bombing). But now they realized that the calculated gamble had come up short. As Mladic stonewalled a vacillating Janvier, the Americans decided that airstrikes needed to be resumed at once. If the pause turned into a permanent halt, then all the credibility NATO had earned—and all the leverage Holbrooke's team had enjoyed—would be diminished, if not altogether gone. Before leaving Germany for meetings at NATO headquarters in Brussels, Holbrooke and Wes Clark worked the phones with their counterparts in Washington and NATO command, lobbying them to restart the air campaign.[22]

THEY CONTINUED TO PUSH THEIR CASE in Brussels during a meeting with NATO's civilian representatives on the NAC, the same group that weeks earlier had implemented the "Gorazde rules" that the Bosnian Serbs were now violating. But rather than being angry, many in the room were reluctant to resume the bombing. Astonished, Holbrooke pointed out that exactly two weeks prior, he and Clark had returned to Washington with the bodies of Frasure, Kruzel, and Drew. Since resuming the shuttles, they had moved things forward dramatically. Milosevic had solved the question of who would speak for the Serbs, and the upcoming Geneva meeting would provide momentum and set the stage for a larger conference. But the Bosnian Serbs were cheating, and they had to be punished.[23]

The decision facing them, Holbrooke said with a hint of melodrama he often used on such occasions, was a "classic dilemma in political–military relations, one we faced but never solved in Vietnam: the relationship between the use of force and diplomacy." NATO's decision to retaliate for the Sarajevo massacre had been necessary and correct, he argued. Now, after the Bosnian Serbs have refused to take the opportunity to comply, the bombing pause needed to end. "It [is] now essential to establish that we are negotiating from a position of strength."[24]

Holbrooke asked U.S. Ambassador to NATO Hunter to assume the familiar position and remain with his divided colleagues to hammer out a new ultimatum. They pressed for specific, verifiable conditions on the Bosnian Serbs: no attacks on any safe area, withdrawal of all heavy weapons from the Sarajevo exclusion zone, complete freedom of movement for the UN and NGO personnel, and unhindered use of the Sarajevo airport—each to be achieved within a "finite" period of time. After a long and "tumultuous" meeting, the NAC agreed and set the U.S.-proposed terms for Bosnian Serbs' compliance, announcing that they had another 48 hours to cooperate.[25]

A LONG LABOR DAY: MACEDONIA, "REPUBLIKA SRPSKA," AND NATO BOMBING

After their meetings in Brussels, the American diplomats fanned throughout the region, with Holbrooke going to Geneva to meet with the Organization of the Islamic Conference (an important group because of its support for the Sarajevo government), and the rest of the team traveling to Zagreb to meet with Sacirbey before returning to Belgrade for another session with Milosevic. Then on September 4—Labor Day in the United States—Holbrooke's team set out for what turned out to be the longest day of their shuttle diplomacy.

Before stopping in Ankara, Turkey, where they planned to meet the Bosnian leadership, the Americans spent most of their Labor Day in Athens and Skopje, where they worked to close the Greece–Macedonia agreement. In Athens, the aged and frail Greek Prime Minister, Andreas Papandreou, had been under considerable pressure to oppose any deal. Holbrooke told him that time was running short. Finally, Papandreou said he would agree to a deal if Holbrooke would call him personally from Macedonia President Gligorov's office in Skopje and, speaking for the United States, "guarantee" that the Macedonians would keep their word.

Holbrooke had no problem providing Papandreou this modest bit of theatre he desired. He immediately flew to Skopje, where after several more hours of additional discussion—"he wanted to make us sweat awhile," Holbrooke recalled—Gligorov agreed. Holbrooke made the phone call to seal the deal.[26]

While the two sides were unable to reach agreement on such contentious issues as the name "Macedonia" or the Macedonian flag, they decided to discuss these later and sign an interim agreement. They agreed to have their Foreign Ministers meet the following week in New York under the auspices of Cyrus Vance and Matthew Nimetz to normalize relations formally. Greece also agreed to lift its embargo on Macedonia, greatly reducing the threat of conflict.[27]

Holbrooke and his delegation spent a relatively small amount of energy to get this deal, but their intervention provided the decisive pressure. Their efforts, beginning with the secret trip of Jim Pardew and Chris Hill (who was later named the first U.S. Ambassador to Macedonia) paid off. They believed that this success would bolster their image as a team that "meant business" and "could get things done." Milosevic had told them the previous day in

Belgrade that they would not be able to solve the Macedonian issue; they hoped he was watching.[28]

WITH THIS VICTORY, the shuttle team flew to Ankara for a late night meeting with Izetbegovic and Sacirbey, who were on an official visit to Turkey, one of their key Muslim allies. Following the previous day's talks in Belgrade with Milosevic, the Americans had reworked the draft constitutional principles for the Geneva meeting—now entitled the "Joint Agreed Statement of Political Principles"—and needed the Bosnians' input. In the new draft, Bosnia would "continue its legal existence with its present borders and continuing international recognition," reflecting what the Americans considered to be a major concession they had extracted from Milosevic. This one sentence revealed that, for the first time, the Serb leader accepted Bosnia as an internationally recognized, single independent state with inviolable borders. Holbrooke believed that "this phrase represented a huge breakthrough, amounting to de facto recognition of Bosnia by the Serbs."[29]

But the Bosnian leaders did not see it that way. They remained deeply concerned that the Americans' draft still did not do enough to preserve the legitimacy and integrity of the Bosnian state. When Owen showed Izetbegovic the new version, the Bosnian President did not even make it past the first line.

Izetbegovic demanded that the Americans change the draft's promise of the continuation of the "legal entity known as Bosnia and Herzegovina" to the more concise "Republic of Bosnia and Herzegovina." This had been in an earlier draft, but Milosevic had insisted that the words "Republic of" be removed. Such a change involved more than semantics; to Izetbegovic, it reflected that the sanctity of Bosnia's geographic boundaries would be preserved. For the Balkan leaders, the word "republic" meant sovereignty—by insisting on continuance of the republic, the Bosnians were arguing for a unitary, sovereign state with unchanged borders.[30]

For this reason, Izetbegovic also reacted strongly against the reference to the Bosnian Serb entity as "Republika Srpska." Milosevic had insisted that the name be added, arguing that the title alone would not threaten the territorial integrity of Bosnia. "What else should the Serbs call themselves?" he had asked. Izetbegovic was not against giving the Bosnian Serbs a legal role in the new state, but he felt that to allow them to use the term "republic" granted them de facto autonomy. Moreover, it seemed to legitimize the actions undertaken by rebel leaders like Karadzic in January 1992 when they declared their "Srpska" republic independent from Bosnia and part of Serbia. "That name is like the Nazi name," Izetbegovic said emotionally. "If you use it, you are letting them win. It contains the word 'republic,' so they will appear to have a separate country."[31]

Holbrooke and Owen tried to convince the Bosnian President that the name did not imply a sovereign Serb State, but rather, like the "Republic of Texas" and the "Commonwealth of Massachusetts" in the United States, it identified a separate (and subordinate) political entity under a central governmental structure. The name didn't matter as much as the political and legal structures binding it. Owen was sympathetic to the Bosnian President's concerns, but could not see how they could tell the Serbs what to call themselves. Milosevic had demanded "Republika Srpska" as his price for agreement. Past 1 A.M., after a great deal of pressure, the Bosnian President finally agreed. Bosnia would be a single state but consist of two entities—the Federation and the Republika Srpska.[32]

As THEY STRUGGLED WITH IZETBEGOVIC over these details, Holbrooke, Clark, and General Don Kerrick went in and out of the meeting to work the phones with Brussels and Washington to get the bombing resumed. It helped to have two Army generals on the shuttle team. Although neither was in the bombing campaign's chain of command—with the three-star Clark representing the Joint Chiefs of Staff and the one-star Kerrick representing the NSC—they could use their contacts and stature to get answers and push for action.

NATO had issued a new ultimatum, and the Bosnian Serbs were not complying. Yet many Europeans and UN officials still resisted a new round of bombing. Holbrooke later reflected that even though NATO Military Commander (and U.S. General) George Joulwan and NATO Secretary General Claes supported restarting the airstrikes, the UN military command "was looking for an excuse to avoid resumption of bombing."[33]

In Washington, it was the Labor Day holiday, but Strobe Talbott, Sandy Berger and others survived on take-out pizzas in the White House Situation Room while keeping in constant telephone contact with NATO officials in Brussels, UN officials in New York, Zagreb, and Sarajevo, and the shuttle team in Ankara. At one point, Holbrooke explained that if the bombing was not resumed, "our chances for success in the negotiations will be seriously reduced. The Bosnians are barely on board for our Geneva draft, and when we see Izetbegovic again in the morning to go over the draft, the bombing must have resumed . . . if we do not resume the bombing, [then] NATO will again look like a paper tiger." After more phone calls between Washington and Brussels, the bombing advocates finally prevailed. When the UN officially confirmed Bosnian Serb noncompliance the next day, the air campaign restarted.[34]

WITH IZETBEGOVIC'S AGREEMENT to the draft constitutional principles, Holbrooke's team returned to Belgrade on September 5 to finalize the document with Milosevic.

They were worried. The Bosnian Serbs' deviousness during the bombing pause raised questions about Milosevic's influence. The authority he supposedly gained by the Patriarch letter didn't help him get Mladic to withdraw his weapons. As Pardew reported to Washington, "[the] bombing pause affair has made clear that Milosevic cannot deliver Mladic, and Mladic is who counts among Bosnian Serbs." This fact cast doubt not only on the conditions for continued bombing, but also the overall negotiations. The very premise of the "Milosevic strategy" was that the Serb leader could deliver his Bosnian clients. Obviously, if the Americans had overestimated Milosevic's power vis-à-vis the Bosnian Serbs, this strategy would not work. Pardew questioned, "is there not a risk we are negotiating Milosevic on a deal that Mladic won't buy, and that will then serve as the starting point for concessions to Mladic?"[35]

The Americans pressed Milosevic to explain himself and describe the degree of control he had over the Bosnian Serbs. He still clearly wanted a deal, and since that's all the Americans had to go with, they kept the focus on him. Holbrooke played on the Serb leader's desire for international acceptance, even going so far as to make hints about a White House Rose Garden signing ceremony. During a one-on-one meeting, Holbrooke got Milosevic to concede nearly all the outstanding issues on constitutional principles, except for Izetbegovic's desire to have the term "Republic" before "Bosnia" in the first line. They agreed to keep the word out, and Milosevic approved to the draft.[36]

Holbrooke and his team had their first agreement. In three days, the U.S. delegation and Contact Group representatives would gather to witness Croat Foreign Minister Mate Granic, Serb Foreign Minister Milan Milutinovic, and Sacirbey officially agree to the principles. It would be the first time the three Balkan parties had met officially in over 18 months.

DEALING WITH WASHINGTON . . . AND PLANNING FOR PEACE

During this second shuttle round, an unusual but enduring decision-making pattern emerged. Negotiating decisions—even ones as important as the basic principles of Bosnia's constitution—did not flow from Washington. They were not approved by formal meetings of the NSC. They were made by Holbrooke and his delegation.

Holbrooke's team checked in by phone several times a day with their respective bosses, and Clark and Pardew provided written reports to their superiors (Clark to General Shalikashvili daily; Pardew to either Secretary Perry or Under Secretary of Defense Walter Slocombe whenever possible). Holbrooke himself called Washington at least four times a day, talking primarily with Talbott or Tom Donilon.[37] The lead negotiator, though, wanted deliberations about the talks kept internal to the team, often keeping deliberations from officials in Washington. Worried that any agreement could quickly unravel if subjected to lengthy bureaucratic discussions or any premature publicity, most of the shuttle team's accomplishments were presented to Washington as a *fait accompli*.

Holbrooke believed that to preserve the integrity of the negotiations—preventing leaks, for example—and to maximize the team's bargaining flexibility and ability to make quick decisions, they had to circumvent the typical interagency deliberative process. He was deeply influenced from his experience as a junior member of the American negotiating team led by former New York governor and veteran U.S. envoy Averell Harriman, that met with the North Vietnamese in Paris in 1968–1969. The internal divisions Holbrooke witnessed inside Harriman's team (particularly between military and political officials) and the mistrust of officials in Washington had hindered the negotiations. As Holbrooke later reflected, "no other experience was as valuable for me" in shaping both the composition and operational style of the negotiating team. "I would not tolerate any similar internal divisions within our team, and the negotiating flexibility we needed could come only with the full backing of the key members of the Principals Committee."[38] Officials in Washington were also aware of this history, and thus willing to trust the team with considerable latitude. Consequently, during these early days in September, Holbrooke and his colleagues did not seek guidance or approval from their superiors on the principles they were negotiating—they just proceeded. Similarly, while Washington officials watched the Greece–Macedonia issue, Holbrooke and his team alone decided to try to forge a breakthrough, and they did so secretly.[39]

As far back as July 1995, when the NSC-driven policy review was underway, Holbrooke believed that regardless of any finalized strategy, the negotiator would require a great deal of decision-making leverage to succeed. In other words, while the broad parameters of the policy might remain (such as 51–49 or maintaining the territorial integrity of Bosnia), how the negotiations proceeded or what was finally approved would be the shuttle team's responsibility. Holbrooke described this as the "jazz" of diplomacy—variation and improvisation on a theme. He had discussed this approach to Tony Lake during their August 14 London meeting, and while Lake urged that Holbrooke use the talking points as a script initially, he conceded that the lead negotiator needed flexibility. Christopher also felt comfortable leaving the tactical negotiating decisions up to the shuttle team, as long as they operated within the "red lines" of the approved policy. Holbrooke recalls that Christopher and Talbott, along with officials such as Sandy Berger at the NSC, "protected the negotiations" by keeping the rest of the Administration informed of the shuttle team's activities, "while keeping at arm's length efforts to intervene in them."[40]

In this sense, with delegation members representing Secretary of Defense (Pardew), the Joint Chiefs (Clark), State (Holbrooke, Hill, and Owen), and the NSC (Kerrick), the interagency process was repackaged in miniature on the road. Through their representatives on the team, each agency could "clear" negotiating decisions. General strategy would be discussed with Washington, but the day-to-day decisions—which cities they traveled to, who they negotiated with, what issues they discussed, and what deals they cut—were the prerogative of Holbrooke and his team. Holbrooke's executive assistant, Rosemarie Pauli, assumed the immense undertaking of ensuring that all the logistical details that made the fast-paced shuttles possible—from airplanes and hotel rooms to meeting sites and meals—were handled.

On this shuttle, the delegation established a rapport that would serve them well throughout the negotiations. "Our negotiating team had already developed an internal dynamic that combined bantering, fierce but friendly argument, and tight internal discipline," Holbrooke reflected. "Complete trust and openness . . . was essential if we were to avoid energy-consuming internal intrigues and back channels to Washington." To avoid the infighting that had plagued many past negotiating teams, he encouraged informality and frankness. "We succeeded in avoiding [internal divisions], in part because our team was so small, and in part because we shared all information and developed close personal relationships," Holbrooke recalled. Foregoing the more spacious front cabin of the airplane during shuttle flights, Holbrooke sat in the more cramped quarters with the rest of the team to discuss strategy, while support personnel sat in front. They agreed that everything would be discussed openly within the group, and that they would present recommendations to Washington as the "consensus view of the negotiating team."[41]

THIS SYSTEM WORKED well so far. But not everything could be managed by the shuttling diplomats, especially while they were flying all over Europe at such an intense pace. So as Washington officials did their best to keep up with Holbrooke's progress, they also began important work concerning implementation of a possible settlement. Quiet planning had already begun on what, in Washington, promised to be one of the most difficult and controversial issues—how the U.S. military would help enforce an agreement.

In late August, the NSC's Deputies Committee (DC) began reviewing planning papers on military implementation and the "equip-and-train" proposal to help the Bosnians. These proposals sketched out the broad parameters of a future NATO-led "peace implementation force," including rules of engagement, exit strategy, and length of deployment. They had also begun to discuss Serbian sanctions relief and a regional arms control agreement. The Deputies agreed that the military would be deployed in Federation territory, would have the ability to use force in self-defense, and would be under full NATO control.[42]

The Deputies sent the first planning paper summarizing the outcome of these discussions to the Principals Committee on September 1. This paper set forth the broad outlines of the key issues concerning both the ongoing negotiations and implementation (in effect enshrining decisions already made officially into policy), including: on sanctions relief, agreement that sanctions against Serbia would be suspended once an agreement was reached and lifted once implemented; on Gorazde, consensus that the Bosnians would not be pressed to give it up; on economic reconstruction, commitment of U.S. support for a multibillion dollar reconstruction program (but no specific financial pledge); and on the equip-and-train program to support Bosnia's military, an offer to lead a multilateral effort to achieve parity of forces among the parties.[43]

THE SHUTTLE TEAM HAD ALREADY started discussions with the Europeans on many of these issues. During their visits to NATO headquarters, Clark and Pardew had briefed the NAC on the key points of these deliberations concerning a NATO-led force, now to be known as an Implementation Force, or IFOR. This briefing (and all aspects of military implementation) was an important exception to the shuttle team's autonomy—it had been written and approved by Defense officials in Washington.[44] Stressing that such a force must be available to deploy quickly following a negotiated settlement, they outlined the broad principles under which the mission should operate: UN-mandated, but operationally under NATO command and control; capable of combat with a "robust" role; and flexible enough to accommodate non-NATO participants. Clark and Pardew also discussed specifics of an IFOR mission—including the duration of its deployment, proposed IFOR tasks, job of theatre commander, and how to include non-NATO countries in any decision-making process. The allies so far were generally supportive of the American plan. They agreed to meet again before submitting a formal proposal for the NAC to debate.

IN WASHINGTON, the Principals met at the White House the afternoon of September 5 to discuss Bosnia. Joint Chiefs Chairman John Shalikashvili, the well-liked and deeply respected Army general universally known as "Shali," began with a detailed presentation on the NATO air campaign, which had restarted shortly after 7 A.M. Washington time.[45] The Principals agreed that the United States would support the strikes as long as the Bosnian Serbs refused to comply, even if that meant an exhaustion of Option Two targets (command and control facilities, radar and missile sites). Shalikashvili pointed out that if NATO chose to escalate bombing and move to Option Three targets (military-related civilian infrastructure, like power grids)—which, significantly, were not authorized by the July 26 NAC decision to implement the "Gorazde rules"—new NAC approval and further consultation with the UN were required. Tony Lake argued that the United States needed to be prepared to "carry the bombing campaign through," whatever that entailed. Agreeing, Shalikashvili recommended that if NATO chose to escalate, there must be a pause or "firebreak" between Options Two and Three.

Regarding the military's role in implementing a settlement, the Principals endorsed the conclusions made by their Deputies. For example, on IFOR, they made the important decision (apparently with little debate) that the force would remain in place for up to a year or when the Bosnians could defend themselves, whichever came first. They also agreed that given the likelihood that a NATO-led IFOR would complicate the U.S. relationship with Russia (the Russians had already made clear that they objected to NATO's involvement), the United States should begin to think of ways to include the Russians in such a force.

Many of these issues were raised again two days later at a meeting with President Clinton—the President's first full meeting on Bosnia since the August 23 memorial service meeting at Fort Myer. The President focused particularly on the bombing campaign. General Shalikashvili explained that NATO was currently working to take out all of the Bosnian Serbs air defenses, particularly in western Bosnia. Recognizing that targeting was around the area where U.S. pilot Scott O'Grady had been shot down in June, Clinton said such strikes were worthwhile not only for their strategic benefits, but also "on principle." Perry recommended that NATO attack Bosnian Serb air defenses around the key stronghold of Banja Luka in northern Bosnia, and Shalikashvili explained that U.S. cruise missiles would likely be used for such an attack. The Joint Chiefs Chairman also raised the possibility that NATO could run out of Option Two targets soon, and that if the Bosnian Serbs had not complied in two to three days, the United States would have to consider going to the NAC for Option Three authorization. They deferred this decision for the coming days.[46]

THE FIRST STEPPING-STONE: GENEVA

While President Clinton and his advisers discussed the status of the air campaign, Holbrooke and his team arrived in Switzerland for the Balkan foreign ministers' signing of the constitutional principles. The three Balkan Presidents had already agreed to the document, so the meeting itself was supposed to be a formality, not a negotiation. Yet Holbrooke and his team were learning never to expect for things to go as planned.

Izetbegovic called Secretary Christopher in Washington early the morning of September 8 to complain about the acceptance of Milosevic's demand to delete the word "republic" before Bosnia. Given this, he said that in Geneva, Sacirbey would ask to include a statement that Bosnia would remain a whole state, and that all contacts with neighboring countries would have to be by mutual consent of both entities. If the Serbs disagreed, the Bosnian President warned, "there could be problems."[47]

THESE LAST MINUTE THEATRICS reflected the deep suspicions held by each side. Shortly before the meeting was supposed to start, Sacirbey called from his hotel and threatened to stay there unless the reference to the Serb entity as a "republic" was removed from the document. Holbrooke told Sacirbey tersely that he would not serve Bosnia's interests by boycotting—and that if he caused the conference to fail, the Americans would blame him.

Sacirbey eventually showed up, but the Bosnian Serbs presented the next problem. Allowed to attend as part of the Serb delegation but not authorized to speak (Serb Foreign Minister Milan Milutinovic would speak for them), the Bosnian Serbs were not even seated at the main table with the Contact Group representatives, Holbrooke and the three foreign ministers. Yet, when the meeting began, the Bosnian Serb Vice President, Nikolai Koljevic, tried to make an opening statement anyway. Holbrooke immediately called for a break, took the Bosnian Serbs into a private room, and told them curtly that they could leave if they wanted, but they would not be allowed to talk. With Milutinovic's support, Holbrooke told Koljevic that he was "certain" that Milosevic didn't want the Bosnian Serbs to walk out, but they could of course do so if they wanted to. After what others only heard as a "heated shouting match," the Bosnian Serbs returned to the room and agreed to abide by the original condition that they stay quiet and be represented by Serbia. With that, the meeting continued and the foreign ministers formally agreed to the draft constitutional principles.[48]

The agreement on the "Geneva Principles" was a modest but important step on the road to peace. By getting the parties to agree to the basic concepts—the recognition of Bosnia as a single state with its present borders and negotiations based on 51–49 percent territorial division—the United States had helped lay the foundation for future negotiations on a more specific settlement. With Milosevic as their negotiator and spokesman, the Bosnian Serbs were now engaged in the process, for the first time accepting concepts they had resisted for the better part of two years. The Geneva Principles outlined the framework for a Bosnia with shared power between the Muslim–Croat Federation and Serbs; a Bosnian state with free elections, human rights standards, binding arbitration of disputes, ability to establish "parallel special relationships" with neighbors, and countrywide institutions on monuments, human rights, and displaced persons. Yet, the Geneva Principles were silent on exactly how this could be achieved.[49]

THE HOLBROOKE TEAM returned to Washington exhausted after nearly two straight weeks of shuttling, but satisfied with the progress they had made. As Pardew reported to Secretary of Defense Perry, "Holbrooke achieved everything that was possible to achieve at this point in the negotiations. The mistrust, hatred, and maneuvering among the parties will not allow a single, big-bang settlement."[50] Nevertheless, they had accomplished quite a bit without giving up anything—for example, Milosevic had none of the sanctions relief he so deeply coveted. The Bosnian Serbs were again experiencing the full fury of NATO airpower. The Americans had opened discussions with their NATO allies on IFOR, and they had the Contact Group's support, at least for the moment. And the Greece–Macedonia settlement, while not central to the Bosnian problem, symbolized the "can-do" nature of the shuttle team and provided some helpful momentum.

Milosevic had provided the real breakthrough with the Patriarch letter; yet, Bosnian Serb belligerence during the bombing pause renewed concerns about how much influence he actually wielded, particularly over Mladic. The Croats were for the most part agreeable, tolerating the Muslim–Croat Federation while focusing mainly on getting back lost territory like Eastern Slavonia. The most arduous negotiations were with the Sarajevo government. Justifiably believing that they had suffered the greatest, and therefore deserved the most out of a settlement, the Bosnians would resist anything they interpreted to be remotely close to a concession—although when pressured, they did make them.

Holbrooke wanted to wait at least a week before bringing the team back to the region. Then they would have to deal with more contentious issues like specific governing arrangements for Bosnia—such as the Presidency, elections, and territorial control. "Round III will be even harder as we move from concept and future structures to the territorial issues that represent reality to the people in the Balkans," Jim Pardew presciently observed.[51]

5

BOMBS AND DIPLOMACY: NATO'S CAMPAIGN ENDS, THE WESTERN OFFENSIVE CONTINUES

As the shuttle team regrouped in Washington, the UN's military leaders on the ground in Bosnia worried about how to end NATO's air campaign. Lt. General Bernard Janvier, who had reluctantly agreed to resume the airstrikes, remained skeptical about their effectiveness. The French UNPROFOR commander had never liked the airstrikes—when the bombing had begun he had written a memorandum revealing his worries about NATO making UN troops "a party to the conflict"—and now he believed that the bombing produced little of value tactically or psychologically, especially under the limited "Option Two" targets. Making matters worse, NATO was running out of things to hit. The top UN military official in Sarajevo, British Lt. General Rupert Smith, was concerned about the diminishing political advantages of bombing, arguing that if the Bosnian Serbs perceived that "Holbrooke doesn't have his hand on the [bombing] lever, they will refuse to talk." Smith recommended a second bombing pause to organize the political–military strategy.[1]

Senior Washington officials agreed that they could not just keep dropping bombs without a strategy. Following meetings with NATO air commanders in Italy, Under Secretary of Defense for Policy Walter Slocombe told Defense Secretary Perry that the "fundamental problem" with the air campaign was that, other than punishing the Serbs, it was not tied to any overarching plan. "We clearly have moved beyond retaliation for the market attacks and even beyond stopping the shelling of Sarajevo," he explained. "Our explicit demands are weapons withdrawal [from around Sarajevo] and full access [to Sarajevo], but these take Bosnian Serb agreement; it is dubious whether this will be forthcoming." The air campaign's initial goals had been achieved, but they had not decided how long bombing should last, and to what end. "Is it then our intention for bombing to continue indefinitely?" Slocombe asked. "Until we get agreement on this, it will be difficult to make decisions on the future of the campaign."[2]

YET NATO PRESSED ON, broadening the use of weapons available in its arsenal even as the targets ran out. On September 10, the U.S. Navy cruiser USS

Normandy fired 13 Tomahawk cruise missiles at 10 Bosnian Serb air defenses around the city of Banja Luka in northwest Bosnia. In military terms, this attack represented two significant departures in the air campaign: it was the first strike outside the primary area of operations in eastern Bosnia, and it was the first time these radar-guided, $1.3 million dollar weapons with 700-pound warheads had been fired at Bosnian Serb targets. General Shalikashvili had informed the President and his top advisors of such an operation during their September 7 meeting, and NATO command had been planning the attack for several days.[3]

The Tomahawk strike upset the Europeans and the Russians. United States and NATO military planners believed that the attack had been authorized by NAC-approved rules, which allowed hitting targets in northwest Bosnia to destroy Bosnian Serb command and control. Yet at an emergency meeting at NATO, France joined Spain, Canada, and Greece to argue that the attack "insidiously slid" the air campaign from Option Two to Option Three.

"We got criticized fairly heavily for [not checking] more carefully with our allies," Perry recalled. "We figured that the authority that NATO had given to go ahead was a broad enough authority that we did not have to go back and check on every mission that we bombed." The Secretary of Defense admitted that the operation was "a significant escalation in the perception of what we were doing." In terms of destructive capacity, the Tomahawks were less powerful than the hundreds of 2,000-pound bombs being dropped by American planes. Nevertheless, Perry explained, the "effectiveness"—and obvious technological capability—of these weapons symbolized to many that the air campaign had reached a more lethal phase.[4]

The Europeans also worried that NATO had become, in effect, the air force for Bosnian Muslim and Croatian troops on the move in western Bosnia. While the Sarajevo government had pledged that it would not take advantage of NATO air operations by attacking areas in and around NATO targets, it still pursued offensive operations in northwest Bosnia, away from the air campaign. These military successes, while relatively small, fueled the perception that they were coordinating attacks with the Alliance. NATO and UN officials admitted publicly that airstrikes "clearly play" to the Bosnian Government's advantage, and understood that this further upset the already unstable consensus in support of the bombing. This was certainly the case with America's newest and most reluctant partner, Russia.[5]

THE RUSSIAN DIMENSION

Russia's role in the Bosnia crisis confronted American officials with a special challenge. Since the end of the Cold War, the United States had sought to create a cooperative relationship with its former adversary, and to encourage its evolution into a democratic state at peace with itself and its neighbors. But the two countries' differences over Bosnia threatened this transformation. And as Bosnia forced itself on the U.S.-Russian agenda, it set the stage for renewed tensions between the two countries. American officials had seen such a moment coming: "Bosnia is the beast that could eat not only NATO but the Russian–American partnership," Strobe Talbott, the Clinton Administration's point man on Russia, had warned Warren Christopher.[6]

The Russians identified culturally and politically with the Serbs, and their policy usually translated into sympathy for Belgrade and skepticism about any action (such as the economic embargo or NATO strikes) that, as they saw it, unfairly punished the Serbs. As long as the Americans were able to sell their ideas to Belgrade, Russia would have a hard time characterizing a settlement as unfairly anti-Serb.

But Moscow's problems went deeper than Bosnia. Less than five years after the collapse of the Soviet Union, Russia also struggled for acceptance as a great power. Its leaders understood that the future of power relations in Europe were being shaped by the Balkan conflict, and that if marginalized now, they would have to live with the consequences for years. Wesley Clark explains that the Russians saw the American peace plan "in Cold War terms, more 'geostrategic competition' to establish spheres of influence." Although its Balkan diplomacy was neither strong nor consistent (reflecting the disjointed decision-making in Moscow), Russia could not be—and would not be—left out of the process.[7]

American officials understood that, like the rest of the Contact Group, Russia needed to be perceived as being involved in the negotiations. They suffered from what Talbott described as the "Rodney Dangerfield Syndrome," in that they felt that they didn't get any respect. "Moscow's primary goal was neither to run nor wreck the negotiations," Holbrooke reflected. "Rather, what it wanted was to restore a sense, however symbolic, that they still mattered in the world."[8]

Yet massaging the Kremlin's ego wouldn't be easy, especially with NATO's planes in the air. The Russians were apoplectic about the bombing campaign. While they had been cooperative during July's London Conference, they had left unhappy—feeling that they had been duped into agreeing to eliminate the dual-key—and therefore did not consider the "London Rules" to be legitimate. Under these procedures, the Russians did not have to be informed that the bombing would begin, and they weren't. Kremlin officials were upset that force had even been threatened; now that it was being used, and in a way far beyond the "pinprick" NATO operations of the past, the rhetoric in Moscow against the United States and NATO became white hot.

ON SEPTEMBER 7, Russian President Boris Yeltsin wrote a scathing letter to Clinton, claiming that the bombing amounted to "an execution of the Bosnian Serbs" and threatened a "conflagration of war throughout Europe."[9] The next day, Yeltsin used his first press conference since recovering from a heart attack he had suffered in July to air his outrage publicly. In a series of bombastic statements reminiscent of the worst days of former Soviet premier Nikita Khrushchev, he condemned NATO, claiming that the alliance had "virtually assumed the role of judge and executioner." He warned that Russia might "reconsider thoroughly our strategy including our approaches to relations with the North Atlantic Alliance," and that NATO expansion—one of the

Clinton Administration's highest foreign policy goals—would be "a major political error" that would lead to the "conflagration of war erupting throughout the whole of Europe."[10]

The Russians were particularly outraged by the appearance of coordination between the Muslim–Croat offensive in western Bosnia and the NATO campaign. The day after the Tomahawk attack, Defense Secretary Perry discussed the issue with the Russian Defense Minister, Pavel Grachev. Over the course of the previous year, Perry and Grachev had established a strong relationship, allowing them to discuss issues with unusual candor. Throughout the bombing campaign, Perry tried to keep an open line of communication with his counterpart, letting him know "what we were doing and why we were doing it." Perry realized that these consultations were never "fully to [the Russians] satisfaction—they wanted to be in on the decision loop."[11]

In this September 11 phone conversation, Grachev complained that NATO and the United States had taken the side of the Muslims and Croats, and that the airstrikes should have been halted immediately after the Geneva agreement. "If the fighting continues," Grachev warned, "we will have to help the Serbs in a unilateral way." Claiming that the West was using a "double-standard" by punishing the Serbs but not the Croats and Muslims, Grachev said that "ignoring Russian opinion casts doubt on the sincerity of Western intentions to settle the warfare." Within a day, Russia unsuccessfully tried to get the UN Security Council to order an immediate halt to the bombing.[12]

As tensions with Moscow escalated, officials in Washington scrambled to get control of the situation. They needed to put a brake on Russia's anxiety before it harmed other areas of the relationship. Some, like Tony Lake, thought that Yeltsin's reaction was little more than bluster: "I expected it, and always thought that after the thunderclouds, the sun would shine." But even such optimists knew that at best, Yeltsin's rhetoric didn't help their efforts, and at worst, his overreaction could strain relations irreparably. No one wanted to spark a conflict with Russia over Bosnia. Russia's "capacity for doing harm here is immense," Talbott warned. "Keeping them sullen but not mutinous over Bosnia is part of the larger task of keeping Russian reform and U.S.-Russian relations more or less on track." Lake and Christopher agreed, and decided that Talbott should get to Moscow immediately to hear the Russians out and calm them down.[13]

Talbott arrived in Russia on September 14 for, as he put it, "quiet consultations at a time of scratchiness in the [U.S.-Russian] relationship over Bosnia." In meetings with Kremlin officials, Talbott hoped to show that the United States wanted to improve consultations between the two sides. According to the 43-page script Talbott wrote for his meetings, he sought "to project steadiness—with regard both to Russia policy and Bosnia policy— and in doing so, steady the Russians." If Bosnia festered, "it would drive an even-deeper wedge between Russia and the West; it would continue to make Russia look desperate for a deal that favors the Serbs; [and] it would continue to undermine the credibility of the UN, in which Russia is heavily invested."

The basic message would be that while the United States understood that NATO bombing was hard for Russia to swallow, allowing the Bosnian war to continue would be worse.[14]

Talbott made this point to Foreign Minister Kozyrev, who agreed. Kozyrev admitted that failing in Bosnia "would be ruinous to our future relations and our ability to cooperate in Europe . . . All we want to do is to end this bloody goddamned war, and to end it in a way that's a visibly cooperative achievement."[15]

They also discussed the possibility of a Russian role in implementing a settlement, possibly as part of the security presence. Talbott believed that "stiffing the Russians is simply not an option." In Washington, thinking about what role Russia could have was still very preliminary—the Defense Department had worked up a proposal for Russia's participation in an implementation force, in which Russian troops could perform "special tasks" under NATO command and control. But at that point, it was far from clear—indeed it remained doubtful—that Russia would be willing to put its troops under NATO command.[16]

RUNNING OUT OF TARGETS

On September 11, the President and his senior national security advisors met with the shuttle team at the White House. Holbrooke explained that the last round of talks "drew the lines on the field, established the team rosters, and wrote the rule book for the next round of negotiations. Now the rough and tumble game begins." There were several clusters of issues to handle: opening discussions on the map; negotiating a cease-fire (when the "time is right"); organizing military implementation of a settlement; and beginning to flesh out the Geneva principles into working government structures.[17]

The discussion then turned to NATO's air campaign. Sandy Berger, Strobe Talbott, and others had become concerned with the open-ended nature of the bombing. They worried that the Bosnians were dragging their feet in the talks in order to keep the campaign going. "At some point fairly soon," Talbott had written to Berger, "we've got to make it clear to the Bosnians that they're not going to play hard-to-get in the negotiations as a means of forcing us to provide them with an air force to use against the Serbs."[18]

Perhaps aware of such concerns, President Clinton asked if the campaign had "reached the point of diminishing returns." Holbrooke responded that the bombing still helped. "We want it to continue," he said, speaking for his team. "We believe that we should tough it out. Our leadership position is getting stronger. We should use it or lose it. Izetbegovic would not have come as far as he has without the bombing." While they may reach a point where continued bombing would hurt the initiative, Holbrooke said, "we're not there yet." Christopher concurred. "The bombing should continue through Option Two targets . . . it would be bad to back off." The President agreed, but expressed frustration that the air campaign was not better calibrated with the diplomatic effort—especially with the surprising news that time was running out.[19]

Perry and Navy Admiral William Owens, the Vice Chairman of the Joint Chiefs, announced that NATO would exhaust all their Option Two targets in a few days. Although the Pentagon had not hidden that the target list was almost finished, some, including Christopher and Holbrooke, did not expect the end to come so suddenly—and were skeptical that the military had actually exhausted all the targets. But as Holbrooke put it, "there was no way to question the military within its own area of responsibility." If they wanted the bombing to continue, they would have to return to the NAC and the UN to receive approval for Option Three targeting.[20]

Everyone knew that this would be very difficult. Recalling the arduous process to get the NAC to approve Options One and Two following the London decisions in July, American officials had little confidence that they could secure the controversial Option Three decision anytime soon, if at all. The Europeans had already made their skepticism known, and now Russian sensitivity seemed to be an overwhelming obstacle.[21]

Some saw the problem not just in other capitals, but in Washington. After almost two weeks of casualty-free bombing, many civilian officials believed that the U.S. military commanders—and their civilian overseers—were reluctant to press forward with more ambitious attacks and wanted another bombing pause. As Holbrooke later reflected, the military "did not like putting its pilots at risk in pursuit of a limited political objective, hence their desire to end the bombing as soon as possible." Moreover, informed by their own contacts with Serbian military officials, some in the U.S. military command believed that continuing or escalating the bombing would hurt, not help, the prospects for negotiating success. The Pentagon's representative on the shuttle team, Jim Pardew, shared this view, advising Perry that "continued bombing will prevent serious negotiations on the map by strengthening the position of both Serb and Bosnian Government hard-liners. We need a face-saving way to suspend [the airstrikes] for the time being to move forward with territorial discussions."[22]

Christopher and Holbrooke felt very strongly that if the NATO attacks paused or ended without a pretext, it would undermine their bargaining leverage. "I thought it was important to carry on the bombing campaign to the point where it would achieve real effectiveness, [and] that the Bosnian Serbs would be impressed with the willingness of NATO to bomb on a continuous basis," Christopher reflected. If the air campaign had to end anyway, he and Holbrooke argued, then the Americans had to use the little time remaining to get something for it.

"Let's not stop it for free," Holbrooke pleaded. "If you pause the [bombing campaign] now you are going to risk losing the Sarajevo government, and if it takes place [as we're] flying in we won't get any credit for it [the pause] with Belgrade," Holbrooke said. "We need to find a way to leverage the end of the bombing."[23]

President Clinton agreed that they needed to extend the bombing for a few days to buy his negotiators some time. "We can't look weak," he said.

"Even if we're having problems with the Russians, we have to stay firm." The military leaders promised to extend the bombing for another 72 hours, and the next day, Holbrooke's team boarded a plane for Belgrade to begin their third round of shuttle diplomacy.[24]

MILOSEVIC'S SURPRISE

Arriving in Belgrade the afternoon of September 13, Holbrooke's delegation met with Milosevic in his hunting lodge.[25] They had to use the last bargaining chip provided by NATO bombing. But as was becoming his custom, Milosevic had another surprise for the Americans. Insisting on addressing the air campaign before any other issue, Milosevic said that the situation needed "calming," and that he thought he could get the Bosnian Serbs to agree to lift the siege of Sarajevo. He then announced that Karadzic, Mladic and other Bosnian Serb leaders were in a nearby villa and were ready to meet with them.

The Americans were shocked but ready. On the flight to Belgrade that day, they had agreed that if given the opportunity, they would meet with Karadzic and Mladic—two indicted war criminals—provided three conditions were met: first, that Milosevic be recognized as the head of the delegation; second, that the Bosnian Serbs be willing to engage in "serious discussions," not digress into irrelevant historical monologues; and third, that Milosevic secure their agreement to these conditions prior to their meeting. He agreed, and Holbrooke led his team into the woods outside to wait.

A few minutes after the Bosnian Serbs arrived at the villa, he called the Americans in. They faced Karadzic and Mladic warily; some members shook their hands, others didn't. From the moment the meeting opened, it was clear that these men were visibly shaken by the airstrikes. The Bosnian Serb Vice President, Nikola Koljevic, complained that the use of Tomahawks was "no fair" and that it was "an outrage" that American jets had struck 150 meters from his office. Karadzic launched into a self-pitying diatribe about the bombing, referring often to the "humiliation the Serbs are suffering." Overall, the group appeared "staggered" by the bombing and the losses in western Bosnia. "The atmosphere in the region indicates a general breakdown of Bosnian Serb will," Pardew reported back to Washington. "[The Bosnian Serbs] argued long and hard, but primarily wanted a face-saving way out of the bombing. They were very concerned with 'humiliation' of the Serbs."

Karadzic, clearly the leader of the motley group, did most of the talking. Mladic, dressed in battle fatigues, did little but scowl. At one point, Karadzic threatened that if he did not get what he wanted, he would call the last U.S. leader he had been in contact with, former President Jimmy Carter. Holbrooke responded firmly that while he had worked for President Carter 15 years earlier, the American team worked only for President Clinton. Later, Milosevic told Holbrooke that it was good to clear this up for Karadzic. "You know," the Serb president said, "that was very smart the way you handled

Jimmy Carter. Those guys are so cut off from the world they think Carter can still decide American policy."

After several hours of tense discussion, the Bosnian Serbs agreed to allow the Americans to draft the terms for an end to the bombing campaign. General Wes Clark joined Owen, Pardew and Chris Hill to write the document. A half-hour later, Clark stood to share the draft with the Bosnian Serbs. One of the most successful military leaders of his generation, Clark had a commanding presence, and his straightforward intensity made him an effective communicator (several years later, the world got to know his skills much better when he served as the NATO commander during the 1999 Kosovo campaign and then, after his military career, as a 2004 Democratic presidential candidate). As Clark read aloud, the Bosnian Serbs, particularly Mladic, became increasingly angry, complaining that the terms were unfair and offended Serbian pride. Mladic burst into a furious tirade, calling the bombing a criminal act and claiming that the United States needed to punish all sides, not just the Serbs. Interrupting Mladic, Holbrooke turned to Milosevic and threatened to leave. "We had an agreement," he said. "This behavior is clearly not consistent with it. If your 'friends' do not wish to have a serious discussion, we will leave now." Milosevic quickly huddled with his Bosnian Serb colleagues, and they agreed to calm down and rejoin the discussions on American terms.

At three o'clock that morning, the Bosnian Serbs accepted the American plan. They pledged to cease all offensive operations around Sarajevo and begin immediately to relocate their heavy weapons. They also agreed to allow road access to Sarajevo and open the Sarajevo airport for humanitarian traffic. In exchange, NATO would suspend bombing for 72 hours to assess compliance. If the Bosnian Serbs cooperated, bombing would end indefinitely and the agreement would be formalized with the Sarajevo government.[26]

The Americans had gone to Belgrade to try to use their remaining leverage to negotiate an end to the bombing, which was going to end anyway, and remarkably, Milosevic delivered. Once again, when doubts had emerged that Milosevic was losing control of his Bosnian cronies, the Serb leader moved decisively to prove that he was in charge. Although some had raised questions about the air campaign's military effectiveness, it seemed clear from this meeting that the Bosnian Serb leadership—as well as their chief patron—wanted the bombing to end. The shuttle team had no doubt that the air campaign had enhanced their bargaining power. Now they had the Serbs' agreement to lift the siege of Sarajevo. The next step would be to sell it to the Bosnians.

ZAGREB AND MOSTAR

After a few restless hours of sleep, the American team flew to Zagreb. The Croat leadership had only passing interest in the Sarajevo deal, discussing instead the progress the Muslim–Croat Federation forces were making against the Serbs on the ground in western Bosnia. The Croats promised that their military campaign would be limited, aiming only to stabilize the confrontation line. Yet their forces continued to press on toward the city of Banja Luka, sending as many as 40,000 Bosnian Serb civilians fleeing. The Bosnian Serb Army was in great disarray, and the Croats confirmed reports that Bosnian Serb soldiers were shooting their officers.[27]

Bolstered by these successes, President Tudjman mused whether the Federation should try to take Banja Luka. The Americans cautioned against doing so, arguing that it would create even larger numbers of refugees. Instead, Holbrooke and General Clark discussed with Croat Defense Minister Susak the areas that Federation forces should fight to take.[28]

THAT AFTERNOON THE TEAM DROVE to meet Izetbegovic and his Prime Minister, Haris Silajdzic, in Mostar, the ancient city on the Neretva River, which had been nearly decimated in 1993 during the Muslim–Croat conflict. The city once represented multiethnic Yugoslavia; now, divided between Muslims and Croats in a tense peace, it symbolized the fragility of the Muslim–Croat Federation.

The Bosnians did not welcome the bombing's end—they believed that they were on the brink of a major military success. Incredibly, Izetbegovic even indicated a willingness to have Sarajevo undergo a few more days of shelling in return for more NATO bombing, and Silajdzic angrily called the agreement "totally unacceptable." Holbrooke explained that while he understood their frustration, they really had no choice; NATO was running out of targets, and continued bombing would require UN and NAC approval. The Bosnians were very unhappy, but understood that there was nothing they could do.[29]

THE DISCUSSION TURNED NEXT to constitutional principles the Americans wanted to expand. The Geneva agreement had established the broad framework for a Bosnian constitution, yet did not address exactly how this would operate. They wanted to get the parties to agree to specific governmental structures that would serve as the connective tissue to hold Bosnia together. Using Geneva's "agreed principles" as a template, Roberts Owen had prepared a draft document of "further agreed principles" outlining the structure of a Bosnian state. This draft called for elections in Bosnia as soon as conditions permitted; a joint presidency that would govern the country; and provisions for creating a new Bosnian parliament.[30]

Owen outlined for Silajdzic his proposal for a three-person presidency that would sit atop the Bosnian government. Visibly upset, Silajdzic said that any consideration of an electoral process or joint leadership would legitimize Serbian ethnic cleansing. In the prime minister's view, elections would only be legitimate after Bosnian refugees resettled in their own land—a process, he pointed out, that could take 5–15 years. The Americans agreed that the current leadership in Pale would make poor partners in any government, yet they hoped that by forcing the Bosnian Serbs to democratize through elections, more reasonable leaders would emerge in the future. Silajdzic also reopened the "Republika Srpska" issue that the U.S. team had fought so hard with Izetbegovic over in Ankara, claiming that the title recognized the "fascist" Bosnian Serbs.[31]

THIS CONVERSATION showed the Americans that Prime Minister Silajdzic could be a big problem. As the most vocal critic of the U.S. plan, Silajdzic seemed reluctant to make any settlement with the Bosnian Serbs. Of the three primary Bosnian negotiators, the Americans had dealt with him the least, and they felt more comfortable with Sacirbey and Izetbegovic. In the past they had worked very closely with Sacirbey on constitutional issues, and were optimistic that the Foreign Minister would be able to bring Izetbegovic around to an agreement. They were less hopeful about Silajdzic, who seemed to distrust the Americans and had a difficult relationship with Holbrooke. Realizing this, Holbrooke asked Owen and Hill to drive back to Sarajevo with Silajdzic the next morning, hoping that by traveling together during the five-hour trip over Mt. Igman, the two Americans and Silajdzic could establish a relationship of trust. Hill and Silajdzic both had a background in U.S.-Albanian relations (Silajdzic had done academic work on the subject, while Hill was an Albanian expert), and Holbrooke hoped that this common interest could break the ice.[32]

Hill and Owen left with Silajdzic for Sarajevo on September 15 while the rest of the U.S. team departed for Geneva to attend a Contact Group meeting. That night in the Bosnian capital, Hill, Owen, and U.S. Ambassador to Bosnia John Menzies (who knew Silajdzic well) met with the Prime Minister over dinner where they went over the draft "further agreed principles."

The two key areas of debate were about elections and the presidency. Milosevic had pressed to hold elections sooner rather than later. Perhaps he hoped to remove his Bosnian Serb rivals, especially Karadzic, through the ballot. Thousands of Bosnian Serb refugees were living in Belgrade, and the Serbian President expected that his influence would turn their vote against the Karadzic-dominated government (as it turned out, early elections allowed the most extremist elements to dominate the Bosnian government). In contrast, the Bosnian Muslims wanted to delay elections until Bosnia returned to its prewar demographic balance. If the thousands of Muslim refugees were allowed to return to their home throughout Bosnia, Silajdzic hoped that they could regain control over much of the country through elections.

Hill and Owen convinced Silajdzic that it was in his government's interest to hold elections while an international security presence remained on Bosnian territory. An outside organization like the OSCE could monitor refugee returns and human rights during a transition period, and then oversee the elections to ensure that they were free and fair. Silajdzic agreed, but refused to commit to anything definitive on the timing. The draft principles outlined only that they would take place "as soon as social conditions permit."

On the joint presidency, Owen's initial idea of a three-person body was expanded to a six person council comprised of two members from each ethnic group. Decisions would be made by majority vote, and the group would have the powers appropriate for a central government, including command over foreign relations, trade, and customs. However, the specifics of the presidency's powers remained vague, particularly on how its decisions would relate to a new Bosnian parliament and what powers would be reserved for the two entities.

By the next day, Silajdzic had agreed to the points on elections and the joint presidency that Owen had incorporated into his draft. Happy with their progress, Hill and Owen thought that Silajdzic seemed looser and less edgy. For the moment, the Prime Minister wasn't the obstacle they worried he would be. He now supported the "further agreed principles," and Hill and Owen believed that they had created a draft that Milosevic could live with.[33]

WHILE HILL AND OWEN were with Silajdzic in Sarajevo, the rest of the delegation met with the Contact Group in Geneva. Hosted by the Russians, Holbrooke had to attend this meeting to help douse some of Moscow's frustration. This was a prime example of using process to compensate for Russia's dismay over substance. In the heavily publicized session held at the Russian embassy, the Contact Group pressed for convening an international peace conference. Holbrooke noted that all three Balkan Presidents had expressed interest in such an event, but that they remained too divided to come together yet. Instead, Holbrooke suggested that the Contact Group agree to meet at another foreign ministers meeting, similar to the one in Geneva, later that month at the United Nations in New York.[34]

A THREE-CAPITAL DAY

Holbrooke's team wanted to dramatize the end of the siege of Sarajevo. They decided to travel to all three Balkan capitals, the first time anyone had made such a one-day shuttle, beginning in Zagreb. With the Muslim–Croat offensive in western Bosnia continuing to advance, they needed to pressure Tudjman not to take Banja Luka. Then, they would fly into the newly reopened Sarajevo airport to send the same message of military restraint to the Bosnians. They hoped that the very act of flying into an airport their efforts had helped reopen would symbolize their accomplishment and potentially improve their relationship with Sarajevo, which remained tense. Finally, they planned to complete their 24-hour diplomatic trifecta with Milosevic in Belgrade.

STARTING IN ZAGREB, Holbrooke met privately with Tudjman while Clark, Pardew, and Kerrick met with Defense Minister Susak. On direct instructions from Washington, Holbrooke had already told Tudjman to slow his offensive, but there was little sign of it abating. Most Washington officials wanted Holbrooke to issue a clearer message of restraint. Yet Holbrooke believed that "both as a matter of simple justice and high strategy," the United States could not oppose the offensive "unless it either ran into trouble or went too far." He was no doubt influenced by his fallen colleague Bob Frasure, who exactly a month earlier, two days before he died, told Holbrooke that "we 'hired' these guys to be our junkyard dogs . . . we need to try to 'control them' . . . this is the first time the Serb wave has been reversed. That is essential for us to get stability, so we can get out." He therefore urged Tudjman to keep going, but warned him to stop at Banja Luka, the largest city deep in Bosnian Serb territory.[35]

There were at least four concerns about Banja Luka. First, Holbrooke believed that taking the city would be useless since the Croatians would have to give it up in a negotiated settlement. Second, some worried (but not Holbrooke) that an attack on Banja Luka would draw Belgrade into the war. Milosevic had not hinted one way or the other, but the Serbian military might feel compelled to intervene to prevent a complete collapse of the Bosnian Serb Army. Third, even if an attack on Banja Luka didn't spark a wider war, it seemed certain that it would create a massive Serbian refugee crisis. The UN estimated that more 250,000 refugees could be sent streaming into Serbia, which on top of the refugees from Krajina, would create a profound humanitarian crisis.[36] Such fallout might significantly disable Milosevic's ability to negotiate; even the Bosnians realized that sparking a massive refugee flow was not desirable, and the American team was very concerned about promoting a moral and humanitarian disaster. Finally, taking Banja Luka might exacerbate the problems between the Muslims and Croats, who were fighting over the spoils. With the Bosnian Serbs on the run, the Federation partnership threatened to be destroyed by each side's diverging battlefield objectives. Territorial greed could rip this "shotgun marriage" apart—and then the entire peace process would unravel.[37]

But the Croatians didn't want to stop. In his meeting with Clark, Pardew, and Kerrick, Defense Minister Susak talked about taking Bosnian Serb positions like "a kid in a candy store." After a heated argument, he eventually pledged that his forces would not go "one inch further." They also raised concerns about reports of clashes between Muslims and Croats, stressing the importance of maintaining comity within the Federation. Susak reacted strongly to what he described as an American "lecture," complaining about the Bosnian Muslims, whose combat logic was "to go as far as possible but cry foul when [they] run into trouble." Susak did say that Muslim and Croat military leaders had met recently in an effort to calm tensions, and, observing that "it takes two to make the Federation work," asked that the U.S. press the Muslims to cooperate.[38]

Despite Susak's pledge that things would calm down, the Americans remained uneasy about the threat to Banja Luka and the possibility for renewed Muslim–Croat fighting. The Croats had been less than reassuring. Holbrooke wanted to reduce the temperature of the Muslim–Croat rivalry, and proposed that Tudjman and Izetbegovic get together to sort things out. They agreed to meet September 19 in Zagreb with the Americans as host—an unusual arrangement, but indicative of the critical role the United States played to keep the fragile Federation together.[39]

AFTER A DISTRESSING MORNING IN ZAGREB, Holbrooke's team boarded a C-130 military cargo plane, donned helmets and flak jackets and, with

F-16 escorts, arrived in Sarajevo for the first time by air. To the long-suffering people of the Bosnian capital, their arrival had the intended effect: when the team arrived at the Bosnian Presidency building, a large crowd gathered outside to wave American flags and shower them with cheers, an event that moved the team deeply.

Yet the adulation stopped at the building's door. Izetbegovic and Silajdzic remained unconvinced that the Bosnian Serbs would comply with the terms for weapons withdrawal, and demanded that the air campaign resume. They reopened issues that had been resolved only days before, such as the definition of "humanitarian." Frustrated, Holbrooke said that by only concentrating on the "smaller picture," Izetbegovic and Silajdzic were missing the opportunity to move forward on what could be a highly favorable settlement. "The situation had changed too fast for these brave but isolated men to recognize how much progress had been made," he later reflected. He cut short any discussion of the "further agreed principles" and the fate of Banja Luka, as the Bosnians were so sourly argumentative that the talks would have only been counterproductive.[40]

THAT EVENING, the American team sat down with Milosevic in Belgrade. Reviewing the day's events, they told him that the "jury was still out" on whether bombing would resume. They explained that the Sarajevo government was still unhappy with the pause, and wanted the campaign to resume "at all costs." Surprisingly, the Serb leader seemed unfazed about the military situation in western Bosnia. After being told that things looked desperate for the Bosnian Serbs, Milosevic confidently stated that they "would bring things under control." Rather than talk about the fighting, Milosevic was anxious to discuss the future negotiations; particularly, the prospect of convening a three-president "Camp David" style summit as soon as possible. The Americans demurred.

After three hours, the team's exhausting three-capital day ended. But they had little time for rest. They had to return to Zagreb the next afternoon to prepare for the critical meeting between Tudjman and Izetbegovic.[41]

FEDERATION RESTRAINT; TAKING CREDIT WITH MILOSEVIC

Holbrooke hoped to get the two presidents to agree to a joint statement reiterating their commitment to the Federation and intent to continue military collaboration. Yet when the two leaders met at the Croatian Presidency the afternoon of September 19, any semblance of goodwill that might have existed between them quickly vanished.

This was the first time the Americans had seen the two presidents together, and as Holbrooke later recalled, "their intense personal animosity was worse than we had imagined." Tudjman angrily berated Izetbegovic on the need for restraint and not to take Banja Luka. The Croat leader had lost his appetite for the city; his forces had recently suffered a setback trying to cross the Una River on the Bosnian–Croatian border, and two Dutch UN peacekeepers had been killed in the crossfire.[42]

When the Bosnian President resisted, Tudjman yelled that he had no place to talk, since Croatian forces had suffered casualties to liberate "eighty percent" of their land. Looking on, Ambassador Galbraith observed that Tudjman "could barely contain his contempt [for the Bosnians]" and "had the smug aspect of superiority while Izetbegovic seemed quite beaten down." The shouting match proceeded for some time, continuing on as though the Americans were not even in the room. As Galbraith noted, "it was like observing a therapy session through a one-way glass mirror."[43]

Despite the poisonous atmosphere, Tudjman and Izetbegovic did agree to a joint statement on cooperation that their foreign ministers had worked out the previous day. Couching their decision in terms of their support for the American peace initiative, the two presidents promised not to take Banja Luka. Revealingly, they asked Holbrooke to make the announcement public—so that they would not appear weak to the Bosnian Serbs, or perhaps, the Americans worried, so Tudjman could walk away from the agreement later. They reaffirmed the commitments made to each other in the July 1995 Split agreement, and declared that their strategic partnership would continue in an effort to liberate "occupied territory." Finally, they agreed that the ownership of any territory taken by the offensive would be settled through a political dialogue and without regard to the ethnicity of the conquering army. Since most of the territorial gains thus far had been accomplished by Croatia, this was of particular interest of the Bosnian government. At least on paper, the Bosnians and Croats remained allies. Unfortunately, as the discussion that day proved, the reality remained far more uncertain.[44]

OTHER THAN BANJA LUKA, Holbrooke's team still believed that further military gains by the Federation in western Bosnia would bring major diplomatic benefits, while Washington officials wanted Tudjman and Izetbegovic to stop completely. To make the case for allowing the offensive to continue, Holbrooke sent Washington his first formal message of the shuttles.

In a handwritten fax to Christopher, Holbrooke argued that "contrary to many press reports, the military offensive has so far helped the peace process." The tough negotiations over territory were "taking place right now on the battlefield, and so far, in a manner beneficial to the [51–49] map." Indeed, by September 17, American intelligence analysts estimated that the Federation now controlled 51 percent of Bosnia to the Serbs 48 percent (compared to July, when the Serbs controlled 63 percent).[45] The issue, then, was how far they should be allowed to go.

Washington and the Holbrooke team concurred that attacks on Banja Luka and Eastern Slavonia were off-limits. Concerning actions in other areas, however, Holbrooke disagreed with many of his colleagues at home. He believed strongly that the negotiations would benefit from Federation victories around the towns of Sanski Most and Prijedor. Both were part of Federation territory under the Contact Group plan, and both were areas that Milosevic said he would not let go. Holbrooke therefore advised that the United States should get out of the "traffic light game." In the past, he wrote to Christopher, "we have weakened our credibility by flashing so many 'red lights' that no one knew which ones we meant and how seriously we meant them." Win or lose, Holbrooke asserted that Federation attacks on these areas would, paradoxically, be better "for the negotiations (although [the U.S.] would exploit them quite differently) than restraint imposed by the U.S." Here was an unusual moment: a small peace negotiating team pushing back for more military force.[46]

IMMEDIATELY AFTER THE BITTER Tudjman-Izetbegovic meeting, Holbrooke and his team flew back to Belgrade to get credit from Milosevic personally that they had gotten his adversaries to stay away from Banja Luka. They told him that while Izetbegovic and Tudjman understood all the military and strategic reasons why not to pursue Banja Luka, the main reason they had pledged not to attack was because "the U.S. had told them not to."[47]

The discussion then turned to the political "further agreed principles," which had evolved since Hill and Owen's talks in Sarajevo. Milosevic expressed his support, but said that he needed help bringing the Bosnian Serbs around. He asked Holbrooke if Owen could return to Belgrade to work on "technology" with the Bosnian Serb leadership. In Milosevic's version of the English language, "technology" meant "theater," and he explained that a "procedure must take place" for the Pale leadership to sign on to these principles. Such a meeting would not be a negotiation, but rather a chance for the Americans to walk the Bosnian Serbs through an agreement to which they would be a party. Holbrooke said that he would send Owen, Hill, and Pardew back to Belgrade over the weekend of September 24–25.[48]

WHEN THE HOLBROOKE TEAM arrived home in Washington early September 20, they believed that things were moving forward. The NATO bombing campaign had finally ended. The siege of Sarajevo was over. Milosevic again proved ready to compromise, forcing the Bosnian Serbs along if necessary. Discussions to expand the Geneva principles had begun. And the Croats and Bosnians appeared to understand the need for restraint.

Despite this momentum, the Americans believed that they didn't have much time. "The next thirty days are critical," Pardew reported to Secretary Perry. "A settlement is possible within a month, although Milosevic wants it to happen before then. If no settlement can be reached in that time, I'm afraid we are in for another long winter in Bosnia."[49]

Milosevic had indicated a great desire to end the conflict. He seemed anxious to enjoy the fruits of a settlement, especially sanctions relief and political relations with the West. Further, he seemed driven by a personal need to enhance his own image, to be viewed as an international statesman. "He is increasingly insistent on a Balkan summit which he hopes will be in the U.S.," Pardew reported.

In a frustrating twist, the Serb leader still proved much easier to deal with than the Sarajevo government. Infuriated by the end of the NATO campaign, they paid almost no attention to its consequences—the improvement of life in Sarajevo. Finally enjoying military success, they showed little desire to settle an agreement anytime soon. As negotiators, they remained moody, disorganized, and conflicted about both objectives and tactics. Their leaders were deeply divided—the Americans had to calibrate their message depending on which of the Bosnian leaders they were with, whether Sacirbey, Silajdzic, or Izetbegovic.

Tudjman had emerged as the swingman for any agreement. His army's successes were critical, keeping pressure on Belgrade and Pale. Yet the Croat president's openly contemptuous attitude toward the Sarajevo government undermined their already fragile alliance. Further, Eastern Slavonia remained a dealbreaker for Tudjman. As Holbrooke wrote to Christopher, "I must warn that [Eastern Slavonia] is a very explosive issue on which we must make major progress if we want to have a Bosnia settlement." The concern was not only that Milosevic would balk at giving it up, but that Tudjman may actually want to take it militarily. "[Tudjman] might rather liberate it by force," Holbrooke wrote, "than get it peacefully, since another military victory which also drives more Serbs out of his country may be more appealing to him than a peaceful but protracted settlement." Keeping the Croat leader in check would be a critical challenge for the Americans in the weeks ahead.[50]

ORGANIZING FOR A SETTLEMENT

While the Holbrooke delegation hopscotched across the region, policymakers in Washington continued to prepare for a possible settlement. In particular, the legal working group at the State Department began to think about the different aspects of an agreement and how they should fit together. They aimed for a comprehensive peace plan, one that would go far beyond than simply ending the war. They wanted to build a new Bosnia.

Since late August, John Kornblum at the State Department had thought that given the complexity of the negotiations and the fact that the signatories would vary according to each particular issue, an agreement should be modeled after the 1971 Quadripartite Agreement on Berlin, in which the United States, Soviet Union, Britain, and France agreed to establish basic governing provisions for the divided German city. Kornblum, heavily influenced by his days as a junior Foreign Service Officer involved in the Berlin negotiations and later as OSCE Ambassador, believed that they needed a "chapeau" document with various attachments—akin to side agreements—on specific issues. Like the Berlin agreement, a Bosnian peace would have a general framework agreement detailing the basic principles of a settlement that all sides would adhere to, such as those agreed to in Geneva. Then, there would be various annexes covering the specifics of a comprehensive peace, such as the internal political structure of Bosnia, an arrangement for military implementation, separation of forces in Bosnia, and resolution of the Serb–Croat dispute in Eastern Slavonia. Not all the parties would have to sign each annex—it would depend on whether it was an internal Bosnian issue or an external regional issue. Such a structure would provide maximum flexibility, matching particular aspects of implementation with the appropriate parties and helping with timing issues by dividing implementation into discrete phases.[51]

On September 17, Holbrooke called Kornblum from the shuttle and asked him to start drafting the documents along these lines. They could then use these drafts to prod the three parties toward specific decisions. "Our talks so far have been useful in clarifying positions and even narrowing many of them," he said, "but we must now move to specifics and that requires a U.S. draft." Following Holbrooke's request, Kornblum and the legal team began fleshing out the contents of a comprehensive settlement, beginning with the "chapeau" framework agreement. They continued to work outside the normal interagency process, which Holbrooke believed was "too cumbersome and time consuming—but he also wanted to maintain complete control.[52]

As KORNBLUM AND HIS TEAM began to write an agreement, other Washington officials discussed how to implement one. In early September the Deputies Committee continued deliberating about possible implementation arrangements—such as the appointment and duties of a civilian implementation coordinator and possible funding.[53] These talks were far enough along that by September 18, the State Department hosted meetings in Washington with French and Russian officials on civilian and military planning for implementation. They agreed that while the Americans would control military aspects of any agreement (because U.S. forces would shoulder most of the responsibility), the civilian effort would be led by the Europeans (who would carry most of the burden for paying for reconstruction).[54] Crucially, UN Secretary General Boutros-Ghali made clear that he would be glad to be rid of the former Yugoslavia—which he believed was crippling the UN's budget and distracting the organization from other priorities—and agreed to allow the organization for all aspects of implementation to be placed outside the UN and under the control of the Contact Group.[55]

THE PRESIDENT'S SENIOR ADVISORS also focused on how to handle the Muslim–Croat ground offensive.[56] Despite Izetbegovic and Tudjman's September 19 pledge to spare Banja Luka, the question remained about how far Federation forces should go—and Washington officials remained deeply divided about the answer. At a September 21 White House meeting, Tony Lake emphasized the importance of the "red lights" the Americans had given the Bosnians and Croats to end their offensive. Holbrooke, who had just returned to Washington, strongly disagreed. Voicing aloud what he had written to Christopher privately, Holbrooke said that "we haven't given them any 'red lights' outside of Banja Luka . . . I made no effort to discourage them about Prejidor and Sanski Most and other terrain that is theirs on the Contact Group map. The map negotiations are taking place on the battlefield right now." Lake wasn't convinced. He remained concerned about the prospect of the Administration being blamed for "encouraging" further bloodshed. He urged that their "public line" should be "no more offensive operations."

"We should emphasize peace," Lake said to Holbrooke. "It may be your view on Sanski Most and Prejidor, but you should say it in a way that doesn't exacerbate differences on other fronts." The Russians were becoming increasingly sensitive about the offensive, and CIA Director John Deutch added that Federation attacks on these two areas would spark huge refugee flows.[57] With Christopher agreeing with the National Security Advisor, Holbrooke conceded that restraint would be the public line—but he reserved the right to keep pushing them in private. If the current military situation stabilized and Muslim–Croat tensions rose, he explained, "then next week may be the time to push for a cease-fire."[58]

6

INCHING FORWARD: THE NEW YORK AGREEMENT AND A CEASEFIRE

While President Clinton's senior advisors debated battlefield traffic lights and State Department bureaucrats prepared for a possible settlement, the shuttle team's diplomats led several intense days of negotiations on two continents to put the finishing touches on the "further agreed principles" they had begun to develop. Bosnian Foreign Minister Sacirbey arrived in Washington for talks on September 22, while Owen, Hill, and Pardew traveled to Belgrade the weekend of September 23–24 to meet with Milosevic and the Bosnian Serbs. The Americans hoped that between these two visits, they would be able to finalize the draft principles in time for another foreign ministers event scheduled during the September 26 Contact Group meeting in New York City—which, like the Geneva meeting, they hoped would be another major step toward a peace agreement.

THE BUMPY ROAD TO NEW YORK

Since the shuttle team had returned to the U.S., Owen and his legal advisors had continued drafting the principles for the New York meeting. The Washington lawyers recommended some revisions—specifically, defining the power of the joint presidency, establishing separation of powers between the executive and legislative branches, and, upon Lloyd Cutler's recommendation, creating a constitutional court.[1] At the State Department on September 22, Sacirbey spent the day with the American legal team and agreed to most of the revisions. He asked for more specificity on others, such as clarifying that the parliament be elected by "direct, popular vote" and empowering the government to raise revenues.[2]

AFTER INCORPORATING SACIRBEY'S CHANGES into the draft, Owen, Hill, and Pardew flew to Belgrade on September 23. Handing Milosevic the latest text, they explained that after the New York meeting, Holbrooke planned to return to the region and hopefully conclude an agreement to convene an international peace conference. Looking over the changes, Milosevic said that he had no problem with the joint presidency, but the Bosnian Serbs would. He also rejected the proposal to hold direct elections for parliament. "This will go too far," he said. "It's too much for the beginning."[3]

This trip was supposed to have been simply "technology" for Milosevic, but the Bosnian Serbs came to negotiate. The Pale group—which included Karadzic, Kraijinik, and Koljevic—didn't want to agree to any new principles, they wanted to re-litigate the ones agreed to at Geneva. They refused to accept the fundamental point of the Geneva agreement: that Bosnia would remain a single, sovereign state. They had no respect for anything Milosevic had negotiated, and no interest in working with the Federation.

On elections, for example, the Bosnian Serbs rejected the idea that both entities would go to the ballot simultaneously. Karadzic claimed that simultaneous elections would remind his people of the "old days," the time when Bosnia was a Federal Republic of Communist Yugoslavia. By holding elections concurrently with the Federation, the Bosnian Serbs would be admitting a political union they wished to ignore.

As Milosevic had warned, they also rejected direct elections. Pale was not ready to empower its people to elect a central "Bosnian" government. Rather, they expected that the Srpska government would send its delegates to the central government, like a country sending an ambassador to an international organization. They did not want even the weak national government of the American plan, nor did they want an elected national parliament. In fact, the Bosnian Serbs rejected all of the central political functions that Milosevic had accepted. To them, the joint presidency's control over "foreign affairs" referred not to external relations, but internal ones among the two entities. Karadzic even complained that the joint presidency, or, as he called it, the "one-half of hell," was unacceptable. Quite simply, the Serbs wanted their own state.

Milosevic had to step in again to deliver the Bosnian Serbs. By Sunday morning, September 24, he had bullied them into agreement, altering the final text only slightly from the one originally presented by the American team. They removed the word "simultaneous" from the elections, and agreed not to hold them "directly." The Bosnian Serbs accepted the joint presidency and the parliament, although they reduced the members of the presidency to its original three (it had been six). They also trimmed the functions of the central government, leaving only foreign affairs and international financial matters as enumerated powers.[4]

WHILE HILL, OWEN, AND PARDEW were on their way back from Belgrade on September 24, Sacirbey met at the White House with Tony Lake.[5] The Bosnian Foreign Minister explained that the "further agreed principles" draft—the one he had seen and edited before the Belgrade talks—was a good one. However, he had just talked with Izetbegovic, who was very concerned that Owen, Hill, and Pardew had gone to Belgrade to meet with the Serbs. Izetbegovic worried that the Americans had been contaminated with "Belgrade air," and insisted that they visit Sarajevo immediately to review the changes. "President Izetbegovic is not going to tolerate your people going to Belgrade and only dealing with Milosevic," Sacirbey said. "This is not a deal between Milosevic and you, but between all of us. The optics look bad; you need to spend more time in Sarajevo to show balance." Lake tried to reassure Sacirbey, promising that Holbrooke would visit Sarajevo first during the next shuttle round.

Some wondered whether this would be enough to satisfy the Bosnians. They did not want to ruin an agreement in New York because they had over-looked Sarajevo for Belgrade, which Holbrooke later admitted was a mistake. Izetbegovic then made the decision for them, announcing that due to the "lack of progress" in the constitutional talks, the Sarajevo government would boycott the New York meetings. Late Sunday afternoon, Holbrooke reached his three colleagues by phone while they were refueling in Shannon, Ireland, on their way home, and asked them to return to the Balkans to save the New York meeting.[6]

Arriving in Sarajevo the morning of September 25, the three tired and unhappy Americans met with Izetbegovic and Prime Minister Silajdzic. They challenged many of the changes, particularly the removal of direct elections for parliament. Silajdzic was especially outraged. But as he described his problems, the Americans saw that the Prime Minister was not upset over the changes made in Belgrade, but with Sacirbey's changes made the Friday before in Washington. Silajdzic objected to the presidential bias of the draft, where the joint presidency would have exclusive responsibility over such areas as foreign relations and international financial matters, as well as the ability to appoint a cabinet. He favored an arrangement closer to a parlia-mentary system, where the legislature would appoint a cabinet, the joint presidency would act as the head of state and, naturally, the prime minister would wield the real governing power.[7]

Exasperated, the three Americans suggested some slight compromises, such as complete separation between the joint presidency and parliament. They tried to blur some areas where agreement was not yet possible. Rather than making the joint presidency responsible to appoint a cabinet, the principles simply stated that a cabinet would exist. And they promised that all aspects of the management and operation of the government would be negotiated in "the immediate future" (presumably at a peace conference). With these changes, the Bosnians finally agreed.[8]

THE MORNING OF SEPTEMBER 25, Owen called his friend Warren Christopher, who was already in New York preparing for the foreign ministers meeting, to tell him that Izetbegovic and Silajdzic had agreed to the new text. Hill immediately faxed the draft to Holbrooke, and Christopher called Izetbegovic to thank him for his cooperation. The Bosnian President assured the Secretary of State that Sacirbey would attend the next day's meeting. But in what had become an all-too-familiar pattern, the "final" agreement was hardly that. When Holbrooke received the draft principles that morning, his aide Philip Goldberg grimly said that the Serbs would never accept the Bosnian revisions. He was right.[9]

Holbrooke and his team began to work the phones, contacting Milosevic in Belgrade to try to work out another compromise. Christopher and Holbrooke briefed President Clinton and the rest of the Principals via video teleconference on the problem.[10] In an afternoon meeting with the three Balkan foreign ministers, Christopher, Holbrooke, and UN Ambassador Albright demanded that the remaining differences be resolved.[11]

Throughout the remainder of that day and long into the night, the Americans in New York worked furiously to hammer out the agreement. Whether by phone or in person, these were difficult negotiations. The concept of direct elections remained a nonstarter for Milosevic. He asked that the provision for elections "by popular vote"—which had been added in Sarajevo—be removed. The Serb leader also argued against "exclusive" foreign policy powers of the new government. The Geneva agreement had stated that each entity could make certain international arrangements, particularly economic ones, with outside countries, and the word "exclusive" seemed to limit that right. In several phone calls late that night, Holbrooke cajoled the Serbian leader, dangling ambiguously the carrot of "good things" to follow if they solved the problem, particularly the "exclusive" issue.[12]

In between calls with Milosevic, Holbrooke pressed the Bosnians. Meeting in his suite at the Waldorf-Astoria Hotel, Holbrooke asked Sacirbey to concede Milosevic's point on direct elections. The Bosnian Foreign Minister argued that the only way democracy could work in Bosnia was if leaders were popularly decided. Otherwise, the Bosnian Serbs would be able to stage sham elections to legitimize their illegal control. Nonsense, Holbrooke said, the Bosnians already had guarantees (in the Geneva agreement) that an international body would supervise these elections to ensure their legitimacy. Even the United States did not have direct elections for its president, he explained.

Holbrooke and Sacirbey were both strong personalities, and they lost their tempers. It was late, they were tired, and the meeting turned ugly. Holbrooke recalled that the meeting "came [close] to physical violence." Things finally calmed down, but nothing got resolved. The night ended without a fight, but the negotiations were not much further along than when they began.[13]

Christopher and Holbrooke were back on the phone with Izetbegovic before seven the next morning. Christopher demanded that the Bosnian President defer the issue of direct elections, and Izetbegovic finally conceded. They also agreed to drop the word "exclusively" concerning foreign policy powers. But they didn't have agreement yet. Two hours later, as Christopher, Holbrooke, and other American officials prepared for the talks on the 12th floor of America's UN mission, Sacirbey called to say that the Bosnians had again changed their minds. Apparently, he had called Izetbegovic and talked him out of his pledge to the Secretary of State. Outraged, Christopher and Holbrooke immediately summoned the Bosnian Foreign Minister to meet with them in Madeleine Albright's office.

This was Christopher's first real taste of the Balkan negotiations, and he was not pleased. Holbrooke later reflected that he had never seen him so mad. When Sacirbey arrived, the normally gracious Christopher ignored his outstretched hand, and sternly asked "what the hell is going on here?" The Bosnian President had made a deal, and now, with time running out, Sacirbey was backing him out of it. Christopher proceeded to have what he called "a firm exchange" with the Bosnian Foreign Minister "about the fact that this had been agreed [to] by his president and we would proceed on that basis."

They didn't have much time to solve the problem, as they all had to attend the previously scheduled Contact Group ceremony where the Balkan foreign ministers were supposed to formalize their agreement. Christopher, Holbrooke and Sacirbey went into the meeting as planned. No one else in the room was aware of the new problems, and waited for the ceremony to begin. Christopher opened the meeting, allowed the press to take some pictures, and then adjourned it quickly. With the other Contact Group members utterly confused, the Americans and Sacirbey returned to Albright's office to continue their talks.

Christopher continued to press the Foreign Minister without success. After coordinating with Tony Lake, he told Sacirbey that President Clinton would soon make an announcement from the White House. He would either praise the New York agreement or announce that it had failed and criticize the Bosnians. It would be up to Sarajevo government to decide which message Clinton would deliver.

After calling Izetbegovic, Sacirbey pledged to abide by their earlier agreement. In exchange, the Americans promised to pursue "direct" elections later in the negotiations, and allowed Sacirbey to speak of an undivided Sarajevo in his acceptance announcement (which was a rare foray into territorial discussions that they had so far avoided). The Contact Group and Balkan Foreign Ministers quickly convened to bless the "further agreed principles" before the agreement unraveled again.[14] Shortly before 4 P.M. in Washington, President Clinton stepped into the White House Briefing Room and announced the agreement.[15]

WITH THESE "FURTHER AGREED PRINCIPLES"—or the "New York principles"— the three parties agreed to share institutions of political power: a joint presidency, a national parliament, and a constitutional court. The New York principles provided the state institutions vital to establishing and maintaining the broader concepts—such as a single Bosnian state—outlined over two weeks before in Geneva. Yet, both the Geneva and New York agreements were only initial steps. Alone, they did not add up to a comprehensive settlement.

The road to New York also starkly illustrated the challenges ahead. The Bosnian Serbs were barely on board with either the Geneva or New York agreements. And the festering divisions within the Sarajevo government remained very troubling. The gyrations of the past 48 hours had not been about problems between the parties, but within the Bosnian delegation, over Izetbegovic and Sacirbey's rivalry with Silajdzic. It seemed that with the

New York principles, the three Muslim leaders began to focus on how their decisions would affect their own personal positions in a future Bosnian state, and each tried to mold the principles in ways that would best reflect their future status. The Americans found themselves not only serving as mediators among the three Balkan parties, but also among the competing personalities and interests within the Sarajevo government itself.

THE FOURTH SHUTTLE

Two days after the drama in New York, the exhausted Holbrooke delegation set off for the Balkans for the fourth time in six weeks. In Geneva and New York, they had pushed the parties to agree to a broad framework for a comprehensive settlement. Now, they wanted to convene a peace conference. President Clinton had already discussed this during a September 23 call to German Chancellor Helmut Kohl. "Many serious issues remain, but I think a settlement can be reached in the coming weeks," the President said. "I believe now we can bring negotiations to a conclusion."[16]

Shuttle diplomacy had produced the basic building blocks of the future Balkan state. But many difficult issues that had been intentionally left out of the Geneva and New York agreements needed to be settled—especially the most contentious subject, the territorial division of Bosnia. Holbrooke's team wanted to get the parties together and conduct "proximity talks," where the three sides would gather in one place and be separately housed for the duration of the negotiations. There, the Americans could continue to mediate through shuttle diplomacy, but by foot rather than by plane.

Holbrooke believed that in order to maximize U.S. leverage, the peace conference must be held on American soil. He knew that this would anger the Europeans—he and Carl Bildt had discussed holding the talks in Stockholm, and French Foreign Minister de Charette had already made a "big pitch" to host the conference in Evian, France (the same place where the agreement was signed to end Algeria's war of independence in 1962).[17] Holbrooke had also raised the issue with Serb and Bosnian foreign ministers, Milutinovic and Sacirbey, who said they needed American prestige to reach a settlement, and that a European venue would be too easy to leave if the talks broke down. Milutinovic "heaped scorn" on holding the conference in France, stating that Evian was the "last place" the Serbs wanted to go. "Who do they think we are, the Algerians?," he said.[18] Moments before he left on this fourth shuttle, Holbrooke also called Vice President Al Gore from New York's La Guardia Airport to discuss the issue. Gore agreed that the logic for a U.S. site was strong, and promised to make this point to the President.[19]

Holbrooke's team detailed its "unanimous views" about the timing and venue of a peace conference in formal document presented to the Principals. They suggested that the talks be held in relative isolation outside of New York City or Washington, which would seal the parties off from the press, but be close enough so that the talks could benefit from high-level intervention (such as Secretary Christopher or Tony Lake). While the three parties would be represented by their presidents, the conference would be co-chaired by Holbrooke, Bildt, and Russian Contact Group envoy Igor Ivanov. If they got an agreement, President Clinton could preside over a signing ceremony at the White House.[20]

DEPARTING FOR SARAJEVO on September 28, the shuttle team had two goals: to get an agreement for a peace conference, and broker a country-wide cease-fire.[21] A cease-fire had been one of the central components of the U.S. peace initiative—it had been outlined clearly in Lake's seven point script. Yet for weeks the shuttle team had resisted this, and Washington had deferred to them despite many views to do otherwise. But as they headed back to the region, the American diplomats now believed that the time was right.[22]

Several factors influenced this shift. First, as was evident from the discussion during the September 21 Principals Committee meeting at the White House, most senior officials were uneasy with encouraging more violence, even if they agreed that it helped the Muslims and Croats.

Second, as illustrated by Tudjman's obnoxious performance with Izetbegovic in Zagreb on September 19, it had become clear that Croatia would not tolerate much more sacrifice. Accomplishing most of their strategic objectives, the Croats now controlled 28 percent of Bosnian territory (over 10 percent *more* land than they were assigned under the Contact Group map), while the Muslims held 23 percent (over 10 percent *less* land assigned to them). Given this, the Croats weren't enthusiastic about risking their own troops to help the Bosnian Muslims. "Frankly, we have one basic problem," an anonymous American official told the *New York Times*, "Tudjman just does not particularly like Muslims."[23] Foreign Minister Granic had told Christopher and Holbrooke during their September 25 meeting in New York that Croatia would stop providing artillery support for the Bosnian forces, and had explained to the press that since the successful military offensive had "established a new reality," it should end. "We believe that this is the right time for the end of war and for a final just peace," Granic told the *Washington Post*.[24]

The Sarajevo government was happy to be finally scoring victories, and wanted to press forward. But they couldn't do it without the Croatians. Every time the Muslims fought without Croat support, they "got their asses handed to them," Chris Hill recalled.[25] If Sarajevo continued to act against Zagreb's wishes, the Federation's problems would certainly get worse. Clashes had already occurred between Muslim and Croat troops. In New York, Sacirbey had told Holbrooke how much he distrusted Tudjman, stressing that "the peace process could be held up by differences in the Federation." President Clinton himself understood this problem, explaining to Chancellor Kohl that a "strong Bosnian–Croat alliance is critical to the success of the peace process," and that "it [the Federation] must not blow up. We don't want to snatch defeat from the jaws of victory."[26]

A third factor fueled these concerns: the apparent revival of the Bosnian Serb Army. By September 24, the battle lines had stabilized, and the UN reported that the Bosnian Serbs were mounting successful counterattacks against Croat and Bosnian forces.[27] Evidence surfaced that Belgrade's cooperation with the Bosnian Serbs, which was apparently minimal earlier that month, had resumed significantly. U.S. intelligence reported that the cooperation between the two armies was "very good and stronger than ever." To Holbrooke, the situation metaphorically resembled the moment of a perfect tennis serve, in which the ball is momentarily stationary over a player's head; it's no longer rising, it's not beginning to fall yet. To many Washington officials, it would be better for the Federation to stop before the "ball" began to drop.[28]

BECAUSE OF THE FRACAS surrounding the Hill/Owen/Pardew trip to Belgrade, the shuttle team stopped first in Sarajevo. Holbrooke believed that the Bosnians were "pathologically unnerved" by the amount of time his team had spent in Belgrade, eroding their sense of trust in the Americans. Pardew felt that the team needed to spend more time with the Bosnians, because "compared to Sarajevo, Belgrade will be easy the rest of the way."[29]

Sitting down with Izetbegovic and Silajdzic the morning of September 29, they discussed the cease-fire and a peace conference. Without committing himself, Izetbegovic outlined three conditions for a cease-fire: restoring gas and utilities to Sarajevo; ensuring the full demilitarization of Banja Luka; and opening a road to Gorazde for humanitarian relief. Each of these seemed fair to the Americans. Holbrooke then outlined his own three ground rules for a future peace conference: that each delegation would be empowered to decide for their government (in other words, no ratification process); that delegations could not threaten to leave the talks; and that no press would be allowed. Also, Holbrooke said that there would not be a separate Bosnian Serb delegation—Milosevic would continue to negotiate on behalf of the Bosnian Serbs.

They also discussed the role of a NATO-led military force in implementing a settlement. For weeks, NATO officials in Brussels had been in the process of planning for an implementation force, or IFOR.[30] The Bosnian President wanted a strong IFOR role, from enforcing the withdrawal of Bosnian Serb forces from Federation territory and providing protection for elections, to guaranteeing freedom of movement and the return of refugees, to defining and enforcing Bosnia's border with Croatia and Serbia. This last request had not yet been considered by military planners as an IFOR responsibility, and Pardew warned Holbrooke that this would be a hugely expensive and dangerous undertaking.[31]

Izetbegovic also envisioned IFOR deploying in Serb-held areas, not just Federation territory. Up to that point, NATO had wanted to limit IFOR's responsibilities only to Federation lands to avoid the threat from conducting activities in "hostile" Serb-controlled territories. It now seemed likely, however, that for Bosnia to remain undivided, NATO troops would have to be deployed in both the Federation and Srpska. As General Clark reported that day to Shalikashvili, "there is a real risk that IFOR would inadvertently solidify the division of Bosnia-Herzegovina" if its deployment was limited to the Federation.[32]

Clark also described the implications of NATO support for elections security, refugee return, and freedom of movement. Obviously, such tasks entailed a far more intrusive mandate for IFOR than mere separation of forces or securing cease-fire lines, and the military was concerned that such duties put troops at greater risk. "Providing security to the elections process in the Serb entity would entail additional risks for our forces," Clark explained. "It will require a degree of international election and police support which will be difficult to muster. Although the total population is only about 60% of Haiti's or Cambodia's, the terrain, returning refugees, and ingrained hatred will add immeasurably to the difficulties in preventing incidents."

ALTHOUGH A PEACE AGREEMENT was still far from certain, the negotiations had entered a phase in which the military—and Washington's civilians—would have to make some hard choices about the risks they were willing to run to implement a settlement. The diplomatic initiative had been premised upon a major military commitment to Bosnia—whether in support of a UNPROFOR pullout under Op-plan 40104 or to implement a peace settlement—but the specific decisions about the shape and scope of the commitment still had to be made. These would be critical to the dangers troops would face. Determining IFOR's tasks and area of deployment were not just questions of military tactics. Such choices cut to the core of the Administration's commitment to this effort: how much was the United States prepared to pay in blood and treasure for peace in Bosnia? Would the military do more than separate the warring parties? How long should the United States stay? At the time, such critical questions were deferred.

THE TEAM'S TIME in Sarajevo reduced some of the tensions in the U.S.-Bosnian relationship. The Americans found Silajdzic, the winner of his government's most recent power struggle, to be much more cheerful and cooperative than before. Ambassador Menzies told Holbrooke that Silajdzic was pleased with the results of New York and was attempting "to salve bilateral bruises" recently inflicted on the relationship.[33] On the other hand, Mo Sacirbey's performance earlier that week had deepened doubts about his reliability. After New York, Pardew noted that Sacirbey was "inconsistent . . . seized with the public limelight for its own sake, and an outsider in Sarajevo." Although the team had once been more wary of Sacirbey's rival, Silajdzic, some now believed that he could be the least troublesome Bosnian negotiator. "If we convince Silajdzic and stay with him in dealing with Izetbegovic," Pardew advised Holbrooke, "our troubles with the fractious Sarajevo government will be reduced."[34]

BEFORE A CEASEFIRE, Holbrooke still wanted the Federation to push its offensive. In Zagreb on October 1, he asked the Croatian leadership to continue their military operations for just a few more days to give the Bosnians an opportunity to take as much territory as possible. In a private meeting with Tudjman, Holbrooke said he expected a cease-fire in ten days. Yet, stressing that some valuable territorial gains were left, Holbrooke urged the Croat President to "do whatever you can militarily in the next week." As he had done before, Holbrooke recommended key towns to take: "I would hope that you can take Prejidor, Sanski Most, and Bosanski Novi. If you take this, you will have land to give away." Tudjman listened carefully to Holbrooke's recommendations, explaining that he would consider helping the Muslims, since "they can't take territory on their own."[35]

A DECISION ON VENUE

After their meetings in Zagreb, Holbrooke's team took a side-trip to Sofia, Bulgaria to discuss European security issues with the former communist government and fledgling American partner. That night, Holbrooke called Strobe Talbott for an update on Washington's decision-making concerning the location of proximity talks. Talbott explained that while there was wide support to convene a peace conference, almost no one favored the idea of holding it in the United States. Apparently even Vice President Gore's support had waned. "The vote is nine to one against an American venue," Talbott explained, "and I'm one of the nine."

The President's top advisers planned to discuss this question during the next two days, and Holbrooke asked that he be allowed to state his case via secure phone. Talbott suggested instead that Holbrooke outline his argument again in writing. After he hung up, Holbrooke spent the rest of the night drafting his case (calling Tom Donilon for advice), which he also discussed with his team on the flight to Sarajevo the next day. When they arrived in Bosnia on October 2, Holbrooke sent the message to Washington from the Sarajevo embassy.[36]

AGAIN PRESENTING the "unanimous views" of the negotiating team, Holbrooke outlined the rationale to hold talks on American soil. "Given the difficulties we will face," Holbrooke explained, "Washington readers of this message may well wonder why they should agree to allow any tripartite negotiations anywhere near the United States. In fact, our recommendation is derived from the difficulties we face." He wrote that having the talks at an American site outside of Washington would significantly enhance the chances for success. "In the U.S., we will have full control of the process; elsewhere, we will probably lose much of our control, reducing our leverage dramatically." All the parties wanted to have talks in the United States he explained, as they felt that it would enhance the prospects for success and, ultimately, help guarantee that an agreement would be respected once signed.

One way an American site would enhance their leverage was by enabling senior officials—such as Christopher, Lake, Perry, and Shalikashvili—to visit the talks to provide extra boosts when needed. Holbrooke described that "Christopher was indispensable in the difficult morning hours in New York last Tuesday; his availability on short notice was critical, and will be again during the talks in ways that are not easily compatible high-profile and hard-to-schedule transatlantic travel . . . this U.S. drop-in advantage, we strongly believe, would immeasurably improve our chances of success." Also, Holbrooke wrote, the rules of the planned conference (such as keeping the media out and confining the delegates to the conference site) would be very difficult to enforce outside the United States.

To preempt concerns that an American venue would increase the costs of failure, Holbrooke argued that "such a risk-adverse calculus misses the main point: this Administration's prestige and standing is already fully engaged in the eyes of both the American public and the world. Failure will be approximately the same whether we meet in New Jersey or New Caledonia. We must maximize the chances of success, not reduce them in anticipation of possible failure." Even if talks were to fail, Holbrooke believed that given nature of the problem, "the world will still give the U.S. credit for its efforts," and the Sarajevo cease-fire, Geneva and New York agreements would still stand.

Finally, he concluded, the parties' willingness to take further chances for peace "will hinge to a great extent on their perception that we—and not the Europeans—are driving the process." Giving away this responsibility to the Europeans, Holbrooke believed, would "stop us in our tracks." The Europeans would undoubtedly complain (particularly the French, who were "making an all-out bid to take over the process by hosting the talks"), but he advised that "they will respect us and come along." Since the American peace effort first began back in August, "it has been viewed by the parties as a powerful signal that . . . 'America is back.' Similarly, the choice of venue will be seen as a critical indicator of whether we are committed to see this process to its conclusion."[37]

THE PRINCIPALS debated this proposal at a White House meeting the afternoon of October 2.[38] Christopher urged his colleagues to consider Holbrooke's views seriously. He felt that the decision should really be the lead negotiator's call: "he had been with the parties; he had a firm recommendation as to where we could be most effective, and that was in the U.S."

The Secretary of State did, however, address the downsides to hosting a conference in the United States. "Although the team denies this," he told his colleagues, "the consequences of failure would be greater because it would be viewed as 'our conference.' We would be rolling the dice." Also, Christopher pointed out that the President could "be drawn into this," that he could not be isolated from such an important event on American soil. Moreover, such a decision would likely cause a "rift" in the Contact Group. "The allies and Russians will go bananas if we're seen as hijacking the process," he warned.

Although Christopher supported Holbrooke's recommendation, his concerns resonated with others. Sandy Berger, perhaps the most politically astute member of the national security team, believed strongly that the United States needed to "hold the rudder," but raised the point that an American venue could become a media-circus and increase tensions with Congress. Playing devil's advocate, he explained that the Europeans would be very angry, possibly creating problems with critical implementation issues—such as support for IFOR. Albright concurred with Berger, observing that "the level of European hostility against us is incredible." In her view, a U.S. site "would only magnify our differences over implementation." She also expressed concern that they would have difficulties allowing suspected war criminals—such as most of the Bosnian Serb leadership and Milosevic himself—on American soil.

Lake spoke up in support of the American site, arguing that no matter how angry the Europeans might become, they would still participate in implementation. As a way to mollify them, Lake suggested that they structure a "two-tiered" peace conference, possibly having some portion of the talks (such as a signing ceremony) in Europe. Although Perry, Shalikashvili, and Deutch supported Lake and Christopher, the group decided to delay sending a decision to the President for a few days. Instead, Lake suggested, they should think harder about "a plan to ameliorate European concerns," and brainstorm about possible venues other than New York or Washington.[39]

The Principals reconvened at the White House two days later to make the final decision. After a brief discussion, they agreed to hold the talks at a secluded location in the United States, removed from Washington or New York but close enough to permit "drop-ins" by senior officials. In a nod to the Europeans, they decided to leave open the possibility that an agreement would only be initialed at the U.S. talks, with an official signing ceremony held at a European venue. Lake lobbied for a final signing at a summit hosted by the President, but others felt that the downsides (presumably from Europe) would be too great. They also decided that the Holbrooke team should work with the Contact Group to develop options for possible follow-on events—such as "implementation talks"—in European capitals or Moscow. Soon after this meeting, officials from the NSC, State Department, and Pentagon began to consider possible sites.[40]

ALTHOUGH THE PRINCIPALS had decided to host the talks, they disagreed about whether the announcement should be packaged with a countrywide cease-fire. Holbrooke team's believed that the two had to be linked—there could not be peace talks if the parties were still fighting on the ground. They were concerned that if the fighting continued, talks would inevitably be delayed—and possibly postponed—while the parties jockeyed for military advantage. Moreover, the Bosnians might begin to lose, weakening the relatively strong negotiating position they currently had.

The Secretaries of State and Defense were sympathetic but less insistent about linking the two. Perry argued that "we should push like hell to get [the cease-fire]," with Christopher explaining that a cease-fire would be beneficial but not essential. "We should not rule out proximity talks if we don't get it," Christopher said. Curiously, Tony Lake, who only days before had pressed Holbrooke to flash red lights to halt the Bosnian-Croat offensive, was strongly opposed to making a peace conference contingent on a cease-fire. "We should press for [a cease-fire]," he said at the October 4 White House meeting, "but not make it a precondition."[41]

NEGOTIATING A CEASE-FIRE

The military situation in western Bosnia had taken a turn for the worse. In a counteroffensive, the Bosnian Serb Army reconquered land taken a month earlier by Croat and Muslim forces. To use Holbrooke's metaphor, the Muslim–Croat "tennis ball" had reached its apex and was on its way down—fast. Despite Washington's desire to de-link a cease-fire and proximity talks, Holbrooke was determined to forge an end to the fighting that could be announced simultaneously with a decision to convene a peace conference. Indeed, he had defiantly told Washington that if he were unable to get a cease-fire, he would hold off on announcing a peace conference and instead continue shuttle diplomacy.[42]

WHEN THE HOLBROOKE DELEGATION met with Izetbegovic and Sacirbey the afternoon of October 2 in Sarajevo, they pressed them to agree to an immediate cease-fire. The Bosnian leaders were reluctant, but said that they might be interested if the Serbs could meet the three terms they had outlined several days before (restoring utilities to Sarajevo, a demilitarized Banja Luka, and a road to Gorazde). Believing that he was on the brink of another military success, Izetbegovic requested that they wait another ten days before pushing for a cease-fire. Holbrooke countered that to let the fighting continue would be a "big risk," and that the Bosnians should accept that they've gained all they could.[43]

The Americans used the Croats and Serbs to pressure the Bosnians. They spent October 3 shuttling between Zagreb and Belgrade to negotiate the terms for a cease-fire. Milosevic agreed that the time was right. The Croats, who only days before had been advised to press forward and support the Muslims militarily, were easily persuaded that the fighting should end. Would this be enough to move Sarajevo? Pessimistic, Holbrooke called Tony Lake to explain that the chances of a cease-fire were 20 percent at best.[44]

On October 4, the Americans joined EU negotiator Carl Bildt in Sarajevo to press their case. The Bosnians said that while they agreed "in principle," they would commit to stop fighting only when their three preconditions—especially opening roads and gas lines to Sarajevo—were met. Izetbegovic sensibly argued that without gas and open access, peace would mean little to his people. Yet it seemed clear that the Bosnian President really wanted more time to try to make further military gains.[45]

Holbrooke needed to reason with Izetbegovic, so he pulled him into a room with Don Kerrick and Sacirbey. Holbrooke wanted to use Kerrick's background in military intelligence (although the Brigadier General was the NSC representative on the delegation, he was on loan from U.S. Army Intelligence) to explain to the costs of further military action. Although Kerrick was then privy only to the same information as other team members, Holbrooke theatrically emphasized his experience as an "Army intelligence specialist" to convince Izetbegovic that the Bosnians should stop and that the Croats would no longer support them. "Kerrick and I had not discussed this meeting in advance," Holbrooke recalled, "but he played his part perfectly." They discussed not only specific intelligence but also the common tendency of Generals to go too far—"[the Bosnian] armies were tired, they weren't well trained, they didn't have the support, and Banja Luka for them would be that one battle too far, which would turn the momentum back to the Bosnian Serbs." Also playing up his connection to the White House and his role as President Clinton's representative on the team, Kerrick described for Izetbegovic the President's "strong desire" for a cease-fire. Holbrooke, never shy of the theatrical, laid it out for Izetbegovic plainly: "Mr. President," he said, "you're shooting craps with your nation's destiny."[46]

Izetbegovic agreed to meet the Americans half-way: he would accept a cease-fire, but only if it took effect in several days. The Bosnian Serbs, he said, needed to prove that they would comply with the cease-fire terms in good faith—he also wanted one last chance to make military gains. The fighting would not end until Sarajevo had gas and an open road to Gorazde. Izetbegovic also insisted that Holbrooke go to Belgrade to get Milosevic's commitment.

So Holbrooke, Clark, Kerrick, and Owen flew to Belgrade that night to meet with Milosevic. Not wanting the deal to unravel in Sarajevo while they were in Belgrade, Hill and Pardew stayed behind to be with Izetbegovic and Sacirbey. As these last terms were being discussed, they worked together for over three hours on an open phone line between the two capitals, and Holbrooke called back to Washington to consult with both Christopher and Lake.

They agreed with the Bosnians that a cease-fire that would take effect in five days. If gas supplies were not turned on by then, the deal would be off. The Bosnians would get an open road to Gorazde, but since mine-clearing would take a few weeks, this condition would not be linked to the cease-fire (though they did make the opening a requirement to attend a peace conference). The cease-fire would last for 60 days or until the completion of a peace deal, whichever came later. Milosevic agreed to the cease-fire as a "witness," and in turn got Karadzic, Krajisnik, and Mladic to sign the document. Also, Milosevic approved a written agreement to convene proximity talks in the United States (as the Serb negotiator for peace talks, he approved on behalf of the Bosnian Serbs).[47]

As THE CEASE-FIRE neared, the Americans drafted a formal agreement to announce a peace conference that would commence "on or about" October 25 in the United States. Holbrooke informed Washington of Milosevic's approval of these two documents early the morning of October 5, although he warned that they only had Sarajevo's verbal agreement. They reserved the right for revision and, as Holbrooke explained in a message to Christopher and Lake, "any changes in Sarajevo could cause a serious last minute problem." At noon, Holbrooke arrived in Sarajevo to get the Bosnians signature.[48]

The Bosnians didn't have a problem with the draft announcing the conference, but remained uneasy with the cease-fire. As shown over a week earlier in New York, the closer they got to an agreement, the colder their feet became. The Americans had been able to get the Serbs to agree to the Bosnians' terms. Sarajevo would get electricity and gas and a road to Gorazde. But Izetbegovic remained reluctant. From the shuttle team's perspective, the agreement ended the bloodshed. From Izetbegovic's perspective, the agreement ended his chance for retribution—the military momentum had shifted and the Bosnians Serbs were on the run, at last having a taste of the suffering that they had inflicted on his people. As Jim Pardew later reflected, "it takes a lot of courage for these men to pick up a pen and sign something that we had negotiated with their arch enemies."[49]

Placing a final obstacle in the way, Izetbegovic said that he would not write his signature on the cease-fire document alongside those of his Bosnian Serb enemies. Holbrooke had a photocopy made of the agreement with the Bosnian Serb signatures removed—since the agreement would not have formal legal standing, he didn't think it mattered if the parties initialed the exact same document—and said to the Bosnian President that now he had no excuse not to sign. Izetbegovic tried one last stalling tactic, saying to Holbrooke, "I don't see your signature on this, Mr. Ambassador." Holbrooke quickly grabbed his pen, signed the document, and pushed it back to the stunned President. He told Izetbegovic that they had to leave Sarajevo to see Tudjman in Zagreb and the Contact Group in Rome. As Holbrooke rose to leave, Izetbegovic, his hand shaking, signed the paper. The parties had agreed. At 11 A.M. Washington time, President Clinton announced from the White House that a cease-fire would take effect on October 10, and that the parties would convene in the United States around the end of the month for proximity talks.[50]

FOLLOWING A QUICK STOP in Zagreb to finalize plans with Tudjman—where Holbrooke made one last plea that the Croats capture as much territory as possible during the five days before the cease-fire took effect—the Americans landed in Rome for another meeting with the Contact Group. While the Europeans had been informed about both the cease-fire and venue for a peace conference, they had not been fully consulted. The French were especially upset about the American location, so as a gesture of compromise, Holbrooke's team decided that the peace talks would be followed by an "international peace conference" in Paris to bless any agreement ceremonially. Washington officials had wanted to leave this issue open, but Holbrooke went ahead and made it part of the formal announcement to lock-in some sort of European event (and, more immediately, to calm a room of angry Europeans). The President announced this in his statement on October 5, and Christopher called his German, French, and British counterparts to inform them of the decision.[51]

THE HOLBROOKE TEAM returned to Washington from their fourth shuttle on October 6 after accomplishing exactly what they had set out to do—negotiate an end to the fighting and set the timing for peace talks that they would host. On October 11, the cease-fire began. It was the thirty-fifth nationwide cease-fire since the Bosnian war started in April 1992. But it was the first to be linked to a meaningful diplomatic process—and genuine hope for a lasting settlement.

7

PREPARING FOR PEACE: A DEAL WITH RUSSIA, A DECISION ON IFOR

The Americans had just three weeks to prepare for the peace conference. Considering that only a few months earlier, America's Bosnia policy had been bogged down and knotted, it was amazing that they had come so far so fast. Not only did they need to locate the site for the talks and make the challenging logistical and diplomatic arrangements, but they still had to draft the texts that would be the basis for negotiations. Many of these efforts were already underway by early October. Yet with the conference now scheduled, this drafting effort would have to intensify.

Policymakers in Washington and Europe also worked to create the arrangements for implementing a peace. Progress toward achieving a settlement—as difficult as that had proved to be—far outpaced planning for implementing one. Many questions needed answers. From the Clinton Administration's perspective, the most critical issue concerning implementation was the same one that it had struggled with for nearly three years: what America's military mission in Bosnia would be.

THERE WAS NEVER ANY DOUBT that the United States—not its European allies, not the UN, and not the Balkan parties—would draft the military component of a peace agreement. "Particularly after UNPROFOR, we wanted to make sure that there would be no question about the authority of a military force," Under Secretary of Defense for Policy Walter Slocombe recalled. "It had always been our position that we would write it."[1] But since this would be a NATO mission, the Americans would have to get agreement within NATO's North Atlantic Council, reaching consensus with its sixteen ambassadors.

The debate on the scope and structure of NATO's implementation force (IFOR) transcended Bosnia; it would set the course for the Alliance in the post–Cold War world. "As NATO prepares to implement a Bosnian peace plan," NATO Ambassador Robert Hunter cabled to Washington, "it faces some of the most consequential decisions of its history, especially in terms of how it is organized and how it operates."[2] Such decisions involved, for example, the UN role in a NATO-led implementation force, the flexibility commanders on the ground would have to make tactical decisions and, crucially, the relationship between NATO and non-NATO countries—such as Russia—participating in IFOR.

NATO AND IFOR

During the third week of September, while most American officials focused on the chaotic New York meetings and the negotiations to secure the "further agreed principles," Slocombe joined Wes Clark and John Kornblum in Europe to begin quiet consultations at NATO on IFOR. Their discussions with the British, French, and Italians revealed broad agreement on the basic organization and goals for the mission.

Everyone believed that there should be a civilian coordinator to supervise the nonmilitary aspects of a peace settlement, and that this person's authority should not interfere with the military chain of command, as had been the case with UNPROFOR. However, the French, backed by the British, demanded that both the IFOR and civilian coordinator "wear a highly-visible UN hat," and be designated by the UN Secretary General. The Americans, resisting any arrangement that would resemble the "dual-key" structure that had made decisions over NATO airstrikes so difficult, insisted that these leaders should only be "validated" by the UN Security Council and remain independent of the international body. In this way, the civilian coordinator would lead a coalition of the willing, not a UN mission. "The U.S. accepts the necessity of NATO authority," Slocombe told British and French representatives in Paris on September 26, "but if there is even a whiff of UN oversight of NATO, congressional approval [for an IFOR mission] would be extremely difficult to win."[3]

But the Europeans wanted strong political oversight of IFOR operations. Citing the lack of coordination within NATO during the air campaign (as shown, they argued, by the dispute about the Tomahawk strike), the British suggested appointing a special political representative of the NATO Secretary General to work alongside the IFOR military commander in Bosnia. The United States opposed this, countering that arrangements for political–military coordination already existed in NATO—the NAC—and that establishing any new arrangement amounted to creating another chain of command.[4]

On September 29, the NAC approved the parameters of an IFOR mission largely along the lines the Americans had pushed for. The NATO ambassadors agreed that the civilian implementation coordinator would have authority granted by the UN Security Council, but would not be a "UN representative." And on the issue of political decision-making within NATO, the NAC decided that political guidance would be conducted through the Alliance's existing structure, not a special representative.[5]

Based on these agreements, and the basic contours for IFOR that had already been established by Washington's deliberations, Slocombe, Clark, and Kornblum began to write the military annex for a peace settlement on the flight home from Brussels. When they returned to Washington, they turned the drafting over to the Joint Chiefs of Staff and NATO commanders.

They completed a preliminary version by October 3, which then circulated among the other agencies for what turned out to be a vigorous debate.[6]

WITH A DRAFT MILITARY STRUCTURE in hand, NATO's defense ministers met on October 5–6 for a previously scheduled summit in Williamsburg, Virginia. During the first day of talks, the news broke that the Bosnian cease-fire agreement had been reached. This development, Secretary of Defense Perry reported to President Clinton, "added urgency" to the Williamsburg discussions. He found a "sense that the time for discussion and debate has passed. The ministers want to get on with the operation." The Americans were gaining confidence and not above self-congratulation, even among themselves. To Perry, the NATO ministers conveyed that the alliance had "emerged from a long dark tunnel of indecision and irresolution. The cure was American leadership."[7]

NATO's military commander, U.S. Army General George Joulwan, briefed the ministers on the military planning for IFOR, urging them to "seize the moment" and commit to troop and financial numbers. Joulwan's concept for IFOR entailed a force of 50–60,000 ground troops in Bosnia, deployed into three zones led by separate American, French, and British commanders. Almost all 16 NATO nations wanted to contribute to the force, Perry wrote to the President, adding that "it is amazing what American leadership has done to bring in other countries." In terms of American commitments, Joulwan explained that the American military would provide roughly one-third of the total troops, at an estimated cost of $1.5 billion.[8]

RUSSIA AND IFOR

While negotiations with the Europeans on IFOR were well underway, there was still a long way to go to work out what role, if any, Russia might play. In a September 27 telephone conversation with Clinton, President Yeltsin stressed the issue's importance. While discussing the agenda for their scheduled summit meeting at FDR's historic estate in Hyde Park, New York, Yeltsin abruptly interrupted the interpreter to stammer "NATO, NATO, NATO, NATO! This is one of the most difficult issues we will have to discuss!"[9]

The Clinton Administration faced a simple challenge: Russia wanted to be a part of the peacekeeping mission in Bosnia, but not under NATO command. The Russians had what American officials described as a "chronic allergy to NATO," flaring most acutely around talk of expanding the Alliance to include former Warsaw Pact nations. NATO's bombing campaign against the Serbs didn't help, as many Russians saw this as further humiliation of a once great power. "The big problem was that NATO's activism in Bosnia would exacerbate Russian concerns about NATO power," Strobe Talbott reflected. American officials worried that Russia's anger over Bosnia could knock it off the path of democratic reform. Avoiding such trade-offs was one of the reasons the Clinton team had sought to avoid Bosnia for so long.[10]

This challenge was particularly difficult given the upcoming parliamentary elections in Russia, where Yeltsin's opponents were using NATO's activism in Bosnia against him. In a September 28 meeting at the White House, Russian Foreign Minister Kozyrev told President Clinton that a NATO-only force could bring down the Yeltsin government. "We can't put our troops under NATO command," Kozyrev said. "President Yeltsin would be under great pressure." Clinton explained that while he realized that NATO command was difficult for Russia, the United States could not recreate the conditions of more recent—and less successful—military operations. "We had some problems in Somalia with ambiguous command and control," he said. "I believe that in part due to this 18 American soldiers died there . . . I am sensitive to Russian concerns, but we need to ensure that we have a practical arrangement, so that we don't get kids killed." Agreeing to work with the Americans, Kozyrev said that "what's important is a nod toward Russian public opinion." The President agreed. "I know the last couple of months have been tough for you and that our actions haven't helped," he said. "We want to help you now as we make peace in Bosnia. I want to help your situation."[11]

MANY CLINTON ADMINISTRATION officials viewed Russian participation in IFOR not only as a problem to be managed, but also an opportunity to be seized. The decision was not driven by military necessity—if anything, including Russia would make military implementation more complicated, not less. "The Russians were so obviously interested in working with us on IFOR, it made little sense not to try and work something out," Tony Lake recalled. "If anything, they were bad bargainers—they undermined their own leverage by signaling to us how bad they wanted in."[12]

Bill Perry and Strobe Talbott agreed with Lake, but they saw a larger purpose at stake. They believed that a Russian role in IFOR would be an important symbol, not only as a sign to the parties in Bosnia that the international community was united and that implementation would be even-handed, but to those in Russia who doubted that the Russia and the NATO Alliance could work together. As Talbott wrote to Christopher at the time, "the good news is that if we can work something out on this issue, it will help us not just with Bosnia now . . . but also with NATO expansion and the NATO-Russia dialogue later on."[13]

They wanted IFOR to become an example of the possibilities of U.S.–Russian partnership. "Really the principal motivation for bringing [Russia] into Bosnia was so that we would have something practical from which to build on this priority relationship," Perry explained. "This effort was 2% about Bosnia and 98% about moving the U.S.-Russian relationship forward," Walter Slocombe recalled. To Talbott, the way to "jujitsu" this difficult issue was "to make NATO's activism in Bosnia proof of the proposition that NATO and Russia could cooperate and that we could turn the Bosnian experience into a reassurance as far as the Russians were concerned."[14]

Including Russia in IFOR would be a way for the West to integrate its former global adversary into the security architecture of Europe. "We saw that IFOR was a metaphor for solving difficult security problems in Europe," Perry said, "and we wanted to have Russia as part of the solution . . . not as a nation creating problems [or] standing outside and watching." If NATO and Russia couldn't cooperate on Bosnia, Perry believed, "you couldn't do it in the rest of Europe." As Perry and his Assistant Secretary for International Security, Ashton Carter, later wrote, "Exclusion [of Russia] would be taken by Russians as a sign that the extended hand of our post Cold War 'partnership' was a false gesture, that our military-to-military relationship was for show but not for real."[15]

BY EARLY OCTOBER, American officials were jetting across Europe to conduct three parallel negotiations—negotiating with the Balkan parties, with NATO allies on IFOR, and with Russia. On the Russia track, a major step would take place in Geneva, and the main players would be Defense Secretary Bill Perry and the Russian Defense Minister, Pavel Grachev.

When Perry and his delegation—which included Talbott and other officials from the Pentagon, State Department, and National Security Council—departed Andrews Air Force Base outside Washington for Geneva the evening of October 7, they were prepared to offer Grachev two proposals for Russia's participation. First, Russian forces could maintain their command links, but operate under IFOR for specific operations or functions; or second, Russia could perform separate "non-combat" tasks, such as logistics or airlift. There were two red-lines Perry would not cross: compromising NATO command and control, and giving the Russians their own sector to oversee (for fear that a Russian zone would bring de facto partition for the Serbs).[16]

The United States insisted on NATO command, and Russia insisted on staying outside of it. As they flew across the Atlantic, Perry's team worried whether that they could find a way out of this box. They thought that if they did not make any progress on this trip, there would be tremendous pressure in Washington to give up the effort.

Gathered around the conference table aboard the National Airborne Operations Center (NAOC)—the giant 747 that had been built during the Cold War to be an airborne command post in the event of a nuclear war—Perry welcomed the group to "mission impossible." One of their biggest challenges was to keep Russia from walking away from even trying to find a solution. They worried that Russian military officials—especially Grachev—did not want to spend scarce military resources in Bosnia, and were pressuring Yeltsin against participation. Thus, along with finding a mutually acceptable formulation for Russia's participation, Perry found himself in the awkward position of having to convince Grachev that the cause was even worth the effort.[17]

THE NEXT DAY in Geneva, the Russian Defense Minister did not budge on the question of NATO command, and insisted that Russia be given a "major" role with its own implementation zone. At one point, he grabbed himself by the throat to show what would happen to anyone in Moscow who would agree to subordinate Russian troops under NATO. "[Grachev] was emphatic that it would be political dynamite for Yeltsin to agree to political subordination under the NAC," Perry reported to Washington. Grachev made clear that such an arrangement "might well produce a communist victory in the coming elections. This would set Russia back seventy years, and we'll be back in the Cold War."[18]

Grachev then played some cards clearly intended to show what he meant. He said that Russia was preparing to solve unilaterally the question of how many Russian troops would be allowed in certain areas under the Conventional Forces in Europe (CFE) treaty, and would not cooperate with a proposed new Nunn-Lugar program to help secure nuclear materials in Russia. The Americans did not take these threats seriously, but that Grachev would even state these positions—making clear that they were connected to Bosnia—was reason for concern.[19]

Yet the conversation did offer a glimmer of hope. The Russian Defense Minister emphasized that above all else, "optics" were important. To avoid even the appearance that Russian forces were under NATO, he urged the Americans not to refer to IFOR as a "NATO force" but rather an "International Implementation Force." Grachev's comments confirmed the Americans' suspicions—the Russians were most concerned about the appearance of equality. As a Pentagon strategy memorandum read, "a good cosmetics job . . . could tip the balance" toward Russian acceptance.[20]

The Perry team returned home uncertain that, even with the potential for a "cosmetic" solution, a deal was within reach. As Talbott told Christopher, the talks showed that "there is a significant chance that we can't get there from here—that is, it may simply be too hard for the Russians to participate in, or even cooperate with, a NATO-led IFOR." Talbott thought that the Kremlin was deeply divided. "I suspect that what Bill [Perry] saw in Geneva was Grachev's own bottom-line. What's not so clear is whether it's Yeltsin's. It's certainly not Kozyrev's: he's got in mind a much more modest (and realistic, and to us acceptable) Russian force that could fit alongside IFOR in a non-combat capacity." Given this confusion, most of the final decisions, both Talbott and Perry reported back to their colleagues, would have to be made by Presidents Clinton and Yeltsin when they next met on October 23 in Hyde Park, New York.[21]

WITH ONLY A WEEK to go before the presidential summit, the Americans intensely engaged the Russians. On October 16, the Holbrooke team traveled to Moscow to meet with the Contact Group, where they were joined by Strobe Talbott and Walt Slocombe to discuss IFOR.[22]

The Russian position had not changed since the Perry–Grachev meeting in Geneva. "Clearly the Russians want to be part of the operation," Slocombe wrote Perry, "but they have not yet really changed their position on political control, independence of action, and a [Russia-only] geographical sector."[23] As Talbott told the NAC in Brussels on October 19, it was now "much clearer how unclear the situation is . . . President Yeltsin is reserving for himself the final say on what has been an extremely contentious issue both within his

Administration and in the legislature." Russian domestic politics were a very large part of the problem. "Virtually every contentious issue [in Russia]," Talbott said, "is the subject of intense debate and exploitation by the government's opponents as further proof of Yeltsin's selling out Russia's interests."[24]

THE FIFTH SHUTTLE

After the meetings in Moscow, the Holbrooke team flew for Belgrade for its fifth and final (and shortest) shuttle before the peace talks. To present a united front, they invited Carl Bildt and Russian minister Igor Ivanov, who would cochair the peace talks along with Holbrooke, to travel with them. Lasting only 48 hours, this trip was only meant to be a "final systems check" with the three parties before negotiations resumed in the United States.[25]

The Americans announced that the peace conference would be held at Wright-Patterson Air Force Base outside of Dayton, Ohio. While Tudjman seemed disinterested, Izetbegovic and Milosevic were disappointed. The Bosnian leaders wanted easier access to the American media to drum up public pressure on their behalf. Milosevic wanted to be closer to New York and Washington, where he could enjoy the highlife and, no doubt, also play to the media. Upon hearing that the talks would be held not in bustling midtown Manhattan but sleepy middle America, he yelled that "I'm not a monk" and "you can't confine us to a military base!" Milosevic also insisted on meeting President Clinton, believing that this would be critical to mending his image. Recognizing that this could provide useful leverage in the negotiations, Holbrooke kept the carrot dangling. "The President will not be involved in the talks," he said. However, if they reached an agreement, he promised they would "consider" having Clinton participate in a signing ceremony.[26]

Milosevic pressed the hardest on sanctions relief since his first meeting with Holbrooke in August. "On sanctions, Milosevic has finally taken the gloves off," Pardew reported to Perry. Calling this the "question of all questions," the Serb leader stressed that sanctions were unjustified given his country's cooperation in the peace process. He argued that they should be suspended before proximity talks started, and then fully lifted once an agreement was signed. Holbrooke rejected this demand, explaining (somewhat disingenuously) that the issue could only be decided by the UN.[27]

HYDE PARK

The Americans had reason to worry about the October 23 Clinton–Yeltsin meeting in Hyde Park. The negotiations were already tough; but Yeltsin's extremely erratic behavior—fueled by illness, alcohol consumption, or probably both—raised concerns that the summit would become a huge diplomatic disaster. It would be a major test for the "Bill and Boris" relationship. At a stop in Paris on his way to New York, Yeltsin told French President

Chirac that he wanted to put as many as 25,000 Russian troops in IFOR and rejected being under the "aegis" of NATO. Chirac agreed that if this were the case, Russia should have its own sector—directly counter to plans the United States had been working with its NATO allies on.[28]

The day before Hyde Park, Yeltsin was, even for him, unusually blustery. In New York City to celebrate the 50th anniversary of the United Nations, Yeltsin used a speech before all the other world leaders seated before him in the General Assembly to stress his concern that the UN Security Council had been "put on this sidelines" in decision-making on IFOR. "It is inadmissible for a regional organization [NATO] to take decisions on the massive use of force, [and] bypassing the Security Council," he thundered. President Clinton clearly had his work cut out for him. As Christopher told the President in the helicopter on the way to Hyde Park, "You'll probably not find Yeltsin in a subtle mood."[29]

DESPITE THIS FOREBODING DRAMA, the Hyde Park talks were a surprising success. Reflecting on the meeting, Talbott recalled that "Yeltsin went to Hyde Park and either caved or got reasonable on all these questions." Clinton had urged Yeltsin to "prove the pundits wrong," and he did. The Russian President's fire-and-brimstone had vanished; his tone "was more pleading than hectoring or threatening." Talbott (who was almost always the notetaker for Clinton's one-on-one meetings with Yeltsin) felt that the meeting was "one of the best between these two presidents, both atmospherically and psychologically, despite expectations that it would be one of the worst."[30]

On IFOR, Yeltsin agreed that, at a minimum, two battalions of Russian troops—up to 2,000 soldiers—would participate in noncombat roles, such as mine-clearing, reconstruction, and airlift. Yeltsin had lobbied for a more substantial Russian role, but Clinton explained that it could only be done under NATO command. In this way, Russia could work "with" NATO, but not "in" NATO. The proposal fell between Washington's two red lines: denying Russia's desire for its own sector, and fulfilling the American demand for unified NATO control.

After weeks of talks, the Russians had agreed to the size and function of its contribution to IFOR, as well as its broad relationship with NATO. However the two leaders did not reach an agreement on the specific command structure for IFOR, and how Russia would fit into this command. These thorny operational decisions could still threaten Russian participation. Clinton and Yeltsin decided to leave these details up to Perry and Grachev, who were scheduled to meet at the end of the week.[31]

CLINTON, TUDJMAN, AND IZETBEGOVIC

Clinton met on October 24 with Tudjman and Izetbegovic together in New York's Waldorf-Astoria hotel (both presidents were also in New York to join the UN's 50th Anniversary Celebrations). This was President Clinton's only meeting with the Balkan leaders during his Administration's diplomatic effort. With only seven days to go before the peace talks began, the President sought to frame the stakes in an historic context. "We have seen things in the last few years that we never expected to see," he said. "Israel and the PLO sitting down after 30 years of fighting; the IRA laying down its arms . . . but what the world wants more than anything else is for a resolution of the war in Bosnia." Clinton stressed the importance of the Federation, praising their successful cooperation thus far: "The significant strengthening of the Croatian and Bosnian armies has helped make a decent peace possible. Without that I am not sure that the NATO bombing or Dick Holbrooke's diplomacy would have worked; the differences might have been too great."[32]

Both Izetbegovic and Tudjman pledged their commitment to success in Dayton. Yet as usual, tensions between the "allied" leaders were not far from the surface. Izetbegovic raised his concerns about the Muslim–Croat Federation. While "all the parties present here support the Federation in words," he explained, "the process of implementation [such as allowing freedom of movement and return of refugees] has not taken place as it should have." Ignoring this complaint, Tudjman restated his wish for including Eastern Slavonia on the negotiating agenda in Dayton. Forced to play referee, Clinton said that the discussion "illustrates my point . . . We need more personal contacts between your representatives to make the Federation work on the ground. Getting a settlement will depend on the two of you having trust. Strength lies in genuine unity."

A PERRY-GRACHEV BREAKTHROUGH

Perry and Grachev and their teams met three days later in Washington to sort out the specifics of their presidents' commitments on IFOR. The Americans had two goals: first, and most important, to work out the practical aspects of the "minimum" Russian role that Yeltsin had agreed to in Hyde Park. And second, to explore if there were any possibilities to achieve what Yeltsin had called a "maximum" Russian role, one with its troops having more responsibilities, yet as part of IFOR with NATO's command and control intact.

Despite the presidential bonhomie of Hyde Park, these were contentious discussions, with both sides arguing over what Clinton and Yeltsin had even agreed to. When Perry began by saying that they had to agree on the practical requirements for Russia's participation in the "special operations unit," Grachev erupted, insisting that this plan was insulting and that Russia needed to be a full partner in IFOR but not under NATO command. Talbott, who had been the only American in the room with Clinton and Yeltsin, explained to Grachev the agreement as he saw it. No one knew whether the Defense Minister was just playing games or if there was a real disconnect within the Russian leadership—there was probably a little of both. Grachev faced pressure from hard-liners in Moscow; as he had told Perry during their talks in Geneva three weeks before, his Kremlin opponents were ready to "get him by the throat" on this issue. Yet as the conversation continued, Grachev's line softened, and they ended their first day of talks by discussing the possibilities of Russian troops reporting to a U.S. commander within IFOR.[33]

The next day, Grachev and Perry flew together on a U.S. Air Force plane to Fort Riley, Kansas to observe a joint U.S.-Russian peacekeeping exercise and then went to Missouri's Whiteman Air Force Base to destroy a Minuteman silo as part of a nuclear disarmament exercise. Perry and Grachev continued their discussions on the plane between these stops. Perry found Grachev's mood far more cooperative; he seemed relaxed and ready to make a deal. Perhaps this was because of the intimate setting of the plane's conference room, without all the Kremlin watchers around him; or perhaps, as Perry later reflected, he was inspired by the Fort Riley joint peacekeeping exercise, where American and Russian troops showed that on the ground, they could work together.[34]

By the time the Defense Ministers returned to Washington on October 28, they had an agreement on the specific arrangements for a "minimum" Russian role: no more than two-thousand Russian soldiers would participate in a "special operations unit" under the command of U.S. General George Joulwan and a Russian military deputy. They based this remarkable compromise on the "hats" Joulwan wore. As the Supreme Commander of Allied Forces in Europe, Joulwan would be the NATO commander of IFOR. But the Russians would only recognize his position as the head of U.S. forces. Perry had initially thought that this idea would have been a "complete nonstarter," but to his surprise, it worked. "The Russians were unbelievably, surprisingly, sanguine about being under American command," Talbott recalled. "It was being under NATO command—NATO being a four-letter word in Russia—that bothered them." Indeed, at one point in these talks, Grachev had proposed that they simply eliminate the name "NATO" from the operation—the Russians could work in IFOR and do what it said, as long as the name "NATO" was not part of the command structure.[35]

Their agreement also left open the possibility that Russia could participate in a more integrated combat role as part of IFOR. Perry and Grachev decided that General George Joulwan and his Russian counter part Leontiy Shevtsov would follow up with talks in Brussels to work out the operational details, which they successfully concluded on November 8.[36]

PREPARING FOR DAYTON

Soon after his shuttle diplomacy began in August, Holbrooke decided that if they ever got to a peace conference, they would push for a big-bang outcome—rather than seek a short, basic agreement formalizing a cease-fire, the goal would be to create a detailed, comprehensive settlement. He wanted to establish the foundation for a new state. Holbrooke believed that they had one good shot at getting such an agreement. "What was not negotiated at Dayton would not be negotiated later," he recalled. "We recognized that implementation would at least be as difficult as the negotiations themselves, but we rejected the minimalist theory that we should negotiate only those matters on which implementation would be easy." Holbrooke's Washington colleagues gave him tremendous flexibility to shape an agreement, and he did not hold back. He wanted a far more ambitious deal than the general points Tony Lake had outlined in his August script.[37]

The small legal working group at the State Department had been working on draft documents since mid-September, starting with the "framework agreement," which would be the chapeau document of the package of annexes that would address specific issues. By early October, they had begun to draft the annexes. The group fleshed out commitments made in the Geneva and New York principles—such as a constitution, elections provisions, commissions on human rights and refugees, an arbitration system, and the territorial division. They also considered other issues that would have to be part of a comprehensive settlement, such as Eastern Slavonia, economic reconstruction, arms reductions, and lifting of economic sanctions. The closely knit State Department group began writing these documents alone, then expanding into larger working groups including officials from other State Department bureaus and the NSC.

The drafting proceeded at an intense pace during the first two weeks of October. On October 15, they assembled the first version of the peace agreement—combining the framework agreement with seven annexes into a 38-page document—and sent it to Holbrooke. The seven annexes were: (1) cessation of hostilities and disengagement; (2) constitutional structure; (3) arbitration tribunal; (4) commission on human rights; (5) commission on refugees and displaced persons; (6) commission to preserve national monuments; and (7) political implementation of a peace settlement. The annexes not contained in this package (but to be included eventually) concerned IFOR, elections, and public corporations.[38] Whereas the framework agreement was cast as an agreement between three independent states (Serbia, Croatia, and Bosnia), the annexes were written as commitments between the Bosnian parties—the Federation and Srpska. The United States and the Contact Group would sign the Framework document as "witnesses." With only a first draft, the working groups continued their efforts, aiming to complete the text about a week before the start of the talks.[39]

THE "GREAT DEBATE" ON IFOR

The only annex handled separately from this process concerned military implementation. "Broadly speaking," Walter Slocombe later explained, "anything Holbrooke could get the parties to agree to was OK, but on IFOR, we had a big interest in how this came out. We would write it, and the parties would agree to it." After the Joint Chiefs of Staff reworked the initial draft that had been created by Slocombe, Clark, and Kornblum during their September trip to Europe, Kornblum had asked that a Pentagon staffer temporarily move to the State Department to help continue work on the IFOR annex. Unlike the other annexes, this one was regularly vetted—and vigorously debated—by the Deputies Committee and their Principals. It was therefore the area of the greatest distance between the peace Holbrooke's team was negotiating with the parties and the settlement that Washington was prepared to implement.[40]

TWO WEEKS BEFORE the Dayton talks began, the Clinton Administration had yet to decide several basic questions about the American military role in implementing a settlement. "This was not a mission the military coveted," Sandy Berger remembered. Pentagon officials had devised IFOR's basic structure, yet substantial issues of policy and practice remained. While it was far preferable for American forces to go into Bosnia to implement a success rather than implement a failure (the situation they faced with UNPROFOR withdrawal and Opplan 40104), two fundamental decisions still had to be made. First, what would U.S. forces actually do in Bosnia, and second, how long would they stay?[41]

Military planners could determine the logistics, but they needed political decisions on the specific objectives and broader strategy. Many of these questions involved operational issues—what, for example, would IFOR's role be in elections security or refugee return? Would IFOR be involved in Eastern Slavonia? How would the civilian administrator and the IFOR commander interact? Will IFOR deploy into Serb areas?[42]

Other questions—perhaps the most difficult ones—addressed the strategic question of the mission's goals and how much the Clinton Administration was willing to gamble on this risky undertaking. How would IFOR avoid mission creep, or becoming drawn deeper and deeper into an extended conflict? What was the exit strategy? What constituted a violation of the peace agreement? Who would decide? What would IFOR's response be? How would IFOR be even-handed in dealing with Srpska and the Federation—would there be a threshold of non-compliance after which IFOR would use force against the Muslim–Croat Federation?

How these questions of military planning were answered would define the fundamental purpose of the U.S. diplomatic effort and the kind of peace settlement the Americans sought. Was the goal to end the fighting, or to help build a new Bosnian state? The former called for a limited military mandate— enforcing the cease-fire and implementing the military aspects of a settlement, which could be done relatively quickly. The latter required a far more intrusive military role—assisting with refugee return, arresting war criminals, ensuring freedom of movement and security for elections, implying a much longer commitment. Holbrooke describes this as a "great debate" between two sides: the "maximalists," like himself and his negotiating team, who believed that American forces should assist with nearly all aspects of implementation to help build a new Bosnia; and the "minimalists," mainly at the Pentagon but also with the support of Tony Lake, who argued for a more limited military mission, designed to keep the peace.[43]

ALTHOUGH SUCH ISSUES had been a frequent topic of conversation for weeks, the Deputies Committee began to consider them formally only in late October.

Officials from the State Department, NSC, and the Joint Chiefs each put together lists of questions about IFOR to answer.[44] After two meetings, the Deputies approved a memorandum outlining their conclusions and recommendations for the Principals to consider.[45]

These deliberations left many unresolved issues, such as: whether IFOR should be deployed in Serb territory; whether the Federation and Serb forces should store their weapons in cantonment sites that could be monitored by IFOR; whether there should be a demilitarized zone along the internal border between the Federation and Srpska; whether IFOR should help provide security for elections and assist in refugee returns; whether IFOR would respond to "over the horizon" attacks against civilian aid workers or gross violations of human rights; whether IFOR should have any police functions for itself or stand ready to support the proposed International Police Task Force (IPTF); or whether IFOR should be deployed along Bosnia's external borders.[46]

The Principals Committee began debating these difficult questions on October 25.[47] The basic disagreements were between the State Department and the Pentagon—the State Department favoring a more expansive role; the Defense Department wanting a limited one. For example, State wanted the parties to be forced to accept an IFOR-monitored cantonment of their forces and a 20 km weapons exclusion zone along the Srpska–federation border. Arguing that IFOR would not have the forces sufficient to monitor and enforce such provisions, the Pentagon wanted the parties to agree to these terms voluntarily. The Pentagon also resisted State's recommendation that IFOR deploy on Bosnia's external border. The military was concerned that such a mission would make troops susceptible to hostage-taking. State made the proposal at Izetbegovic's request; it assumed that the Defense Department's fears were greatly exaggerated. Moreover, without IFOR protecting the external border, the Serbs would never allow Bosnian forces to regulate official border crossings into Srpska.[48]

This debate continued when the Principals Committee met again two days later. On many of the specific disagreements, they compromised between the minimalist Pentagon and maximalist State Department positions. For example, on a weapons-free Federation–Srpska border, they agreed that, at a minimum, IFOR would require the parties adhere to a 4 km zone. Reduced from the original 20 km zone, a 4 km zone was small enough to satisfy the military's concerns about having enough troops for enforcement. On external border security, the Principals decided to have IFOR provide "a presence" at crossings where heavy traffic in support of the IFOR mission occurs.

The Principals were most deeply divided about whether IFOR should provide election security, support refugee returns, or hunt down war criminals— the most intrusive military responsibilities. After a spirited and at times heated tense argument, General Shalikashvili offered a compromise: IFOR would have the "authority," but not the "obligation," to implement such tasks. If IFOR's completed its "primary" mission of implementing the military aspects of an agreement, then ground commanders could choose to implement these "secondary" tasks. The maximalists understood that this was the best they could do. "This was a big step forward," Holbrooke recalled. "But the meaning would not be determined until the commanders on the ground decided how to use their 'authority.' "[49]

Urged on by Holbrooke, Albright and others, the Principals also decided to ensure that the IFOR commander's authority to take decisive action would be virtually limitless. By adding this so-called "silver bullet clause" to the military annex—which read that the IFOR commander could use force to stop any activities that he "deems a threat or potential threat to [IFOR] or its mission, or to another party"—they addressed the fundamental weakness of UNPROFOR. As General Clark explained, "under UNPROFOR, the obligations of the force had been unlimited . . . about its authority was very limited. Under our agreement, we were seeking . . . to give the commander unlimited authority to accomplish . . . limited objectives." True, but the maximalists also hoped that by empowering IFOR commanders to take interventionist actions, they might choose to do so.[50]

DECIDING WHAT AMERICAN FORCES should do begged another key question: how long would they stay in Bosnia to do it? Few senior officials believed it should be very long. Nearly two months earlier, in a White House meeting on September 5, the Principals had decided that the military force should remain until the Bosnians could defend themselves or up to twelve months, whichever came first. This decision was made public on October 17, when in a joint appearance before the Senate Armed Services Committee, Christopher, Perry and Shalikashvili said that NATO would "complete its mission in twelve months and [then] withdraw." This critical issue had been decided without much debate in Washington or any consultation with the negotiating team, as senior policymakers understood that for both military and political reasons, they needed a clear exit strategy to avoid such crises as the october 1993 "black hawk down" debacle in Somalia. President Clinton openly worried about mission creep. Sandy Berger recalls that most senior officials—but especially Tony Lake—believed that "if we did not delimit our involvement, the American people would not tolerate something similar down the road . . . we wanted to show success."

But this decision had enormous consequences for what role IFOR would have in implementing a settlement—and therefore, what kind of peace they could try to achieve. How long IFOR stayed would have a major impact on its ability to address the challenges the Principals had been debating, most of which would take considerable time to meet. "[One] year was not sufficient to succeed, no matter what happened at Dayton," Holbrooke believed. Yet the "decision had been made, and we had no choice but to defend it publicly."

The Principals understood the dilemma they were in, and at their October 27 meeting, discussed what a "clear and defensible" end-state IFOR should seek to accomplish before departing. In other words, what should they want—and realistically expect—Bosnia to look like after one year? Although they didn't reach a conclusion that day, they began to consider what milestones would have to take place to measure the success of the mission.[51]

A Sanctions Squabble

In addition to these crucial decisions on IFOR, the Principals also had to decide what to do about economic sanctions against Serbia. Since the beginning of the diplomatic initiative, the Administration's policy on sanctions had been simple: sanctions would be suspended if a peace agreement was signed, and permanently lifted once an agreement was implemented. After his last shuttle to the region, however, Holbrooke believed that this policy should be slightly modified. Milosevic had begun pushing publicly and privately for sanctions relief, claiming he already had a commitment to it.[52] Although Holbrooke had told Milosevic that there was nothing he could do about sanctions, he worried that the Serb leader would be less willing to compromise at Dayton if he did not see some relief soon.

Holbrooke proposed accelerating the timetable for lifting sanctions, suspending them at the beginning of Dayton. He argued that this would place more pressure on Milosevic to reach a deal—letting him nibble on the carrot of sanctions relief would increase his desire to have the whole thing. Furthermore, he thought that it would help Milosevic domestically, allowing him to address dire humanitarian needs (exacerbated by the influx of Krajina refugees) while also strengthening him against domestic critics who opposed an agreement. For the Bosnians, the proposal would put them on notice that any obstructionism on their part would mean that Serbian sanctions would not be reimposed. Suspending sanctions during the height of the negotiations, Holbrooke argued, would create a more even-handed atmosphere, enhancing the American role as honest broker.[53]

Many in the Administration had serious doubts about Holbrooke's argument. Strongest opposed were the two Administration officials perhaps most familiar with the sanctions issue—UN Ambassador Albright and Vice President Gore's National Security Advisor, Leon Fuerth. Both believed that giving in on sanctions would fritter away vital leverage. "The [sanctions] lever was fully in our hand," Albright reflected, "and if we were to give it up, it had to be given up for something good."[54] Moreover, sanctions would be tough to reimpose, and Serbia could blunt the effect of reimposition by stockpiling during the suspension period. Sanctions relief was not needed to "help" Milosevic compromise; U.S. intelligence assessed that the Serb leader faced "remarkably little" internal political pressure to achieve immediate sanctions relief, and it would not enhance his bargaining position over the Bosnian Serbs. Lastly, such a decision would have troublesome side-effects— it would directly contradict the President Clinton's commitment to Congress that sanctions relief would come only with an agreement (made most prominently in a August 29 letter to Robert Dole), and only anger the Bosnians and Croats.[55]

At the October 27 meeting, the Principals decided that sanctions should stay in place. Holbrooke let the issue rest. "In light of the situation," he told his colleagues, "I'm holding off on my recommendation. It's too much water to carry." Nevertheless, the Principals pledged that they would be prepared to revisit the issue if Holbrooke requested.[56]

THE LAST PUSH TO DAYTON

With only five days to go before the Dayton talks started, the Washington bureaucracy was a flurry of activity. The working groups had produced a revised draft of a peace agreement. The document had ballooned to 92-pages and 9 annexes—adding new annexes on elections and a proposed International Police Task Force. To prepare internally for the upcoming talks—and introduce other officials to the specifics of the draft agreement—the State Department organized several large interagency meetings. On October 25, Holbrooke and lead members of the drafting team briefed senior officials in Secretary Christopher's seventh floor conference room. The next day, this group held a five-hour off-site meeting in Warrenton, Virginia, chaired by Christopher, to review the draft text and the general strategy for the talks.[57]

The Warrenton talks were a dress rehearsal for Dayton. As host, the Americans would take the lead in presenting the annexes to the parties and shepherding them through the negotiating process. Holbrooke outlined the sequence of events for the first day: when Secretary Christopher would arrive, the plans for an opening ceremony, and how negotiations would begin. They planned to introduce the entire package on day one. "The parties expect external leadership, and the European don't understand the need to lean on the parties," Holbrooke said.[58]

THAT SATURDAY, OCTOBER 28, Holbrooke traveled to New York to meet with Bosnian officials. Joined by Roberts Owen and Jim O'Brien, they reviewed the constitutional draft and elections annex with Mo Sacirbey and Paul Williams, an American lawyer hired by the Sarajevo government. Since early October, both the Americans and Europeans had worked with Bosnian legal experts (and their consultants) to help get them better prepared for Dayton. Rather than have the Bosnians simply reacting to outside proposals, "we wanted them to begin thinking more seriously about what they wanted out of an agreement," the American Ambassador to Bosnia John Menzies said.[59] This meeting was intended to be a final push in this effort; a "desperate attempt," Holbrooke recalled, for the Bosnians to "think more strategically" about these issues.[60]

Foremost on Sacirbey's mind, however, was the grave condition of the Muslim–Croat Federation, insisting that the United States do something about it. Sacirbey's comments were only the most recent warning about the sorry state of this alliance; Izetbegovic himself had told President Clinton on October 24 that the Federation was in trouble. Both the State and Defense Department assessments were very pessimistic about the entity's future viability. "A peace agreement in Bosnia removes the strong tactical basis for [the Federation's] continuance," a Pentagon analysis explained. "Even with moves to strengthen the Federation, I have doubts about its long-term prospects," a State Department planner warned.[61]

Little had changed since the late Joe Kruzel outlined his concerns about the Federation before the Mt. Igman accident over two months earlier.

"The Federation is seen as a marriage of convenience," he wrote. Now, on the eve of Dayton, it seemed that the "fundamental conceptual flaw" Kruzel had described could bring an agreement down in flames.[62] The peace being brokered by the Americans relied upon a healthy, fully functioning Federation. Yet at that point, no such entity existed. From Izetbegovic and Tudjman on down, the Muslims and Croats simply did not trust each other. Holbrooke understood that they would have to work immediately at Dayton to rebuild this fractured yet vital relationship.[63]

ALSO THAT WEEKEND, the Contact Group came to Washington, where they saw the draft texts for the first time. The Europeans complained bitterly that they had been shut-out of drafting agreements that they were supposed to help implement. Carl Bildt remembers that the discussions revealed "a deep gulf between European and U.S. perceptions on what peace implementation really meant." The Europeans were particularly concerned with the IFOR annex. In discussions led by General Clark, the Europeans and Americans performed an exhaustive, line-by-line markup of the document. Others went over the political and civilian implementation annexes, with the Europeans playing close attention to the constitution (which they believed was unworkable) and an international police force. They were amazed that the Americans had failed to produce an annex on civilian implementation—confirming their view that Washington was too obsessed with military implementation—and demanded that it create one. These difficult discussions on the eve of the conference made it clear that the Americans still had a long way to go to reassure the Europeans and, where necessary, bring them into the process.[64]

THE MORNING OF OCTOBER 31, the Holbrooke team joined President Clinton and other senior officials at the White House for their final meeting before Dayton.[65] Christopher began by outlining the planned schedule as well as the rules the negotiations would follow. "There will be radio silence after the opening ceremony," he said. Holbrooke wanted to lower expectations for the conference. Fond of football metaphors, he described that "we're on our own 30-yard line." Although he didn't know how long the talks would last, there were "practical limits" to how long they could go. "We'll hit a wall by day ten," he said, explaining that they would use the upcoming travel of Clinton and Christopher (in mid-November, both were scheduled to attend an Asia-Pacific summit and a state visit in Japan) to set benchmarks for progress. "Even if we fail," Holbrooke concluded, "the U.S. can be proud." The Geneva and New York principles provided a sound political foundation to build upon, with a Sarajevo at peace and a countrywide cease-fire in place. "Dayton's a gamble, but the shuttle phase has been exhausted."

President Clinton expressed deepest concern about IFOR. If Dayton was successful, he faced a prospect that no president ever welcomed: sending thousands of American soldiers into a dangerous, possibly hostile environment, for a cause that few Americans fully understood. This decision weighed heavily on Clinton's mind. According to his political advisor Dick Morris, Clinton was "quite adamant" that U.S. troops "would not be rummaging around in the mountains looking for war criminals." He sometimes pondered with his closest advisors about the risks of success, saying that "we've got to counter the downside of troops with the upside of peace." He was haunted by earlier events under similar circumstances—when troops were killed and his presidency was thrown into a crisis. "Given Somalia, we must have a clear mission so there's no 'mission creep,' " he said. Moreover, Congress was becoming a real problem, and IFOR threatened to hurt him politically. The day before this meeting, in a vote that House Speaker Newt Gingrich called "a referendum on this Administration's incapability of convincing anyone to trust them," the Republican-controlled House passed overwhelmingly a nonbinding resolution stating that the United States should not send troops to Bosnia without congressional approval.[66]

On the substance of what would be negotiated in Dayton, the President told his team that he wanted the Bosnian capital to remain unified. "I have strong feelings about Sarajevo," he said. "It would be a mistake to divide the city. We don't want another Berlin." He also suggested that negotiators not feel constrained by artificial deadlines. He advised that they continue the stepping-stone approach of the shuttles, ensuring that at least some agreements would be locked-in if talks failed. "If you can't get all the way to a final agreement, the credibility of an interim agreement will depend on whether there are concrete confidence-building measures without a reversion to slaughter and chaos." On Serbian sanctions, the President stated his view that they should stay in place until there were assurances that Milosevic would honor a peace agreement. "But we can't ignore the negotiating dimension," Secretary Christopher responded. "We need to keep Milosevic on the reservation. We want to be able to say to him that when we initial [an agreement] we'll start a process of suspension." With Lake and Holbrooke's support, the President agreed.

Following this final briefing, Holbrooke and his delegation boarded a plane for Wright-Patterson Air Force Base. "This is the best chance we've had for peace since the war began," President Clinton said to the press later that day. "It may be the last chance we have for a very long time."[67] After four long and bloody years, Bosnia's future would be decided in Dayton, Ohio.

8

A Slow Start: Dayton,
November 1–10

The delegations began arriving at Wright-Patterson Air Force Base on the afternoon of October 31, the day before the opening of what were officially called the "Proximity Peace Talks." Wright-Patterson is one of the major Air Force bases in the United States—partly named for the Dayton-born Wright brothers, the enormous facility housed Air Force test pilots in the 1950s and later served as a training center for NASA's Mercury astronauts. The area around the sprawling, 8,000-acre military base is typical of the American Midwest—flat, sparse, and in November, often cold and grey. Ohio itself is larger than Bosnia (and U.S. negotiators had created a map showing such), and far away from the New York air that Milosevic claimed to want to smell. Dayton, like many communities in middle America, is a quiet city, large enough to have its own television station but small enough to still have a drive-in movie theater. Although delegates rarely strayed far from base, the city enthusiastically played host, and it was easy to see the Dayton Chamber of Commerce envisioning a tourist industry centered upon a new city of "international peace."

The negotiations would be conducted in secrecy. The delegates were not allowed to talk to the press; as Christopher had told President Clinton, there would be "radio silence" once the opening ceremony was over. The Americans alone would speak publicly for all the delegations, and State Department Spokesman Nicholas Burns's briefings from Washington would be the only on-the-record press statements. They wanted to keep delegates from grandstanding—complete seclusion would allow the talks to proceed with minimal concern about how victories or concessions might play in the next day's papers. Maintaining such isolation was easier then than it would be only a few years later, with the prevalence of cell phones and blackberries.

In many ways, Dayton was not only radio silent to the public, but also to the rest of the American government. As with the negotiations during the shuttles, officials in Washington were not always aware of the precise substance of the discussions, especially given the complexity and speed with which things happened inside the compound. Although they stayed informed by frequent phone calls, written updates, or even meetings by secure videoconference, it was almost impossible for them to keep up with the fast-paced talks. Only the most sensitive negotiating decisions were submitted for high-level review. Indeed, as the 11 annexes were developed at Dayton, there was only one up-to-date draft in all of Washington.[1] Among the entire U.S. negotiating delegation, only General Wes Clark, Don Kerrick and Jim Pardew regularly provided brief written reports for their superiors, and Holbrooke asked to clear them all.

Yet like the shuttle efforts, the negotiators operated within clear policy "red lines," such as sanctions relief for Serbia or specific U.S. military commitments on IFOR. Inside these boundaries, however, Holbrooke and his team were free to use their own judgment and improvise about how to proceed. Although such senior officials as Secretary Christopher said that they did "watch the negotiations very closely," receiving frequent telephone updates from Holbrooke or others, and visited the talks at decisive moments, they rarely intervened from Washington unless asked.[2]

HOLBROOKE AND HIS CORE TEAM—Owen, Hill, Pardew, Clark, and Kerrick—would conduct the negotiations, and were joined in Dayton by most of the staff that had served as their "backstops" in Washington. With everyone in one place, Dayton became a sort of autonomous bureaucracy, capable of making most decisions without support from Washington. John Kornblum and the legal working group responsible for drafting the annexes were there, as well as officials from the State Department's European Bureau to assist on specific aspects of the negotiations. The three American ambassadors in the region—Perina, Menzies, and Galbraith—were present, and would help negotiate with their respective Balkan counterparts. Assistant Secretary of State for Human Rights John Shattuck and Ambassador-at-Large Robert Gallucci (who had been the architect of the 1994 Framework Agreement to halt North Korea's nuclear program and was in Dayton at the request of Christopher and Talbott) also came to assist in their areas of expertise. The Pentagon sent several staffers to handle the military aspects of the negotiations, and U.S. and European intelligence personnel were on site as well. Indeed, since for most of that month the federal government was shutdown due to the fierce budget battle between the Clinton Administration and Congress, the "Dayton bureaucracy" often was one of the *only* parts of the U.S. government at work.[3]

The Bosnian, Croat, Serbian, and Contact Group delegations were of similar size; in all, nearly 200 officials were present to support the negotiations. In addition, hundreds of U.S. administrative personnel—from clerical support and public affairs officers to communications specialists and security guards—were involved in the talks. While many of these people were loaned from Wright-Patterson, a considerable number of them had come from their offices in Washington.

The five delegations lived in Wright-Patterson's Visiting Officer Quarters, or VOQs. Covering roughly three square blocks, the VOQ area had been fenced off from the rest of the base, with security checkpoints to regulate access. These modest two-story accommodations looked a lot like college dorms. They had sleeping quarters for the delegates, as well as offices and conference rooms for negotiations. In the two weeks since Wright-Patterson had been chosen as the conference site, Air Force crews worked round-the-clock to spruce-up the suites that would house the heads of each delegation—Tudjman, Milosevic, Izetbegovic, Bildt and Holbrooke. They wanted to make the rooms appear presidential; while hardly the grandeur of Versailles (or even Evian), or the relaxed intimacy of Camp David, the VOQ's were nicely improved from what was 1970's era military housing. Notwithstanding these renovations, the accommodations struck Bosnian Foreign Minister Sacirbey as "a little like Motel 6."[4]

The VOQ area would be the primary location of the proximity talks; the Croat, Bosnian, Serb, and U.S. quarters faced one another in a quadrangle (while Carl Bildt and some of his senior team were on the upper floor of the American VOQ, the Russians and the rest of the Europeans from the Contact Group were housed in a building adjacent to the quadrangle). Here is where negotiators could shuttle back and forth among the delegations. Yet, unlike the lush lawned quads that grace many university campuses, this quad was an empty parking lot.

About 100 yards away from the VOQ complex sat the Bob Hope Hotel and Convention Center, named after the famous entertainer who grew up in Ohio. A concrete path, known as the "peacewalk," had been constructed by the Air Force for the short stroll between the VOQ and the Hope complex. Like a university campus' student union, the Hope Hotel was the central place where the delegates could meet, eat, and work. The main dining facility for the talks was also in the Hope Hotel, at a sports-bar named Packy's, where CNN played alongside sporting events on its wide-screen TV's. The Officers Club, which was only a short driving distance from Hope Hotel, also served as a place where high-level officials could eat. Office suites for American support staff were also in the Hope complex, and the convention center would hold any large group meetings, starting with the opening session.

Day One: Wednesday, November 1

"The eyes of the world are on Dayton, Ohio," Secretary of State Christopher said from the tarmac after his plane landed at Wright-Patterson on a chilly November morning. "We have come to the heartland of America to try to bring peace to the heart of Europe."[5] He then joined Holbrooke to meet with each of the Balkan Presidents and with the Contact Group to ensure that each party would respect the groundrules (such as not talking to the press) and, hopefully, create a serious and positive atmosphere for the negotiations.

These opening meetings gave Christopher a chance to set the tone. "You will need to make clear to all the parties that they will each be required to make compromises and sacrifices," a State Department strategy paper to Christopher read. Yet, the United States understood that the odds weighed against achieving a comprehensive settlement at Dayton. "Bosnian officials, buoyed by their battlefield successes, are ambivalent about any agreement which in their view would rescue the Serb entity from collapse. Meanwhile, the Serb side is deeply distrustful of the process, and Milosevic will have his hands full delivering the Bosnian Serbs into a unitary state with the sort of superstructure which is envisioned in our draft documents." Given the remaining divisions on map and constitutional issues, U.S. intelligence analysts were skeptical that a comprehensive agreement could be reached. "Working out agreeable solutions to the numerous contested issues is likely to extend beyond the 1–2 weeks which the parties appear prepared to spend in Dayton," one such memorandum read.[6]

The step-by-step negotiating process of shuttle diplomacy had brought the parties within close range of a settlement, but many contentious issues had not yet even been addressed. The Geneva and New York Agreements created a strong political and legal framework for a future Bosnian state, yet constitutional details would have to be fleshed out further. Moreover, serious discussions about the most critical issue—territory—had been left entirely for Dayton. The strategy throughout the shuttles had been to tackle the easier issues first. By doing so, Holbrooke had hoped to develop a sense of trust among the parties as well as bolster his team's credibility as a mediator, both of which would be essential as the parties moved to the tough issues at Dayton. Now this strategy would be put to the test.

CHRISTOPHER FIRST MET with Tudjman. The Croat President had one main goal at Dayton: get Eastern Slavonia back. Up to that point, Tudjman had been disinterested about almost everything but Eastern Slavonia (the only exception being the Federation military offensive). However, the Americans believed that since Tudjman also desperately wanted Croatia to be accepted as part of Western Europe—thus being eligible for financial support and participation in defense programs like NATO's "Partnership for Peace"—he would cooperate on other issues as long as he got a favorable resolution in Eastern Slavonia.

Christopher made this point to Tudjman, stressing the importance of his support for the Muslim–Croat Federation. Recent tensions in the Federation, coupled with Bosnian Muslim concerns about Croatia (as Izetbegovic expressed to the President on October 24 and Sacirbey discussed with Holbrooke on October 27), placed this problem at the top of the Dayton agenda. U.S. intelligence reported that while Tudjman was "sitting on the fence," he would likely support the Federation as "the lesser of two evils." The State Department's European Bureau believed that "Zagreb formally supports the Federation but shows little interest in loosening its hold over areas controlled by the Bosnian Croat and regular Croatian forces."[7] Given this attitude, Christopher wanted to reiterate to Tudjman what President Clinton had told him personally only eight days before—that the United States looked to his country, "as the stronger party" of the Federation, to use its considerable influence to make the alliance work.[8]

THE SECRETARY next saw Milosevic. The Serb leader had recently signaled his flexibility on such key issues as Eastern Slavonia, and apparently felt that the elements of an agreement were less important than the act of agreeing.[9] The State Department's European Bureau described Milosevic as a leader squeezed on all sides. Under pressure from sanctions, military defeats and political isolation, he still had to confront a Bosnian Serb leadership "that is trying to walk back commitments contained in the Geneva and New York principles, and the nationalist opposition in Serbia [that] is accusing Milosevic of selling out." It remained an open question whether he could deliver them. Yet the Americans believed that "Milosevic has already taken a major leap by agreeing to represent the Serb side in Bosnia, and he probably believes that now is the time to cut a deal."[10]

Milosevic started the meeting with Christopher in his customary manner, blunt and a bit crude. Having already tasted the sports-bar cuisine at Packy's, the Serb leader complained about the "shit food," but commented favorably on a friendly waitress named Vicki (which with his thick accent, Milosevic pronounced as "Wicki").

Turning to serious issues, Christopher pressed the Serb leader on human rights. John Shattuck remembers that "Milosevic had clearly decided to go on a charm offensive to rehabilitate himself before Dayton," and the Americans wanted to knock him down a few notches. Throughout the past week, both the *Washington Post* and *New York Times* had run lengthy articles outlining Serb atrocities in Srebrenica during July 1995.[11] The State Department had helped provide information for these articles, and their publication caused Milosevic to complain bitterly to Christopher and Holbrooke about a "media conspiracy." The Americans did want to pressure Milosevic, making clear to the Serb leader that his presence at Dayton was itself an act of goodwill on their part.[12]

CHRISTOPHER'S SESSION WITH the Sarajevo delegation, by far the most divided of the parties, aimed to reassure them. "They want peace, but not at any price," the U.S. embassy in Sarajevo described.[13] As the opening of the conference neared, Izetbegovic was apparently tired, distracted and deeply ambivalent about ending the war just as his side had begun fighting back successfully. He even considered staying home and letting others lead the talks. Haris Silajdzic, himself pessimistic that a deal could be reached, characterized the prospects for success as "unclear and uncertain." In an attempt to brighten this dour outlook, Christopher and Holbrooke wanted to remind the Bosnians about the "carrots" for cooperation—such as equip-and-train and economic reconstruction.[14]

As he had with Tudjman, Christopher also urged the Bosnians to strengthen the Federation. Izetbegovic and Silajdzic agreed, but demanded that a new Federation agreement—one that provided a specific governing structures and an implementation outline—be reached *before* they addressed key issues with the Serbs. This Bosnian demand for an additional set of negotiations was a new wrinkle in the gameplan, but the Americans knew that unless they patched-up the Muslim–Croat alliance, any agreement reached at

Dayton had no chance of succeeding. Yet in order to ensure that they spent most of their energy on the core issues, Holbrooke asked Michael Steiner, a well-trusted and highly capable member of Germany's delegation to the Contact Group, to take charge of drafting a new Federation agreement. In the eyes of the Americans, Steiner would thus become the most influential European at Dayton.[15]

Finally, Christopher demanded that Izetbegovic curb the support the Bosnian military was receiving from Saudi or Iranian-backed Mudjahadeen paramilitary groups. Known as the "Muj," these were Islamic fighters that, after the September 11, 2001 attacks, the world came to know as jihadists or Al Qaeda. Many Muj, in fact, had come to Bosnia after training in Al Qaeda terrorist camps in Afghanistan or Sudan (as the Bosnian war—a conflict with Muslim victims—had become a rallying cry for some Islamic extremists; in fact, two of the 9/11 hijackers had traveled to Bosnia in 1995 to fight). The British had recently raised similar concerns with the Sarajevo government, threatening that if such forces were not withdrawn from Bosnia, they would consider withdrawing aid workers and support for Bosnian reconstruction efforts. Christopher explained that the Administration could not justify either to Congress or the American public helping the Bosnians militarily—whether by deploying U.S. troops there or participating in an equip-and-train program—under such circumstances. "I must be very clear with you," he said, "one Mudjahadeen is too many."[16]

CHRISTOPHER'S FINAL MEETING before the opening ceremony was a working lunch with Carl Bildt and the Contact Group. Although Bildt and Russian representative Igor Ivanov were, along with Holbrooke, officially the co-chairs of the conference, they had no clear role in the negotiations. Almost all of the planning and organizing for Dayton had been done by the United States; the Europeans had seen the first drafts of the negotiating texts only the previous weekend. The Americans would drive the talks. Everyone expected that the Contact Group would press the Secretary to outline a role for them in the negotiations, to be certain "that they are kept fully in the loop as events develop." Christopher played to this, stressing the importance of working closely together and delivering a unified message to the parties. He also tried to reassure them that while "some of us" were not happy with the various aspects of negotiating process, "it is a result we are all pursuing together. That result has to be a peace agreement that works. Let us not lose sight of that."[17]

CHRISTOPHER AND HOLBROOKE then joined all the delegates at 2:30 P.M. in the "B-29 Superfortress" Room of the Hope Convention Center (to the chagrin of some of the Europeans, all of the conference rooms were named for U.S. military planes) for the formal opening ceremony. At the center of the large fluorescent-lit ballroom, Christopher and Holbrooke joined Bildt, Ivanov, French representative Jacques Blot, British representative Pauline Neville-Jones, German representative Wolfgang Ischinger and the three Balkan Presidents around a small circular table.

After everyone took their seats, Secretary Christopher rose to motion the three Balkan leaders to shake hands. Like the 1993 handshake between Israeli Prime Minister Yitzhak Rabin and Palestinian leader Yasir Arafat on the White House's South Lawn, the image of these three men clasping hands was the photo-op the Americans wanted. The embrace, like Rabin and Arafat's, was equally awkward and dramatic. "We thought it would be a constructive beginning," Christopher recalled. "It seemed likely there would be a good deal of tension in the room when they first got together, so it would be symbolically important for them to shake hands."[18]

In his opening comments, Christopher tried to set the agenda both thematically and substantively. "We are here to give Bosnia and Herzegovina a chance to be a country at peace, not a killing field," he began. In order to do so, he outlined four key conditions that needed to be met: first, Bosnia was to remain as one state with "a single international personality"; second, that a settlement must take into account "the special history and significance" of Sarajevo (a diplomatic way of saying that the city must remain unified); third, that human rights must be respected and that those responsible for atrocities be held accountable (a message to Milosevic); and finally, that a solution must be brought to Eastern Slavonia (a sop to Tudjman). All of these issues had already been raised privately, but now America's top diplomat had presented them publicly as the necessary ingredients for an "enduring peace."[19]

FOLLOWING THIS CEREMONY, Christopher joined Milosevic and Tudjman for the first negotiation of the talks, on Eastern Slavonia. Meeting in the living room of the "Carriage House," a small military VIP cottage about a mile from the VOQ area, the two Presidents faced each other while Christopher and Holbrooke sat together on a couch. Milosevic had arrived late, but seemed very relaxed—in fact, too relaxed. He had just come from the Officers Club, and as he sauntered in, it was clear that he had been drinking. He greeted Tudjman and his delegation (including Foreign Minister Granic and Defense Minister Susak) informally by first-name. Already feeling loose, Milosevic ordered a glass of red wine. Christopher and Holbrooke each joined in with a glass of white.

U.S. Ambassador to Croatia Peter Galbraith opened the meeting by describing the state-of-play on the Eastern Slavonian negotiations. Galbraith explained that the two Presidents needed to overcome their remaining (and, in his view, small) differences. Tudjman responded that these "technical" matters were no problem, the issue was whether the Serbs would accept the reintegration of Eastern Slavonia into Croatia. Milosevic did not see the remaining issues as merely "technical." As the conversation heated up, the two Presidents began to talk to each other in Serbo-Croatian, leaving the interpreter behind. As the Americans looked on in puzzled shock, Milosevic tried to bully Tudjman into accepting his proposals, such as leaving the territorial decision to a local referendum. The Croat President responded coolly, not giving in to Milosevic's pressure. Holbrooke remembered this as a "wild meeting," characterized by the two Presidents "screaming and yelling each other."

The only result was that Milosevic caved to the fact that Eastern Slavonia had to be included in an overall settlement in Dayton. Up to that point, he had refused to involve himself with problems in Eastern Slavonia; these were issues, he contended, between Zagreb and the local Serbs in the region. Now, Milosevic agreed to negotiate something in Dayton that he could then "recommend" to the local Serbs to accept. Although a small step, it was at least something to start with.[20]

THE SECRETARY OF STATE returned to Washington that evening. His trip to open the talks had been largely a success: the opening ceremony set the desired tone, and a substantive foundation had been established with all the parties. Now they had to get to work. That night, the Americans presented the delegations the draft Framework Agreement and annexes on the constitution, elections, and IFOR.

Day Two: Thursday, November 2

Holbrooke had devised a tiered approach to conduct the talks: he and his core team would work to lock-in agreements on political and constitutional arrangements while opening discussions on the map, which he expected to be the most difficult issue. Alongside these efforts would be two parallel negotiations, in which the Americans hoped only to participate when necessary: talks to secure agreements on Eastern Slavonia and the Federation. At the outset, Holbrooke's primary objective was to avoid early setbacks and let the talks evolve naturally. Again falling back on a football metaphor, he later recalled that the initial goal at Dayton was "of course to score touchdowns to win the game. But first, you have to get some first downs."[21]

Work began immediately on the Federation. Throughout the morning and afternoon, Holbrooke and Michael Steiner mediated lengthy meetings between Izetbegovic, Tudjman, and Federation President Kresimir Zubak (a hard-line Croat) to establish broad parameters of a proposal.[22]

During one of these sessions, Holbrooke asked John Shattuck to join the discussion to report on his investigations of human rights violations and stress the importance of his gaining entry into key areas of western Bosnia. In addition to ensuring access for America's top human rights official, Holbrooke thought that they would also be able to forge a deal to provide the Muslim and Croat refugees the right to return to their homes in four select towns in western Bosnia (Jajce, Bugojno, Travnik, and Stolac). Although the refugee numbers would be relatively insignificant, Holbrooke hoped that such a confidence-building measure would help improve Bosnian–Croat relations (since these refugees were a product of the 1993–1994 Muslim–Croat war) and smooth the Federation talks along. He also wanted to ensure that human rights remained high on Dayton's agenda—as Shattuck's presence attested to.[23]

Both Izetbegovic and Tudjman put up "incredible resistance" to the refugee proposal. Tudjman claimed that such an agreement would be "absurd" this early in the negotiations. Visibly annoyed, Holbrooke abruptly got up and told them that if they could not even agree to this minor deal, he might as well call in the press to tell them that further negotiations would be fruitless. Putting on his coat as if to leave, Holbrooke yelled that "I've got this human rights guy [Shattuck] who's willing to risk his life to visit these areas, and you can't even assure us that you can get a few people to relocate." After this outburst, Izetbegovic and Tudjman agreed to the proposal, signing a paper that briefly outlined the relocation arrangement.[24]

Later that day Holbrooke got Milosevic to guarantee access for Shattuck to the main Bosnian Serb city in Bosnia, Banja Luka. Holbrooke and Shattuck also pressed the Serb leader on the whereabouts of David Rohde, a young American journalist for the *Christian Science Monitor* who had been missing in Bosnian Serb territory since October 30. Rohde's status had become a major issue for the media, who were camped out at Dayton and starved for stories. Milosevic agreed to work with the Bosnian Serbs on the issue, and that evening, Shattuck left for Bosnia.[25]

TUDJMAN AND MILOSEVIC got together over lunch at the Officers Club to discuss Eastern Slavonia. The Croats believed that a deal on Eastern Slavonia "was there," with an agreement being centered on elections in Eastern Slavonia within one year, with a UN-sponsored military force, separate from IFOR, to assist with implementation. But the duration of the UN implementation phase remained hotly contested. That evening, Tudjman left Dayton (as previously scheduled) to return to Croatia for their national elections. In order to continue negotiations in the region—as Milosevic insisted—Holbrooke asked Galbraith and UN representative Thorvald Stoltenberg to travel with the Croat President back to Zagreb and go immediately to Eastern Slavonia.[26]

While the Croats and Galbraith were confident that they were close to a deal, Holbrooke and Chris Hill (who became deeply involved in these talks) remained skeptical. They had always assumed that the key issue would be the length of time for the return of Eastern Slavonia to Croatia—Tudjman wanted the process completed in one year, Milosevic insisted on at least two years—and neither side seemed willing to compromise. Although Galbraith had been sent back to negotiate with the local parties, Holbrooke knew that the real action would remain in Dayton. He sensed that Milosevic realized he would have to concede Eastern Slavonia, but was looking for a way to do so without aggravating the Serbs in the area.[27]

THE AMERICANS also spent a substantial amount of time that day negotiating with the Contact Group on the remaining draft annexes. They had briefed their European partners on the military, constitution, and elections annexes the weekend prior to Dayton, but had not yet given them the remaining documents, some of which were still being finalized within the U.S. team. As Holbrooke later observed, not only were they negotiating with the three Balkan delegations, but "we were trying to negotiate with and within the Contact Group," obviously slowing the entire process down. They had set up a daily coordinating session at 9 A.M. with the Contact Group representatives in the Hope Hotel, but the Americans (especially Holbrooke) found the meeting overcrowded, unwieldy, and time-consuming.[28]

THE ATMOSPHERICS throughout this first day of serious negotiations were characterized to officials in Washington as "generally positive . . . even light-hearted." Don Kerrick reported to Tony Lake that "all sides seem willing to deal—even anxious to do so." The Americans were encouraged by the Milosevic–Tudjman lunch discussion, giving hope that the two sides could get results without intensive supervision, and thus far, no real problems had emerged over the three annexes presented to the parties. Milosevic, for his part, had demonstrated his desire to complete a settlement. As Jim Pardew observed, "Milosevic is maneuvering at every level to move toward an agreement while he keeps the Pale Serbs under control and away from the decision-making process."[29]

Day Three: Friday, November 3

Dayton's third day began with a 9 A.M. meeting between the Americans and the Contact Group. Sitting in the B-29 Room at the Hope Convention Center, the two sides finalized several of the draft annexes, but Holbrooke left frustrated, believing that "we wasted almost two hours on trivial matters." The Europeans were particularly focused on the newly-created civilian implementation annex, considering the senior civilian official as the critical player in implementing any settlement. IFOR would be run by the Americans, but the Contact Group had agreed that the civilian process would be under European oversight (the Europeans wanted Bildt to assume the role, and he reluctantly accepted). This was apparently one of their only "instructions" from the EU Council of Ministers going into the Dayton talks.[30] The Americans agreed, figuring that this would help ensure that the Europeans would handle most of the bill.[31]

IMMEDIATELY AFTER THIS MEETING, Holbrooke and his core team met for four hours with Milosevic in the American VOQ. In contrast to his cocky and loose manner of the past few days, that morning they found Milosevic prickly and insecure. He griped about the beating he had been taking in the American press, claiming that these stories were part of a U.S.-Bosnian coordinated effort to soil the Serbs. Holbrooke didn't deny this, and pressed him to deliver the unconditional release of David Rohde. That day, Rohde, imprisoned in a jail in the northwest Bosnian town of Bijeljina, was formally convicted of illegally entering Bosnian Serb territory and falsifying ID papers. While serving a two-week sentence for these crimes, there were reports that Rohde could be charged with espionage, which would carry a sentence of five years. Holbrooke made clear to Milosevic that they could never conclude any agreement while an American journalist remained imprisoned.[32]

Turning to the draft Bosnian constitution and other annexes, Milosevic seemed generally supportive of the draft "framework agreement," the broad statement of principles to which the 11 annexes would be attached. However, he argued that Karadzic should be permitted to participate in future elections. Since Milosevic did not believe that the Bosnian Serb could win an election, he thought that forcing him to face the ballot was a way to get rid of him. Otherwise, he would end up a martyr. It was out of the question that the Americans would allow an indicted war criminal to run for office. They wanted Karadzic arrested.[33]

THAT EVENING, the Americans hosted a dinner for all the delegates at Wright-Patterson's Air Force Museum. Holbrooke wanted to have a social event during the beginning of the talks, thinking it would be a nice way to unwind after three full days in Dayton. The event had many attributes of a high school dance, with the delegates dividing into cliques, some mixing and gossiping, and others warily eyeing each other. An Air Force orchestra was on hand to belt out big band music in the style of Glenn Miller. As Kerrick reported the next day to Lake, the mood of the evening was one of "laughter and camaraderie amongst both sides." The setting for the first group dinner of this peace conference drew attention; held in the cavernous main room of the Museum, the guests dined in the shadows of an enormous B-29, several Stealth F-117 fighters, and, appropriately to some, a Tomahawk cruise missile that seemed to be pointed right at Milosevic's table. The Europeans noted that it was a strange place to hold a "peace dinner." The symbolism served a purpose but was coincidental—Holbrooke had simply intended to stage a social event, not send the parties a message. But few believed him.[34]

Day Four: Saturday, November 4

It had only been three days, but on the first Saturday of the talks, some of the participants hoped to get some rest. The American support staff organized a bowling trip, and provided soccer balls and footballs for use. To Holbrooke's annoyance, Mo Sacirbey took Izetbegovic away for most of the day to see his alma mater Tulane University play football against nearby Louisville. That night, Milosevic hosted the American delegation at the Officers Club for a lobster dinner, with the food shipped in from Maine by Chris Spirou, an American citizen and former New Hampshire Democratic Party leader who was at Dayton as an advisor to the Serb delegation. Although the cold and blustery Midwest winter weather was settling in, Don Kerrick reported to Lake that the "parties remain warm and receptive to one another, but [are] showing almost no movement on key issues—yet."[35]

Before Izetbegovic and Sacirbey departed for the football game, they met with Holbrooke, Hill, Owen, and Kerrick. Holbrooke tried to talk about the map, but didn't get very far. Sacirbey responded that since there "wasn't a better place to start," the talks should stick to the map created for the 1994 Contact Group plan. They then asked for Izetbegovic's views on the political structures of a democratic Bosnian state—the presidency, parliament, and national elections. As Kerrick reported, "Milosevic and Izzy retain opposite views on election of national parliament and presidency." Little had changed in their respective positions since the intense negotiations over the New York principles in late September. Izetbegovic still supported broad powers for a federal presidency and parliament, both of which would be elected directly. Milosevic wanted narrowly defined powers without direct elections. When Holbrooke asked Izetbegovic what the solution should be, the Bosnian President responded honestly: "convince one side [to] compromise to our position."[36]

THE AMERICANS also continued to struggle with the David Rohde situation. Holbrooke was worried that if Rohde's status worsened—if he were held indefinitely or even sentenced for espionage—the media outrage would side-track the negotiations. Ten members of Rohde's family had arrived in Dayton on Friday to plead for their son's release, and Ambassador Menzies had spent most of his time during the past few days with them. Nikola Koljevic, the Bosnian Serb Vice President, joined Menzies to meet with Rohde's family for several hours. He arranged a phone call with the imprisoned journalist, and both Menzies and several family members spoke with him. Holbrooke also met with Rohde's family, providing the most recent news and reassuring them that the United States was working for his release.[37]

TRAGICALLY, the biggest news of the day had nothing to do with the Balkans—but symbolically, everything to do with the negotiations. As these would-be peacemakers worked or rested that Saturday, a Nobel–Peace Prize-winning peacemaker, Israeli leader Yitzhak Rabin, was killed by a gunman in Tel Aviv. Rabin was a bold, brave statesman who accepted considerable risk to compromise and make peace with his neighbors. For all these attributes, he had been gunned down by the hate and violence that his leadership had tried so hard to overcome. Although none of the Balkan leaders showed the slightest sorrow for Rabin personnally, the assassination hit close to home for many of them, serving as a reminder of the real risks these negotiations presented.

Day Five: Sunday, November 5

Discussions resumed with the Bosnians on the map, with Pardew, Kerrick, and Sacirbey grappling over the future status of Sarajevo. The Bosnian Foreign Minister explained that the night before, he, Croatian Foreign Minister Granic and Defense Minister Susak agreed that the 1994 Contact Group map should be the baseline for any territorial negotiations. "[The] quality of terri-tory under the Contact Group plan [is] better," Sacirbey said. With this, the Bosnian Foreign Minister outlined his position: Sarajevo would be a unified city, and the Muslims would be compensated for the areas around Srebrenica and Zepa, which they were supposed to control under the Contact Group map. Sacirbey argued that any trades had to be "adequate" in, for example, vital resources and economic value. The Muslims had to get something in exchange for their territorial losses—"[one] shouldn't assume [that the] Serbs can enjoy success [in this] peace plan," Sacirbey said.

The Americans raised the idea to keep Sarajevo unified but politically autonomous—like Washington, DC, it could be a separate federal capital. The city could be divided into several semiautonomous political districts (called Opstinas) and, like the proposed Bosnian presidency, have a three-person mayoral council whose chairman would rotate among the three ethnic groups. The municipal government would be responsible for such citywide services as transportation, utilities, and sanitation, while the local Opstinas would control education, cultural services, and local health services. The city would be policed by a multiethnic force, which the international community could help train and monitor. Sacirbey agreed to consider the proposal.[38]

WORK CONTINUED on an Eastern Slavonia agreement, with Chris Hill shuttling between the Croats and Serbs. The Serb side objected to any hint that the territory would be under Croatian sovereignty, which was exactly what the Croats wanted. The Croats were willing to be flexible on many details, including Serb rights and an international transitional administration, but they were not prepared to forego the threat of the military option without some kind of recognition of sovereignty.[39]

In a private meeting that day with Croat Defense Minister Susak, Pardew discussed the role of international troops in implementing an Eastern Slavonian peace. Tudjman was scheduled to return to Dayton in three days (Wednesday, November 8), and Pardew explained to Secretary Perry that "we can expect quick decisions on both the Eastern Slavonia and Federation arrangements." Susak believed that an implementation force for Eastern Slavonia was part of an overall settlement and therefore part of IFOR, with American forces included. "To Susak, the requirement for U.S. troops [in Eastern Slavonia] is tied directly to the Serb demand for the Russian battalion to remain in Eastern Slavonia," Pardew reported to Perry. "His logic is this: If the Russians must be there, the Croatians want an equivalent NATO force; Russians will not accept NATO command and control, therefore, a Russian arrangement with the U.S. is required." The Croat Defense Minister struck Pardew as more interested in American command than a large number of troops, yet, Susak "does believe that some U.S. troops would be required to justify the command position." Holbrooke supported the idea of making an Eastern Slavonia part of IFOR command, but the Pentagon (who feared any expansion of IFOR's responsibilities) strongly opposed to the idea.[40]

Day Six: Monday, November 6

Holbrooke began this sixth day in Milosevic's suite to discuss sanctions. Over the weekend, the Serb leader had started to peddle a new argument for sanctions relief: to help him deal with an energy crisis plaguing Belgrade before the harsh Balkan winter set in. Although this directly contradicted with the Administration's policy reaffirmed immediately before Dayton—lifting sanctions only upon initialing of a final peace agreement—Holbrooke relayed this request back to Washington.

Milosevic threatened that it would be hard for him to agree to anything without some immediate relief. Holbrooke explained that sanctions would not be negotiated as a part of a peace deal, but would be lifted as a result of one. If Milosevic cooperated, he explained, Serbia would get all the sanctions relief it needed. The "real point is [to] get real peace," Holbrooke said. Then U.S.–Serbia relationship could be restored with "no restrictions."

He also pressed Milosevic to get more engaged in the negotiations. "[We've spent] six days here," Holbrooke said. "[We] can't stay forever. You may want to stay to make Dayton your capital—I want to go home. [We] can't stay beyond November 15."[41]

FROM THE PERSPECTIVE of the U.S. team in Dayton, the sanctions problem embodied three separate issues, and each required decisions from their colleagues in Washington.[42] The first issue was the UN Security Council's consideration of humanitarian agencies' emergency request to allow 23,000 tons of heavy heating oil into Belgrade. Officials in Dayton felt that the United States should support this proposal, urging Washington to make this happen soon.

The second issue concerned natural gas supplies for Belgrade. According to the October 5 Bosnian cease-fire agreement, which reopened natural gas supplies to Sarajevo, the same access was supposed to have been guaranteed to Belgrade. The problem was that the Russians (Belgrade's chief gas supplier) believed that they needed the authorization of the UN sanctions committee to supply Serbia, which they claimed the United States was blocking. According to Kerrick, Milosevic argued that he needed "concrete action for people in Belgrade (now in subzero weather) while he is in beautiful, sunny Dayton. [The U.S.] delegation believes that even after discounting exaggeration, this argument has validity."

The third sanctions issue was Milosevic's proposal to export a limited amount of grain to pay for fuel imports. The Serb leader claimed that he could not pay his main energy supplier, Russia, for fuel he desperately needed for winter heating. He had initially made this "grain-for-oil" request in an October 26 letter to the UN Security Council, but now pressed for immediate action. In Washington, Leon Fuerth produced a detailed assessment of the idea, concluding that the Serb leader was being disingenuous. The amount of fuel requested "far exceeds the narrowly defined uses cited," Fuerth explained, concluding that Serbia could profit $20–$80 million on such a deal. While he thought Milosevic's request excessive, he agreed that "a tightly controlled [relief] package could be designed to meet the most immediate needs without seriously undermining the overall sanctions regime." The delegation in Dayton concurred, recommending that Washington authorize Serbia to trade a more limited level of grain for less fuel.[43]

For the most part, officials at the NSC supported Fuerth's analysis and recommendations. In a phone call that day with Kerrick, Sandy Vershbow argued that the issue wasn't as "humanitarian" as Milosevic was framing it. Nevertheless, Vershbow said the NSC was reviewing ideas in the context of a larger agreement, and that Lake was "seized" with the issue. Things seemed to lean toward Fuerth's scaled back plan, and apparently he was trying to get the "definitive answer" that day. They were "prepared to do something," Kerrick records Vershbow as saying, "but less than what Milosevic wants. [The] President is taking [a] hard line."[44]

DEPUTY SECRETARY OF STATE (and Dayton native) Strobe Talbott also became involved. That afternoon, he arrived at Wright-Patterson as the first of what Holbrooke planned as a series of visits by senior Administration officials. These trips were designed, Holbrooke later explained, to impress upon the parties that the "full weight of the U.S. government was behind the negotiating team" and to "educate Washington officials on the complexities and realities of these negotiations."[45]

Since the Principals Committee planned to discuss the sanctions issue soon, the U.S. delegation in Dayton urged Talbott to engage. The Bosnians recognized the importance of his visit—and surprisingly, intervened on behalf of Milosevic. During a dinner hosted by Holbrooke in Talbott's honor, Izetbegovic and Silajdzic told the two American officials—in Milosevic's presence—that the October 5 ceasefire agreement mandated unrestricted gas flows to *both* Serbia and Bosnia and that "millions of people are freezing in both countries." When the Americans pressed Milosevic that he was asking for more gas than was necessary for humanitarian purposes, Silajdzic told Holbrooke to "knock this off—don't make an issue out of quantity; this is for confidence building." To help guide the decision-making process in Washington, Talbott asked Kerrick to draw up a "checklist" of sanctions issues and what the negotiating team wanted. As Kerrick wrote the next day, "[We] need help to clear decks on sanctions issues today. [The] goal is to have U.S.G. position by COB [close of business]. Position should be sent to Dayton for leverage in negotiations."[46]

THE TALKS ON EASTERN SLAVONIA limped along. In Holbrooke's morning meeting with Milosevic, the Serb leader complained that he was confused by the way the negotiations were split between Dayton and the Galbraith-Stoltenberg talks in the region. Holbrooke and Chris Hill agreed, realizing that they would have to start acting independently of Galbraith's efforts. Galbraith's negotiations were not going well anyway, and he realized that the local Serbs would only cooperate if "instructed" by Milosevic. In an effort to move the talks forward, officials at Dayton wrote a new draft agreement. Written mainly by Hill, this new version reworded and simplified Galbraith's original text. The most significant change was the elimination of the provision for mutual recognition between Croatia and Serbia, which Holbrooke and Hill believed should be negotiated separately.[47]

DESPITE THE OCCASIONAL FLARE-UPS, the atmosphere among the delegates in Dayton remained congenial. The Talbott dinner that night seemed to be the pinnacle of goodwill; the evening's mood was later described as "giddy." Milosevic and Izetbegovic spent much of the night sharing jokes in Serbo-Croatian. To Holbrooke, Izetbegovic's comment that Serbia deserved gas supplies gave reason for optimism: "For the first time, it seemed that Milosevic and Izetbegovic had found common ground on an issue." Holbrooke reflected that Talbott "went home [to Washington] completely blown away" by the good cheer found in his hometown. "We often talked [since Dayton] that his visit was the high emotional point."[48]

Day Seven: Tuesday, November 7

Giddiness could only take the talks so far. It had been a week, but meaningful movement over contentious issues—such as the constitution and the map—had not yet occurred. In fact, the subjects had barely been discussed. "All going well," Kerrick wrote, "just unclear where all is going."[49] The parties seemed loose—too loose—and the Americans feared that they were enjoying themselves too much. While it was good that the parties were talking to one another, Holbrooke wanted to see more progress. After studying other peace conferences, like the 1978 Camp David peace talks between Egypt and Israel, he believed that Dayton could not last any longer than two weeks. While he knew the first week would be slow, he had planned to end the conference around mid-November, to coincide with Secretary Christopher's travel to Asia. It now seemed, however, that this timetable would not be met.

Negotiations on the annexes had been sidetracked by lengthy bargaining sessions with the Europeans, as well as work with the parties on the Federation and Eastern Slavonia. Because the Americans first had to negotiate with the Contact Group on each annex even before it went to the parties, progress on the texts was much slower than anticipated. Making the process even more cumbersome, the rest of the Contact Group did not accept Bildt's authority as the EU representative and the titular head of their delegation, requiring the Americans to hold talks with each European representative as well as the group. And, while the Federation and Eastern Slavonia were critical to getting to a final settlement, the parties essentially used them as excuses not to move in other areas. To many members of the U.S. delegation, each party, Balkan and European alike, were unwilling to engage tough issues. "[There is] no evidence anyone—parties or Euros—want to close a deal," Kerrick reported to Washington that morning.[50]

So the Americans increased the pressure, starting with Holbrooke's one-on-one meetings Izetbegovic and Milosevic. According to a written report Holbrooke sent to Washington that night (the first and one of the very few he sent from Dayton), he told both leaders that "after one week of increasingly good vibrations without any significant progress on core issues, it was time to get serious."[51] At Holbrooke's suggestion, the two Presidents had met privately several times since Sunday, but had yet to produce anything significant. "Although they are both sometimes giddy after their private Izzy-Slobo meetings," Holbrooke explained, "three days of these have done nothing more than create a better atmosphere." As a way to make these talks more productive, Holbrooke got the two Presidents to pledge to continue their private dialogue, but now mediated under "U.S. only" auspices. The first meeting, scheduled for the next day in the Hope Hotel, would focus on the constitution, map and electoral issues. "If this happens," he reported back to Washington, "it will mark a clear transition to a second phase here."[52]

SERBIAN SANCTIONS were again a major topic of conversation; but this time, most of the action was in Washington. That afternoon, the Principals Committee met at the White House to discuss the issue.[53] This was the first PC meeting since Dayton began, and Holbrooke, Clark, Kerrick, and Pardew joined the session via secure video teleconference.

The Bosnians and Serbs had reached an agreement, but Washington had not yet joined. After a contentious discussion—one in which Holbrooke recalls Lake actually "banging his head on the oak table in frustration"—the Principals decided to allow a limited supply of oil and gas to Belgrade. Holbrooke later reported that the Serbs were unhappy with the delay, as were the Bosnians. "Slobo was increasingly angry today about the sanctions issue. Silajdzic repeated to me again (after [the] PC) that his government wanted movement on unrestricted natural gas and generous heating oil as a confidence-building measure."[54]

The Principals also discussed the proposed "equip-and-train" program for the Bosnian military. They reviewed the Pentagon's plan, which outlined that the Administration should develop a program utilizing contractors rather than military personnel.[55] To get the project moving, a team of civilian contractors from the Institute of Defense Analysis (IDA) was scheduled to go to Dayton the next day to talk with the Bosnians.[56]

THE AMERICANS also wrestled with the Europeans over Annex 11, the "Police Annex," which had emerged as the most troublesome as far as allied relations were concerned. The U.S. team in Dayton pushed for a strong police force; the Europeans, led by the British, objected, arguing that an international police force should only monitor civilian violations but not have enforcement capabilities. They also did not want the police to carry arms, comparing them to the unarmed British "bobbies." Carl Bildt argued that what the Americans wanted made sense "only if we were ready to take total control of the entire legal system in the country." NATO and U.S. military officials also were opposed to a robust police force, worrying that if it got into trouble, IFOR would have to come to the rescue. Given these concerns, combined with the Administration's reluctance to pledge funding for such a force (paying others to take the risk)—the bitter budget battle with Congress was then in full fury—the Americans were playing with a weak hand.[57]

THE DAVID ROHDE PROBLEM lingered, as the journalist still sat in jail in Bijeljina.[58] Although Holbrooke believed that Milosevic was trying to get Rohde's release, he figured that a little more pressure on the Serb leader might help. Menzies continued to work with the families, and Holbrooke even dispatched his wife, Kati Marton, a journalist and chair of the Committee to Protect Journalists, to press Milosevic aggressively.[59] During Monday night's dinner, Talbott had raised the issue with the Serb President. Now Holbrooke needed Secretary Christopher to weigh in. Although Talbott's intervention had "laid down a strong marker over our concern for Rohde's well-being," Holbrooke drafted a tough letter from Christopher to Milosevic. Upon returning to Washington from Yitzhak Rabin's funeral in Israel, the Secretary approved the letter, and Holbrooke presented it to Milosevic. It seemed to have an immediate effect. Late that night, he told Holbrooke that Rohde would be released at 6:00 A.M. the next morning.[60]

Day Eight: Wednesday, November 8

The news of David Rohde's release buoyed everyone's spirits. His family, still holding a vigil in Dayton, was ecstatic, and asked Holbrooke to pass on their thanks to Milosevic. President Clinton and Secretary Christopher called Rohde and spoke to him just after he arrived at the U.S. embassy in Belgrade. Admirably, Rohde told them that he hoped his situation had not "screwed up" U.S. efforts in Dayton, but in fact it had been a time consuming diversion.[61]

This promising start gave the Americans high hopes for their session with Izetbegovic and Milosevic in the Hope Hotel's B-29 Room. This meeting, the first major one held with the parties in the Hope Hotel rather than the VOQ's (which created an atmosphere of formality and seriousness), focused almost entirely on the map. The Americans wanted this event to mark the beginning of the next phase of the negotiations—"the period of bringing the parties to closure."[62] But rather than signaling the beginning of the end, these talks revealed how far the parties had to go.

"This six-hour map marathon was one of the great revealing meetings for us," Holbrooke reflected. "Up to that point, these people had been reasonably cordial to each other—but the sight of the maps drove them nuts." Kerrick described the scene as "reminiscent of *The Godfather*, [with] Don Slobo and outcast Bosnian Serbs, Don Izzy and the Federation." At one moment the parties would be "glaring across the table [at each other], screaming, while, minutes later they could be seen smiling and joking together over refreshments."

Most of the discussion centered on Sarajevo and the "Washington, DC" plan. "Despite hours of heated, yet civil exchanges," Kerrick reported, "absolutely nothing was solved." The parties stuck to their entrenched positions—the Serbs wanted a divided Sarajevo and the Bosnians wanted the whole city. The two sides just talked—or rather screamed—past each other. Bosnian Serb leader Kraijsnik delivered a long monologue on the benefits of a split city, while Sacirbey explained that the Bosnians would leave Dayton and return to war rather than accept division.[63]

The Americans had wanted to submit their own map proposal to serve as the basis for discussions, but were reluctant to do so with the parties still so far apart on basic concepts. As the day wore on, the Serbs eventually came around to accept in principle the "Washington, DC" idea for Sarajevo. With this modest concession, the United States offered some revisions to the 1994 Contact Group map, identifying Sarajevo as a federal city and reflecting changes as a result of the lost Bosnian enclaves (Srebrenica and Zepa) and the gains from the Federation offensive. Milosevic reacted favorably to this plan. Pardew explained that the United States "will hold serious map talks with [the parties] tomorrow now that we have an agreement on a concept for a unified Sarajevo." Others were less optimistic that an agreement "in principle" on Sarajevo meant that a genuine consensus had been reached. Kerrick reported to Lake that it was "not clear [whether] Sarajevo is solvable," and Holbrooke's report to Washington stated only that on the map, "we have decided to go back to a shuttle."[64]

The map session had been a disaster. Milosevic had warned the Americans about the potential for trouble, and told them afterward not "to try this again." Holbrooke agreed. Never again would the Americans assemble all the delegations together for a negotiation. Henceforth, while the Balkan parties remained in their VOQ's, U.S. negotiators traveled back and forth, delivering various proposals on such issues as the constitution, Sarajevo, elections, and the map.

WHILE THE MAP TALKS deadlocked, there was a breakthrough on the Federation. Michael Steiner's negotiations produced an interim agreement to build a stable and fully functioning Muslim–Croat entity in Bosnia. Starting with the premise that "strengthening the Federation and building trust between its constituent peoples has still not produced satisfactory results," the text outlined steps to integrate the entity economically, politically, and socially. The agreement created a federalist separation of powers between the Federation and the future central government of Bosnia; split customs revenues between the Federation and the central government; and provided a new governing statute for Mostar, which would be the Federation's capital. Although U.S. negotiators believed that "implementation will require lots of international pressure," achieving a strong Federation was "a must [to] make progress in overall talks." They hoped to reach final agreement in time for Christopher's second trip to Dayton, scheduled for Friday, November 10.[65]

AN UNUSUAL ADVISOR arrived in Dayton that day: Richard Perle, a former aide to Democratic Senator Henry "Scoop" Jackson, Defense Department official in the Reagan Administration, and an influential Washington neoconservative hawk. Perle, referred to by some as the "Prince of Darkness," joined the Bosnian delegation as a consultant on military issues, where he was joined by Douglas Feith, then a Washington lawyer who would later become a much-discussed senior Pentagon official in the George W. Bush Administration and leading advocate of toppling Saddam Hussein in Iraq. Before accepting the Bosnian invitation, Perle had called Holbrooke to discuss his role. Holbrooke agreed immediately, believing that despite the objections by many in Washington (especially Tony Lake) about his presence, Perle's advice "would help bring rigor and discipline to the Bosnian camp." In one key area,

Holbrooke and Perle were tactical allies—they both rejected the Pentagon's "minimalist" interpretation of its role in implementation.[66]

Perle focused the Bosnian unhappiness with the draft annex on IFOR. They wanted a far more robust IFOR than the Pentagon was willing to provide—including a mandate to arrest war criminals, commit to elections protection, and guarantee the return of refugees. "We are going to have big problems with them on these issues in the next few days," Pardew reported to Perry, and Kerrick warned Lake that the PC might have to take up the issue soon. That night, Perle told Holbrooke and General Clark—who had taken charge of the IFOR talks—that the current draft military annex would be the basis for moving forward, but hinted that he would advise changes.[67]

For the most part, the annex had remained unchanged since it was first presented to the Contact Group the weekend before Dayton. But with Perle's presence, Kerrick described, "storm clouds [begin to] thicken over IFOR." Clark led extensive discussions with Perle and the Bosnians. The main thrust of Perle's revisions was to increase IFOR's obligations, particularly on securing Bosnia's border and providing security for elections, the very issues that had been so intensely debated in by the Principals in Washington before Dayton. In its current form, IFOR would be authorized to do almost anything but obligated to do very little. Perle believed it had to have a "stronger mandate"—meaning, more obligations—to be effective.[68]

The Pentagon especially worried that the Bosnians would hold an agreement hostage to their demands for a more obligated and responsible IFOR. They could make such conditions the price for compromise on issues like the map, constitution and elections. Kerrick warned Lake that such a showdown might be looming, and that Washington officials would need to decide how to respond. While Perle's presence seemed to increase the possibility of such a trade-off, gaining his support was seen to have value, especially for those, like Holbrooke, who believed that IFOR needed to have a more robust mandate. With the President and other senior Administration officials currently involved in tough negotiations with Congress over the scope of U.S. involvement in IFOR, Perle's solidly Republican credentials and contacts could prove to be valuable assets. "The potential benefit of Perle's involvement," Kerrick wrote to Lake that night, "is his willingness to influence key members on [Capitol] Hill in favor of strong U.S. participation."[69]

SANCTIONS REMAINED A PROBLEM, Holbrooke complained to Washington. "While we tried to shift gears today," he explained, "we had a difficult time due to the sanctions issue which turned the day into a shambles." Milosevic remained interested in little else. The PC had agreed to provide some relief, but there had been a delay, so the U.S. delegation pressed for action. Holbrooke was especially enraged with his colleagues, and had several heated phone conversations with Albright and others. Finally, after Tony Lake's critical intervention, Washington pledged to allow a limited supply of natural gas to flow to Belgrade for home heating. The next day, Milosevic grudgingly accepted this offer.[70]

Day Nine: Thursday, November 9

After Wednesday's acrimonious "map marathon" between Izetbegovic and Milosevic, the Americans hoped that Tudjman's arrival and a Federation agreement might give the talks a boost. "President Tudjman's return to Dayton on November 8 begins a critical phase of the proximity talks," Christopher reported to the White House. "The parties need to move from discussion and engagement on the issues to reaching specific agreements." In the next two days, the Americans wanted to finalize an Eastern Slavonia settlement along with the Federation agreement. "There are still major obstacles ahead," the Secretary of State wrote, "and we should not assume a successful outcome. I plan to travel to Dayton on November 10 to try to give the parties a push."[71]

In an attempt to accomplish as much as possible before Christopher's arrival, Holbrooke resumed shuttling between the parties. As Kerrick described it to Lake, the Americans conducted "a full court press."[72]

TERRITORIAL ISSUES DOMINATED THE DAY, as the Bosnian Serbs presented their counterproposal to the U.S. map. The Americans expected that this back-and-forth would continue for several days, with each side likely to hold key concessions until other issues unfolded. Sarajevo's status continued to be a major roadblock. Milosevic ridiculously pledged to "finish maps today," but then he reversed his earlier commitment to accept the "Washington, DC" Sarajevo plan. His Bosnian Serb colleagues would never buy it, he said.[73]

With the negotiators now facing the toughest issues, decisions seemed to weigh more heavily on each Balkan leader. Meeting over lunch, Milosevic implied that he could pay the ultimate price if he compromised too much. "General Kerrick," the Serb leader said, "while America's professional prestige is on the line, my head and life are at stake—literally." It was hard to tell whether Milosevic genuinely believed this or was merely posturing. The Serb President vacillated from being the "Godfather" of the Serbs to the vulnerable martyr for peace. The character he assumed depended upon how badly he wanted a particular deal. Kerrick told Lake that "[Milosevic] wants us to believe that Krajisnik and others are capable and willing to remove him if he goes too far," concerns Holbrooke dismissed as "theatre." Nevertheless, as Kerrick pointed out, it seemed that for many of those at Dayton, "Rabin remains a fresh memory."[74]

TUDJMAN RETURNED to Dayton and initialed the Federation agreement, which they planned to sign formally the next day with Christopher presiding. Yet the talks on Eastern Slavonia went nowhere. Galbraith's efforts in the region had broken down completely. "Milosevic clearly sees the Eastern Slavonia card as a valuable one," he cabled to Dayton, "and will play it when it will have maximum impact in the overall negotiations." The Croats seemed to be ratcheting up the pressure militarily, as reports came in that they were moving forces closer to the Eastern Slavonian border. While U.S. intelligence analysts did not anticipate violence in the near-term, they predicted that Croatia would "seek a military solution" by the end of the year. Recognizing this, Galbraith noted that while Milosevic "must be mindful of looming Croatian military action, he does not yet appear ready to settle."

Day Ten: Friday, November 10

Shortly before 9:30 A.M. Friday, Christopher returned to Wright-Patterson, where he immediately went to work to save the Federation agreement. Overnight, Tudjman found a problem with the draft he had initialed: there was no guarantee that a Croat would hold one of the top three leadership positions—President, Prime Minister, or Foreign Minister—in the country. Tudjman refused to sign unless he had this commitment.[75]

With the formal signing ceremony planned for that afternoon, Christopher and Holbrooke rushed to the Bosnian VOQ, where they pressed Izetbegovic to compromise and allow a Croat Prime Minister. Tudjman's request seemed reasonable. As Kerrick explained to Lake the next day, "[The] Croats have a point. [It's] hard to justify Muslims holding all three [positions]." Unhappy, Izetbegovic conceded that the issue could be "delinked" and resolved later. He had a good reason to try to defer this decision, since giving up one of these posts would mean either Sacirbey or Silajdzic being replaced by a Croat. Prior to the scheduled ceremony at the Hope Conference Center, Christopher met briefly with Kresimir Zubak, a Bosnian Croat who, as the current President of the Muslim–Croat Federation, had been the source of Tudjman's compliant. Christopher told Zubak that Izetbegovic had offered to "delink" the issue, setting it aside for now but solving it before leaving Dayton. With this pledge, Zubak agreed to sign the document as long as the problem was resolved soon.[76]

THIS LAST MINUTE FIGHT over the Federation illustrated why the Americans were deeply distressed about the disarray within the Bosnian delegation. They had seen this episodically throughout the shuttles, but now that they were with the Bosnian leaders for hours everyday, the problems were obvious. "Their internal splits, which were becoming increasingly acrimonious, were paralyzing us," Holbrooke recalled. In their meeting that morning, Christopher pushed Izetbegovic to engage key issues like the map. "Territorial issues are in a deadlock," he said, "in good measure due to your side's failure to make realistic offers." He reminded Izetbgeovic that there was still the possibility of "lift-and-leave"—the United States would not support the Bosnians if they were the source of diplomatic failure. "I know that these issues are difficult," Christopher's talking points read, "but given our original carrots and sticks approach for peace last August, we do not want to get into a position where Sarajevo is responsible for failure to reach agreement."[77]

CHRISTOPHER REITERATED many of his private comments to the Balkan Presidents in his public remarks at the signing ceremony in the B-29 Room. "As implemented, today's agreement will bring the Federation to life," he said to the delegates and press gathered at the Hope complex (this was the first time the media was allowed onto the base since the opening ceremony). However important the paper signed that day was, Christopher did acknowledge that the "true test" of the agreement would be in the way it was carried out. Izetbegovic echoed this sentiment, saying that history would judge the accord according to "what is done" rather than "what is said."[78]

BEFORE LEAVING DAYTON to return to Washington, Christopher also tried to breathe life into the Eastern Slavonia talks. Chris Hill's mediation had brought the Croats and Serbs close to an agreement, but the Presidents still differed over the duration of Eastern Slavonia's reintegration into Croatia— Milosevic wanted at least two years while Tudjman wanted one. Christopher created a compromise: the transitional authority would govern the area for one year but its mandate could be extended for another year if requested by either of the parties. Milosevic and Tudjman went off by themselves to discuss the idea.

As Christopher and Holbrooke waited in the American VOQ with their team, they looked out the window to an unusual scene: across the quad, Milosevic and Tudjman were walking side-by-side toward them. Entering Holbrooke's conference room, the two Presidents sat next to each other on a couch, and proudly announced that "we have solved Eastern Slavonia," accepting Christopher's compromise. Milosevic explained that this phased approach would give the East Slavonia Serbs time to adjust to the new realities. They insisted that the agreement not be announced at Dayton but in the region—he wanted to maintain the illusion that he was not in control of the Serbs in Eastern Slavonia. The Americans agreed, but Christopher told Milosevic and Tudjman that by the time he returned to Dayton on November 14, he wanted an agreement completed.[79]

THIS INTERVENTION helped put the finishing touches on the Federation and brought Milosevic and Tudjman to the doorstep of an Eastern Slavonian deal. Yet the Americans understood that they had a long way to go. After the Federation agreement signing, Christopher "harbored no illusions about how far this small step left us from the finish line, and how difficult reaching that line would be." The overall mood in Dayton remained positive, but it seemed that the talks constantly teetered on the brink of collapse. "If these guys want peace," Holbrooke told his wife, Kati Marton, that evening, "they can get it in a week." After ten days, Kerrick observed that the parties were "still enjoying each other's company, but [the] more they see of each other, [the] more they seem to be willing to chuck it all and return to war." The chances for success at Dayton seemed to come and go like the tide—"every twelve hours [we're] sure we will fail only to find real chances for success at next high tide."[80]

9

ENDGAME: DAYTON, NOVEMBER 11–21

Days Eleven and Twelve: Saturday and Sunday, November 11–12

Dayton's second weekend was a moment of transition. It had taken ten days to clear away such issues as the Federation and Eastern Slavonia, and the parties had become comfortable with the surroundings and each other. Yet despite hours of intense negotiating and prodding by the Americans, the core issues remained largely untouched. There had been some discussion about territory—such as the status of Sarajevo—with little success. The Bosnian government had done little more than restate their previous positions, and Milosevic remained defiant. With the two-week mark approaching fast, the Americans wanted to use the weekend to jump-start things. "Saturday," Kerrick informed Lake, "is a day of maps."[1]

It would be a disappointing day. Hours of talks produced nothing new. In a Saturday meeting in Holbrooke's suite, Izetbegovic and Silajdzic pored over the maps in detail, but agreed to nothing. Izetbegovic simply repeated that the Contact Group map would be the basis for negotiations. "They would not discuss the map for a long time, arguing that there is only one map, and that's the Contact Group map," Chris Hill recalled. This map still included the lost enclaves of Srebrenica and Zepa, areas that the Bosnians had no hope of getting back, but they still insisted on claiming.[2]

The Serbs didn't help. Milosevic seemed to be playing around, and the Bosnian Serbs were even worse. Although they had been isolated throughout most of the negotiations, the map was the one area where they had been included. Jim Pardew had spent the most time with them during the first week, and Holbrooke had allowed Krajisnik to have the floor during the November 7 acrimonious "map marathon."

After enduring hours of speeches about the sanctity of Serb land and the threat of encroaching Islam, Pardew knew that the Bosnian Serbs were hardly a constructive presence. He had suffered through their lecturing, and been witness to downright bizarre behavior. Some Bosnian Serbs had loaded up on hunting knives and camouflage gear at the Wright-Patterson PX, although the Americans drew the line at firearms. At one point, John Shattuck went to meet with Bosnian Serb Vice President Koljevic, only to find him alone in his room and so drunk that he "was barely able to talk, complaining that his phone had been cut off—apparently on Milosevic's orders." Holbrooke asked Pardew not to meet with the Bosnian Serbs anymore, leaving responsibility for involving the Bosnian Serbs to Milosevic.

The weekend's map talks destroyed all the goodwill of the previous week—or any momentum the Americans had hoped that the Federation agreement or Eastern Slavonian deal could bring. "Both sides are in over their heads . . . Shouts, anger highlight talks," Kerrick reported. Carl Bildt described that when it came to the map discussions, "Holbrooke was banging his head against a brick wall."[3]

As RELATIONS between (and within) the delegations soured, so did the Europeans' attitude toward their American partners. The Contact Group had never been entirely happy with a U.S.-led peace process—they felt slighted, belittled, and constantly complained of being sidelined. Bildt explains that as the Dayton talks approached, they had been willing to put up with a certain amount of American "flag-waving" as long as they agreed with the substance of the negotiations. But they had grown uncomfortable with the American goal of an ambitious, comprehensive settlement, believing that it tried to do too much—and in certain areas, like civilian implementation, did not do enough.

As during the shuttles, at Dayton the Americans saw the Contact Group as a problem to be managed rather than a partner to be included. As the Contact Group's British representative, Pauline Neville-Jones, later wrote, she and her colleagues "were informed but not consulted, and their primary role was to assist as far as needed, witness and ratify the outcome. But they were not to interfere." The Contact Group's accommodations at Dayton symbolized the role they would play: their VOQ was the fifth building, near the quad, but not part of it.[4]

By that weekend, the effects of neglect—both perceived and real—began to show. "These were relatively high-level officials who were at a negotiation with no negotiating power; they were there just to bear witness," Robert Gallucci observed. "It was really tough on their egos."[5] European delegates rumbled more loudly about their treatment, and rumors spread that Carl Bildt might leave Dayton. The French complained (both at Dayton and in Paris, where President Chirac berated the American Ambassador, Pamela Harriman) about American "heavy-handedness," characterizing the U.S. attitude as "we take the credit, you get the bill." Their unhappiness was complicating the negotiations, particularly on the parts of the agreement where Europe would have to play a key role—such as the annexes on police, civilian implementation, and OSCE monitoring of the elections. They thought the Americans were too focused on the map and military implementation. Bildt remembers "getting seriously worried about how everything would work out in purely technical terms . . . details that might be of great importance later were handled with a nonchalance that I considered almost irresponsible."[6]

But the Americans believed that the Europeans were so consumed by these technical details—as well as being sidelined—that they would prefer to leave Dayton empty-handed. They were amazed with the Europeans' preoccupation with their own piece of the peace instead of the deal itself. Holbrooke had become increasingly impatient with the amount of time he spent everyday with the Europeans (and they had become frustrated with him), starting with the large Contact Group meeting every morning. He finally decided this was a waste of time, and asked John Kornblum to take over the Contact Group portfolio. As an old European hand, Kornblum had a knack (perhaps it was just patience) for soothing the Europeans, and they respected him. He became their primary daily contact, keeping them informed of overall progress, negotiating select issues with them and, of course, receiving healthy doses of their anger. "Holbrooke stared at his maps, and visited us when he could," Bildt recalled.[7]

THE OTHERWISE DISMAL WEEKEND brought one positive development: a final agreement on Eastern Slavonia. The parties delivered the text Saturday in Dayton, and on Sunday it was signed by Galbraith, Stoltenberg, and local officials in Zagreb and the town of Erdut. As Christopher and Holbrooke had negotiated two days before, the final document struck compromises on the last dividing issues. The UN Transitional Authority would govern the area for at least twelve months but no longer than two years. When the UN's mandate expired, the region would become part of Croatia. Local elections would be held toward the end of the transitional period; and the international community would monitor human rights and refugee relocation.[8]

WITHOUT ANY PUBLICITY, the families of Robert Frasure, Joseph Kruzel, and Nelson Drew visited Dayton that Sunday. It was an emotional moment, serving as a stark reminder of the real human sacrifices that had gone into this massive diplomatic undertaking. There was a small luncheon for them with the American delegation, and they met with the three Balkan Presidents in their respective VOQs.

Day Thirteen: Monday, November 13

In anticipation of Christopher's return, the pace of negotiations accelerated on all fronts. The drafting experts worked to get as many of the annexes cleaned up as possible, while Holbrooke and his core team conducted intense shuttling between the three Presidents on the map. The atmosphere remained sour. Izetbegovic was in an awful mood, refusing to see either Tudjman or Milosevic, while Tudjman refused to see Milosevic. "That is why they call these proximity talks, of course" Holbrooke wrote to Christopher that night. "But it did constitute retrogression."[9]

The Americans remained most worried about the rancor inside the Bosnian delegation which Holbrooke referred to as a "mini-Yugoslavia." Silajdzic had emerged as the most level-headed and cooperative. But every time the Prime Minister tried to make a deal, he would be undermined by either Izetbegovic or Sacirbey. "Time and again," Holbrooke reflected, "Silajdzic's frustrations became so intense that his emotions took over and prevented him from making rational decisions." Seeing the psychological toll this was having on the

Prime Minister, Holbrooke tried to give him confidence, taking him for a midday walk around Wright-Patterson's grounds.

As they strolled along the perimeter of the compound, Holbrooke stroked the Bosnian leader's ego, saying that as "the leading proponent at Dayton of a multi-ethnic Bosnia," Silajdzic had an "historic role" to play. Without quick progress, Holbrooke said, Secretary Christopher would consider ending the talks. Silajdzic exploded, angrily saying that such threats "would only stiffen their spines." Holbrooke told Silajdzic that the Americans would finally unveil their own map. "I told him that we would no longer negotiate from their map, or Milosevic's, or the Contact Group map."[10]

THE AMERICANS spent the rest of the day working on the map, peddling different ideas and options back and forth. The Bosnians pressed for swaths of land in northwest Bosnia (for key railroad lines) and areas south of Gorazde (for major power plants). They insisted on having the northeast Bosnian town of Brcko. Milosevic fought all of these demands, only giving up areas that were already in Federation hands that he had intended to relinquish anyway.[11]

By the time these sessions ended around midnight, the Americans were even more frustrated with the Bosnians. They were reluctant to compromise on anything, and seemed "clearly prepared to return to war." Yet, oddly enough, Silajdzic thought that the negotiations had taken a turn for the better. Earlier, Holbrooke found the Prime Minister "emotional, gloomy, and threatening." But during a second walk together that night, Silajdzic said that "it had been the best day of Dayton so far." Tired and frustrated, Holbrooke "thought [Silajdzic] must be on some controlled substance, since it seemed to me that the tortoise of our progress was being outrun by the hare of the calendar. But he was serious, and perhaps he is right."[12]

THE SARAJEVO GOVERNMENT only seemed to operate effectively when it had outside help from those like Richard Perle. On Sunday, the U.S. delegation sent back to Washington the Bosnian edits of the draft military annex for the Deputies Committee to review. The Bosnians offered over 150 changes, which were primarily the handiwork of Perle and Doug Feith, and had been vetted by both Holbrooke and General Clark. Many Administration officials, especially at the NSC and Pentagon, were outraged that Perle was even in Dayton and that he was trying to undo decisions that they had already made. "Tell Perle to shove his goddamn changes up his ass," one angry Defense Department official screamed at Holbrooke. Most of Perle's suggestions were minor. But some were significant, and while Holbrooke supported most of them, he tried to reassure his skeptical colleagues that he had prevented changes that promote "mission creep."[13]

This draft had become so controversial that it had even earned its own name: the "Perle markup." It reflected the desire for a stronger, more interventionist IFOR. Perle added language that would oblige the IFOR commander to carry out the force's mandate "to the maximum extent consistent with its resources" to improve the climate for elections, remove the one-year limit for deployment, and apprehend war criminals. Using Perle's edits, Holbrooke and Clark tried to revisit many of the issues that the Principals had decided before Dayton, such as elections protection and the one-year limit for IFOR. Holbrooke remained deeply frustrated by the Pentagon's resistance to a more robust military role, and at times his emotions spilled over. At one point, he and Clark got into a heated debate on the issue, and Holbrooke asked "Wes, do you understand that there are members of the Joint Chiefs who want our effort to fail, and they probably won't admit it even to themselves?" As the Joint Chiefs' senior representative at Dayton, Clark loyally defended his superiors, but even he acknowledged later that "I sensed a lot of truth in what Holbrooke was saying."[14]

That afternoon, Clark and Pardew joined the DC meeting via secure video teleconference to discuss the "Perle markup." The Deputies accepted most of their recommendations, only rejecting changes that radically altered the scope of IFOR—such as the removing the force's one-year limit, or creating a "mechanism" to investigate suspected war criminals. Perle's efforts had succeeded in bringing some specificity to IFOR's mission, but it still essentially remained a force of nearly unlimited authority with relatively few concrete responsibilities. Yet he had helped move IFOR closer to the interventionist force that Dayton's maximalist negotiators envisioned. "There was no question about it: the military annex had been improved by Richard Perle's involvement," Holbrooke later wrote.[15]

Day Fourteen: Tuesday, November 14

When Christopher arrived in Dayton for his third visit, the mood had turned from frustration to desperation. "There is a certain feeling among most people that success here is highly likely because of the momentum we had going into Dayton and the effort and commitment of the U.S. [government] has put into these talks," Holbrooke wrote Christopher. "As you know, I do not share this view—and not because I am 'low-balling' expectations."

Holbrooke thought that the minimal progress they had made had taken too long. "My concern over the situation here is based on the amount of time we have lost on such issues as sanctions arguments, the time spent on Federation-building (although it was productive and unavoidable, it consumed eight days), and, above all, the immense difficulty of engaging the Bosnian Government in a serious negotiation . . . So, on Day 14, we are about where we should have been on Day 8 or 9." Each of the parties challenged the prospects for success in their own way: the Bosnians were disorganized, Milosevic dishonest, and Tudjman disengaged. "While the Bosnians are the sort of friends that try one's patience, Milosevic has often lied outright about factual data or changed his position after we thought we had locked something in. As for Tudjman, he is fast becoming the King of Dayton."

Christopher intended to stop at Wright-Patterson on his way to Asia to finish the deal. But given the remaining differences on every core issue, the negotiations needed a middle-reliever, not a closer. "We have to recast your trip," Holbrooke wrote. "It now becomes a last warning to get serious." Christopher would leave that night to attend the APEC ministerial meeting in Osaka, Japan, and then he was supposed to join the President in Tokyo for an official state visit. However, given the bleak status of the negotiations, he decided to cut his Asia trip short to return to Dayton immediately. Holbrooke advised him to leave the parties "with the clear message that when you return [from Japan] we must have either closure or close-down . . . That, pure and simple, is the message of your trip."[16]

THE SECRETARY OF STATE SPENT the day shuttling continuously among the three delegations. By the time he left around midnight, he had seen Dayton's highs and lows. Although he departed without any breakthroughs, he reported to President Clinton that the day "offered tantalizing hints that a peace agreement might indeed be possible."[17]

As planned, his meetings concentrated on the issues where the parties remained deadlocked: the map and Sarajevo. The map talks were the most difficult. Christopher prodded Izetbegovic and Milosevic to begin exploring possible territorial trade-offs. Although doing so "in an angry and vitriolic manner," he found that the two Presidents exposed enough common ground to provide a glimmer of hope. "It is possible, in the good moments, to see the final shape of the final map," Christopher wrote to the President. "But it is a very fragile system."[18]

Christopher recognized what everyone who had been there the entire time could see: that while the issues alone were difficult, the parties' internal divisions had become a huge obstacle. As Holbrooke had warned, the biggest problems were with the Sajajevo government. "The Bosnians are very divided among themselves and still not fully convinced that a peace agreement is in their interest," Christopher explained to Clinton. He believed that Izetbegovic was most reluctant because "he was giving up sole leadership of his country—flawed as it was—for a power-sharing arrangement."[19] During one of their three meetings that day, Christopher had a "heart-to-heart" dis-cussion with the Bosnian President "to remind him of all the benefits that a genuine peace would bring." He also wanted to reiterate the consequences of failure—that they had "put an enormous amount on the line for peace" to save Bosnia, and therefore would not assist the Sarajevo leadership if they blocked a reasonable settlement.[20]

When the Secretary of State departed that night, it was clear that whether heading toward an agreement or not, the talks had entered the endgame. He later characterized that day "as one of those times when you can feel [that] the negotiation is either going to succeed or fail in a few days." He could see the fatigue on the faces of the Balkan leaders as well as those of his own del-egation. Christopher thought that "they were reaching the point where they were getting on each other's nerves. However attractive Dayton was . . . they were beginning to get 'cabin fever'; it was beginning to get cold." He knew he needed to get back quickly. Christopher's presence had a calming influ-ence on everyone, especially in contrast to Holbrooke's relentless (and at times overbearing) intensity. Both in stature and style, the Secretary of State exuded control and steadiness. When he arrived in Dayton, Carl Bildt remembered, "he became the house psychiatrist . . . without him, the whole thing would have exploded."

Looking forward, Christopher told the President that "I believe we should take a shot at bringing these [talks] to a conclusion." Although he admitted that success was "a very optimistic scenario that may well not happen," he decided to cut short his own visit to Japan to return to Dayton. If talks were successful, Christopher suggested that they aim to conclude them as the President returned from Tokyo, "so that you could be involved in any possible announcement." On the other hand, if they failed to reach closure by early the next week, "it will probably be necessary to suspend the negotiations on the best basis possible."[21]

Day Fifteen: Wednesday, November 15

As he traveled to Japan, Christopher hoped that Holbrooke's "aggressive tutelage" would be able to "fill in the success" of his visit. While there was some progress on the annexes concerning IFOR and civilian implementation, these also happened to be the annexes that the Balkan parties themselves had the least to do with. On the core issues, they were going in circles. "Everyone has a sense of progress," Kerrick reported to Lake that night, "but [it's] hard to put a finger on concrete achievement . . . [we] seem to be near a deal, but far away at the same time."[22]

The Bosnian Serbs, who Christopher had described to Clinton as "present but quite invisible," began to clamor more loudly for attention.[23] By this point, it was no secret that Milosevic would sell them out for any deal. Although the Bosnian Serbs were supposedly part of Milosevic's delegation, he was rarely seen with them, and they were rarely seen at all. Desperately looking for an outlet for their frustrations, the Bosnian Serbs tried to reach out to the Americans. In a memorandum to Roberts Owen, Bosnian Serb leader Momcilo Krajisnik commented on the "unacceptable provisions" of the latest draft constitution. They opposed the most fundamental aspects of an agreement; most of their changes would have reversed the Geneva and New York principles, and every one of their changes divided Bosnia. Complaining of being shut out of the process, Krajisnik said he "wondered whether there is any point" in making any comments, observing that the "method of work adopted by the international mediators is, needless to say, seriously threatening to undermine the overall peace effort in Dayton."[24]

IN WASHINGTON, the Principals Committee finished work on several of the most important implementation issues: the "equip and train" program for the Bosnians and the civilian and police annexes.[25] Joined by Wes Clark, John Kornblum and Robert Gallucci (who had become the lead negotiator for the police and civilian implementation annexes), who participated from Wright-Patterson via secure video, the PC debated the controversial program to arm the Bosnian Muslims. Many understood the contradiction between having

Bosnia remain a single state yet allowing it to have, in effect, three separate armies, one of which would be helped by the Americans. Yet, because "equip and train" had been such an important carrot for the Bosnians, and since there was considerable pressure from Congress and elsewhere to "level the playing field" militarily inside Bosnia, they had to live with what Holbrooke later called a "fundamental flaw in our postwar structure."

But to make this flaw less glaring, the Principals agreed to include an arms control section with the IFOR annex (thus creating Annex 1-A, on IFOR; and Annex 1-B, on "regional stabilization"), placing the "equip and train" program within a broader context of arms reductions between Serbia, Bosnia, and Croatia. While Holbrooke realized that this "build up/build down" plan was itself contradictory, it was "the best course available" to ensure that the Bosnian Muslims could protect themselves while at the same time reduce the likelihood of renewed fighting. Yet, as he later acknowledged, making arms control a "goal" of implementation rather than an "obligation"—which would have required a more interventionist IFOR, a prospect the Pentagon continued to resist—meant that enforcement of Annex 1-B was "left to the goodwill of parties who had no goodwill."[26]

The Principals' also discussed Gallucci's efforts on the police and civilian implementation annexes. While deciding to keep the mission of an international police task force separate from IFOR's (except in the event of gross human rights violations or attacks on civilian aid organizations), they approved the drafts. With this, Gallucci went back to the parties the next day for the finishing touches. Shortly after midnight the morning of November 17, the parties reached final agreement. Of the 11 draft annexes, these were the first two finished.[27]

THAT NIGHT in Washington, one of the most important—and deeply troubling—events of the Clinton Presidency took place. The President of the United States had his first interaction with a young White House intern, Monica Lewinsky. Incredibly, during this encounter the President managed to conduct two telephone conversations with members of Congress, briefing them on the Dayton talks and the prospects for American troops implementing an agreement. This ugly episode set off a chain of events that in three years would lead to the President's impeachment and trial by the U.S. Senate.[28]

Day Sixteen: Thursday, November 16

With Christopher scheduled to return Friday evening, the American team hoped to use several visits by other top officials to help push the talks toward conclusion. Tony Lake would arrive that afternoon, and Secretary of Defense Perry, NATO Commander General George Joulwan, and Major General William Nash, the Commander of the First Armored Division in Europe, were scheduled to come the next day. As the senior U.S. military leaders in Europe, Joulwan and Nash would lead the IFOR effort (Joulwan from NATO headquarters, and Nash on the ground in Bosnia).

Before Lake arrived, the Americans helped to orchestrate an important tête-à-tête between Milosevic and Silajdzic. For the past few days, Holbrooke had hoped that the Bosnian Prime Minister would step up and push his government to a settlement. On the big issues that remained—the map and Sarajevo—Izetbegovic and Sacirbey were unrealistic and unyielding, while Silajdzic would at least entertain compromise offers. The problem was that as the intra-Bosnian struggle escalated, so did the mental toll on Silajdzic. He was exhibiting mercurial, some thought manic-depressive behavior. To John Menzies, who had had a lot of experience with the Prime Minister in Sarajevo, Silajdzic had so much nervous energy that at times he was like a "caged panther." When the pressures become too great, the Prime Minister would often go into a funk, essentially disappearing from the talks.[29]

Holbrooke continued to reach out to Silajdzic, and asked Menzies and Rosemarie Pauli to befriend the Prime Minister, taking him for walks, joining him for meals, or talking with him about his family and future. Holbrooke's wife, Kati Marton, also spent time with him, talking about her books or ones he wanted to write. Bizarrely, Silajdzic even asked Marton to co-author the book he wanted to write on the war. On Wednesday night, Holbrooke and Marton had even taken Silajdzic off base for a private dinner at a French restaurant in Dayton.[30]

ON THAT BITTER COLD Thursday morning, Menzies and Pauli took Silajdzic for a walk outside the VOQ compound. Holbrooke and Chris Hill, meanwhile, set out with Milosevic on a long stroll around the base, ending up at the Officers Club for lunch. Braving the winter weather, the Americans asked the Serb leader what kind of gestures he could make to break the map impasse. They did not press for any specific territorial concession, but rather a symbolic goodwill gesture, "like Anwar Sadat"—referring to the late Egyptian President's historic 1977 trip to Jerusalem—to show the Bosnians that he was willing to go the distance and make meaningful sacrifices. One idea was to offer a special highway connecting Sarajevo to Belgrade. Milosevic seemed amenable, replying that he was also thinking about what kind of move he could make.[31]

Holbrooke, Hill, and Milosevic arrived at the Officers Club shortly before noon. The place had become a favorite haunt of the Serb leader's, who enjoyed the country club ambiance compared to the crowded VOQ quad and burgers and fries at Packy's. Soon after they arrived, Menzies and Pauli came in with Silajdzic and sat at the opposite end of the large, wood-paneled dining room. Before he had left with Milosevic that morning, Holbrooke had called Pauli to tell her where he was going, and she had decided to take Silajdzic there too.

As they ate, Holbrooke went over to Silajdzic's table to say hello, and they began to discuss some points Milosevic had raised on the status of Gorazde. They began to draw different options out on table napkins and, as other diners looked on in amazement, Holbrooke shuttled the ideas between the two leaders. After several trips back and forth across the dining room, Holbrooke finally got Silajdzic to join Milosevic at his table. Sitting down together for one of the few times since the Bosnian war had begun, the two leaders talked in Serbo-Croatian about creating a land corridor between Gorazde and Sarajevo. Milosevic at one point told Silajdzic that after withstanding three years of shelling by "Bosnian Serb cowards," the Muslim government had "earned" Sarajevo. Although nothing was solved, this napkin diplomacy was an important breakthrough: the two sides had started negotiating seriously over a territorial issue.[32]

Following this dramatic lunch, Tony Lake and Sandy Vershbow arrived at Wright-Patterson. Holbrooke took Lake to meet with Izetbegovic and Milosevic (Tudjman was still away). Making clear that he was speaking for President Clinton, Lake strongly emphasized the need for closure in the next few days. America's patience with the entire effort was waning, Lake explained, and if success was not achieved here, then Europe would assume more responsibility in any future negotiations.

"Tony said there was no second chance for the U.S.," Holbrooke described in a report to Christopher that night. "[He said] that this was our last, best shot and that Congress was going south on us; that if they don't reach agreement when you get here we will turn them over to Pauline [Neville-Jones, the British Contact Group representative], Jacques [Blot, the French representative], and Wolfgang [Ischinger, the German representative], and our role will greatly diminish." The parties took this threat very seriously. No one—not Milosevic, not Izetbegovic—wanted the Europeans to be in charge. As an additional carrot, Lake explained that if they succeeded in reaching agreement that weekend, President Clinton might visit Dayton (wanting to get credit for a deal, Clinton remained interested in bringing the parties to the White House, but eventually was talked out of it). This point intrigued Milosevic but not Izetbegovic. Instead, the Bosnian President asked if he could visit Congress.[33]

As expected, Milosevic pressed Lake on sanctions. "I understand you're the most anti-Serb official in Washington," Milosevic said to Lake. The National Security Advisor explained the policy that had been reaffirmed the day before in the Principals Committee: while suspension would come with initialing, complete lifting of sanctions would only come with full implementation. Milosevic said he accepted this, but then argued with Lake and Holbrooke about the exact meaning of "implementation."[34]

After Lake and Vershbow left Dayton that evening (with Lake telling his Washington colleagues that Dayton was "an insane asylum"), Holbrooke invited Milosevic over to the American VOQ. He wanted to talk with him about the Sarajevo-Gorazde land corridor they had discussed at the Officers Club with Silajdzic. In a map room set up in the U.S. VOQ, General Clark used the Defense Mapping Agency's highly technical, highly classified 3-D imaging system called "PowerScene" to show Milosevic the terrain between Sarajevo and Gorazde. Two months earlier, this $400,000 computer system helped NATO planners choose targets in the bombing campaign; now, it helped negotiators at Dayton plan for peace. By rendering scenes from actual terrain imagery down to two yards in detail, PowerScene enabled the negotiators to travel through Bosnia in virtual reality, visually surveying the geographic details via computer. All the delegations at Dayton were completely fascinated with PowerScene; the Americans quickly saw that the computer program had at least as much value psychologically as it did substantively, serving as an impressive reminder of American technological-military prowess. PowerScene also became one of the rare forms of entertainment for many at Dayton, who passed what little spare time they had "flying" through Bosnia. The map room became such a popular attraction that the U.S. delegation began to refer to it as the "Nintendo Room."

Milosevic had offered the Bosnians a thin two-mile road corridor to connect Sarajevo to Gorazde, which, as Clark's PowerScene tour of the mountainous terrain revealed, was completely unviable. After two hours and a bottle of Scotch (of which Milosevic consumed four glasses), they reached an agreement on a wider corridor through the mountainous terrain. "We have found our road," Milosevic pronounced. Because of the circumstances surrounding this event, many began to call this agreement, suitably, as the "Scotch Road" or the "Clark Corridor." Although Holbrooke deliberately downplayed this as a "minor concession"—and dismissed the influence that alcohol might have had over Milosevic's decision-making—it did represent the first substantial breakthrough on a key issue in days. The American team hoped that it might be the first crack in the dam blocking a final settlement.[35]

As the negotiations entered their third week, a fundamental question remained: Would these leaders summon the courage to make the final decisions necessary to reach an agreement? Watching from afar, Washington officials believed that while success was hardly certain, they had to press on. As Strobe Talbott described the situation in a "Strobegram" to Sandy Berger, the American effort was "a bit like the crew of a badly damaged B-17 returning from a bombing run from Germany, two or three engines out, gaping holes in the fuselage, flying on vapor from our tanks, landing field barely in sight on the horizon; Dick [Holbrooke] in the pilot's seat. Question is whether to let him try to land the thing. Answer: yes. But buckle up, because it ain't going to be pretty or smooth."[36]

In many ways, the problems that Holbrooke's team had encountered during the two months of shuttle diplomacy were replayed more intensely in Dayton. Tudjman, who had already gotten his primary objective in Dayton—Eastern Slavonia—played along, helping the Bosnians when it was in his interest but otherwise remaining aloof. His lack of interest in the details of other issues was evident in the amount of time he spent *away* from Dayton—ten of twenty-one days. Milosevic, on the other hand, had great interest in success. Desperate for sanctions relief and acceptance from the West, he had proven willing to make concessions. His idiomatic (and frequently vulgar) command of the English language and desire to please the Americans made him, in many ways, the easiest of interlocutors. The Sarajevo government, with its internal strife and uncertain goals, seemed dangerously close to torpedoing the peace, however flawed it may be, that Milosevic and Tudjman were ready to give them.[37]

"The Bosnians still wish us to believe that they are getting a lousy deal," Holbrooke wrote to Christopher that night. "But they know it is not only a good deal but the best they will ever get." While the Americans believed that it would seem rational that the Bosnians take this best chance for settlement, their clashing personalities and competing visions of a just peace stood in the way.

To Holbrooke, Izetbegovic was more of a "movement" leader than a - "governing" leader. "Izzy spent nine years of his life in jail," Holbrooke explained to Christopher, "he has no understanding of, or interest in, economic development or modernization—the things that peace can bring." Izetbegovic struck Holbrooke as concerned not about the citizens he represented, but about an idea: "He shows remarkably little concern for the suffering his people have endured; after all, he has suffered greatly for his ideals. To him, Bosnia is an abstraction, not several million people who overwhelmingly want peace."

Silajdzic, on the other hand, seemed to be more realistic about governing, and had concentrated on establishing viable political structures and engaging such issues as economic reconstruction. Yet, Silajdzic's mood swings undermined his ability to take the lead. "If Haris did not have such an unpredictable personality, he would have played the hero here; we still have hopes that he will do so."

Finally, Sacirbey, who had assumed such an important role when America's shuttle diplomacy was launched in August, had grown increasingly isolated and gloomy as Dayton went on, creeping further behind Izetbegovic's shadow. And his relationship with Holbrooke had become embittered. At one point, Sacirbey snuck his mistress into the talks—an obvious distraction in clear violation of the rule against allowing unauthorized outsiders within the compound—and Holbrooke demanded that she leave. Aside from such extracurricular activities, Holbrooke saw Sacirbey as driven by two contradictory motives: "he wants to be liked by the Americans, but his primary goal seems to be to undermine Haris at all times." In all, Holbrooke hoped that Christopher's return to Dayton might force the Bosnians to unify, as least momentarily, to finish a deal.[38]

Day Seventeen: Friday, November 17

Defense Secretary Perry and Under Secretary of Defense Walter Slocombe arrived at Wright-Patterson shortly before 10 A.M. Generals Joulwan and Nash arrived at noon. Holbrooke planned this display of American military leadership to impress (and intimidate) both the Balkan leaders and Europeans "that we were serious" about using troops to lead military implementation. Moreover, like Tony Lake, Perry and Joulwan could continue to ratchet up the pressure on the parties. "Lack of a settlement would be a problem for the United States. It would be a catastrophe for your country," Perry planned to tell Izetbegovic and Milosevic.[39]

Perry's toughest meeting that day was with Izetbegovic. The Bosnian leader was prickly, probing the Secretary of Defense on his commitment to the "equip and train" program (Izetbegovic knew from Richard Perle that the Pentagon had been opposed). Perry confirmed that the United States would honor its promise to help the Bosnians restore their army through an equip-and-train program, as long as the parties agreed to a suitable arms control agreement. "I told them that I believed, and that our government believed, that the imbalance of forces back in 1992 had been a contributing factor to the war starting in the first place," Perry recalled. "Therefore, when NATO forces left in a year, we did not want to leave an imbalance . . . we would work with them to get a balance of forces."[40]

BY THE EVENING NOVEMBER 17, five of the eleven annexes—Human Rights, Refugees, National Monuments, Civilian Implementation, and Police—were complete. The General Framework Agreement, plus the annexes concerning Arbitration and Public Services, IFOR, and arms control, were almost finished.

The three most contentious issues remaining were the constitution, elections and, of course, the map. Drafting the constitution was nearly done, although some at Dayton (especially Europeans like Bildt) wondered whether it would ever be workable. It looked good in principle, but like the Geneva and New York agreements, the constitution masked fundamental disagreements between the Pale and Sarajevo leaders on the desirability and role of a central government. The Bosnian Serbs had still not accepted that Bosnia would be a unified state controlled by the center. "The Serbs would prefer to give maximum powers to Republika Srpska but know that this is out of the question," Pardew reported to Perry. "So they have sought to sabotage the central government . . . [keeping its] the powers limited." On the positive side, while the constitution alone could not guarantee a viable, multiethnic, and democratic Bosnia, it would "provide the Bosnians the opportunity to build such a state." But "for this opportunity to be realized," Pardew observed, "the current leadership in Pale will have to change this, either through election or indictment."[41]

On the elections annex, the two parties were at odds over two issues: voting rights for refugees and displaced persons, and the responsibilities of the Organization of Security and Cooperation in Europe (OSCE) in overseeing the elections. Holbrooke considered the first issue a deal-breaker. Milosevic was taking the position that voters must be physically present to register to vote (since so many Muslims had fled their homes, this helped the Serbs). The Bosnians, in contrast, wanted voters registered (and have their votes applied) to where they lived in 1991, the last time a census was taken in Yugoslavia.

The Americans offered a solution, recommending that voters themselves be able to determine where their votes would be applied. If both sides remained inflexible, a back-up option would be to defer the issue until after Dayton to be decided by a special electoral commission. The Europeans rejected this, believing that elections would be the most important part of Bosnia's future. They considered the Americans' willingness to punt on this issue as symptomatic of their overall approach to the negotiations. Bildt worried that Holbrooke was spending too much time on the map, while "absolutely crucial and much more difficult issues of how the wounds could be slowly healed . . . were being swept under the carpet.[42]

While it was true that the Americans were deeply focused on the map—and considered it the core of the conflict—it is unfair to claim that they underappreciated or ignored outright issues like elections. In fact, the Americans wanted a strong hand for the OSCE in conducting the elections, while the Europeans and Milosevic wanted to narrowly define the OSCE's role to that of "observers and monitors." The U.S. delegation believed that such a limited mandate for the OSCE would doom the elections—perhaps the most critical political benchmark of any settlement—and it was therefore worth delaying a decision to get it right. They stood firm for giving the OSCE responsibility for "supervising" the elections. Since the word "supervise" could be interpreted in different ways, Holbrooke argued that no matter which other civilian implementation jobs were headed by Europeans, the OSCE representative overseeing elections had to be an American.[43]

THE AMERICANS wanted to finish in time for Thanksgiving. "Saturday," Holbrooke wrote to Christopher, "will shape up as the decisive day of Dayton." For the first time, he suggested that they consider setting a deadline to end the talks, to "make them realize we mean it is our only chance for success." After two days of warnings by high-level U.S. officials, Holbrooke saw that "both sides are fully primed for this [deadline] approach; indeed, they half dread it." Holbrooke recognized this as "a high-risk strategy," but he now thought it was probably going to be essential.

The Secretary of State's big Boeing 707 plane touched down at Wright-Patterson from the whirlwind, 72-hour trip to Osaka around 5:00 that afternoon. Following short meetings with Izetbegovic and Milosevic, Christopher joined the rest of the senior delegates at the Officer's Club for the second lobster dinner hosted by Milosevic and Chris Spirou. In retrospect, this dinner proved to be the short respite before the final drama.[44]

Day Eighteen: Saturday, November 18

That morning the Americans announced that this would be the last weekend of negotiations—setting a deadline for midnight Sunday. Holbrooke had always figured that they might have to take such a "pay or play, drop-dead time" step to close the talks. "These people had fought one another for a long time," he recalled, "and were ready to sit in Dayton for a long time and just argue." That night, the Americans began to prepare the documents and organize a signing ceremony.[45]

WHILE THE PACE INTENSIFIED to finish work on the three most difficult issues—elections, the constitution, and the map—the American team's main concern remained getting the Sarajevo government to cooperate. In an attempt to rally them, Holbrooke asked Menzies to put together a sales pitch. In it, he listed eight ways in which the Bosnians would benefit under what had already been agreed to at Dayton—and which they would lose if the talks failed: (1) a single national government with democratic constitution and central institutions; (2) an economic reconstruction package; (3) a NATO-led implementation force under an American command; (4) a strengthened Federation; (5) a territorial gain from 50 percent of Bosnia to over 55 percent, (6) an extensive civilian police structure, (7) additional human rights protections, and (8) a commitment by Belgrade to normalize relations, including additional confidence building measures. As Carl Bildt acknowledged, "it was hard to imagine a better opportunity [for peace] and better terms." They presented this package to the Bosnians that afternoon.[46]

Christopher and Holbrooke also enlisted several key allies to weigh in with the Bosnians, including British Prime Minister John Major and Turkey's leader, Suleyman Demeriel. As a key Muslim country and NATO partner, Turkey's support for the Bosnians was essential. Ankara and Sarajevo had already begun to coordinate economically and militarily, and Turkey would play a central role in an "equip and train" program. Holbrooke hoped that a phone call from President Demeriel would convince Izetbegovic not to leave Dayton empty-handed.[47]

THAT NIGHT, Milosevic delivered a critical and stunning concession. After dinner, the Serb leader arrived at Holbrooke's VOQ suite unannounced. He wanted to talk about Sarajevo. He thought the city should remain unified, and was prepared to give total control to the Muslim government. "Izetbegovic has earned Sarajevo by not abandoning it," he said, echoing what he had told Silajdzic two days earlier. "He's one tough guy. It's his."[48]

The Bosnians would get Sarajevo. Hearing words that they thought would never be uttered voluntarily from Milosevic's mouth, Christopher and Holbrooke pressed for details. To Milosevic, the deal was simple: in exchange for some minor territorial concessions in northwest Bosnia, the Federation would get total control over Sarajevo. No "Washington, DC" plan, no ethnically divided city—"it's too complicated, it won't work," Milosevic said.

With one dramatic decision, Milosevic simply capitulated on one of the most divisive issues of the negotiations (and delivered on one of the Bosnian and American core goals). By doing so, he also completely sold out his Bosnian Serb colleagues. Holbrooke believed that Milosevic's move had more to do with the internal dynamics of post-Dayton Serbian leadership than a genuine desire to reach agreement with the Bosnians. This was "a strategic decision to break the back of the Pale Serbs," Holbrooke reflected later. Milosevic's move aimed to weaken the current Srpska leaders (especially Karadzic and Krajisnik), who had pledged to make Sarajevo their own, thus preserving Belgrade's power over Serbs in Bosnia. At that time, Holbrooke could not see how Milosevic would convince the Bosnian Serbs to accept this asymmetrical "deal" without having a mutiny on his hands. Clearly aware of this, Milosevic asked the Americans not to tell them anything about this conversation—he would have to break the news to them himself.[49]

Crescendo—Days Nineteen and Twenty:
Sunday and Monday, November 19–20

The deadline was set for midnight Sunday. To create a sense of imminent closure, Christopher and Holbrooke asked the U.S. team to pack their bags, requesting that the other delegations do the same. They also told everyone that the phones would be disconnected the next day, and began to collect bills. As the suitcases lined up outside the American VOQ, it became clear that the other delegations saw right through the bluff. Deadline or not, they didn't take the American threat to leave seriously.[50]

While talks continued at the working levels to finalize the annexes on political and legal issues (which were close to agreement), Christopher and Holbrooke zeroed in on the map. At this late hour, it was clear to everyone—even the Europeans—that the negotiations hinged on territory. This had been a three-year war about the control of land—if they could not reach consensus on a map, then there would be no peace. But for every step forward, they seemed to take two back. That weekend, Milosevic's two significant territorial concessions—on the Gorazde corridor and Sarajevo—came back to haunt them.

For the American sales pitch outlining the reasons why the Bosnians should sign an agreement, the Air Force graphics staff had produced large posterboards detailing the points, headlined as the "Gains of Dayton." After the presentation, Holbrooke and Menzies left the posterboards with the Bosnians, who innocently placed them near the couch in Izetbegovic's suite. On Saturday night, Milosevic entered Izetbegovic's suite for a meeting. From behind the couch, only the top edge of one poster could be seen—what the Serb President saw, in large bold letters, was: "Federation Territory has been increased from 50% to 55% during Dayton Talks."

Milosevic stopped dead in his tracks. His concessions over the last few days had meant that Srpska would get less territory than allotted by the 51–49 Contact Group plan, and his Sarajevo concession made the percentages even more imbalanced. Furious, the Serb President marched right to Holbrooke's suite to complain that the Americans had tricked him (for the past day, the U.S. delegation, knowing they had gotten the Bosnians at least 55 percent of the territory, had deliberately withheld the percentage from Milosevic). Anything other than 51–49 was totally unacceptable, he said. He could compromise a great deal, but "he would not be able to survive or impose a deal," which was not based on the Contact Group map. The Americans knew they had to yield. Christopher had personally signed the 51–49 proposal in 1994, this split had been a key part of Tony Lake's seven points that framed the American initiative earlier that summer, and it had been enshrined by the Geneva principles. In order to prevent Milosevic from reneging on all the territorial concessions he had already made, Christopher and Holbrooke conceded that they would have to shave the map back to 51–49.[51]

Milosevic suggested creating a wider land corridor in northeast Bosnia, near the town of Brcko, the narrowest part of Srpska territory. Under the original 1994 Contact Group map, the Brcko corridor, also referred to as the "Posavina corridor," would narrow to about 30 meters, consisting entirely of an underpass below a railroad bridge. It was unclear whether this incredibly thin "land corridor" would ever be workable, but Izetbegovic insisted on it, reminding Christopher each time they met that he had agreed to this personally. From Milosevic's point of view, a wider corridor would reduce the vulnerability of dividing Srpska in two (and isolating the Banja Luka region within the Muslim–Croat Federation). Holbrooke concluded that, given the immense amount of bloodshed over the corridor, the best they could do would be to maintain the status quo. But in discussions with Milosevic that day, Silajdzic agreed to be flexible on the corridor, and, apparently with the reluctant approval of Izetbegovic, conceded to the Serbs the town of Brcko.

THE MAP TALKS started again at 8:30A.M. Sunday, continued throughout the day, and went long into the night. Christopher and Holbrooke tried all sorts of negotiating combinations—meeting separately with Izetbegovic or Milosevic, bringing the two of them together, or including Silajdzic and Sacirbey. Tudjman returned to Dayton shortly before 10P.M., and Christopher and Holbrooke met with him for an hour. Finally, at around 11:30P.M. Sunday night—a half-hour before the midnight deadline, which they obviously would miss—Holbrooke asked Milosevic and Silajdzic to come to the American conference room. While Holbrooke, Christopher, Wes Clark and others waited down the hall in Holbrooke's suite, Milosevic and Silajdzic set out to finish the map and get the Serbs back to 49 percent. Chris Hill, who was fluent in Serbo-Croatian, moderated the meeting.[52]

Milosevic and Silajdzic began horse-trading, seeking to gain slivers of land, some more valuable symbolically than strategically. Milosevic asked to have Mladic's hometown back, and Silajzdic worked to acquire as many historically Muslim areas as possible. At one point, Silajdzic asked for a town with an old mosque. "Oh Haris," Milosevic said, "didn't you hear those [Bosnian Serb] idiots blew it up." They decided on the final contours of the Gorazde Pocket, and concluded the lines for the "Scotch Road."[53]

WHILE MILOSEVIC AND SILAJDZIC worked on the map, Holbrooke asked to see the draft "failure" statement. Over the last few days, State Department speechwriter Tom Malinowski had written two statements—one praising success, another regretting failure—that Christopher could read at the conclusion of the talks. Malinowski, who kept both drafts with him, had become a sort of Dayton weather vane; others gauged the prospects for an agreement by whether Christopher or Holbrooke wanted to see the "success" or "failure" statement. At this late hour, things looked bad. Holbrooke asked to look at the failure statement, and after giving it a quick read, he threw it up in the air in outrage. As the pages floated to the ground, he said the statement was not "final" enough: the parties needed to be told that the United States was out of the game.

Standing over a computer, a visibly tired and agitated (and some thought crazed) Holbrooke dictated the language to Malinowski while the other

Americans looked on in astonishment. His redraft reflected the frustration of the moment. "To put it simply," his statement concluded, "we gave it our best shot. By their failure to agree, the parties have made it very clear that further U.S. efforts to negotiate a settlement would be fruitless. Accordingly, today marks the end of this initiative . . . the special role we have played in the recent months is over. The leaders here today must live with the consequences of their failure."[54]

BUT THAT NIGHT'S roller-coaster ride was not over. Just as the Americans were preparing to call it quits, the momentum suddenly shifted. Silajdzic had an idea how to get the Serbs up to 49 percent. Milosevic and Silajdzic took their maps and joined Christopher, Holbrooke, Hill, and Clark in the American conference room. The Federation would give Srpska a wide swath of territory in a mountainous, relatively unpopulated area in western Bosnia. Since this egg-shaped area had few towns (which both sides were reluctant to give away), and had been recently captured during the Croat military offensive, the exchange seemed fair. Suddenly, slightly before 4 A.M., Milosevic and Silajdzic shook hands, turned to the Americans, and said they had a deal. Christopher opened a bottle of his favorite California Chardonnay to celebrate the breakthrough.

Silajdzic went off to get Izetbegovic. Minutes later, the Bosnian President appeared, clearly annoyed and sleepy, wearing an overcoat over his pajamas. Meanwhile, Christopher, Holbrooke, Clark, and Hill studied Milosevic and Silajdzic's map. Upon close inspection, they saw a problem. Silajdzic had just given away Croatian-controlled territory, land that Croatia's army had fought for. Even as they drank Christopher's wine, Chris Hill went into the night to get Tudjman.[55]

The Croatian President was asleep, so Hill returned to the American VOQ with Foreign Minister Granic. Granic refused a drink, asking only to see the map. As soon as he saw it, the celebration bubble burst. "Impossible, impossible," Granic yelled, slamming his hand against the map. "Zero point zero zero chance that my President will accept this!" He left abruptly, got Defense Minister Susak, and returned to continue his tirade.

Christopher, Holbrooke and Hill had been worried about how the Croats would react, but did not expect such a venomous outburst from the normally mild-mannered Granic. The foreign minister was outraged that Silajdzic had the audacity to trade territory that the Croats had won back. "You have given away the territory we conquered," Granic screamed at Silajdzic. Trying to salvage something, the Americans went back to work, "shaving a little but here and a little bit there," scrambling to finish by sunrise. While the fuming Granic paced nervously, Holbrooke turned to Izetbegovic and asked what he thought. "I cannot accept this agreement," he said quietly. "I stand with our Croatian allies." At this point, Silajdzic exploded. He had once again been undercut by his President, this time in front of the Americans, Croats, and Milosevic. "I can't take this anymore," he screamed, throwing his papers down on the table. Glowering at Izetbegovic, Silajdzic stormed out of the room. The "agreement" had lasted 37 minutes.[56]

What little optimism that had existed at 4 A.M. was completely shattered. These early morning hours seemed to encapsulate all the anger and passion of the Balkans. Christopher, still remarkably composed and impeccably dressed at such a late hour, went back to his suite, showered, changed clothes, and prepared to return to the drawing board.[57]

SHORTLY AFTER DAWN Monday morning, Christopher and Holbrooke were back at it, talking first with Izetbegovic, then with Milosevic. Since the midnight deadline had long passed, they decided to give it one more day. If things were not solved by Tuesday morning, the talks would be over.

Christopher and Holbrooke decided that after the "37-minute map" debacle, President Clinton needed to get involved. They called Washington and recommended that the President call both Izetbegovic and Tudjman to press them to accept the deal. Christopher believed that Tudjman's "desire to make Croatia part of the community of Western Europe would make a call from President Clinton very effective." Pressure also needed to be brought on the Bosnian President. "Izetbegovic is on the verge of collapse," Tom Donilon, who was with Christopher in Dayton, reported that night to Sandy Vershbow. "It's clear that Izzy has zero commitment to life in one [multi-ethnic] state." From Washington, Tony Lake strongly opposed a Clinton call to Izetbegovic, fearing the appearance of American pressure on the Bosnians to concede. Finally, they decided that Clinton would only call Tudjman and try to get him to agree to the "37-minute map."[58]

"I must say I'm impressed with how much has been achieved in the overall agreement and the benefits that will come to all of the parties," Clinton said to Tudjman that afternoon. "I understand a very difficult trade-off will have to be made to resolve the map. I'm calling you again to ask you to give back a small percentage of non-traditional Croatian territory in western Bosnia to bring the map back in line with the basic 51–49 territorial concept." Surprisingly, Tudjman told the President that the Croats had already made such a proposal, explaining that they hoped to reach final agreement in one to two hours. Thanking Tudjman for his cooperation, Clinton urged him to close things out. "We have to get an agreement. We don't want to go back to the killing."[59]

What Tudjman didn't tell the President was that his proposal had a price— he would only agree if the Bosnians also made their own territorial concessions. Once again, the burden fell on the fractured Sarajevo leadership.

WHILE HOLBROOKE BELIEVED that Clinton's call had given them "a new lease on life," by 9 P.M. Monday night, everyone thought the negotiations would end in failure. The Bosnians still would not budge. The only compromise they offered was to sign an agreement without a map. Carl Bildt recalls that the "Americans believed—not without reason—that they had done more for the Muslims during the talks than anyone could reasonably ask. And everything was now about to collapse because the Muslims were unable to make the transition from a war to peace."[60]

Thinking the talks were over, Christopher, Holbrooke, and their core team gathered in their VOQ and debated how the Americans should be involved in any future diplomatic efforts. Was it in the U.S. national interest to pursue peace if the parties weren't genuinely committed to it? And, crucially, if Dayton failed, how much control would the United States retain over any future negotiations? Holbrooke, exhasted and emotional, was completely fed up. He argued that they should terminate the talks and step aside from Bosnia altogether; as his version of the failure statement read, the United States had given its best shot, and it was time to back off. "Holbrooke doesn't want to restart shuttle diplomacy—he says this should be the end of our initiative," Tom Donilon told Sandy Vershbow by phone. Christopher, on the other hand, felt that they should keep the process going, that they could end what he called the "Dayton Phase" of the talks by agreeing to preserve the cease-fire—which was scheduled to end on December 11 if peace talks failed—and resume shuttle diplomacy (this also reflected the advice President Clinton gave to his team during their meeting the day before the talks began).[61]

THE AMERICANS BELIEVED that the Sarajevo government deserved one last chance. That night, they would give them a final ultimatum, with one hour to decide. It had all come down to this. On a secure phone line, Christopher called President Clinton at 9:30P.M. to ask his approval. "[I] told the President that there was a very substantial chance that we would not succeed," Christopher recalled. "Basically, he gave me authority to do the best I could. In my judgment, trying to keep it going longer there [in Dayton] would set back the ultimate [peace] process."[62]

Shortly after 10P.M., Christopher and Holbrooke met with Izetbegovic, Silajzdic, and Sacirbey in the Bosnian VOQ. Christopher tried to persuade Izetbegovic that the agreement was a good one, and that the Unites States had obtained for them almost everything they had asked for. Yet, the Bosnian President remained unwilling to commit. "Izetbegovic knew I was right," Christopher later wrote, "and he knew that he had within his grasp the peace he wanted." Yet after years of war with the Serbs, "he couldn't quite bring himself to accept an agreement that would result in sharing power with them." Visibly angry, the ordinarily reserved Christopher raised his voice and told Izetbegovic that they had one hour.[63]

Five minutes after Christopher and Holbrooke left the Bosnian VOQ, Silajdzic burst into Holbrooke's suite in a rage, almost completely out of control. "You and Christopher have completely ruined everything," he screamed. "We can't ever give in to a U.S. ultimatum, we can't ever accept it." Firing back, Holbrooke told Silajdzic that the Bosnians had 95 percent of what they sought from Dayton, and that the United States was not about to let him "piss it away." He asked Silajdzic to leave and use the remaining time to get his President to accept this final offer.[64]

As the end of the hour neared, Holbrooke and others put the finishing touches on the failure statement. Based on Christopher and Donilon's suggestions, this draft was a better reflection of Christopher's (and Clinton's) views—that Dayton was largely a success, that the parties should work to build on the progress achieved there and continue the peace process.

Explaining that they had reached an understanding on every major issue but territory, the statement read that "the future of these negotiations is wrapped in the details of the map we are negotiating. But we did not want an agreement that was artificially reached, for such an agreement would surely fall apart." They decided that if the talks indeed failed, which seemed likely, the parties would sign an interim agreement to extend the cease-fire, reaffirm the Eastern Slavonia and Federation agreements, lock-in the commitments made in Geneva and New York, and pledge to resume negotiations at a later date— but not in the United States. "In the final analysis," the draft statement concluded, "as our experience in Dayton makes so very clear, only the parties can make the critical choices that peace requires. We will continue to help them in any way we can."[65]

At 11:30P.M., they sent John Kornblum to the Bosnian VOQ for an answer. Sacirbey told him that the Bosnians would agree to a final settlement only on one new condition: that they get the town of Brcko. The town's status had already been decided—the Serbs were supposed to get it. Kornblum gave the draft failure statement to Sacirbey. As Kornblum later recalled: "I said that we had been trying valiantly all day, [but] there just seemed to be too many issues that could not be bridged, in particular, that the Bosnians had just been coming up with one point after another." Sacirbey refused to accept the deal without Brcko, and Kornblum told him that the talks would be over the next morning.

Kornblum returned to tell the rest of the U.S. delegation that the Bosnians would not agree without getting Brcko. Holbrooke called Christopher— who, despite having shown amazing stamina for someone 70 years old, had gone off to his Hope Hotel suite for some well-deserved rest—to tell him "it's over but it's not over," pending a miracle concession on Brcko. "I recommend you get some sleep, and we'll keep working it from here." Christopher, though, felt that the introduction of Brcko into the endgame was "finally the [deal]-breaker." After long hours of negotiating in other areas, this "new issue, in addition to [Izetbegovic's] general reluctance, might be the final straw," he later recalled.[66]

The End—Day Twenty-One: Tuesday, November 21

At daybreak, the weary negotiators awoke to a fresh blanket of snow on the ground. It seemed a fitting note to end on. They had scheduled a press conference for 11:00A.M. Everyone finished packing, and several in the U.S. delegation met at Packy's for a last breakfast. Wes Clark remembers "thinking that at least the failure meant that our military wouldn't have to wrestle with the stresses and strains of ground operations in Bosnia" a feeling that many of President Clinton's political advisors shared. When told during the White House morning staff meeting that the talks would end without agreement, Mack McLarty, the President's Counselor and his oldest friend, passed a note to a colleague that summed up this mood: "Like the AlkaSeltzer commercial— oh what a relief it is!"[67]

But soon word spread that Milosevic had gone to see Tudjman to suggest that the two of them sign the agreement without Izetbegovic. Holbrooke wasn't sure whether this was acceptable, but at least it provided another opening to keep talking. He knew it would put incredible pressure on Izetbegovic—enough so that he might actually break down and sign. Holbrooke notified Christopher, and then joined the rest of the American delegation for the 8A.M. staff meeting—which was supposed to be their "shut-down" meeting.

The Americans debated the merits of Milosevic's gambit. Christopher strongly opposed the idea. He felt that it directly contradicted their goal of only accepting a comprehensive peace. The talks had gone too far to give up and exclude the Bosnians. Moreover, from a legal perspective, the Secretary argued that you could not have a viable contract with only two of three parties as signatories. And, finally, he was uncomfortable with "leaving Izetbegovic twisting in the wind."[68]

As they discussed what to do, Holbrooke's wife, Kati Marton, burst into the room to tell them that a coatless Milosevic was standing alone outside in the snowy parking lot. He wanted to see Christopher and Holbrooke immediately. Marton ran out in the quad to catch Milosevic (who, finding no one, had already turned around to leave), bringing him back to Holbrooke's suite as the American staffers shuffled out. In the room alone with Christopher and Holbrooke, Milosevic made his proposal that the Serbs and Croats sign without Izetbegovic. Christopher rejected it. Milosevic then made a final offer: that the status of Brcko be deferred for later, pending the decision of an appointed international arbitrator.[69]

Christopher liked the idea and hoped that it would be enough to bring the Bosnians back. "Suddenly [Milosevic] was prepared to agree to arbitration and did not insist on trying to define the [Brcko] corridor, [which would] enable us to reach agreement." Milosevic asked Christopher to be the arbitrator. Christopher explained that he couldn't be, but would support an arbitration process headed by a respected international lawyer. The Secretary then asked Roberts Owen to draw up the language for an arbitration clause for Brcko, to be decided within one year. Meanwhile, Christopher and Holbrooke went to see Tudjman.[70]

Tudjman, hearing Milosevic's arbitration offer, agreed and, banging his fist on the table, said that they had to "get peace now" by forcing Izetbegovic to accept. Christopher and Holbrooke then walked through the light snow to the Bosnian VOQ where they met with Izetbegovic, Silajdzic and Sacirbey. As they talked, over 700 journalists waited at the press center across the base, all reporting imminent failure. The press conference was scheduled for 11A.M.; it was already after 9A.M.[71]

The two American diplomats outlined Milosevic's latest proposal to the three Bosnians. Everything agreed to at Dayton would be implemented, they explained, except for Brcko, whose future would be decided by arbitration.[72] Christopher said that they had run out of time for new deadlines. They needed a response immediately.

After a long pause, Izetbegovic said "it's an unjust peace." Then, forcing the words out, he quietly muttered his answer: "but my people need peace." The Bosnians had agreed. Holbrooke, realizing that things could quickly unravel if he and Christopher stuck around to talk about details, whispered to the Secretary, "let's get out of here fast!"[73]

Christopher and Holbrooke immediately called President Clinton, who despite his political advisors' apprehensions, was pleased. He said that he was ready to fly out to Dayton to participate in the announcement. They recommended that the President stay in Washington to make the announcement from the Rose Garden. "Mr. President," Holbrooke said, "you don't want to be anywhere near these people today. They are wild." The President said he would make the announcement as soon as possible, in order to lock-in the agreement and avoid any last minute shenanigans before the afternoon signing ceremony in Dayton.[74]

SHORTLY BEFORE NOON in Washington, President Clinton stepped into the White House Rose Garden, as Christopher, Holbrooke and Donilon watched on a television in the Secretary of State's Hope Hotel suite. "After nearly four years of 250,000 people killed, 2 million refugees, and atrocities that have appalled people all over the world, the people of Bosnia finally have a chance to turn from the horror of war to the promise of peace," the President said. With an agreement achieved, he called on the American people to support implementing peace—particularly through the use of U.S. troops in IFOR. "We are at a decisive moment," he said. "The parties have chosen peace. Americans must choose peace as well. Now that a detailed settlement has been reached, NATO will rapidly complete its planning for IFOR . . . Now American leadership—together with our allies—is needed to make this peace real and enduring. Our values, our interests, and our leadership all over the world are at stake."[75]

In Dayton, Christopher and Holbrooke briefed the Contact Group representatives on the details of the final compromises. Throughout the tumultuous past few days, the Europeans had been largely isolated from the Americans' last-ditch negotiating effort (even more shut out than usual), and at best, had heard only rumors and snippets of details about an agreement.

After Holbrooke and Christopher's quick briefing for the Contact Group, they joined the three Balkan Presidents in the Hope Hotel for a celebratory lunch. President Clinton called, and over a speakerphone, congratulated the group on the accomplishment. "Following this long, scratchy negotiation," Christopher reflected in his unassuming way, "there was an aura of some modest good feeling."[76]

THE CEREMONY began at 3 P.M. in the B–29 room, in the same place where the conference had opened three long weeks before. The small circular table from the opening ceremony had been replaced by a long table where the three Balkan Presidents sat alongside Christopher, Holbrooke and Bildt on a dais facing an enormous crowd. The room seemed twice as packed as three weeks earlier, with hundreds of journalists wedging into any tiny space they could find. While Christopher and Holbrooke had advised against President

Clinton's attendance, they did ask several senior Washington officials, including General John Shalikashvili and Deputy Secretary of Defense John White, to fly out to Dayton to join them.

Consistent with almost every other step in this process, the ceremony went forward while chaos raged on the sidelines. Shortly before the event began, Milosevic presented the maps to the Bosnian Serbs. Until that moment, they didn't know that he had given away Sarajevo. When Krajisnik saw the map—and the fact that not only had he lost Sarajevo, but also his cherished villa in western Bosnia—he fainted. When asked what happened, Milosevic chortled, "he went into a coma." The Bosnian Serbs were outraged by what Milosevic had done—not only on the map, but also on the elections and constitution. They refused to initial the agreement, and would not participate in any part of the closing ceremony. Milosevic promised that he would get their signature within a week.[77]

"Today, you will leave Dayton with a comprehensive agreement in hand," Secretary Christopher said to the overflow crowd, while the three Presidents at the dais looked on. "On this Thanksgiving weekend, our joint work has made it possible for the people of Bosnia to spend New Year's Day in peace for the first time in four years." Then, in a scene that filled the next day's airwaves and newspapers around the world, the three Presidents initialed the Dayton Accords.

ALTHOUGH THE CEREMONY that afternoon reflected a sense of relief and accomplishment, everyone recognized that the challenges ahead were daunting. Indeed, the American diplomatic effort had brought a comprehensive agreement, but its value was worth nothing more than the paper it was written on until its terms were implemented on the ground. President Clinton expressed as much that morning from the Rose Garden, and Christopher and Holbrooke reiterated this point that afternoon in Dayton. "The agreements and territorial arrangements initialed today are a huge step forward, the biggest by far since the war began," Holbrooke said in his concluding remarks. "But ahead lies an equally daunting task: implementation. On every page of the many complicated documents and annexes initialed here today lie challenges to both sides to set aside their enmities, their differences, which are still raw with open wounds . . . To make [peace] work is our next and greatest challenge." Secretary Christopher echoed this sentiment. "This victory will not be secure unless we all get to work to ensure that the promise of this moment is realized. The parties have put a solemn set of commitments on paper. In the coming days and weeks, they will have to put them into practice— extending them to every mayor, every soldier, every police officer in their territory."[78]

THREE WEEKS LATER, President Clinton joined the rest of the Contact Group leaders in Paris to witness the formal signing of the Dayton Accords. Soon after, U.S. General George Joulwan ordered 60,000 NATO forces to deploy to Bosnia. Over four years after then-Secretary of State James Baker proclaimed that the Unite States "didn't have a dog" in the Yugoslav fight,

20,000 American troops were on the ground in Bosnia as part of this NATO force. The Clinton Administration had indeed gone over the Balkan "waterfall," as Bob Frasure had warned it would, but it had steered a course that few thought was possible during the summer of 1995. With Dayton, there was now genuine hope that a lasting peace could be accomplished and a new Bosnia could be made. Implementing Dayton's terms would not be simple; as Warren Zimmermann aptly noted, the agreement "mirrored all the complexities and contradictions" of the Balkans.[79] American negotiators had spent over 18 weeks preparing this complex blueprint for peace. Now, working with the Europeans and the rest of the international community, they had to set forth and build it.

Epilogue: America and Dayton

The successful conclusion of the Dayton talks ended one of the most intensive diplomatic undertakings the United States had pursued since the end of the Cold War (comparable efforts up to that point were the 1989–1990 Two-Plus-Four process that led to Germany's unification, the 1990–1991 effort to put together the Gulf War coalition, and the ongoing Middle East peace process). Although the guns fell silent, events in Bosnia continued to occupy the attention of senior officials in Washington for years. In the weeks after Dayton, 20,000 U.S. soldiers were on their way to Bosnia and a massive international reconstruction effort began. A decade later, the United States and its European allies remain deeply involved there. While the nature of their commitment has changed—for example, in 2004 the European Union took over NATO's security role, and American military forces withdrew—they still have a tremendous stake in Bosnia's success.

Looking forward, the story of America's efforts to end the Bosnia war and establish the foundation for a new state offers many lessons, such as how the United States can work to solve conflicts; the improvisation of shuttle diplomacy and international peace talks; the relationship between military force and diplomatic negotiations; managing relations with key allies; and how to rebuild societies and governments torn apart by war. Today, with the United States engaged in major peace-building and reconstruction efforts in Kosovo, Afghanistan and Iraq, as well as potentially in places like the Palestinian territories and elsewhere, many of the lessons of Bosnia's peace process endure.

This diplomatic history also helps answer important questions about the implications of Clinton Administration's engagement in Bosnia, not only for the future of that country, but also for the future of American foreign policy. With the availability of new evidence about the Clinton Administration's internal decision-making and the course and conduct of its diplomatic effort, as well as the benefit of further perspective, several questions warrant deeper analysis.

First, why in the summer of 1995 did the United States government reverse months of indecision and determined distance from the Bosnia conflict to launch an all-out effort to end the war? Second, once engaged, why did it succeed? Third, what were the Dayton Agreement's consequences for Bosnia—in hindsight, what can we learn from these negotiations about the benefits or flaws of the agreement as it has been implemented? Finally, what did the effort to bring peace to Bosnia mean for President Clinton's foreign policy, and America's role in Europe?

GOING OVER THE BOSNIA WATERFALL

The first puzzle is why President Clinton and his team finally decided to break away from their "muddle through" approach toward Bosnia in August 1995 to pursue a major diplomatic initiative. Was this the result of the foresight and determination of strong policymakers? Or, to paraphrase Winston Churchill, was it an instance of the United States finally doing the right thing after exhausting all of the alternatives? Did events push the American government to do what it would never do otherwise?

The answer is a little of each. The Clinton Administration decided to create its "endgame strategy" for Bosnia and implement it when it did because of five factors that, like a perfect storm, came together in the summer of 1995: first, the potential downfall of the UN mission in Bosnia, triggering the U.S. military commitment to assist with withdrawal; second, the July 1995 massacre in Srebrenica; third, the destructive impact both of these events had on the NATO alliance and the Clinton Administration's larger goals in Europe; fourth, domestic political pressures, especially congressional efforts to lift unilaterally the arms embargo against Bosnia; and fifth, the Croatian military offensive into western Bosnia and the Krajina region. While other analysts have offered similar explanations, the new historical evidence detailed here provides a more complete picture about how these factors worked together to influence the Clinton Administration into acting when it did.[1]

THE POLICY TRANSFORMATION started when events in Bosnia began to spin out of control. Throughout the spring and summer of 1995, American policymakers watched with great concern as the United Nations mission there crumbled. The Bosnian Serbs' aggressive hostage-taking of European troops capped months of American frustration with the UN mission, especially the "dual key" decision-making structure for NATO airstrikes. But the Clinton Administration's deepest fear was the consequences of the U.S. commitment to help the UN forces withdraw, as set forth in Op-Plan 40104 that outlined a deployment of 20,000 American troops.

For over two years, the Clinton Administration had worked to prevent putting ground troops in Bosnia. Yet because of the commitment to help their allies—a commitment that the president did not fully appreciate and certainly came to regret—this was exactly the situation they had placed themselves in. Throughout May and June 1995, the Clinton team worked to convince the Europeans to keep their forces on the ground and bolster the UN mission. They also conducted an intense internal debate about how long these efforts could last, and whether it made more sense to push UNPROFOR out and get the mission over with. Finally, they began to consider ways to end the crisis diplomatically, pursuing discussions—at first outside the formal decision-making process, and only later through normal interagency deliberations—that eventually led to its "endgame strategy."

As these debates were getting underway, the crisis in Srebrenica shocked the Clinton Administration and clarified the difficult choices it faced. The United Nations had been unable to stop the Bosnian Serbs from massacring thousands of innocent civilians in this so-called safe area, and because of the "dual-key" decision-making structure, neither had NATO. The Srebrenica crisis did three things: it provided further proof that the UN mission was barely hanging on, increasing the likelihood of its withdrawal; it placed other "safe areas" in immediate danger, forcing policymakers to figure out how to protect them from suffering a similar fate; and it showed the fundamental impotence of the West's policy, humiliating the Clinton Administration and its European allies, compelling them to respond.

The failure of the UN mission and the horrors of the Srebrenica massacre were two reasons why President Clinton's senior advisors began crafting a new approach in the summer of 1995. Also important is how these factors contributed to a third: the danger that these events—and the costs of a failed Bosnia policy—would destroy the Clinton Administration's ambitions for the NATO alliance and its larger goals in Europe. President Clinton's highest policy priority in Europe was to strengthen NATO and work toward enlarging it to include states from the former Warsaw Pact. But events in Bosnia directly threatened the Alliance's credibility (as well as America's leadership of NATO). The desire to maintain NATO's unity was the reason that the Administration had committed to assisting with the withdrawal of European troops from the UN mission in the first place (and why it felt that it could not renege on the commitment); it was why the United States refused to overrule European objections to lifting the UN arms embargo against Bosnia; it was also the reason that President Clinton proved reluctant to push harder for NATO airstrikes and eliminating the "dual-key."

But the prospect of Bosnia plunging into complete chaos overshadowed all of these concerns, threatening the very premise of President Clinton's policy. In the absence of America's leadership, countries like France began to assert their role, creating even move pressure on the Administration. As Secretary of State Christopher asked, "did NATO have a mission worth enlarging for if it could not solve Bosnia?"[2] The answer of course was no, and the Clinton Administration understood that by solving Bosnia it would prove that NATO remained relevant—and that American leadership remained essential. It used the July 1995 London conference to push through a bold new NATO policy, forging Alliance unity to threaten the Bosnian Serbs with sustained airstrikes. It also accelerated its deliberations about pursuing a diplomatic solution to the crisis.

This explains why President Clinton and his team began to change course and create their "endgame strategy" to end the war, but not why they pushed their new diplomatic initiative when they did in August 1995, rather than waiting until September or October, or even after the 1996 presidential campaign. The Congressional vote to lift the arms embargo against Bosnia is one reason for this timing; Croatia's successful military offensive is the other. While President Clinton had pledged to block the legislation to lift the arms embargo unilaterally, Congress had enough votes to override his veto. Clinton understood that to prevent this—and to protect himself from a major political defeat on the eve of an election year—he needed to prove to Congress that he had a better alternative. With Congress going out of session for the summer recess in early August and not returning until after the Labor Day holiday in early September, the President and his advisors knew they had a few weeks to act. Then, in late July, the day before the U.S. Senate voted to lift the arms embargo, Croatia launched its successful attack on the Bosnian Serbs around Bihac. Soon after it rolled into Krajina, creating new momentum on the ground against the Serbs. This military offensive, combined with the likelihood that Congress would vote to override the President's veto when it returned to Washington, created the precise window of opportunity in August 1995 through which the Clinton Administration launched its peace initiative.

THE SOURCES OF SUCCESS

While this answers why the Clinton Administration decided to pursue a diplomatic initiative and acted when it did, the second question is why these efforts succeeded in creating the Dayton agreement. For three years, many other diplomats had tried and failed to bring peace to Bosnia. What made this process different? Reflecting on this history, these negotiations succeeded because of the confluence of four factors: first, NATO's bombing campaign against the Bosnian Serbs; second, the success of Croatia and Bosnia's military offensive; third, the decision to simplify the negotiations by forcing Milosevic to speak for the Bosnian Serbs and relying on the Muslim–Croat Federation; and fourth, the ingenuity and tenacity (and sometimes unique powers of persuasion) of the lead American negotiator, Richard Holbrooke, and his talented shuttle team.[3]

The Clinton Administration's success at giving new backbone to NATO—and its efforts to ensure that the Alliance followed through on its threats after the Bosnian Serbs violated the "London Rules" by attacking Sarajevo—is the first reason the Dayton process succeeded. After months of resisting pinprick attacks and dividing the United States and Europe by exploiting the "dual-key" decision-making structure, the Bosnian Serbs were rattled by the sustained air campaign. With the bombing, "the psychological balance had changed," Madeleine Albright later wrote. "The Bosnian Serbs could no longer act with impunity, while NATO was no longer barred from using its power."[4]

This use of force gave Holbrooke's shuttle team leverage that previous diplomatic efforts lacked. As Christopher describes it, they had the "full fury of NATO military power behind them" giving credibility to their efforts in both Belgrade and Sarajevo. The bombing also helped boost the Bosnian government and got it to engage in the process. The American negotiators (and their counterparts in Washington) worked to coordinate the air campaign with their diplomacy as best they could, pushing first for the bombing to begin, then asking for a pause to test the Bosnian Serbs, and then demanding its resumption. Looking back, this military resolve had a decisive impact on the negotiations during at least two moments: when Milosevic forged the "Patriarch letter" shortly after the bombing began; and two weeks later, when the Bosnian Serbs agreed to the terms for a cease-fire.[5]

GENERAL WESLEY CLARK recalls that a few weeks after Dayton, Milosevic took him aside and said that the Americans "must be pleased that NATO won this war . . . it was your bombs and your missiles, your high technology that defeated us . . . we Serbs never had a chance against you." Clark told the Serb leader that he was wrong, "you lost [the war] to the Muslims and Croats."[6] This exchange helps illustrate the influence of NATO's air campaign on Milosevic. But it also is a reminder that Dayton also owes its success to a second factor, the Muslim–Croat military victories on the ground.

After helping open the window of opportunity for the American diplomatic initiative with its initial strike against the Serbs in August 1995, Croatia's military gains, along with the Bosnian Muslim victories, continued to bolster the negotiations throughout the shuttle diplomacy. Like NATO's bombing, the Serb military losses changed the situation psychologically, with the Croats and Muslims exacting revenge against the aggressors. It also increased the pressure on Milosevic to strike a deal. He not only faced the prospect of his clients losing all the ground that they had captured, but also the destabilizing impact of the massive refugee crisis sparked by the thousands of Bosnian Serbs who had fled the fighting to Serbia.

The Clinton Administration had initially worried about the consequences of a Croatian offensive against the Serbs, warning President Tudjman and his aides in July 1995 not to attack Krajina for fear of triggering a wider Balkan war. But after Croatia's lightning success, they quickly realized that the campaign worked to their advantage. As Holbrooke explained it at the time, the map negotiations were taking place on the battlefield, with the Muslims and Croats winning back territory by force that would be hard for them to get back through dialogue. The American negotiators improvised their approach to fit what was happening on the ground and repeatedly sought (with some success) to influence the battlefield strategy to fit the negotiating strategy, coordinating with the Croats and Bosnians about what territory to take and, importantly, warning them that certain areas should be off limits. At the end of September, as the military campaign's successes decreased and tensions between the "allied" Muslims and Croats increased, the Americans pushed the parties to end their operations and agree to a cease-fire. By the time the fighting stopped, many of territorial issues had been solved, leaving the most difficult ones—like Sarajevo, the land corridor for Gorazde, or the town of Brcko—for Dayton.[7]

TOGETHER WITH NATO's bombing campaign, the ground offensive gave the negotiations the military backing that made Dayton possible. But the peace agreement was an achievement of diplomacy, not a military triumph.

Force alone did not end the Bosnian war. It worked alongside several key diplomatic decisions, the most important of which was to simplify the negotiations by reducing the number of parties involved from five (Croatia, Bosnian Croats, Serbs, Bosnian Serbs, and the Bosnian Muslims) to two (the Muslim–Croat Federation and Serbia).

This was the rationale behind the "Milosevic strategy" to demand that the Serb leader alone speak for his Bosnian Serb clients and, when necessary, force them into agreement. Originally proposed by Robert Frasure, this approach was not uncontroversial, as some senior officials and most Europeans (although not Bildt) thought that it was wrong not to deal with one of the parties (Pale) directly involved in the conflict. But the strategy looked more attractive after the two most powerful Bosnian Serb leaders—Karadzic and Mladic—were indicted for war crimes, which allowed the Americans to bar them from Dayton on international legal grounds. The Americans also believed that they needed to increase a sense of accountability, and that they had greater leverage over Milosevic with better carrots and sticks (sanctions relief or further isolation) to get him to cooperate. Milosevic responded to this pressure, forging the "Patriarch Agreement" that effectively cut the Bosnian Serbs out of the negotiations over their future. During the few times that the Americans ever dealt with the Bosnian Serbs (including two show-downs in Belgrade) Milosevic was always there to strong-arm them when needed. U.S. negotiators did not worry how to bring the Bosnian Serbs along—all that mattered to them was that Milosevic was on board.

A similar logic drove the American effort to create and then strengthen the Muslim–Croat Federation. Although this strategy proved far more frustrating and less successful, it still contributed to the negotiation's success. The Clinton Administration had engineered the Federation in 1994 to unify the Bosnian Muslim and Croats against a common enemy. Whenever the two sides worked together—whether at the negotiating table or on the battlefield—their alliance proved very effective. Yet the Americans were forced to put forth an enormous amount of energy to hold the Federation together, often spending as much time mediating differences between the Croats and Muslims as they did between them and Milosevic. At the same time, this approach, along with the "Milosevic strategy," presented the Clinton Administration with a moral dilemma and created problems for implementation, both of which will be discussed below.

THE FOURTH FACTOR that made Dayton different from previous diplomatic efforts—and was a key part of its success—was the many decisions made by Richard Holbrooke and his core negotiating team. Looking back, historians can sometimes overemphasize the importance of individuals on particular outcomes and overlook larger trends at work. To be sure, during the Dayton process, such events as NATO's bombing campaign or the Croat offensive were far beyond the efforts of a few individuals, even though the Americans worked to manipulate these events to their advantage. Like most major nego-tiations, there were many individuals involved: the Balkan parties, the Contact Group, NATO and UN leaders, and American civilian and military officials in Washington. Yet one cannot reflect back on this history and fail to recognize the crucial role that such key individuals as Holbrooke and his shuttle team played in deciding not only the substance of what was or was not negotiated, but the ways these talks were conducted and how they turned out.

Several Washington officials—especially Tony Lake and Madeleine Albright—deserve credit for acting during the summer of 1995 to bring order and discipline to a policymaking process that had broken down, to push for a new diplomatic initiative, and to get President Clinton and the European allies on board. Given the chaos that preceded the launch of this effort—with endless and inconclusive meetings and confusion about America's military commitment to help UN troops withdraw—that is no small accomplishment. But the policy they handed to the negotiators was mainly a broad set of goals, not a plan; it established only the most basic guidelines, some of which (like urging the Bosnians to give up specific territories) were discarded immediately. Nor did this initiative outline how to execute the negotiations going forward—such as how to conduct shuttle diplomacy, involve the Europeans or the Russians, or whether and when to conduct a peace conference. Once the peace mission was underway, Holbrooke and his team decided nearly every aspect of the timing, course, structure and content of these fast-moving negotiations. The support they received from President Clinton, Warren Christopher, William Perry, General Shalikashvili, Strobe Talbott, Sandy Berger, Lake, Albright, and many other senior officials allowed them to assert such control and were essential to their success, and the intervention of many officials (especially Christopher) at critical moments proved decisive.

When compared with the role of negotiators (below the level of President and Secretary of State) in other major American diplomatic efforts to solve conflicts—such as ending the war in Vietnam, the work to bring peace to Northern Ireland, or the many twists and turns of the Middle East peace process—the degree of control Holbrooke and his team had over both the process and substance of these negotiations was rare, if not unprecedented. That said, they did not drive every decision, nor did they win every bureaucratic fight—their inability to convince their Washington colleagues to be more flexible on economic sanctions against Milosevic is one example, and their unsuccessful effort to create a more robust, "maximalist" mandate for IFOR's military implementation is another.

Yet throughout the shuttles and especially at Dayton, Holbrooke and his team made countless decisions—both large and small, and often improvised without any guidance from their superiors in Washington—that helped bring peace to Bosnia and shape its future. They devised and negotiated the step-by-step process that led to the Geneva and New York agreements. They structured the Dayton text as a framework agreement with annexes, decided what the annexes would be, and negotiated their content. They determined the schedule for the talks, and successfully advocated (over the strong opposition of many) to hold the peace conference in the United States. They championed the "Milosevic strategy," worked hard to keep the Federation together, and used breakthroughs like the Greece-Macedonia deal to create a sense of success. They lobbied for NATO's bombing campaign, negotiated the terms of its end that lifted the siege of Sarajevo, advised the Muslims and Croats about the course of their military offensive, and eventually pushed them stop it. And most important, they aimed far beyond simply formalizing a cease-fire or a basic agreement, instead pursuing a comprehensive settlement that aimed to solve the conflict and create a detailed blueprint for the governance of a new Bosnia.

ALL OF THESE decisions helped make Dayton possible and influenced the agreement's outcome. But given what we now know, one must ask whether in some instances better choices could have been made. If these negotiations reflect what Holbrooke describes as the "jazz" of diplomacy—variations on a theme—then did some of the riffs prove to be off-key? For instance, was it a mistake to press the Muslims and Croats to end their military offensive when they did, rather than let the campaign run its course? Perhaps allowing the ground campaign to continue for a few more days and weeks would have made the Serbs even more desperate for a deal, strengthening the bargaining position of the Muslims and Croats. At the time, Clinton Administration officials debated which traffic lights to flash, with Washington policymakers for more anxious for a quick cease-fire than the shuttle team. Yet since the Muslims and Croats had already taken back significant territory (some of which they ended up returning at Dayton)—and since the campaign itself was starting to increase tensions between the Muslim and Croat leaderships, endangering that critical relationship—it made sense for the Americans to push for a ceasefire when they did, before Banja Luka would have fallen.

Also important were the choices the negotiators made about which issues to include or exclude from the talks. For example, in addition to solving the problem of Bosnia, the Clinton Administration's "endgame strategy" aimed for a regional settlement, including issues like a deal on Eastern Slavonia (which was an important part of Dayton), while the Holbrooke team, with no guidance from Washington, improvised a solution to the Greece-Macedonia dispute (which was not directly related to the talks but gave the shuttle team valuable momentum). Both of these accomplishments helped bolster the overall goal of ending the war. However, for the same reason, American negotiators decided not to make other issues—like seeking an end to Milosevic's repression within Kosovo, the small Muslim-majority province of Serbia—a part of the peace settlement. Since NATO fought a massive air war to end Milosevic's stranglehold on Kosovo less than four years later, it is worth asking if this was the right choice, and whether the 1999 conflict could have been prevented if the United States had dealt with the issue at Dayton.

The decision not to deal with Kosovo at Dayton seems like the right choice because it was probably the only choice. Excluding Kosovo, like including Eastern Slavonia and Greece–Macedonia, helped the Bosnia peace process. As Holbrooke describes it, Izetbegovic and Tudjman had "zero interest" in Kosovo. Carl Bildt agrees. "There is no way we could have done

Kosovo at Dayton," he recalled. "Kosovo would have broken the back of that camel very fast." While the Americans pressed Milosevic on the subject several times during the talks, they had to use their leverage on many other issues to end the war that was ongoing, instead of the one that had yet to happen. In retrospect, most troubling for Kosovo's future was not what happened at Dayton, but what came after. Milosevic's involvement in Bosnia did not end in November 1995—since the United States and the Europeans continued to need and use their leverage over him to help implement the agreement, they had less ability to influence his behavior in Kosovo, and the consequences were tragic.[8]

Perhaps the most consequential decision—or rather, series of decisions—worth reexamining are those that shaped the kind of comprehensive peace settlement Dayton sought to achieve. The agreement went for beyond a cessation of hostilities, and given the sustained international attention Bosnia has required since November 1995, it must be asked whether it made sense to seek such an ambitious outcome. To answer this, one must assess Dayton's success by its own high standards and address some of the difficult challenges of implementation.

DAYTON AND BOSNIA

Looking back with the advantage of ten years perspective, did Dayton meet its aims?

The first answer is an unqualified yes. The fundamental objective of the Clinton Administration's intervention in Bosnia was to end the war, and Dayton did that. For three years, Bosnia was the worst conflict in Europe since the end of World War II; for ten years, it has been peaceful. That is no small accomplishment. What many feared about a post–Dayton Bosnia—especially worries about renewed fighting between the parties that would draw the NATO-led implementation force into a quagmire and kill or wound many American troops—never came true. Hundreds of thousands of refugees have returned to their homes and towns. Cities like Sarajevo have come back to life and are beginning to thrive again. Bosnia's economy, although still propped up by the international community, is improving. The key figures of the Dayton process have left the scene—Tudjman and Izetbegovic have passed away, and Milosevic sits in jail in The Hague. A new generation of leaders in Bosnia and throughout the region is emerging, many of whom embrace the future of hope and opportunity that the negotiators in Dayton envisioned.

But forging peace among Bosnia's three nationalist factions was only one part of the Dayton Accords. The other goal was far more challenging and controversial—to create a single, democratic, tolerant, multiethnic state. Some commentators and even senior officials believed that this objective was unrealistic and unwise to pursue—Clinton's own CIA Director, John Deutch, describes Dayton's ambitious aims as "fantastical" and one of the U.S. Administration's "failing(s)." As Carl Bildt explains, Dayton "is the most ambitious document of its kind . . . a traditional peace treaty aims at ending a war . . . while here it is a question of setting up a state on the basis of little more than the ruins and rivalries of a bitter war."[9]

By this measure, Dayton's record is mixed. While Bosnia's political evolution has had some significant successes, including several nationwide elections, it is hardly a smoothly functioning state. In fact, it remains deeply corrupt and troubled. To some extent, this was expected: no one was more familiar with the agreement's weaknesses and shortcomings than the diplomats who negotiated it. Since 1995, many of these officials involved, including the lead negotiator himself, have been very candid about its flaws. They understood that their ambitious goal of creating a unified Bosnia at peace with itself would be very hard to fulfill quickly, if at all. They knew that creating a peace agreement was not the same thing as producing peace, accepting that much would depend on decisions made by those responsible for implementation. And they realized that like any complex negotiation, Dayton contained many compromises that were necessary to end the war but would make implementing a settlement difficult. Some of these challenges were inherent in the governing structures the agreement created, others stemmed from the specifics of its implementation. What follows is a broad overview of what these challenges are, and why they exist.

Unification or Partition?

If Dayton's first goal was to end the war, its second goal was to maintain Bosnia as a single state. Bosnia has not broken apart, but relations among its three ethnic groups remains tense. In too many ways, Bosnia still operates as two semi-independent entities—the Republika Srpska and the Muslim–Croat Federation. This ethnic tension is fundamental to Dayton; in many ways, this was unavoidable once the Contact Group had agreed to the 51–49 percent territorial split in 1994. While many parts of the agreement sought to push the country together, other parts work to pull the country apart. Because of this, while Bosnia is one country, the core question of the war—what Bosnia's identity should be—remains unresolved.

One reason for this is that the central government created by the agreement remains too weak. Holbrooke realized this almost instantly after Dayton and has regretted it ever since. The Americans always wanted a stronger central government, but each of the Balkan leaders resisted. They all had powers they wanted Dayton to enshrine. The result is that the agreement created many institutions that have not worked very well. As Holbrooke puts it, "the good news" about Dayton was that "joint institutions actually existed; the bad news was that they barely functioned." The agreement's dizzying array of overlapping jurisdictions and authorities at the national, entity (state), and local level, allocated among two entities and three ethnic groups, made governing very difficult. Given this, as Holbrooke told the Bosnians in a speech in 2000, "even the simplest governing decisions are very difficult . . . the agreement allows the extremist, separatist parties to block legislative approval of many basic needs . . . [and] to hold up reforms and progress."[10]

Dayton also institutionalized ethnic politics. In order to agree to a deal, the Muslim, Croat, and Serb leaders demanded that they would each be guaranteed a piece of the pie, embroidering ethnicity into the machinery of government. Because power within the state structures has been divided along ethnic lines (allowing each ethnic group to hold a certain number of leadership posts, etc.), rejectionists have had ample opportunities to undermine Bosnia's common institutions.

Holbrooke regrets that the agreement gave so much power to ethnic groups instead of encouraging an issue-based, inter-ethnic political process." The Americans especially lament allowing the Bosnian Serbs to call their entity Republika Srpska. Some assert that an agreement would have been impossible without this concession—Carl Bildt explains that Republica Srpska was "the essence of the deal." Yet Holbrooke believes that, in retrospect, Izetbegovic was right and that they should have tried harder to "cram a different name down Milosevic's throat."[11]

Another reason for the weak central government and virulent ethnic politics is that those least invested in Dayton were the ones most responsible for implementing it. By design, the negotiations left out significant factions within each party who remained opposed to the idea of Bosnia as a single, multiethnic state.

For example, as discussed above, one of the key reasons the United States succeeded in getting a deal was that it simplified the negotiating process by concentrating on Milosevic and the Federation. Yet this strategy placed significant obstacles in the way of successful implementation. Because many aspects of Dayton were imposed on the parties within Bosnia—by Milosevic, by Tudjman, and by the United States and the Europeans—political reconciliation has proved very difficult. The Bosnian Serbs and Croats claimed that they had nothing to do with the agreement, and some Bosnian Muslims argued that they had been coerced into it.

Nearly every step of progress in Dayton's implementation has thus required a heavy hand from the outside. Most of the attributes of a single state (everything from a common currency, passports, and license plates to a state border and customs service) have come only after significant intervention by the international community or U.S.-induced pressure from Zagreb or Belgrade. Importantly, each externally mandated decision has been respected. Yet looking back, few doubt that Dayton should have sought to do more to reconcile the differences between these opposing visions of Bosnia, rooting out those rejectionists who still stand in the way of tolerance and multiethnicity.

Pressure for Bosnia's continued division is also fueled by what Holbrooke has called "our biggest mistake at Dayton"—allowing the country to have, in effect, three separate armies—one of which is armed and trained by the United States. Even though "equip and train" for the Bosnian Muslims defied the unifying logic of Dayton's goals, the program was a key carrot to get the Sarajevo government to agree. Throughout the negotiations,

Holbrooke and his team tried to obligate NATO to take on the task of disarming these armies to consolidate the force, but military leaders rejected this as too dangerous. He admits that this left Bosnia "with a situation that was clearly untenable in the long run." The existence of three armies, organized and motivated by different objectives and loyalties, made the security situation more like a military stalemate than a peace agreement for a single state. Although these three armies have not come to blows, their very existence has worked against fulfilling the concept of Bosnia as one country.[12]

Considering these centrifugal forces embedded within the Dayton agreement—creating a weak central government, institutionalizing ethnicity, leaving out the parties most responsible for implementation, and allowing separate armies—it is remarkable that Bosnia has made the progress it has during the past decade. It is important to remember that despite these obstacles and its many imperfections, Bosnia today is a single state at peace. While the path to fulfilling Dayton's ambition of "one state, two entities, and three peoples" has hardly been easy, it has not failed. As one analyst of post–Dayton Bosnia explained, "it is not only unfair but inaccurate to dismiss and demonize the Dayton settlement as a deal simply legitimizing partition." Nor is it wise to look at the challenges Bosnia faces and assert that it would be better off divided, as some have argued. Doing so would not only unravel much of the good that Dayton has accomplished—it would likely trigger new refugee flows, create even weaker states with even fewer resources, increase the likelihood of fighting, and ultimately legitimize aggression.[13]

Minimalists versus Maximalists

Some of Bosnia's post-Dayton challenges originate from the details of the agreement or how it was negotiated; others come from the ways the agreement has been implemented. As the history of these negotiations makes clear, the American effort to bring peace to Bosnia revolved around a core argument that the Dayton Accords themselves did not solve: whether the goal was to help implement a cease-fire or help construct a new Bosnia state. This debate is most clearly illustrated by the bureaucratic struggle over the role and responsibility of IFOR between what Holbrooke describes as the "minimalists" in the Pentagon and the "maximalists" like himself, but it can be found in many other parts of Dayton's implementation as well.

Dayton itself was as "maximalist" an agreement as possible; it aimed to create an ambitious blueprint for a new state. Yet many areas of Dayton's implementation have suffered from "minimalism," whether because of the limits placed on the instruments the agreement created for implementation, or because those responsible for implementation have interpreted their roles, responsibilities and powers narrowly. This tension between Dayton's ends and means created what some have described as an "enforcement gap" that slowed implementation immediately after the peace agreement and still plagues Bosnia to this day.[14]

One place where this gap has been especially troubling is in civilian implementation. For too long after Dayton, the international civilian authority was not led or structured in a way that could make it an effective player in implementation. As a recent analysis of reconstruction efforts in post–Dayton Bosnia explains, "a major weakness of the international effort was the fragmented nature of civilian implementation, poor coordination between the military and civilian elements, and disparity among the civilian elements themselves." To many of the Europeans at Dayton, part of the problem was that throughout the negotiations, the Americans were far more focused on the military aspects of implementation than the civilian ones, leaving the responsibility primarily to others. As Carl Bildt remembers, "the U.S. would focus on military matters and limit its involvement in the civilian arena, while the European countries were wary of a peace effort that was too military in a narrow sense." While the Americans spent hours negotiating among themselves over the parameters of IFOR's role in implementation, they spent comparatively little time poring over the same kinds of details for the civilian aspects of the agreement. Civilian implementation was never a central part of the discussions in Dayton, as the issue was left to the Europeans and someone from outside the core American team, Robert Gallucci. The result was that there were many questions about how the civilian aspects of the agreement would actually work in practice, resulting in years of drawn out negotiations between the United States and Europe about how civilian implementation should proceed.[15]

Another part of the problem was the conceptual gulf between the Clinton Administration and the Europeans about the powers of those in charge of civilian implementation, particularly the "High Representative." Throughout the negotiations, the Europeans sought more powers for the High Representative grounded in authority from the United Nations. Yet because of the problems with the "dual key" for NATO bombing, as well as the catastrophe of U.S.–UN relations in Somalia and the 1994 tragedy in Rwanda, American officials focused on empowering the IFOR commander at the expense of the High Representative, and keeping the UN out of the process entirely. The Clinton Administration—especially Pentagon officials—did not want the High Representative—especially a European one—to have any control over American military forces on the ground. But at the same time, the Europeans did not want the military commanders to have a role in civilian implementation.

The result was, in the words of one of the Contact Group representatives at Dayton, an international civilian authority that operated "in uncomfortable and unconvincing limbo." The Americans came to regret this decision, and they later prodded the High Representative to assert more oversight (in 1997, the U.S. and Europe supported creating the so-called Bonn powers, which gave the High Representative greater tools to assert his authority). Holbrooke cites Carl Bildt's "valid" criticism that "the Americans initially stressed purely military aspects and did not want any cohesive civilian or political authority" (after Dayton, Bildt went on to serve two years as Bosnia's

High Representative). Explaining that he opposed this view, Holbrooke says that the compromise reached at Dayton about the High Representative's limited powers "was a mistake . . . [the] mandate should have been stronger."[16]

EVEN IF the instruments of civilian implementation had been stronger, they still would have been hindered by the other major contributor to Dayton's ends-means gap: the self-imposed limits on military implementation. The 12-month deadline for IFOR, and later the 18-month deadline for its successor "Stabilization Force" (SFOR) was the single greatest contradiction between Dayton's aspirations and reality. David Halberstam correctly describes the decision to set these deadlines as a "waffle of the first order." As this history shows, the Clinton Administration agreed to the original time limit for IFOR early in the process and without much debate—and no input from the negotiating team. It lived in fear of "mission creep" and wanted to guarantee an exit strategy from Bosnia. American military officials insisted on these deadlines for the same reasons they fought so hard to limit IFOR's obligations: to keep U.S. forces out of danger, and to end the mission as soon as possible. Also, Administration officials understood that without such an explicit commitment to leave, gaining congressional approval and sustaining public support would be difficult, especially as they headed into a presidential election.

Perhaps true, but these arbitrary deadlines were inherently minimalist and wholly unrealistic. They only made sense if the goal was to create a stable military balance on the ground (which could arguably be done in a year) not a lasting peace (which would take much longer). Looking back, Sandy Berger admits that the concerns that drove this decision were "perfectly reasonable, but turned out to be wrong."[17]

The deadline undermined the ability to implement the maximalist parts of the agreement. It gave Dayton's opponents hope that they could simply outwait the international community. It also weakened civilian implementation, since the High Representative had no incentive to act forcefully if NATO's 60,000 troops were going to withdraw soon.

The American negotiators at Dayton understood this dilemma. Yet they still publicly defended the deadline as realistic. Since they had given the IFOR commander the "silver bullet" authority to take any action he considered necessary, they argued—skeptically, but honestly—that if the military intervened forcefully from the moment it entered Bosnia, it could accomplish its objectives by the end of a year. When IFOR deployed, however, its commanders interpreted their responsibilities in the most limited terms, often refusing to use the authority given to them. Holbrooke (who had left government in early 1996) recalls watching "with growing anxiety" as IFOR forces stood aside while Dayton's opponents blocked implementation, refusing to take such essential actions as seeking to arrest wanted war criminals, especially Karadzic and Mladic. "What NATO/IFOR demands happens," Holbrooke wrote to President Clinton in a June 1996 message. "But the reluctance of NATO to go beyond a relatively narrow interpretation of its mission has left a gaping hole in the Bosnia food chain. . . . the Bosnian Serbs have increasingly defied Dayton's powers [and] the Bosnian Muslims have moved further from a multiethnic state." Madeleine Albright, who became Secretary of State during Clinton's second term, agreed with this assessment, describing that NATO "was engaged in what I call reverse mission creep, taking no risks and doing little to help achieve civilian-related goals."[18]

This struggle over IFOR's "authority" versus its "obligations," which had been the subject of intense debates inside the White House Principals Committee during October 1995, continued to be the most contentious issue during the initial years of Dayton's implementation. The first IFOR deadline came and went, and the Administration set a new one. Slowly, the argument that NATO troops needed to exercise their authority gained support inside the Administration (it helped that many fears, like major bloodshed, were never realized). Finally, at the end of 1997 President Clinton announced that U.S. troops would continue to be part of the NATO force indefinitely, measuring their progress by accomplishing tasks (such as refugee returns, political and economic reforms, and cooperation with the war crimes tribunal) rather than by arbitrary deadlines. "The President had finally made it explicit that we would not walk away from Bosnia," Holbrooke recalled, and the pace of implementation accelerated dramatically. Albright told Clinton at the time that this was "one of the most important decisions of your second term." Two years after Dayton, the maximalists had finally prevailed.[19]

The same can now be said of civilian implementation. Since the first few difficult years after Dayton, the international civilian authority has assumed a far more intrusive role to keep Bosnia on the path of reform, frequently making and enforcing decisions over the opposition of local officials, or even dismissing obstructive Bosnian leaders from office. International authorities have worked to stitch Bosnia together, including by creating a national flag, common currency, unified economy, and national license plates, as well as fighting corruption and strengthening the judiciary. Greater coordination between civilian and military authorities has also developed, and many indicted war criminals have been arrested.

A decade after Dayton, these efforts have started to pay dividends. As a measure of how far the country has come, consider how the strategic debate in the United States and Europe has shifted—rather than thinking of Bosnia as a perpetual ward of NATO and the EU, many see a future in which the country could start heading toward joining these institutions. Although realistically this possibility remains years away, the fact that some (including the current High Representative, Paddy Ashdown) are even discussing this is evidence of significant progress.

Country or Project?

Yet the international community's eventual success in pursuing maximalist implementation of the peace agreement reveals a paradox. Dayton was designed to create a single, independent state, yet Bosnia's evolution has largely depended on decisions made by outsiders. As Carl Bildt describes it, Dayton was "half-negotiated and half-imposed." Partly because of the deep scars of war, and partly because of the tensions that stem from compromises within the agreement itself, Bosnia still cannot stand on its own. A decade after Dayton, an anonymous Sarajevan has been quoted as saying, "we don't live in a country, we live in a project." This is a more direct way of explaining what a 2005 high-level international commission on the Balkans concludes: that Bosnia's greatest challenge now is to create a "sustainable self government."

Some have criticized Dayton as an attempt to impose democracy from above. These skeptics blame the international community for violating Bosnia's sovereignty, suppressing its self-determination and operating without enough accountability. Although many of these critiques are hyperbolic—some critics decry Dayton as "liberal imperialism" or a "European Raj"—they do highlight a fundamental challenge of post-conflict democratization. At what point does outside implementation actually hinder, rather than enhance, the process of creating a self-sustaining peace? The past decade in Bosnia has shown what happens when there is too little oversight, but at what point is there too much? Has Bosnia become too dependent on outside help? Or what happens when the overseer's appetite for engagement runs out? Such questions and their answers should inform other democratization efforts now underway—from Kosovo, to the major undertakings in Afghanistan and Iraq.[21]

Empowering Evil

Another challenge that American diplomats had to confront is, in retrospect, one of the most difficult. Throughout the negotiations and far into implementation, they had to bargain with—and to a great extent rely upon—individuals such as Franjo Tudjman and Slobodan Milosevic, who bore responsibility for some of the worst crimes against humanity in Europe since the end of World War II. A key factor behind the "Milosevic strategy" was that the Americans would not negotiate directly with indicted war criminals such as Mladic and Karadzic. Yet this was hardly an appealing choice. While Milosevic would not be indicted for war crimes until 1999 (and Tudjman died before he could be indicted), the Americans knew at the time that his hands were dirty, placing them in the moral dilemma of dealing with evil to end evil.

Such dilemmas are not new to international diplomacy or unique to Bosnia. Holbrooke often cites the example of Raoul Wallenberg and Folke Bernadotte, two Swedish leaders who negotiated with two of the most notorious Nazis, Adolf Eichmann and Heinrich Himmler, during World War II to save thousands of Jews (and about whom Holbrooke's wife, Kati Marton, has written books). For years, American diplomats also negotiated with figures such as Yasir Arafat in an effort to bring peace to the Middle East, or even once worked with and supported dictators such as Iraq's Saddam Hussein against mutual enemies like Iran.

Yet these precedents did not make the dilemma any less troubling. Holbrooke and his team dealt with Milosevic but they did not let him off the hook. They knew about his culpability, and frequently pressed him on the subject. The Serb leader refused to acknowledge Serb war crimes as a legitimate issue, countering with lectures on crimes committed by Muslims and Croats and the impact of sanctions on his people. Milosevic also denied that he had any control over those Serbs who had committed atrocities—which was ridiculous considering that when it served his interests, he could make Mladic or Karadzic appear in Belgrade at a moment's notice.

Take one example of how the Americans worked to counter this line of argument: Holbrooke recalls that at one point during his shuttle diplomacy, he asked the CIA to prepare an unclassified document detailing links between Bosnian Serbs who had committed war crimes and Milosevic's Internal Affairs Ministry.[22] During a meal in Belgrade the evening of October 19, Holbrooke pressed the issue, eliciting the expected response from the Serb leader: "No, no, no," Milosevic said defensively, they had it all wrong. With this cue, Holbrooke said that Jim Pardew had a piece of paper outlining how the United States had it right. Pardew placed the CIA paper on the table next to Milosevic. The Serb leader refused to look at it or touch it. It seemed as though Milosevic saw the paper itself as the "smoking gun that connected him to all of this. And that, of course, is his greatest fear." If they linked Milosevic to war crimes, his entire strategy of rehabilitation and international acceptance would be completely undermined. After the meal, Pardew left the paper at Milosevic's place. A Serb aide told the American negotiator that he had forgotten something. "No, I didn't forget it," Pardew said. "It's for [Milosevic]. He can have it."[23]

Despite occasionally reminding Milosevic that they had the goods on him, the Americans constantly grappled their larger dilemma. "I felt like washing my hands every time I came out of a meeting with the man," Holbrooke later told the author Michael Ignatieff. The Clinton Administration's lead human rights official, John Shattuck, recalls that they often struggled with whether it was right to deal with Milosevic, especially knowing that doing so created the dangerous byproduct of empowering him. "The bottom line," Shattuck later wrote, "is that we made a choice in 1995 to save lives and secure peace in Bosnia, but Milosevic survived and the larger crisis continued."[24]

Sadly, the demands of implementation often conspired to prolong the dilemma. For Dayton to work, Milosevic had to be made into a legitimate partner for peace—and despite negotiators' best attempts to keep the pressure on him, this process of empowerment inevitably obfuscated his guilt. Because of his central role in delivering the Bosnian Serbs, the "Milosevic strategy" continued for the early years of implementation. American negotiators often returned to Belgrade to secure his agreement to some aspect of Dayton's implementation.

Many said that Milosevic was not only the arsonist of the Balkans, but also its fireman. As long as the international community needed his help in Bosnia, it remained difficult to press him too hard in other areas, like political repression inside Serbia or, initially, his ethnic cleansing campaign against ethnic Albanians inside Kosovo that ultimately led to the 1999 NATO bombing that liberated that tiny province from Belgrade's control. Today, as the world learns more about Milosevic's criminality through his war crimes trial at The Hague, the difficulties these trade-offs presented are even starker.[25]

But a Bosnia peace agreement could not have been accomplished without working with Milosevic. And while the aftermath of empowering him is one of Dayton's greatest tragedies, it is also clear that without the agreement—which established a precedent of justice and set an example for international intervention to enforce accountability—Milosevic might not be sitting where he is today, behind bars.

THE UNITED STATES, EUROPE, AND DAYTON

Dayton's core accomplishment is what it did for Bosnia: it ended a war and gave hope (and a return to their homes) to millions who have suffered immense hardship. But it did more than that. It helped define a new purpose for the Transatlantic Alliance and organizations like NATO, and ultimately, restored the credibility of American leadership.

Dayton brought to an end one of the most difficult periods in the history of U.S.-European relations. It gave life to the Clinton Administration's strategy for Europe and that strategy's core element, NATO enlargement. President Clinton and his team saw an expanded NATO—one with new missions and members—as the engine of their policy to create a Europe whole and free. Yet for years, the Alliance's inability to solve Bosnia raised serious questions about its future relevance, let alone enlargement. Dayton helped reaffirm the strategy's rationale and gave confidence to its propo-nents—by helping end the war through its air campaign, NATO showed it could be a peace maker; and by taking on the commitment to implement the peace agreement with 60,000 troops, NATO proved it could be a peace enforcer. Without Dayton, one of the top scholars of NATO enlargement put it plainly, "NATO enlargement would never have happened." In fact, if the Bosnia conflict had continued, NATO itself might have become virtually meaningless. As Warren Christopher later described it, Dayton "reinforced the central role of NATO in Europe's security architecture." With the agree-ment, "impotence had been replaced by determination . . . the divisions that haunted us from the beginning of the war in the former Yugoslavia had been replaced by unity."[26]

Dayton also blazed important new paths in U.S.–Russian relations and NATO–Russia relations, proving that the former adversaries could work together to solve common problems. Instead of reducing their challenge by isolating Russia from the Dayton process, the Clinton Administration—led by Secretary of Defense William Perry and Deputy Secretary of State Strobe Talbott, who as individuals deserve as much credit for their diplomacy with Russia as Holbrooke and his team do for grappling with the Balkan parties at Dayton—sought to make Russia a part of the solution. By including Russia in IFOR to work alongside NATO, the United States helped ease Russian con-cerns that the Alliance was not inherently adversarial. This success launched a new era of cooperation between Russia and NATO, leading to such accomplishments as the 1997 NATO–Russia "Founding Act" and eventually the 2002 NATO– Russia Council. It also established a precedent for seeking to include Russia in regional problem solving, as later shown by the American efforts to work with Russia to end the 1999 war in Kosovo.[27]

Finally, Bosnia showed NATO's importance as a security organization that could move beyond its original mission of collective defense to help solve conflicts and enforce peace agreements.[28] Bosnia was the first time that NATO used military power and deployed its troops outside the treaty area. This not only introduced a new concept for NATO's role in world, but at a practical level, taught a generation of military commanders and soldiers important lessons about how to organize and conduct peace enforcement operations. When NATO finally turned over the responsibility for Dayton's military implementation to the European Union in December 2004, the Alliance found itself in charge of major missions in Kosovo and Afghanistan, and many were calling for it to take a greater responsibility for security in Iraq and even play a larger role to end the genocide in Sudan's Darfur region. In ways large and small, all of these efforts draw on NATO's experience in Bosnia. Without its first intervention there, today's NATO is unthinkable.

DAYTON WAS A TURNING POINT for the Clinton Administration's foreign policy specifically and America's role in the world generally. After a difficult first few years in office, this was President Clinton's first major foreign policy success.

The course he chose fit within a well-established American diplomatic tradition: a policy that challenged the status quo and rejected incrementalism, reflecting an all-or-nothing approach that was driven less by concerns about niceties or allied consensus than by getting something done. The position of leader of the free world had gone from being, in Jacques Chirac's stinging words, "vacant," to again being asserted by the President of the United States.

This mattered for America's global standing; it mattered for Clinton personally. John Harris, a leading historian of the Clinton presidency, explains that Clinton "emerged from the fall of 1995 as a vastly more self-confident and commanding leader." In less than six months during 1995, he had taken charge of the Transatlantic Alliance, pushed NATO to use over-whelming military force, risked America's prestige on a bold diplomatic gamble, and placed 20,000 American military men and women on the ground in a dangerous environment. That the President and his Administration ran such risks successfully gave them confidence going forward. Holbrooke recalls that after Dayton, "American foreign policy seemed more assertive, more muscular . . . Washington was now praised for its firm leadership—or even chided by some Europeans for too much leadership."[29]

The Bosnia experience has taught many lessons, but the most important one is this: when it comes to solving global problems, American leadership remains indispensable. America's failure to lead during the early 1990's contributed to the international community's inability to solve Bosnia's crisis; but its bold action in 1995 stopped the war. Perhaps it is fitting that the best description of this comes from the leading European involved in these negotiations, Carl

Bildt. The "simple and fundamental fact" of this story, Bildt writes, is that the "United States was the only player who possessed the ability to employ power as a political instrument and, when forced into action, was also willing to do so."[30] This lesson from Dayton is sometimes easy to overlook today, especially in the wake of September 11 and the war on terrorism, when many around the world are questioning the purpose of U.S. leadership, bristling at the exercise of American power, or claiming that American assertiveness is something new. It is therefore important to remember the important place of one of the last great American diplomatic achievements during the twentieth century—Dayton—in the character and reach of America's twenty-first-century leadership.

NOTES

FOREWORD

1. The Pentagon had the same initial view of the NATO deployment; like Kissinger, they thought Bosnia would resemble the two Koreas or divided Cyprus. Of course, the concept of the negotiating team was exactly the opposite: we wanted *no* NATO troops dividing the two sides, but rather as much integration as possible of the two entities. This is, in fact, what has happened. NATO troops never patrolled the "inter-ethnic boundary line," and today, people move, interact, and drive freely across all of Bosnia without incident or interference.
2. In the Senate, the policy got what the press accurately called "lukewarm support"; by a strong 69 to 30 vote, the Senate approved the troop deployment, but on support of the policy itself, the vote was a narrow 52 to 47 in favor.
3. Among the most important exceptions: Senate Majority Leader Bob Dole, who complained endlessly about the details of the policy because he wanted a more vigorous and earlier involvement, but who supported the deployment; and Senator John McCain, whose initial support was later tempered by his fury at the Administration's ill-conceived and unrealistic pledge to bring the troops home after one year.

PROLOGUE

1. Warren Christopher, *In the Stream of History: Shaping Foreign Policy for a New Era* (Stanford University Press, 1998), pp. 344–345.
2. For the history of Yugoslavia and the origins of the Bosnia conflict, see Laura Silber and Allan Little, *Yugoslavia: Death of a Nation* (TV Books, 1996); Misha Glenny, *The Fall of Yugoslavia* (Penguin Books, 1994); Steven L. Burg and Paul S. Shoup, *The War in Bosnia-Herzegovina* (M.E. Sharpe, 1999); Roger Cohen, *Hearts Grown Brutal: Sagas of Sarajevo* (Random House, 1998); and Mark Mazower, *The Balkans* (The Modern Library, 2000).
3. Warren Zimmermann, *Origins of a Catastrophe* (Times Books, 1996), p. 164.
4. James A. Baker, III, *The Politics of Diplomacy* (G.P. Putnam's Sons, 1995), p. 651.
5. Richard Holbrooke, *To End a War* (Random House, 1998), pp. 41–42; Ivo Daalder, *Getting to Dayton: The Making of America's Bosnia Policy* (Brookings, 2000), pp. 6–7.
6. Madeleine Albright, *Madam Secretary* (Miramax Books, 2003), p. 180; Christopher, *In the Stream of History*, pp. 345–347; Elaine Sciolino, "Bosnia Policy Shaped by U.S. Military Role, *New York Times*, July 29, 1996.
7. John Harris, *The Survivor: Bill Clinton in the White House* (Random House, 2005), p. 47.

8. Christopher, *In the Stream of History*, p. 347; Bill Clinton, *My Life* (Alfred A. Knopf, 2004), p. 513.

9. Albright, *Madam Secretary*, p. 181; Silber and Little, *Death of a Nation*, pp. 309–318.

10. See Glenny, *The Fall of Yugoslavia*, p. 247; Christopher, *In the Stream of History*, p. 354; Silber and Little, *Death of a Nation*, pp. 319–323; Daalder, *Getting to Dayton*, pp. 26–27.

11. Holbrooke, *To End a War*, p. 61; Daalder, *Getting to Dayton*, 31–36.

12. See *Washington Post* editorial, "Bosnia in a Free Fall," May 2, 1995.

13. For Frasure's reports, see "Contact Group—Milosevic's Proposal," Cable, Belgrade 1050, March 4, 1995; "Contact Group Proposal on Recognition/Sanctions Suspension," Cable, State 86669, April 8, 1995; "Milosevic on Bosnia Recognition: No," Cable, Belgrade 1773, April 12, 1995; "Talks with Milosevic: First Round," Cable, Belgrade 2352, May 16, 1995; "The Milosevic Discussions: An Analysis," Cable, Belgrade 2419, May 19, 1995; "Saturday Night with Milosevic—'We Are Right on the Edge of the Blade,' " Cable, Belgrade 2436, May 21, 1995; "A Sunday Lunch With Milosevic," Cable, Belgrade 2437, May 21, 1995; "Milosevic Negotiations—Demands for More Concessions," Draft Cable, Belgrade, June 3, 1995; and "Farewell Session With Milosevic," Cable, Belgrade 2742, June 7, 1995.

14. Albright, *Madam Secretary*, p. 185; Daalder, *Getting to Dayton*, pp. 40–42.

15. See Cohen, *Hearts Grown Brutal*, p. 400; John Pomfret, "Shaky Truce in Bosnia Ends Today; UN Fails to Forestall Resurgence To War," *Washington Post*, May 1, 1995; and "The United States and the Breakup of Yugoslavia: 1980–1995," Chronology prepared by the U.S. Department of State, Office of the Historian, pp. 209–219.

16. "Milosevic and the Good Serb/Bad Serb Game," Cable, Belgrade 2699, June 5, 1995; "Milosevic Talks—No Movement on Reimposition, Saying the Right Things on Hostages," Cable, Belgrade 2621, June 1, 1995.

17. "Letter from the Secretary Re Contact Group," Cable, State 135194, June 4, 1995.

18. See "Summary of Conclusions of Principals Meeting on Bosnia," NSC memorandum, June 6, 1995; Jan Willem Honig and Norbert Both, *Srebrenica: Record of a War Crime* (Penguin, 1997), pp. 160–185.

19. Daalder, *Getting to Dayton*, pp. 46–48.

20. Wesley Clark, *Waging Modern War* (Public Affairs, 2001), p. 48; Carl Bildt, "Holbrooke's History," *Survival* (Autumn 1998), p. 188.

21. Quoted in Daalder, *Getting to Dayton*, p. 50.

1 OVER THE WATERFALL: MAY–JULY 1995

1. Don Kerrick interview, July 15, 1996; see also "Key Bosnia Meeting/Event chronology" (White House paper prepared for media backgrounders on U.S. policy toward Bosnia, August 1995); and Daalder, *Getting to Dayton*, pp. 87–88.

2. "Bosnia: Strategic Choices: NSC Discussion Paper," NSC memorandum, May 17, 1995.

3. Chaired by National Security Advisor Anthony Lake, the Principals Committee met in the White House Situation Room and included Cabinet-level officials (or in their absence, their deputies) from the State Department, the Defense

Department, the Joint Chiefs of Staff, CIA, the U.S. Ambassador to the UN, Office of the Vice President, and NSC staff. The PC would often work from conclusions that had already been reached by their deputies in the Deputies Committee, or the "DC."

4. See memorandum from Richard Holbrooke (EUR) to Secretary Christopher, "Principals Committee Meeting, May 23," May 22, 1995; and "Summary of Conclusions of Principals Meeting on Bosnia," May 23, 1995, NSC memorandum.

5. Chirac had been inaugurated into office on May 17. See David Halberstam, *War In A Time of Peace: Bush, Clinton and the Generals* (Simon & Schuster, 2001), p. 303; and Brian Rathbun, *Partisan Interventions* (Cornell University Press, 2004), pp. 141–143.

6. See Memorandum of Telephone Conversations between Secretary Christopher and French Foreign Minister de Charette, May 24, 1995 (Cable, State 129348); May 26, 1995 (Cable, State 130130); and May 27, 1995 (Cable, State 13144).

7. "Telcon with President Chirac of France," NSC memorandum, May 17, 1995.

8. "Telephone conversation between UK Prime Minister John Major and President Clinton, May 27, 1995," Cable, State 151264, June 22, 1995; William Shawcross, Deliver Us from Evil (Simon & Schuster, 2000) p.157.

9. See Memo from Toby Gati (INR) to Strobe Talbott, "UK/French Plans for the Rapid Reaction Force," June 21, 1995; Daalder, *Getting to Dayton*, pp. 44–45.

10. See Vershbow interviews, July 23, 1996 and September 26, 1996; Memorandum from John Kornblum (EUR) to Secretary Christopher, "Principals Committee Meeting on Bosnia, May 28, 1995;" Daalder, *Getting to Dayton*, p. 51; and Anthony Lake, *Six Nightmares: Real Threats in a Dangerous World and How America Can meet Them* (Little, Brown, 2000), p. 144.

11. "Remarks by the President at the U.S. Air Force Academy Graduation Ceremony," May 31, 1995; and Daalder, *Getting to Dayton*, p. 52.

12. See Vershbow interview, September 26, 1996; Daalder, *Getting to Dayton*, pp. 52–55; Harris, *The Survivor*, pp. 193–194; Elizabeth Drew, *Showdown: The Struggle Between the Gingrich Congress and the Clinton White House* (Simon & Schuster 1996), pp. 245–247; Dick Morris, *Behind the Oval Office: Getting Reelected Against All Odds* (Renaissance Books, 1999), p. 253; George Stephanopoulos, *All Too Human: A Political Education* (Little, Brown, 1999), p. 355.

13. O'Grady, a U.S. Air Force pilot, had been shot down by a Bosnian Serb missile over Banja Luka on June 2, and rescued six days later. See Francis X. Clines, "The Rescue; Downed US Pilot Rescued in Bosnia During Daring Raid," *New York Times*, June 9, 1995; on Clinton's difficult political situation, see Nancy Soderberg, *The Superpower Myth: The Use and Misuse of American Might* (Wiley, 2005), p. 81.

14. See memorandum from Secretary Christopher to President Clinton, "Your meeting with French President Chirac," June 9, 1995; Holbrooke, *To End a War*, p. 65; Bob Woodward, *The Choice* (Simon and Schuster, 1996), p. 255.

15. See "Memorandum of Conversation of the President's Meeting with President Jacques Chirac of France, June 14, 1995" NSC memorandum, June 21, 1995.

16. Vershbow interview, July 23, 1996.

17. On June 16, the UN Security Council approved the RRF, although it left open the question of how to pay for the force. See Barbara Crossette, "Security Council Approves Additional Troops for Bosnia," *New York Times*, June 16, 1995.

18. See Anne Swardson, "Chirac, New to G-7 Summitry, Proves Top Attention-Getter," *Washington Post*, June 18, 1995.

19. Sandy Berger interview, February 25, 2005; Talbott to Christopher, June 16, 1995, Talbott personal files.

20. Peter Tarnoff interview, October 23, 1996; Jim Steinberg interview, August 20, 1996.

21. Talbott to Christopher, June 21, 1995, Talbott personal files.

22. Albright interview, October 28, 1996.

23. Vershbow interviews, July 23, 1996 and September 26, 1996.

24. See "Elements of a New Strategy," fax to Albright from Jamie Rubin, June 21, 1995; and Albright, *Madam Secretary*, p. 186.

25. Albright interview; Daalder, *Getting to Dayton*, pp. 92–93.

26. Vershbow interviews, July 23, 1996, and September 26, 1996; Vershbow interview with Brian Lapping Associates, "Death of Yugoslavia," Roll C7; Peter Bass interview, September 10, 1996; Woodward, *The Choice*, pp. 257–58.

27. Harris, *The Survivor*, p. 117; Talbott personal files.

28. Bass interview; Woodward, *The Choice*, p. 258; Daalder, *Getting to Dayton*, pp. 94–95; and David Rothkopf, *Running the World* (Public Affairs, 2005).

29. See John Shattuck, *Freedom on Fire: Human Rights Wars and America's Response* (Harvard University Press, 2003), p. 149; and memorandum faxed to Strobe Talbott, "Bosnia," June 23, 1995.

30. "A Diplomatic Initiative for ex-Yugo," no date.

31. See memorandum from Frasure to Christopher, "Bosnia—Choosing Which Waterfall We Will Go Over," July 1, 1995.

32. Memorandum for the President from Secretary Christopher, "Night Note," July 6, 1995.

33. Vershbow interview, July 23, 1996; Bass interview.

34. Talbott note to Christopher, June 16, 1995, Talbott personal files.

35. Account from Vershbow interview, September 26, 1996; Holbrooke interview with author (notes), October 17, 1996; Christopher interview, October 22, 1996; Christopher, *In the Stream of History*, p. 348; Holbrooke, *To End a War*, pp. 67–68; and Woodward, *The Choice*, pp. 256–257.

36. Talbott personal files.

37. See July 6, "Night Note"; and Christopher interview, October 22, 1996.

38. In a. note to Christopher, Talbott suggested that on 40104, he emphasize the danger—which he wrote was "acutely on the President's mind"—that the plan may result in a large number of casualties and a possible quagmire. See note to the Secretary from Talbott, no date, cover of draft memo. Despite the President's interest, there is no evidence that the Pentagon began to explore other planning options; however, Christopher later noted that the memo "may have been a spur to energize [the President] to try to find a different strategy." See Christopher interview, October 22, 1996; Daalder, *Getting to Dayton*, p. 98.

39. See Silber and Little, *Death of a Nation*, pp. 345–361; Honig and Both, *Record of a War Crime*, pp. 3–67; David Rohde, *Endgame: The Betrayal and Fall of Srebrenica, Europe's Worst Massacre Since World War II* (Farrar, Straus and Giroux, 1997); Samantha Power, *"A Problem From Hell": America and the Age of Genocide* (Basic Books, 2002), pp. 391–421; and *The Fall of Srebrenica*, Report of the Secretary General Pursuant to General Assembly Resolution 53/35, November 15, 1999, available at <http://www.un.org/peace/srebrenica.pdf>, pp. 57–87.

40. Clinton, *My Life*, p. 666.

41. "Memorandum of Telephone Conversation Between the President and French President Jacques Chirac, July 13, 1995," NSC memorandum, July 17, 1995; Vershbow interview, July 23, 1996; Harris, *The Survivor*, pp. 195–196.

42. See "Memorandum of Telephone Conversation with Chancellor Kohl of Germany, July 13, 1995), NSC memorandum, July 15, 1995; and "Telephone Conversation Between UK Prime Minister Major and President Clinton, July 14, 1995," Cable, State 175869, July 22, 1995.

43. See Tarnoff interview; Christopher interview, October 22, 1996; "The Secretary and British Foreign Secretary Rifkind," Cable, State 171422, July 17, 1995; Rathbun, *Partisan Interventions*, p. 145; Holbrooke, *To End a War*, p. 71; and Clinton, *My Life*, p. 666.

44. Berger interview; Stephanopoulos, *All Too Human*, p. 381; Soderberg, *The Superpower Myth*, p. 76; Woodward, *The Choice*, pp. 260–261.

45. Perry interview, January 13, 1997; Vershbow interview, July 23, 1996; Woodward, *The Choice*, pp. 260–61.

46. Vershbow interview, July 23, 1996; Woodward, *The Choice*, p. 261.

47. "Bosnia Endgame Strategy," NSC memorandum, July 17, 1995.

48. Atop the State Department's copy of the Lake draft is Talbott's handscribbled notation: "Sec, Perry, Shali don't like, Tony and Mad do." See Talbott interview, July 30, 1996.

49. Vershbow interview, July 23, 1996; Bass interview; Woodward, *The Choice*, p. 261; Daalder, *Getting to Dayton*, pp. 100–101.

50. "Options Paper: Position on French Request for Assistance in Defense of Gorazde," NSC memorandum, July 17, 1995.

51. Vershbow interviews, July 23, 1996, September 26, 1996; Woodward, *The Choice*, p. 262; Soderberg, *The Superpower Myth*, p. 82.

52. Perry interview; Vershbow interview, September 26, 1996.

53. "Secretary's Conversation with Spanish FM Solana and German FM Kinkel, July 18, 1995," Cable, State 173739, July 20, 1995.

54. "French President Chirac and President Clinton, July 19, 1995," NSC memorandum, July 19, 1995; "The Secretary and FM De Charette, July 19, 1995," Cable, State 174561, July 21, 1995.

55. "Memorandum of Telephone Conversation Between the President and British Prime Minister Major, July 19, 1995," NSC memorandum, July 20, 1995.

56. "Memorandum of the President's Conversation with President Chirac, July 20, 1995," NSC memorandum, July 21, 1995. Clinton had also talked with Bosnian President Izetbegovic, to whom he reassured that the United States would work hard at London to secure an agreement on airstrikes and elimination of the dual key. See "Presidential Telephone Call with Bosnian President Izetbegovic, July 20, 1990," Cable, State 180778, July 28, 1995.

57. See Vershbow interview, September 26, 1996; Boutros Boutros-Ghali, *Unvanquished: A U.S.-UN Saga* (Random House, 1999), p. 239.

58. See Perry's memorandum to the President, "Special Defense Report—London Conference," July 21, 1995; Perry interview.

59. See Tarnoff interview; for Major's statement, see "International Meeting on Bosnia, Lancaster House, London, Friday, 21 July 1995: Chairman's Statement."

60. Perry interview; Perry memorandum to the President, July 21, 1995; Christopher, *In the Stream of History*, p. 348.

61. See Perry memorandum to the President, July 21, 1995.

2 Through the Window of Opportunity: The Endgame Strategy

1. Perry memorandum for the President, July 21, 1995; Christopher statement, U.S. Department of State *Dispatch*, July 24, 1995.
2. See Vershbow interview, September 26, 1996; Albright interview; and Christopher interview, October 22, 1996.
3. See "Bosnia: P-3 Meeting with UN Secretary General Boutros-Ghali," Cable, State 176444, July 24, 1995; "Bosnia at NATO, July 24," Cable, USNATO 3029, July 24, 1995; "July 24 NAC on Implementing London Meeting Conclusions on Bosnia," Cable, USNATO 3027, July 24, 1995; "Informal NAC, 22 July 1995, Situation in the Former Yugoslavia," Cable, USNATO 3016, July 24, 1995.
4. "Memorandum of Telephone Conversation, President Clinton and French President Chirac," NSC memorandum, July 24, 1995.
5. The specific NAC planning decisions concerning these options were based on plans made in August 1993. See Fax from Bob Clarke (USNATO) to George Glass (EUR/RPM), July 28, 1995, enclosing NAC decision for the July 25, 1995 meeting; and "Operational Options for Air Strikes in Bosnia-Herzegovina," Memorandum of the NAC Military Committee to the [NATO] Secretary General, August 8, 1993.
6. "The Secretary and French Foreign Minister de Charette, July 24, 1995," Cable, State 178191, July 26, 1995.
7. See "Summary of Conclusions for the July 24 NSC Deputies Committee Meeting," NSC memorandum, July 27, 1995; and "Perm-3 Non Paper For the SYG Regarding Use of Air Power in Bosnia," Cable, USUN 2907, July 25, 1995.
8. "The Secretary and UN SYG Boutros-Ghali, July 25, 1995," Cable, State 178623, July 26, 1995.
9. Holbrooke interview with author (notes), October 17, 1996; "July 25 NAC on Bosnia Air Operations (Gorazde)," Cable, USNATO 3059, July 26, 1995; Hunter interview.
10. See "The Secretary and British Foreign Minister Rifkind, July 25, 1995," Cable, State 178624, July 26, 1995.
11. See Draft Cable from Frasure to Hunter, EUR files, July 24, 1995; "Summary of Conclusions for Meeting of the NSC Deputies Committee," NSC Memoranda July 24 and 25, 1995.
12. See Hunter interview.
13. See "Follow-up to Secretary's Call with Silajdzic," Cable, State 179135, July 27, 1995. The decision still left unresolved, however, the question of who could authorize Option Three bombing. On August 10, UNPROFOR Force Commander Janvier and NATO Commander Admiral Leighton Smith agreed that launching Option Three strikes would be "subject to political approval." See "August 1 NAC- Texts, Agreed Decisions and IAU on the Safe Areas of Sarajevo, Bihac and Tuzla," Cable, USNATO 3107, August 1, 1995; and "Memorandum of Understanding (MOU) Between CINCSOUTH and FC UNPF Pursuant to the North Atlantic Council (NAC) Decisions of 25 July 1995 and 1 August 1995 and the Direction of the UN Secretary General," August 10, 1995.
14. "The Secretary and UN Secretary General Boutros-Ghali, July 25, 1995, (9:57am)" Cable, State 179742, July 27, 1995; "The Secretary and UN Secretary General Boutros-Ghali, July 25, 1995, (12:30pm)" Cable, State 179743, July 27, 1995;

"Bosnia: SYG Statement on Air Strike Authority," Cable, USUN 2938, July 26, 1995; Christopher, *Chances of a Lifetime* (Scribner, 2001), p. 349.

15. See Silber and Little, *Death of a Nation*, pp. 353–357.

16. Galbraith interview, August 2, 1996; Galbraith Diplomatic Diary, pp. 19–21; "Letter from Croatian Foreign Minister Granic on Bihac," Cable, USUN 2867, July 21, 1995; "Tudjman Decides for Direct Military Intervention To Save Bihac, Says Susak," Cable, Zagreb 2758, July 22, 1995.

17. See "Summary of Conclusions of Deputies Committee Meeting, July 24, 1995," NSC memorandum, July 27, 1995; "President's Discussion with Yeltsin on Bosnia, Chechnya, July 28, 1995, " NSC memorandum, July 31, 1995.

18. Vershbow interview, September 23, 1996; Kerrick interview, July 15, 1996; Perry interview with BBC, January 18, 1996; "Urging Croatian Restraint in Bihac," Cable, State 177066, July 25, 1995; and "Croatia Welcomes U.S. Demarche," Cable, Zagreb 2785, July 25, 1995; and Galbraith Diplomatic Diary, p. 20.

19. The United States had some knowledge of Croatia's rearming, although it remains unclear whether it actively helped. See, for example, Cable, Zagreb 2758 for reports of artillery shipments from Turkey for Croatia. Also, former U.S. military personnel, working as independent contractors, were hired by the Croatian government to help reformulate their military strategy. See "MPRI Back to Zagreb," Memorandum to Holbrooke from Chris Hoh (EUR/SCE), August 25, 1995; and Roger Cohen, "U.S. Cooling Ties to Croatia after Winking at its Buildup," *New York Times*, October 28, 1995.

20. See Galbraith interview, October 2, 1996; "Updates on Livno Valley Bihac," Cable, Zagreb 2805, July 25, 1995; and "Croat Operation Against 'RSK'— Probable, But Only Several Days From Now," Cable, Zagreb 2807, July 26, 1995.

21. See Galbraith interview; "Six Points from July 30 Negotiations in Knin," Cable, Zagreb 2867, July 31, 1995; "text of SRSG Akashi's Clarification on the Six-Point Plan," Cable, Zagreb 2872, July 31, 1995; "President Tudjman Responds to Akashi on the Six Points From Knin Negotiations," Cable, Zagreb 2881, July 31, 1991; and Galbraith Diplomatic Diary, pp. 23–32.

22. See "Tudjman Letter to Clinton," Cable, Zagreb 2970, August 4, 1995; "Croatia Informs USG of Decision to Begin War, Provides Unconvincing Justification," Cable, Zagreb 2969, August 4, 1995. Tudjman did admit to Galbraith that the United States had not provided Croatia with a "green light." See Galbraith interview, August 2, 1996; Galbraith Diplomatic Diary, pp. 28–29; Silber and Little, *Death of a Nation*, p. 356; Daalder, *Getting to Dayton*, p. 122.

23. On August 6, Croatian Foreign Minister Mate Granic told Galbraith that Croatia and Bosnia would cooperate militarily, as Croatia would "supplement" Bosnian troops that could create conditions for a peace agreement—"the new realities in Bosnia could mean an end to the war by the fall." See "Foreign Minister Says GOC and GOBH Cooperation Will End the Bosnian War by Fall," Cable, Zagreb 2989, August 6, 1995.

24. Christopher interview, October 22, 1996; Perry interview with BBC, January 16, 1996; Clinton, *My Life*, p. 667.

25. See "Urging Serbs Restraint in Bihac and ICFY Caution in Serbia," Cable, State 181865, July 29, 1995; "Pointing the Serbs in the Right Direction," Cable, Belgrade 3837, August 7, 1995.

26. Berger interview; Lake, *Six Nightmares*, pp. 144–145. Background on Congress' role from Wendy Sherman interview, December, 11, 1996; Daalder, *Getting to*

Dayton, 61–64; Power, *The Age of Genocide*, pp. 423–430; Drew, *Showdown*, pp. 248–253; Woodward, *The Choice*, pp. 264–265; and Elaine Sciolino, "In Washington, Defiant Senators Vote to Override Bosnian Arms Ban," *New York Times*, July 27, 1995.

27. "Memorandum of Conversation of the President's Meeting with President Jacques Chirac of France, June 14, 1995" NSC memorandum, June 21, 1995; "Telephone Conversation Between UK Prime Minister Major and President Clinton, July 14, 1995," Cable, State 175869, July 22,1995.

28. Stephanopoulos, *All Too Human*, p. 383.

29. See cover note from Anthony Lake to the President, "Balkan Strategy: Options for Discussion at Foreign Policy Group Meeting, August 7, 1995," August 5, 1995.

30. Lake cover note, August 5, 1995.

31. "Memorandum for the National Security Advisor," from Albright, August 3, 1995.

32. See, respectively, "Bosnia Endgame Strategy: What Kind of Bosnian State?" OSD/JCS memorandum, August 2, 1995; and "Endgame Strategy: A Sustainable Defense of a Viable Bosnia after UNPROFOR Withdrawal," State Department memorandum, no date.

33. Vershbow interview, July 26, 1996; Bass interview; Daalder, *Getting to Dayton*, pp. 106–107.

34. See "Talking Points for the Secretary's Conversation with the President on ex-Yugoslavia," no date, Steinberg S/P files; Christopher hand-written notes for meeting with the President, August 13, 1995, Secretary's August 1995 out-box files/Bosnia.

35. For details, see Tarnoff interview.

36. For quotes, see Woodward, *The Choice*, pp. 265–266; Stephanopoulos, *All Too Human*, p. 383; Albright, *Madam Secretary*, p. 190.

37. Daalder, *Getting to Dayton*, p. 107.

38. Harris, *The Survivor*, p. 201; Elaine Sciolino, "Bosnia Policy Shaped by U.S. Military"; *New York Times*, July 29, 1996.

39. See Holbrooke, "America, a European Power," *Foreign Affairs* (March–April 1995), p. 40.

40. Holbrooke, *To End a War*, pp. 73–74.

41. See Christopher, *Chances of a Lifetime*, p. 256; Holbrooke interview with author, September 19, 1996 (notes); and Albright interview.

42. See "Memorandum of Telephone Conversation Between the President and British Prime Minister Major; French President Jacques Chirac; and German Chancellor Helmut Kohl, August 7, 1995," NSC Memoranda (3 separate telcons), August 8, 1995. Christopher also cabled his counterparts in Europe to inform them of the mission, see "Secretary's Letter to Counterparts, RE: Lake Trip," Cable, State 190102, August 10, 1995.

43. "Talking Points on Bosnia for Consultations with Allies," Draft version, August 8, 1995; Woodward, *The Choice*, p. 266; Daalder, *Getting to Dayton*, pp. 110–111.

44. "Talking Points on Bosnia for Consultations with Allies: August 10–14, 1995," Final version as delivered, August 13, 1995.

45. Bass interview; Christopher interview, October 22, 1996; Tarnoff interview; Woodward, *The Choice*, p. 267; Daalder, *Getting to Dayton*, p. 111.

46. As the Lake team brought the initiative to Europe, officials in Washington continued high-level contacts with both the Croatians and the Bosnians, urging them not to allow the military conflict to escalate. While their military successes had

helped open the window, U.S. officials remained concerned that the Croats and Bosnians might overplay their hand. In calls to Croatian President Franjo Tudjman and Defense Minister Gojko Susak, Vice President Gore and Defense Secretary Perry asked that the Croats cease further military actions, so as "not to lose all the positive benefits of the last week." See "Telephone Conversation: Secretary of Defense Perry and Croatian Defense Minister Susak," DoD memorandum, August 11, 1995; "Vice Presidential Telephone Call: Vice President Gore, Croatian President Tudjman," State Department Operations Center Telcon, August 12, 1995; "Vice-Presidential Telephone Call: Vice President Gore and President Izetbegovic of Bosnia," State Department Operations Center Telcon, August 13, 1995.

47. For reports on Lake's meetings, see: "Germany Supports US Bosnia Initiative," Cable, Bonn 16359, August 14, 1995; "Lake Delegation's Talks in Paris, August 11," Cable, Paris 19356, August 16, 1995; "Visit of APSNA Lake to Spain, August 12, 1995," Cable, Madrid 8551, August 17, 1995; "NSA Lake Meetings with Italian Officials On Former Yugoslavia," Cable, Rome 11349, August 14, 1995; "NSA Lake's Meeting with FM Inou," Cable, Ankara 9594, August 17, 1995; "Official-Informal (memcon of Lake's meeting with PM Ciller)," Cable, Ankara 9384, August 14, 1995; "Kozyrev-Lake Balkan Meeting in Sochi," Cable, Moscow 26215, August 17, 1995; Clark interview, September 18, 1996; Vershbow interview, September 26, 1996; Bass interview; Lake, *Six Nightmares* pp. 149–151; and Daalder, *Getting to Dayton*, pp. 112–114.

48. See Tim Weiner, "Clinton's Balkan Envoy Finds Himself Shut Out," *New York Times*, August 12, 1995; Vershbow interview, July 23, 1996; Bass interview.

49. See Holbrooke, "The Road to Sarajevo," *The New Yorker*, October 21 and 28, 1996.

50. "Talking Points for the Bosnian Government," NSC Memorandum, August 13, 1995.

51. See Bass interview; Vershbow interview, July 23, 1996; Holbrooke interview with author (notes), October 16, 1996; Holbrooke, *To End a War*, pp. 74–75; Lake, *Six Nightmares*, p. 151; Cohen, *Hearts Grown Brutal*, pp. 448–450; and Woodward, *The Choice*, pp. 268–269.

3   Tragedy as Turning Point: The First Shuttle, Mt. Igman, and Operation Deliberate Force

1. See State Department paper, "Proposals for Next Round of Negotiations: Gameplan for Regional Mission (Draft), no date.

2. See Memorandum from Kornblum (EUR) to Christopher, "Holbrooke Mission: Meeting with Sacirbey," August 15, 1995; and, Kruzel notes, "Conversation with Sacirbey—Comments of Peace Agreement," undated; Hill, Clark, Kerrick and Holbrooke comments, Dayton History Seminar.

3. See "Frasure Readout of Holbrooke-Tudjman Discussion, August 16, 1995," notes taken by Kornblum (EUR); "Tudjman Hears U.S. Proposal, Agrees 'In Principle' But Sees the Opportunities Differently," Cable, Zagreb 3146, August 17, 1995; and Galbraith's Diplomatic Diary, pp. 41–42.

4. "Granic Accepts Main Points of U.S. Regional Peace Proposal," Cable, Zagreb 3150, August 17, 1995; and Galbraith Diplomatic Diary, p. 42.

5. "The 'Old' Tudjman Resurfaces in Anti-Muslim Tirade, New Map for B-H," Cable, Zagreb 3151, August 17, 1995.

6. "Milosevic the Gambler," Cable, Belgrade 4039, August 15, 1995.

7. Memorandum for Holbrooke from Perina, "Playing Hardball with Milosevic," no date, EUR/SCE files.

8. See Perina interview; "Readout of Holbrooke-Milosevic Discussions, August 17, 1995 (notes from Holbrooke phone report); General Clark's "Daily Update" to CJCS/VCJCS, August 17, 1995; and Cohen, *Hearts Grown Brutal*, p. 456.

9. Details from Perina interview; Holbrooke, *To End a War*, pp. 4–5.

10. Clark interview, September 18, 1996.

11. See Holbrooke's report, "The Road to Sarajevo," undated document, EUR files; "The Road to Sarajevo"; and *To End a War*, pp. 5–7; Notes of Frasure phone call with Kornblum, "Report on Holbrooke meeting with Milosevic, August 18, 1995, 9:00am."

12. "Tudjman reacts to brief on Milosevic meetings," Cable, Zagreb 6977, August 18, 1995.

13. Clinton, *My Life*, p. 667; Holbrooke, *To End a War*, p. 72.

14. "Trip Update" from Kruzel to Secretary Perry, August 18, 1995.

15. See Holbrooke, *To End a War*, pp. 7–18; Roger Cohen, "Taming the Bullies of Bosnia," *The New York Times Magazine*, December 17, 1995; and Holbrooke interview on the PBS television program, *Charlie Rose*, December 15, 1995, Transcript #1531.

16. "Secretary's Conversation with de Charette: August 19, 1995," Cable, State 198590, August 21, 1995; "Deputy Secretary and UK Ambassador on Bosnia," Cable, State 20278, August 25, 1995.

17. See John Pomfret, "Three U.S. Peace Negotiators Die in Car Wreck Near Sarajevo," *Washington Post*, August 20, 1995.

18. See Todd Purdum, "Clinton Vetoes Lifting Bosnia Arms Embargo," *New York Times*, August 12, 1995. Letter from Dole to Clinton, August 17, 1995; Letter from Clinton to Dole, August 28, 1995.

19. Christopher interview, October 22, 1996; Owen interview, September 11, 1996; Owen/Holbrooke interview; Steinberg interview; Sapiro/O'Brien interview.

20. See Holbrooke, *To End a War*, pp. 85–86.

21. Lloyd Cutler interview, October 8, 1996; Owen interview, September 11, 1995; Kornblum interview, July 26, 1996; Sapiro/O'Brien interview; Price interview.

22. The group usually comprised Cutler; Sapiro; James O'Brien, an Albright aide in the State Department's UN office; Tim Ramish of the Legal Advisor's office; with the assistance of Laurel Miller, an associate with Covington and Burling; and either Chris Hoh, Phil Goldberg, or John Burley, the State Department desk officers for Croatia, Bosnia, or Yugoslavia, respectively.

23. Owen interview, September 11, 1995; Owen draft document, "A Proposal Re the Political Structure of a Bosnian State," August 27, 1995.

24. Holbrooke, *To End a War*, p. 88; Albright interview.

25. Leon Fuerth interview, October 23, 1996; Memorandum from Holbrooke to Christopher, "Principals Committee Meeting on the Balkans Crisis," August 22, 1995; Holbrooke, *To End a War*, p. 88.

26. See Fuerth interview; Holbrooke, *To End a War*, p. 88.

27. The Bosnian Serb problem was best illustrated by an August 22 meeting between British Lt. General Rupert Smith, the UNPROFOR head, and Bosnian Serb General Ratko Mladic. Smith reported that Mladic clearly "had little understanding

of the Holbrooke initiative," and expressed that the United States had to open a channel to the Bosnian Serbs. See "Mladic: Talking to the Bosnian Serbs," Draft Cable, Sarajevo (no number), August 22, 1995, and "Official-Informal" from John Menzies, charge in Sarajevo, to Chris Hill and Phil Goldberg, EUR, Cable, Sarajevo 485, August 22, 1995. See also Gary Jonathan Bass, *Stay the Hand of Vengeance: The Politics of War Crimes Tribunals* (Princeton University Press, 2000), pp. 232–233.

28. Roger Cohen, "Shelling Kills Dozens in Sarajevo; U.S. Urges NATO to Strike Serbs," *New York Times*, August 29, 1995; "Investigation of Sarajevo Market Attack: 28 August 1995," USUN document (IO/UNP files), September 13, 1995; and "Horror again fills Sarajevo's Market," *New York Times*, August 29, 1995.

29. Holbrooke interview, July 10, 1996; Holbrooke interview with author (notes), October 18, 1996; Holbrooke, *To End a War*, pp. 91–92; Clark interview, Owen interview; Talbott interview. According to State Department Operations Center Telephone Logs, Holbrooke called Talbott at 7:44 A.M., only 90 minutes after initial reports of the shelling. See Shift I, August 28, 1995; Perry interview; Bass interview.

30. See "Bildt: Contacts with Pale," Cable, Belgrade Telno 540, August 15, 1995; "Bildt Offering His Own Map in the Balkans," Cable, London 11587, August 16, 1995; "Readout of Bildt-Krajisnik Meeting in London," Memorandum to S/S-O files, August 26, 1995; "Bildt Paints Gloomy Picture of Balkan Settlement Prospects for Germans," Cable, Bonn 16751, August 18, 1995; "Carl Bildt as Mediator in Former Yugoslavia: The 'Besserweisser Moves to the World Scene," Cable, Stockholm 4874, August 15, 1995; Carl Bildt, *Peace Journey: The Struggle for Peace in Bosnia* (Weidenfeld and Nicolson, 1998), pp. 22–91; Carl Bildt interview with author, June 22, 2005.

31. "No French Green Light For Bosnian Military Actions; Chirac Invites Izetbegovic to Paris," Cable, Paris 19434, August 17, 1995.

32. Zimmerman, *Origins of a Catastrophe*, p. 173; Holbrooke, *To End a War*, pp. 97–98.

33. Holbrooke, *To End a War*, pp. 103–104.

34. Clark interview, July 15, 1996; Holbrooke comment, Dayton History Seminar; and "Official-Informal" (Message from Kornblum to Holbrooke), Cable, State 198023, August 19, 1995.

35. See Pardew's report, "Second Meeting with Izetbegovic," August 29, 1995; and General Clark's "Daily Update" to the Joint Chiefs of Staff, August 28, 1995.

36. See "August 29 NATO Political Committee Meeting—former Yugoslavia," Cable, USNATO 3409, August 29, 1995; fax from Charles Skinner (USUN Brussels) to George Glass at the State Department (EUR/RPM), August 31, 1995; and Hunter interview.

37. "Undersecretary General Annan Says UNPROFOR to Respond by Air to August 28 Shelling of Sarajevo Market," Cable, USUN New York 3295; August 29, 1995.

38. The first wave of NATO planes left Aviano Air Force Base in Italy at 8 P.M. EDT August 29 (2 A.M., August 30 Paris/Belgrade time), hitting radar, artillery, and C3 targets. In addition to the U.S., Italy, France, The Netherlands, Spain, Turkey, and the UK all contributed aircraft to these initial strikes. Augmenting the air campaign, French RRF heavy artillery launched a 90-minute barrage from atop Mt. Igman, hitting ammunition bunkers and weapons. See State Department Operations Center Spot Reports, "NATO Action in Bosnia," 0300 EDT and 0600 EDT, August 30, 1995.

39. As expressed by Pardew in his August 29 update to Slocombe.

4 The Way to Geneva: The Patriarch Letter and NATO Bombing

1. Kerrick interview; Perina interview; Holbrooke interview, June 18, 1996; Owen interview, September 11, 1996.
2. Holbrooke, *To End a War*, pp. 105–106.
3. See Wesley Clark testimony before the International Criminal Tribunal for the former Yugoslavia, December 15, 2003, p. 30429 <http://www.un.org/icty/transe54/031215ED.htm>; Silber and Little, *Death of a Nation*, pp. 365–366; p. 379 (footnote 7).
4. See Pardew report to Slocombe, "Peace Initiative in the Balkans—Belgrade," August 30, 1995.
5. Holbrooke interview, September 30, 1996; Pardew interview, July 26, 1996; and Holbrooke, *To End a War*, pp. 105–106.
6. See Roger Cohen, "Serb Shift Opens Chance for Peace, A U.S. Envoy Says," *New York Times*, September 1, 1995; and Holbrooke interview, Dayton History Seminar.; Pardew notes for phone call with Slocombe, August 30, 1995.
7. See "Acting Secretary Talbott and Bosnian Foreign Minister Sacirbey, September 1, 1995" Cable, State 209772, September 5, 1995.
8. Holbrooke interview with author (notes), September 30, 1996.
9. See "Constitutional Organization of Bosnian State: Proposed Basic Principles," Draft, September 1, 1995; Owen/Holbrooke interview, June 18, 1996; Holbrooke interview with author (notes), October 17, 1996.
10. Details from Holbrooke/Hill comments, Dayton History Seminar; Hill interview with author (notes), December 19, 1996.
11. See "Two Hours with Gligorov; 12 with Milosevic," Pardew report to Slocombe, September 1, 1995; Pardew interview, July 31, 1996; and comments by Holbrooke, Hill, and Pardew, Dayton History Seminar.
12. Pardew report to Slocombe, September 1, 1995; Clark interview, July 15, 1996; Holbrooke, *To End a War*, pp. 113–115.
13. Pardew report, September 1, 1995; Owen/Holbrooke interview.
14. Holbrooke, *To End a War*, p. 107. Also see "Constitutional Organization of Bosnian State: Proposed Basic Principles," draft presented to Milosevic (with Owen's handwritten edits), September 1, 1995.
15. Pardew report, September 1, 1995.
16. See "The Acting Secretary and Russian Foreign Minister Kozyrev, September 1, 1995," Cable, State 209771, September 5, 1995.
17. Holbrooke, *To End a War*, p. 117; Bildt, *Peace Journey*, p. 96.
18. Holbrooke, *To End a War*, pp. 83–84.
19. Clark interview; passim comments, Dayton History Seminar.
20. See memorandum to Christopher from Holbrooke, "The Contact Group," August 1995; and Holbrooke, *To End a War*, pp. 84–85.
21. "Presidential Telephone Call, September 2, 1995," Cable, State 215056, September 11, 1995; Shawcross, *Deliver Us from Evil*, p. 183.
22. See Clark interview, July 15, 1996; Holbrooke interview (notes), September 30, 1996; and Holbrooke, *To End a War*, pp. 118–119.
23. See "Assistant Secretary Holbrooke Briefs NAC on Peace Negotiations," Cable, USNATO 3457, September 4, 1995; and Holbrooke interview (notes), September 30, 1996.
24. Holbrooke, *To End a War*, p. 119.

25. See "NAC Press Statement," UK Cable, Telno 343, September 3, 1995; and "NAC Conclusions," UK Cable, Telno 345, September 3, 1995; "Proposed NATO/NAC Statement," September 2, 1995 (no author, located in Pardew notebook, Shuttle II; Book II); and Holbrooke comment, Dayton History Seminar.

26. Holbrooke interview with author (notes), October 17, 1996; Hill interview with author (notes) December 17, 1996; Pardew interview, July 31, 1996; "Official-Informal to Marshall Adair (EUR/SE) from Thomas Miller (DCM Athens)" Cable, Athens 8227, September 4, 1995; and Holbrooke, *To End a War*, pp. 121–127.

27. See "Greece-FYROM Agreement," Cable, State 209743, September 5, 1995; Steven Greenhouse, "Greece and Macedonia Ready to Settle Dispute, U.S. Says," *New York Times*, September 5, 1995; Christopher S. Wren, "Greeks to Lift the Ban on Trade that Crippled Macedonia," *New York Times*, September 6, 1995.

28. See "FYROM Agreement: All Cool with PM Papandreou," Cable, Athens 8148, September 12, 1995; Christopher S. Wren, "Greece to Lift Embargo Against Macedonia if it Scraps Flag," *New York Times*, September 14, 1995.

29. See Holbrooke, *To End a War*, pp. 129–130.

30. See Holbrooke, Hill, Owen, and Zetkulic comments, Dayton History Seminar.

31. Owen interview, June 18, 1996; Holbrooke, Owen, Hill comments, Dayton History Seminar; Holbrooke, *To End a War*, pp. 130–131.

32. See Holbrooke, Owen, Hill, Clark comments, Dayton History Seminar; "A/S Holbrooke's meeting with Turkish Prime Minister Ciller," Cable, Ankara 10444, September 12, 1995.

33. See Holbrooke, *To End a War*, p. 131.

34. Holbrooke comment, Dayton History Seminar; Walter Slocombe interview, January 6, 1997; Holbrooke, *To End a War*, p. 132; Strobe Talbott, *The Russia Hand: A Memoir of Presidential Diplomacy* (Random House, 2002), p. 172.

35. See report to Secretary of Defense Perry from Slocombe, "Pardew Report at 1400Z," September 5, 1995.

36. See report to Slocombe from Pardew, "Meeting with Milosevic," September 5, 1995.

37. Average from calls patched through the State Department Operations Center during August 28–September 8, 1995. Additional calls likely were made, although through direct dialing.

38. Holbrooke interview, October 18, 1996; Holbrooke, *To End a War*, p 83.

39. According to members of EUR staff, officials in Washington were confused by Hill and Pardew's Skopje trip—not sure who went or why. As a result, the European Bureau had to place a staffer in the Operations Center whose sole responsibility was to keep track of the delegation's whereabouts.

40. Holbrooke interview with author (notes), October 17, 1996; Christopher interview, October 30, 1996; Holbrooke, *To End a War*, p. 171.

41. See Holbrooke interview with author (notes), October 17, 1996; Pardew interview, June 27, 1996; and Holbrooke, *To End a War*, p. 111.

42. See "Summary of Conclusions of DC meeting on Bosnia," August 18, 1995; and "Summary of Conclusions for NSC Deputies Committee Meeting, August 28, 1995," NSC memorandum, August 31, 1995.

43. See Memorandum for Principals from Deputies Committee, "Achieving a Bosnia Peace Settlement: Summary of Conclusions and Recommendations," NSC Memorandum, September 1, 1995.

44. See "Implementing a Balkan Peace Settlement," Department of Defense memorandum, revision 30, September 1, 1995. See also "NATO Implementation Force (IFOR)," Pardew report to Slocombe, September 3, 1995; and Cable, USNATO 3457.

45. See "Summary of Conclusions for NSC Principals Committee Meeting, September 5, 1995," NSC memorandum, September 11, 1995; Memorandum to Deputy Secretary Talbott from John Kornblum (EUR), "Principals Committee Meeting, September 5, 1995," no date; and Vershbow interview, September 18, 1996.

46. Vershbow interview, September 18, 1996.

47. "The Secretary's Conversation with Bosnian President Izetbegovic, September 8, 1995," Cable, State 213439, September 8, 1995; "Secretary's Conversation with Bosnian PM Silajdzic, September 8, 1995," Cable, State 213441, September 8, 1995.

48. See "September 8 Meeting Between the Contact Group and the Foreign Ministers of Bosnia-Herzegovina, Croatia and FRY," Cable (draft), Geneva 6808, September 11, 1995; Holbrooke comments, Dayton History Seminar; and Holbrooke interview with author (notes), October 17, 1996; and Holbrooke, *To End a War*, pp. 137–141.

49. See " 'Agreed Basic Principles' For a Peace Settlement for Bosnia-Herzegovina: An Analysis," memorandum drafted by John Kornblum and Jack Zetkulic (EUR), September 8, 1995.

50. Pardew report to Perry and Slocombe, "Balkan Peace Initiative: Round II," September 10, 1995.

51. Pardew report to Perry, September 10, 1995.

5   Bombs and Diplomacy: NATO's Campaign Ends, the Western Offensive Continues

1. See "General Smith: What Does Holbrooke Want Us to Do?," Cable, Sarajevo 555, September 10, 1995; Shawcross, *Deliver Us from Evil*, p. 181.

2. See Slocombe interview, January 6, 1997; Slocombe to Perry, "Trip Report: Vincenza," September 8, 1995.

3. See Eric Schmitt, "NATO Shifts Focus of Its Air Attacks on Bosnian Serbs," *New York Times*, September 11, 1995; "The Fighting: U.S. Officials Say Campaign Might Shift Bombing Targets," *New York Times*, September 9, 1995.

4. See "Permreps Express Concern Over Possible Escalation in Air Strike Operation With Use of Cruise Missiles," Cable, USNATO 3555, September 11, 1995; Perry interview.

5. See "Izetbegovic: 'You Can Expect a Statement by Late Afternoon,' " Cable, Sarajevo 554, September 10, 1995; Kit Roane, "Bosnian Muslims Said to Push Back Rebel Serb Forces," *New York Times*, September 13, 1995.

6. Talbott to Christopher, December 12, 1994; Talbott personal files.

7. See memorandum to Talbott from Toby Gati (INR), "Bosnia—How Mad Are the Russians and What Can They Do?" September 13, 1995; Memorandum to Holbrooke from John Herbst (S/NIS), "Managing the Russian Side of our Balkan Diplomacy," August 26, 1995; and Clark, *Waging Modern War*, p. 57.

8. Holbrooke, *To End a War*, p. 117.

9. In President Clinton's September 9 response to the Russian President, he largely side-stepped disagreements and thanked the Russians for their support. See Message from Clinton to Yeltsin, Cable, White House 92005, September 9, 1995; Talbott, *The Russia Hand*, p. 173.

10. On Yeltsin's comments, see Lee Hockstader, "Yeltsin Attacks NATO Drive as Raids Continue; Moscow Might Reconsider Ties to Alliance, Russia Says," *Washington Post*, September 8, 1995; Steven Erlanger, "Politics on His Mind, Yeltsin Warns West on Bombing in Bosnia," *New York Times*, September 8, 1995.

11. Perry interview.

12. See Perry-Grachev Telcon, September 11, 1995 (Pardew notebook; Shuttle 2; Book 2); Christopher Wren, "Russia Fails in UN to Bar Raids on Serbs," *New York Times*, September 13, 1995.

13. Tony Lake interview, November 5, 2001; Talbott to Christopher, September 15, 1995, Talbott personal files.

14. "Moscow Mission: September 14–15—Talking While Bombing," EUR/RPM files, September 1995. As a way to organize his own thoughts as well as set the agenda for his negotiations, Talbott frequently prepared by writing detailed, and lengthy, scripts. He would usually write them himself, with help from a few members of his inner circle. These scripts served two purposes: they helped Talbott prepare for the task at hand, and as written capsules of the policy goals and red-lines, they became vehicles to coalesce policy around which, to a certain extent, helped discipline and drive the bureaucracy.

15. See Ronald D. Asmus, *Opening NATO's Door: How the Alliance Remade Itself for a New Era* (Columbia University Press, 2002), pp. 129–130.

16. See "Transcript of Talbott Briefing," Cable, Moscow 29798, September 15, 1995; Talbott to Christopher, September 15, 1995; and Talbott, *The Russia Hand*, pp. 173–174.

17. See Memorandum for Christopher from Holbrooke, "Principals Committee Meeting: September 11, 1995," September 11, 1995; Holbrooke, *To End a War*, p. 144.

18. Talbott memo to Berger, September 10, 1995; Talbott personal files.

19. Vershbow interview, December 17, 1996.

20. See Christopher interview, October 30, 1996; Christopher, *Chances of a Lifetime*, p. 247; and Holbrooke, *To End a War*, p. 146; "USUN Secretariat Understanding of Category III Air Strikes," Cable, USUN 3422, September 8, 1995.

21. For example, in a letter to Christopher on September 8, British Foreign Secretary Malcolm Rifkind doubted that getting further NAC approval would be possible. See cable, State 951710, September 20, 1995.

22. See Holbrooke, "The Road to Sarajevo," *The New Yorker*, October 21 and 26, 1996; and Holbrooke, *To End a War*, p. 145. Admiral Owens had been in contact with the General Perisic, the Chief of Staff of the Yugoslav (Serbian) Army. In a phone call at 4 P.M. September 11 (a half-hour before the White House PC meeting), Owens and Perisic discussed the course of the bombing campaign. Perisic said that the "further dimension of the TLAMs (Tomahawks) further exacerbated the situation and that it is imperative to the overall peace process that we achieve a cease-fire." See "Owens-Perisic Telcon," Cable, VCJCS Washington 111853, September 11, 1995; Pardew memorandum to Perry and Slocombe, September 10, 1995.

23. Christopher interview, October 30, 1996; Holbrooke, *To End a War*, p. 146.

24. Vershbow interview, December 17, 1996; Holbrooke/Owen interview; Holbrooke, Owen, Hill, Clark, Kerrick comments, Dayton History Seminar; and Holbrooke, *To End a War*, p. 145.

218   Notes

25. See Holbrooke, *To End a War*, pp. 147–152; Holbrooke/Hill interview; Holbrooke, Hill, Clark, Kerrick, Owen, Pardew comments, Dayton History Seminar; Pardew reports to Slocombe, "Meeting with Milosevic," September 13, 1995; "OPS Report #1/1800L," September 13, 1995; "Meeting with key Bosnian Serb Leaders," September 14, 1995; and Kerrick personal notes, September 13, 1995.
26. See "A Framework for A Cessation of Hostilities Within the Sarajevo TEZ," document faxed to Washington by Kerrick, 3:15 A.M., September 14, 1995. Holbrooke discussed the document in a conference call with Christopher, Lake, Perry and Tarnoff. See call at 2123 EDT, September 13, 1995, from "Bosnia Action Log, September 13–14, 1995," EUR/RPM files.
27. See "A Topic For Your Meeting with FM Granic: Croatia's Appalling Treatment of the Krajina Serbs," Cable, Zagreb 3501, September 11, 1995; "Granic Tells Christopher Croatia Need Slavonia Settlement, Will Support U.S. Peace Initiative," Cable (draft), September 13, 1995; and "Meeting Between National Security Advisor Lake and Croatian FM Granic, September 12, 1995," NSC memorandum, September 21, 1995.
28. See Pardew report to Slocombe, "Federation Offensive in Central B-H," September 14, 1995; Kerrick notes, September 14, 1995; Galbraith Diplomatic Diary, pp. 50–51; and Clark report to CJCS/VCJSC, "Daily Negotiations Update, 14 September."
29. See Pardew report to Slocombe, "Discussion of NATO Air Strikes with Federation," September 14, 1995; Kerrick notes, September 14, 1995; Holbrooke phone readout, September 14, 1995 (EUR files); Clark report to CJCS/VCJSC, September 14, 1995; and Holbrooke, *To End a War*, pp. 154–155.
30. Owen had discussed this approach during a September 12 meeting in Washington with Kornblum and the legal working group. See handwritten notes from September 12 meeting between Kornblum and Owen, EUR files.
31. See Clark CJCS/VCJSC report, September 14, 1995; Holbrooke phone report (EUR files), September 14, 1995; Kerrick notes, September 14, 1995; Owen interview, June 18, 1996; and Hill interview.
32. Holbrooke/Hill interview.
33. See Hill interview; Owen/Kornblum interview. For the version of the principles that came out of the Hill/Owen talks in Sarajevo, see "Eyes Only" fax to Secretary Christopher from Owen, September 16, 1995.
34. See Kerrick notes, September 15, 1995; "September 15 Contact Group Meeting," Cable, Geneva 7052, September 15, 1995; Holbrooke/Hill interview; and Holbrooke, *To End a War*, pp. 155–156.
35. See Galbraith Diplomatic Diary, pp. 55–56; Holbrooke interview with author (notes), December 20, 1996; and Holbrooke, *To End a War*, pp. 158–162; p. 73.
36. See "Serbia: Krajina Serb Resettlement Threatens Broader Balkan Conflict," INR Intelligence Warning, September 21, 1995; Memorandum to Secretary Christopher from Toby Gati (INR), "Resettlement Options for Krajina Serb Refugees," August 17, 1995.
37. See Holbrooke, Hill, Clark comments, Dayton History Seminar; Galbraith Diplomatic Diary, pp. 55–56; memorandum to Holbrooke from Charles Thomas (EUR) and Daniel Sewer (EUR), "The Bosnian Federation: Acting Now to Shore it Up," September 11, 1995.
38. See "Meeting: Croatian Minister of Defense Susak with LTG Clark, BG Kerrick and Mr. Pardew; 17 September 1995; Croatian MOD, Zagreb," Typed meeting

notes (no author), September 17, 1995; Pardew report to Slocombe, "Defeat of the Bosnian Serb Army in the West," September 17, 1995; Clark CJCS/VCJSC update, "Daily Negotiations Update, 17 September 1995"; Kerrick notes, September 17, 1995.

39. Holbrooke interview with author (notes), December 20, 1996.

40. See Pardew report to Slocombe, "Sarajevo," Clark CJCS/VCJCS September 17 update; Kerrick notes, September 17, 1995; Holbrooke/Hill interview; Holbrooke, Hill, Pardew, Clark comments, Dayton History Seminar; Holbrooke, *To End a War*, p. 163.

41. See Pardew report to Slocombe, "Three More Hours with Milosevic," September 17, 1995; Clark CJCS/VCJSC September 17 update; Kerrick notes, September 17, 1995.

42. See Galbraith Diplomatic Diary, p. 57. For reports on UN peacekeepers, see "Two Danish Peacekeepers in Croatia Killed, Eight Wounded, By Serb Shelling," Cable, Copenhagen 4856, September 19, 1995; and "More Danish Casualties in Croatia: Serbs Attack Again, Danes Soldier On, Defmin Angry at UN," Cable, Copenhagen 3843, September 20, 1995.

43. See Holbrooke/Hill interview; Holbrooke, Hill, Clark, Kerrick, Pardew comments, Dayton History Seminar; Kerrick notes, September 19, 1995; Galbraith Diplomatic Diary, pp. 57–58; and Holbrooke, *To End a War*, pp. 164–166.

44. See press statement from meeting in Pardew notebook, Shuttle III; Galbraith Diplomatic Diary, pp. 56–57.

45. See memorandum to Talbott from Toby Gati (INR), "Bosnia: The Pendulum Swings," September 19, 1995.

46. This message was faxed to Christopher on September 19. Holbrooke phone interview with author, September 17, 1996; Christopher interview, October 30, 1996; and Holbrooke, *To End a War*, pp. 167–168.

47. Holbrooke, Clark comment, Dayton History Seminar.

48. See Hill/Holbrooke interview; Holbrooke, Clark, Hill, Pardew comments, Dayton History Seminar; and Kerrick notes, September 19, 1995.

49. Pardew report to Perry and Slocombe, "Balkan Peace Initiative—Round III," September 20, 1995; Walter Slocombe memorandum to Perry, "Bosnia Developments," September 20, 1995.

50. See Pardew report, September 20, 1995; Holbrooke message to Christopher, September 19, 1995.

51. See Jim O'Brien e-mail to Sapiro and Ramish on "peace pieces," September 11, 1995; "Peace Settlement" e-mail, no author (L files), September 13, 1995; memorandum to Kornblum from Sapiro, "Outline of a Peace Settlement," September 13, 1995; "Structure of a Peace Settlement for Bosnia-Herzegovina," Sapiro memorandum, September 15, 1995; hand-written notes (no author) from Kornblum, Sapiro, O'Brien meeting, September 15, 1995; Kornblum interview; Sapiro/O'Brien interview.

52. Message from Holbrooke to Kornblum, "Official-Informal," Cable, Zagreb 3622, September 17, 1995; Holbrooke, *To End a War*, p. 171.

53. See "Summary of Conclusions for Meeting of the NSC Deputies Committee," NSC, memorandum, September 8, 1995.

54. See "Summary of Conclusions for SVTS Meeting of the Deputies Committee," NSC memorandum, September 15, 1995; "U.S.-French Talks on Bosnian Settlement Implementation Planning, September 18," Cable, State 227479, September 23, 1995; and memorandum for Albright and Ambassador Rick

Inderfurth from Jim O'Brien, "U.S.-Russian Consultations on Bosnia Peace Plan, September 21, 1995," September 21, 1995.

55. See "Bosnia Peace Process: Amb. Albright's Dinner with the SYG," Cable, USUN 3672, September 23, 1995.

56. See memorandum for Secretary Christopher from Kornblum, "Principals Committee Meeting, September 21, 1995," with attached paper on "Implementation Structure in a Bosnian Settlement," September 20, 1995; and Slocombe memorandum, "Notes for PC on Bosnia, 21 Sept 95."

57. See "Bosnia/Croatia: Russians Push a Draft Resolution Demanding an End to Bosnian/Croat Offensive, Settle for a Presidential Statement But Will Reraise Resolution on September 19," Cable, USUN 3771, September 19, 1995.

58. Details from Vershbow interview, December 17, 1996; and Holbrooke, *To End a War*, pp. 172–173.

6 INCHING FORWARD: THE NEW YORK AGREEMENT AND A CEASEFIRE

1. See fax from Owen to Kornblum, "Constitutional Principles," September 18, 1995. Details of September 20 meeting from hand-written notes, (L files), September 20, 1995. See also Miriam Sapiro/James O'Brien interview; Cutler interview.

2. See Hill/Holbrooke interview; Holbrooke, *To End a War*, p. 176.

3. See "Meeting with Milosevic, September 23, 1995," type-written notes by EUR's John Burley.

4. See "Meeting with Bosnian Serbs, September 23–24, 1995," type-written notes by John Burley (EUR); Holbrooke, Hill, Pardew, Owen comments, Dayton History Seminar; Holbrooke/Hill interview; and Pardew report to Perry, "Secret talks in Belgrade.," September 24, 1995.

5. See Kerrick comment, Dayton History Seminar; Vershbow interview, December 17, 1996; and Kerrick notes, September 24, 1995.

6. See Holbrooke, Hill, Kerrick comments, Dayton History Seminar; Holbrooke/Hill interview; and Holbrooke, *To End a War*, pp. 178–179. For announcement of Bosnian pullout, see Kit Roane, "Bosnian Says it Will Shun Peace Talks in U.S.," *New York Times*, September 25, 1995.

7. Hill/Holbrooke interview.

8. See "Further Agreed Principles," Working Draft as of 2030 September 25, 1995; and Holbrooke, *To End a War*, pp. 179–180.

9. Hill/Holbrooke interview; "The Secretary and President A. Izetbegovic, September 25, 1995," Cable, State 229436, September 27, 1995; Holbrooke, *To End a War*, p. 180.

10. See memorandum for Christopher from Kornblum, "Principals Committee Meeting, September 25, 1995," September 23, 1995.

11. "Secretary's Meeting with Balkan Foreign Ministers, September 25, 1995, Waldorf-Astoria, New York," Cable, State 233299, September 30, 1995.

12. Holbrooke/Hill interview; Fax to State Department Operations Center (to be passed to Embassy Belgrade and Sarajevo) from Holbrooke, September 25, 1995, 9:40 P.M. EST.

13. Holbrooke comment, Dayton History Seminar; Holbrooke/Hill interview; Holbrooke fax to Perina/Menzies, September 25, 1995; and Holbrooke, *To End a War*, pp. 180–181.

14. See Christopher interview, October 22, 1996; Holbrooke comments, Dayton History Seminar; Holbrooke/Hill interview; Holbrooke, *To End a War*, pp. 182–184. For final copy of Further Agreed Principles and accompanying joint statement, see U.S. Department of State *Dispatch*, "The Dayton Peace Accords," March 1996.

15. See "Remarks on the Peace Process in Bosnia and an Exchange with Reporters," September 26, 1995, *Weekly Compilation of Presidential Documents*, pp. 1714–1715.

16. "Telcon with German Chancellor Kohl, September 23, 1995," NSC memorandum, September 25, 1995.

17. "A/S Holbrooke's September 27 Meeting with GOF Foreign Minister de Charette," Cable, State 233374, September 30, 1995; Bildt interview; Holbrooke, *To End a War*, pp. 185–186.

18. See memorandum for Christopher from Holbrooke, "Meeting with Sacirbey and Milutinovic," September 29, 1995.

19. Philip Goldberg interview, October 31, 1996; Holbrooke interview with author (notes), December 20, 1996.1.

20. See "Issue for Decision: Venue for Balkans Proximity Peace Talks," no date, no author; Vershbow interview, December 17, 1996.

21. See "Briefing Contact Group on Ongoing Negotiations," Cable, State 232176, September 29, 1995.

22. See memorandum to Holbrooke from Toby Gati (INR), "Bosnia—Cease-fire Consideration," September 19, 1995.

23. See Roger Cohen, "A 'Piecemeal' Peace," *New York Times*, September 28, 1995.

24. For quote, see John Pomfret, "Bosnian Serb Losses Could Aid Peace Efforts; Officials Begin to See 'The Right Time' for End to War, but Settlement Hurdles Remain," *Washington Post*, September 25, 1995.

25. Hill interview with author (notes), December 19, 1996.

26. Holbrooke interview, July 10, 1996; "Bosnian Federation: International Pressure is Still the Only Counterweight to Increasing Polarization," Cable, Madrid 10242, October 2, 1995; Holbrooke to Christopher, September 29, 1995; Clinton-Kohl telcon.

27. See, for example, Reuters report, "Serbs Reported to Recapture Town in Northwestern Bosnia," *New York Times*, September 24, 1995.

28. Holbrooke interview, July 10, 1996; Clark interview, July 15, 1996; Holbrooke, *To End a War*, p. 193.

29. Pardew memorandum to Holbrooke, September 28, 1995.

30. See, for example, "September 8 Trilateral Meeting at NATO on Bosnia Peace Plan Implementation," Cable, USNATO 3525, September 8, 1995.

31. Details from this meeting from Pardew phone call to KC Brown, OSD (Dale Waters [EUR/RPM] notes), September 29, 1995; and Kerrick notes, September 29, 1995.

32. Memorandum to CJCS/VCJSC from Clark, "Daily Negotiations Update, 29 Sept," October 2, 1995. Unless otherwise noted, all references below are from this document.

33. See "Silajdzic Makes Nice," Cable, Sarajevo 666, September 28, 1995.

34. See Pardew memorandum to Holbrooke, September 28, 1995.

35. See Galbraith Diplomatic Diary, p. 65; Holbrooke, *To End a War*, p. 191.

36. Holbrooke comment, Dayton History Seminar; and Holbrooke, *To End a War*, pp. 191–193. According to State Department Operations Center Phone Logs

(Shift III), Talbott and Holbrooke talked at 1748 EST. Later that evening (2218 EST; 4:18 A.M. in Sofia), Holbrooke called Christopher's Chief of Staff Tom Donilon.

37. See "October 3 Principals Committee Meeting," Cable, Sarajevo 637, October 2, 1995.

38. In addition to Holbrooke's cable, the PC had the interagency document, "Issue for Decision: Venue for Balkans Proximity Talks." See memorandum for Christopher from Kornblum (EUR), "Principals' Committee Meeting: October 2, 1995," October 2, 1995.

39. See Vershbow interview, December 17, 1996 (Vershbow was the only notetaker at this meeting); Christopher interview, October 22, 1996; Berger interview; Holbrooke comment, Dayton History Seminar; and Kerrick notes, "PC debrief: From TL (Tony Lake)."

40. See notes of October 4 Principals meeting, EUR/SCE electronic files; Vershbow interview, December 17, 1996; "Summary of Conclusions for Meeting of the NSC Principals Committee Meeting on Bosnia, October 4, 1995," October 12, 1995.

41. See Vershbow interview, December 17, 1996; Holbrooke interview with author (notes), December 20, 1996; Hill interview with author (notes), December 19, 1996; memorandum for Christopher from Kornblum, "October 3 Principals Committee Meeting on Bosnia," October 3, 1995; and October 4 "Summary of Conclusions."

42. See Kornblum to Christopher, October 3, 1995.

43. See Kerrick notes, October 2, 1995.

44. See Kerrick notes, October 3, 1995; Vershbow interview, December 17, 1996.

45. See "Bildt Meeting in Sarajevo," Cable, Geneva 7579, October 5, 1995; Kerrick notes, October 4, 1995.

46. See Holbrooke Comment, Dayton History Seminar; Holbrooke interview, July 10, 1996; Kerrick interview; Kerrick notes, October 4, 1995; Holbrooke, *To End a War*, p. 194.

47. According to State Department Operations Center Phone Logs, Holbrooke informed both Christopher and Lake of his progress in Sarajevo that day including two conference calls with both (743 and 2022 EDT). See "Read-out from Sarajevo: October 4, 1995, 1:55am," memorandum from EUR/SCE files; Kerrick notes, October 4, 1995; and Holbrooke, *To End a War*, pp. 196–198.

48. Holbrooke faxed the latest texts of both the cease-fire and proximity talks agreements early the morning of October 5 (7 A.M. Belgrade time). See hand-written note to Secretary Christopher and Tony Lake (apparently also delivered to Talbott, Tarnoff, and Kornblum) from Holbrooke, October 5, 1995.

49. Pardew interview, July 31, 1996.

50. See Holbrooke interview, July 10, 1996; Kerrick interview; Pardew interview, July 31, 1996; *Weekly Compilation of Presidential Documents*, October 5, 1995, p. 1765; Holbrooke, *To End a War*, pp. 197–198; and Alison Mitchell, "Bosnian Enemies Set a Cease-fire; Plan Peace Talks," *New York Times*, October 6, 1995.

51. See Christopher interview, October 30, 1996; "The Secretary and French FM de Charette, October 5, 1995," Cable, State 238061, October 6, 1995; "The Secretary and German Foreign Minister Kinkel, October 5, 1995," Cable, State 238062, October 6, 1995.

7 PREPARING FOR PEACE: A DEAL WITH RUSSIA, A DECISION ON IFOR

1. Slocombe interview, January 6, 1997.
2. "Planning for Peace Implementation in the Former Yugoslavia," Cable, USNATO 3626, September 15, 1995.
3. "French-Hosted Trilateral on Bosnia Peace Implementation Force—September 26," Cable, Paris 23323, September 29, 1995.
4. See Paris 23323; "U.S.–UK Senior Level Consultations on IFOR," Cable, London 13401, September 27, 1995; and "USDP Slocombe Delegation Meeting With Italian CHOD Venturoni—September 26," Cable, Rome 13287, September 27, 1995.
5. See "September 29 NAC Authorizes NMA's to Develop Concept of Operations for Peace Implementation," Cable, USNATO 3822, September 30, 1995; and "Council Decisions on NATO's Role in Implementing a Peace Agreement," DOD Document, Pardew Notebook, Shuttle 5.
6. See "Bosnia Peace Implementation Agreement (Draft)," Joint Staff Document, October 3, 1995; Kornblum interview, Clark interview.
7. Memorandum for the President from Secretary Perry, "Special Defense Report," October 10, 1995.
8. See "SACEUR Concept of Operations for Peace Implementation in the Former Yugoslavia," October 6, 1995.
9. "President's Discussion with Yeltsin on Bosnia, CFE, Hyde Park and a Vice Presidential Meeting with Chernomyrdin, September 27, 1995," NSC memorandum, September 28, 1995.
10. See memorandum for Deputy Secretary Talbott and Under Secretary of State for Political Affairs Tarnoff from Andrew Weiss (S/P), "Engaging the Russians on Bosnia Settlement Implementation," September 13, 1995; Talbott interview, July 30, 1996.
11. "Meeting with Foreign Minister Andrei Kozyrev, September 28, 1995" NSC memorandum of conversation, September 29, 1995.
12. Lake interview with author, November 5, 2001.
13. Talbott memo to Christopher, September 15, 1995; Talbott personal files.
14. Perry interview; Slocombe interview with author, December 6, 2001; Talbott interview.
15. Perry interview; Talbott interview; Slocombe interview; Ashton Carter and William Perry, *Preventive Defense* (Brookings, 1999), p. 33.
16. See "Summary of Conclusions for Meeting of the NSC Deputies Committee, October 6, 1995," NSC memorandum, October 12, 1995.
17. See Carter and Perry, *Preventive Defense*, pp. 34–37; Talbott, *The Russia Hand*, pp. 174–175; and "Talbott-Mamedov meeting: October 3, 1995," undated notes, EUR files.
18. See Secretary Perry's "Trip Report: Meeting with Russian MOD Pavel Grachev, Geneva, 8 Oct 95," October 8, 1995; and "Discussions During 8 Oct Perry-Grachev Meetings," DoD memorandum (draft), October 8, 1995. For Perry's talking points, see "SecDef Talkers for 1-on-1 w/ Grachev," Strobe Talbott draft, October 7, 1995; "Options for Russian Relationship with IFOR," no author, no date, D files; "Two options [on IFOR] from Perry-Grachev Trip," no date, D files; Carter and Perry, *Preventive Defense*, pp. 37–41; and Talbott, *The Russia Hand*, pp. 174–176.

19. Carter and Perry, *Preventive Defense*, pp. 38–39. See also Steven Erlanger, "U.S. Message for Russians: Complaining Pays Off," *New York Times*, September 23, 1995.

20. See "Russian Participation in the Bosnia IFOR: Strategy for SECDEF-MOD Grachev Meeting, 8 October 1995," DoD memorandum, October 5, 1995.

21. Talbott "private" letter to Christopher, attached to Perry October 8 trip report. See also Talbott, *The Russia Hand*, pp. 175–176.

22. See memorandum for Secretary Perry and Deputy Secretary of Defense John White from Walter Slocombe, "Moscow Meeting: 17 Oct 95," October 18, 1995; "Deputy Secretary's 10/17–18 Meetings with DFM Ivanov and Afanasyevskiy," Cable, Moscow 33943, October 23, 1995; Clark report to CJCS/VCJCS, October 17, 1995; Kerrick notes, October 17, 1995; and Clark, *Waging Modern War*, pp. 56–57.

23. Slocombe to Perry and White, October 18, 1995.

24. See "Deputy Secretary Talbott and Under Secretary Slocombe Brief the NAC on Talks in Moscow," Cable, USNATO 4171, October 25, 1995; Clark report to CJSC/VCJSC, October 17, 1995.

25. See "Peace Initiative in the Balkans—Round V," October 19, 1995; "Discussion with Milosevic about Cease-fire Violations and Banja Luka Ethnic Cleansing," Cable, Belgrade 5030, October 12, 1995; and "Milutinovic Says 'Everything is Threatened by Continued Muslim-Croat Offensive," Cable, Belgrade 5045, October 13, 1995. "First Joint Meeting of Proximity-Talks Co-Chairmen with Milosevic," Cable, Belgrade 5122, October 18, 1995; Kerrick notes, October 17–18, 1995; and Pardew report, October 19, 1995.

26. See Kerrick notes, October 17–18, 1995; Pardew memorandum to Perry and Slocombe, "Motivation of the Parties in Bosnia," October 11, 1995; Holbrooke interview with author (notes), December 20, 1996.

27. See Pardew report, October 19, 1995; Kerrick notes, October 17–18, 1995; and Belgrade 5122.

28. See "Yeltsin/Chirac Summit," Cable, Paris 25639, October 21, 1995.

29. Talbott, *The Russia Hand*, p. 179.

30. See "The Acting Secretary and German Foreign Ministry Political Director Ischinger," Cable, State 253723, October 27, 1995.

31. See "Lunch with Boris Yeltsin, President of the Russian Federation, October 23, 1995" NSC Memorandum, November 1, 1995; Talbott, *The Russia Hand*, pp. 179–186; Carter and Perry, *Preventive Defense*, pp. 41–42; Clinton, *My Life*, pp. 675–676; Asmus, *Opening NATO's Door*, p. 131; and Harris, *The Survivor*, pp. 209–211.

32. "Meeting with Presidents Alija Izetbegovic of the Republic of Bosnia-Herzegovina and Franjo Tudjman of the Republic of Croatia, October 24, 1995," NSC memorandum, October 30, 1995.

33. Perry memo to the President, "Special Defense Report," October 27, 1995; Carter and Perry, *Preventive Defense*, p. 42.

34. Carter and Perry, *Preventive Defense*, p. 43.

35. See Perry interview; Talbott interview; "The Deputy Secretary and Russian FM Kozyrev, October 27, 1995" Cable, State 256907, October 31, 1995; Carter and Perry, *Preventive Defense*, p. 43.

36. See Carter and Perry, *Preventive Defense*, pp. 43–44; Joulwan interview with author.

37. Holbrooke, *To End a War*, p. 205.

38. See fax to Roberts Owen from Jim O'Brien, Miriam Sapiro, and Tim Ramish, October 15, 1995.

39. See Sapiro/O'Brien interview; and Sapiro, O'Brien, Ramish comments, October 31 group interview. For the Holbrooke team's response, see "The Wisdom of Holbrooke," O'Brien computer e-mail, October 18, 1995; "Official-Informal," Cable, State 245826, October 17, 1995.

40. Slocombe interview; Sapiro/O'Brien interview; Kornblum interview, July 26, 1996.

41. Berger interview.

42. See "Memo for the Record: Notes from briefing of IFOR preliminary planning to Sec. Christopher," no author, October 13, 1995, D files.

43. Holbrooke, *To End a War*, pp. 215–216; Daalder, *Getting to Dayton*, pp. 145–146.

44. See "Summary of Conclusions for October 18 Deputies Committee on Bosnia," NSC memorandum, October 26, 1995; NSC memorandum, "Revised List IFOR/Unresolved Issues (draft)," drafted by John Feeley, no date; JCS "Information Paper" on Bosnia, October 20, 1995, drafted by John Roberti; and State paper, attached to memorandum to Talbott from Kornblum, "Deputies Committee Meeting, October 20, 1995," October 20, 1995.

45. See "Summary of Conclusion for October 20 Meeting of the Deputies Committee," NSC memorandum, November 3, 1995; Memorandum to Talbott from Kornblum, "Deputies Committee Meeting, October 24, 1995," October 23, 1995; and "Summary of Conclusions for October 24 Meeting of the NSC Deputies Committee," NSC memorandum, November 2, 1995.

46. See Memorandum for Principals from Sandy Berger, "IFOR Issues," October 24, 1995.

47. See "Summary of Conclusions for October 25 Meeting of the NSC Principals Committee," NSC Memorandum, November 9, 1995.

48. See memorandum to Secretary Perry and Slocombe from Pardew, "IFOR Issues for PCL Breakfast and PC Tomorrow," October 26, 1995.

49. See "Summary of Conclusions for October 27 Principals Committee Meeting on Bosnia," NSC Memorandum, October 30, 1995; Holbrooke, *To End a War*, pp. 220–223; Daalder, *Getting to Dayton*, pp. 146–148.

50. Clark, *Waging Modern War*, pp. 58–59; Holbrooke *To End a War*, p. 223.

51. See "Summary of Conclusions for October 27 Principals Committee Meeting on Bosnia"; Berger interview; Holbrooke, *To End a War*, p. 211; Daalder, *Getting to Dayton*, pp. 149–153.

52. See Letter from Milosevic to Christopher, October 19, 1995.

53. See Kornblum to Christopher, "Principals Committee Meeting, October 27, 1995," October 26, 1995; and attached "Sanctions Relief Talking Points."

54. See Albright interview; Fuerth interview.

55. See "Reimposition Mechanisms," State Department paper drafted by E. Bloom (L), October 26, 1995; "Options for Suspension of Sanctions on Serbia-Montenegro," State Department Sanctions Task Force paper drafted by Angel Rabasa (no date), and "Sanctions Relief," NSC memorandum, October 24, 1995.

56. See Vershbow interview, December 17, 1996; "Summary of Conclusions" from October 27 PC; Elaine Sciolino, "Administration Rejects Call to Lift Serbia Sanctions During Talks," *New York Times*, October 29, 1995.

57. See memorandum to Christopher from Holbrooke, "Bosnia Off-Site: An Annotated Agenda," October 24, 1995. See also Gallucci interview; Vershbow interview, December 17, 1996; John Price interview.

58. Vershbow interview, December 17, 1996.

59. See Menzies interview; and "EU Prepared to Help Bosnians on Constitution," Cable, Brussels 10438, October 6, 1995.

60. Holbrooke interview with author (notes), November 26, 1996; Holbrooke, *To End a War*, p. 224.
61. See memorandum to Holbrooke from Daniel Serwer (EUR), "The Bosnian Federation: Requirements for Survival in Dayton and beyond," October 30, 1995.
62. See Kruzel "Trip Report" to Perry, August 18, 1995.
63. Holbrooke interview, November 18, 1996; "The Bosnian Federation: Of Critical Importance, Yet in Critical Condition," Cable, Sarajevo 666, October 14, 1995.
64. For details, see Pardew interview, June 26, 1996; Kornblum interviews; Sapiro/O'Brien interview; Hoh, Goldberg, O'Brien comments, October 31, 1996 interview; Vershbow interview, December 17, 1996; Bildt interview; and Bildt, *Peace Journey*, p. 118.
65. See Vershbow interview, December 17, 1996; Holbrooke, *To End a War*, pp. 226–227.
66. See Bass, *Stay the Hand of Vengeance*, p. 239; Talbott personal notes; Elaine Sciolino, "House Tells Clinton to Get Approval to Send Troops to Bosnia," *New York Times*, October 31, 1995; and John Yang, "House Votes to Limit Role of U.S. Troops in Balkans," *Washington Post*, October 31, 1995.
67. "Statement by the President," October 31, 1995, White House Press Office.

8 A SLOW START: DAYTON, NOVEMBER 1–10

1. This draft was in the hands of John Price of the State Department's European Bureau, who was the "backstop" for the talks from Washington. He would receive periodic updates to the annexes by phone, and annotate the changes on his copy. See Price interview.
2. See Christopher interview, October 22, 1996.
3. As further evidence of Dayton's autonomy, the State Department arranged for the facility to be able to receive and send classified cables to Washington or embassy posts abroad. A new locator line was created temporarily for such cable traffic—"U.S. Office Proximity Talks."
4. See Michael Dobbs, "Bosnia Talks Open With Warning to Leaders; Failure to Reach Agreement Could Lead Europe to Wider War, Christopher Says," *Washington Post*, November 2, 1995.
5. See "Statement by Secretary Christopher upon arrival at Wright-Patterson Air Force Base, Dayton, Ohio, November 1, 1995," U.S. Department of State *Dispatch*, December 1995.
6. See Memorandum to Christopher from John Kornblum, "Scope Paper: Your Participation in the Opening of Bosnia Proximity Talks," October 31, 1995.
7. See memorandum to Christopher from John Kornblum, "Your Meeting with Croatian President Tudjman at the Proximity Talks, Wright-Patterson AFB, November 1, 1995," October 31, 1995.
8. See talking points, "Meeting with Tudjman," Pardew notebook from Dayton, no date.
9. See "Milosevic's Goal: Get an Agreement," Cable, Belgrade 5408, November 1, 1995.
10. See memorandum to Christopher from Kornblum, "Your Meeting with Serbian President Milosevic at the Proximity Talks, Wright-Patterson AFB, November 1, 1995," October 31, 1995; and "Bosnian Serbs Lay Down Markers For Dayton," Cable, Belgrade 5331, October 27, 1995.
11. See Michael Dobbs and Jeffrey Smith, "New Proof of Serb Atrocities; U.S. Analysts Identify More Mass Graves," *Washington Post*, October 29, 1995; and

"Massacre in Bosnia; Srebrenica: The Days of Slaughter," *New York Times*, October 29, 1995.

12. See talking points, "Meeting with Milosevic," Pardew notebook from Dayton, no date; Shattuck, *Freedom on Fire*, p. 186; p. 197.

13. "Bosnia: Peace Agreement Faces Tough Sales Pitch, But IFOR and Economic Aid Are Key Trumps," Cable, Sarajevo 733, November 1, 1995.

14. See memorandum to Christopher from Kornblum, "Your Meeting with Bosnian President Izetbegovic at the Proximity Peace Talks, Wright Patterson AFB, November 1, 1995," October 31, 1995; also see Sarajevo 733.

15. Holbrooke interview with author (notes), December 20, 1996.

16. See talking points, "Meeting with Izetbegovic," Pardew notebook from Dayton, no date; Holbrooke interview with author (notes), December 20, 1996; and Memorandum for Chris Hill from Bill Mozdzierz (EUR/SCE), "UK Warning to Bosnia on Mujahedin," November 1, 1995.

17. See memorandum and talking points to Christopher from Kornblum, "Your Meeting with Contact Group Representatives at the Proximity Talks, Wright-Patterson AFB, November 1, 1995," October 31, 1995.

18. Christopher interview, October 22, 1996.

19. See "Statement by Secretary Christopher at the Opening of the Balkan Proximity Talks," U.S. Department of State *Dispatch*, December 1995; Christopher, *In the Stream of History*, pp. 252–253.

20. See Belgrade 5122; message for Galbraith from Chris Hill, "Official-Informal," State 250182, October 21, 1995; Holbrooke, *To End a War*, pp. 237–238.

21. Holbrooke interview with author (notes), December 20, 1996.

22. See Kerrick to Lake, "Dayton SITREP #1, November 2, 1995, 9:00pm."

23. See Shattuck interview, July 25, 1996; Holbrooke interview with author (notes), December 20, 1997.

24. See Shattuck interview; Galbraith Diplomatic Diary, p. 78.

25. See Shattuck interview; Shattuck, *Freedom on Fire*, pp. 201–203. On Rohde's situation, see "CSM Correspondent David Rohde," Cable, Belgrade 5431, November 2, 1995.

26. See Galbraith Diplomatic Diary, pp. 78–79; and Galbraith interview, October 2, 1996.

27. Holbrooke interview with author (notes), December 20, 1996; Hill interview with author (notes), December 5, 1996.

28. Holbrooke comment; Dayton History Seminar.

29. See Kerrick SITREP #1; Pardew November 2 report to Perry.

30. See Pauline Neville-Jones, "Dayton, IFOR and Alliance Relations in Bosnia," *Survival* 38 (Winter 1996–1997), p. 50.

31. See "November 3 Dayton Update," no author, EUR/SCE files; Gallucci interview; Holbrooke, *To End a War*, pp. 241–242; Bildt interview; Bildt, *Peace Journey*, pp. 130–131.

32. See Kerrick notes from meeting, November 3, 1995; Holbrooke interview with author (notes), December 20, 1996; "Rohde in Bijelina Jail, Convicted of Illegal Entry, Doctored Papers," Cable, Sarajevo 749, November 4, 1995.

33. See Kerrick notes and "November 3 Dayton Update."

34. Kerrick to Lake, "Dayton SITREP #2; November 4, 1994, 10:20pm"; Holbrooke interview with author (notes), December 20, 1996; Holbrooke, *To End a War*, pp. 244–245; and Bildt, *Peace Journey*, pp. 128–129.

35. Kerrick to Lake, "Dayton SITREP #2."

36. See Kerrick SITREP #2 and Kerrick notes, November 4, 1995.

37. See Kerrick SITREP #2; Menzies interview; "Pale Rejects U.S. Terms For Attending Meeting Re Journalist David Rohde," Cable, Sarajevo 745, November 4, 1995; Holbrooke, *To End a War*, pp. 246–247.

38. See Kerrick notes, November 5, 1995; "Agreed Principles on Sarajevo," November 6, 1995 draft, Pardew Dayton notebook.

39. Chris Hill interview with author (notes), December 19, 1996; Chris Hoh comments to author, passim.

40. Details of this discussion from Pardew report to Perry, "Dayton Talks—Implementation Forces in Croatia/Map," November 5, 1995; Holbrooke interview with author (notes), December 20, 1996.

41. See Kerrick notes, "Meeting with Milosevic," November 6, 1995; Holbrooke, *To End a War*, pp. 248–249.

42. Kerrick to Talbott, "Sanctions Issues Checklist," faxed to Washington at 12:22 A.M. on November 7, 1995.

43. See "A Grain-for-Oil Swap," memorandum drafted by Leon Feurth, November 5, 1995 (faxed to Dayton on November 6); and Kerrick to Talbott, November 7, 1995.

44. See Kerrick notes, November 6, 1995; and "Sanctions Update," paper prepared by Chris Hoh, November 6, 1995, 2:00 P.M.

45. Holbrooke interview with author (notes), December 20, 1996; Holbrooke, *To End a War*, pp. 249–250; Talbott, *The Russia Hand*, p. 187.

46. See Kerrick to Talbott, November 7, 1995; Talbott personal notes, November 10, 1995; Talbott interview; Kerrick interview; and Holbrooke interview with author (notes), December 20, 1996.

47. Kerrick notes, November 6, 1995. "Revised Eastern Slavonia Draft Agreement," Cable, Zagreb 4403, November 4, 1995; Hill interview with author (notes), December 19, 1996; and "Eastern Slavonian Talks Deadlock Over Serb Intransigence," Cable, Zagreb 4441, November 6, 1995.

48. Holbrooke comment, Dayton History Seminar; Holbrooke interview with author (notes), December 20, 1996; Holbrooke, *To End a War*, p. 250.

49. See Kerrick report to Lake, "Dayton SITREP #3; November 7, 1995, 9:00am," and unidentified notes, no date, attached to Kerrick report to Talbott, November 7, 1995.

50. Kerrick SITREP #3; Bildt interview.

51. During his visit to Dayton the previous day, Talbott had urged Holbrooke to provide Washington with a one-page report each night. See Kerrick SITREP #4; November 4, 1995, 1:00 A.M.

52. See Holbrooke report to Principals and Deputies, "Dayton Update: Tuesday, November 7, 1995, 11:50pm"; and Kerrick SITREP's #3 and #4.

53. See memorandum for Secretary Christopher from John Kornblum, "Principals Committee Meeting, November 7, 1995," November 7, 1995.

54. See "A Grain for Oil Swap," memorandum for Principals, November 6, 1995; "Bosnia SVTS, November 8, 1995," State Department computer electronic mail files, Megan E. Driscoll (PM-ISP), November 8, 1995; Holbrooke report, November 7, 1995.

55. See memorandum for Talbott from Richard E. Hecklinger (EUR), "Deputies Committee Meeting on Bosnia, November 1, 1995," November 1, 1995; and "Summary of Conclusions for Deputies Committee Meeting on Bosnia," NSC memorandum, November 8, 1995.

56. See "Sustaining a Peace Agreement in Bosnia—Military Stabilization Measures: Equip and Train," attached to memorandum from Kornblum to Christopher, November 7, 1995.

57. Review from Holbrooke report, November 7, 1995; Holbrooke interview with author (notes), December 20, 1996; Holbrooke, *To End a War*, pp. 251–252; Bildt, *Peace Journey*, pp. 132–133.

58. See "Arrest Case of Christain Science Monitor Journalist David Rohde; Consular Visit In Bijelina," Cable, Sarajevo 751, November 6, 1995.

59. See Michael Dobbs, "For Rohde, the Power of a Well-Placed Writer Paid Off," *Washington Post*, November 9, 1995.

60. See letter from Christopher to Milosevic (unsigned), dated November 6, 1995; and "David Rohde Case: Karadzic Raises the Ante," Cable, Sarajevo 762, November 6, 1995; memorandum to Christopher from Holbrooke, "Draft Letter to President Milosevic Regarding David Rohde," November 7, 1995; Holbrooke report, November 7, 1995. See also Kit Roane, "Bosnia Serbs Free U.S. Newsman After 9 Days," *New York Times*, November 9, 1995; Holbrooke, *To End a War*, p. 254.

61. See Holbrooke report to Principals and Deputies, "Dayton Update: Wednesday, November 8, 1995, 10:00pm."

62. Pardew report to Perry, "Dayton Talks—Update," November 8, 1995.

63. Holbrooke interview with author (notes), December 20, 1996; Holbrooke report, November 8, 1995; Kerrick notes, November 8, 1995; Kerrick report to Lake, "Dayton SITREP #5, November 9, 1995, 2:00am," and Holbrooke, *To End a War*, p. 255.

64. See, respectively, Pardew report to Perry, November 8, 1995; Holbrooke report, November 8, 1995; and Kerrick SITREP #4.

65. See "Dayton Agreement on Implementing the Federation of Bosnia and Herzegovina of 9 November 1995"; fax to Kornblum from Daniel Serwer, "Federation Agreement Ready for Signature Tomorrow," November 8, 1995; and Holbrooke report, November 8, 1995.

66. Holbrooke interview with author (notes), December 20, 1996; Holbrooke, *To End a War*, pp. 253–254.

67. See Pardew report to Perry, November 8, 1995; and Kerrick SITREP #4; Holbrooke report, November 8, 1995; and Pardew report to Perry, "Dayton Talks—Update," November 7, 1995 (misdated, November 8, 1995).

68. See Kornblum interview, July 26, 1996; Pardew interview, June 27, 1996.

69. See Kerrick SITREP #6; Clark, *Waging Modern War*, pp. 62–63.

70. See Holbrooke report, November 8, 1995; Pardew report to Perry, November 8, 1995; Kerrick SITREP #5; and Michael Dobbs, "U.S. Announces Easing of Fuel Sanctions Against Yugoslavia," *Washington Post*, November 10, 1995.

71. See Christopher's Memorandum for Leon Panetta, "Weekly Report from the State Department," November 9, 1995.

72. Kerrick report to Lake, "Dayton SITREP #6; November 10, 1995, 1:30am."

73. See Kerrick notes, November 9, 1995; Kerrick SITREP #6; Holbrooke, *To End a War*, p. 259.

74. Kerrick SITREP #6; Holbrooke, *To End a War*, p. 259–260.

75. See Christopher's talking points, "Points for Tudjman," Pardew Dayton Notebook; and Kerrick report to Lake, "Dayton SITREP #7; November 11, 1995, 9:10am."

76. Kerrick SITREP #7.
77. See Christopher's talking points, "Points for Izetbegovic," Pardew Dayton Notebook; Holbrooke interview with author (notes), December 20, 1996; Holbrooke, *To End a War*, p. 261.
78. See "The Federation: An Essential Building Block of Peace in Bosnia and Herzegovina," State Department *Dispatch*, December 1995, p. 10.
79. See Christopher interview, October 22, 1996; Hill interview with author (notes), December 5, 1996; Holbrooke interview with author (notes), December 20, 1996; Holbrooke, *To End a War*, pp. 264–265.
80. Kerrick SITREP #7; Christopher, *Chances of a Lifetime*, pp. 261–262; Holbrooke, *To End a War*, p. 266.

9 ENDGAME: DAYTON, NOVEMBER 11–21

1. Kerrick SITREP #7.
2. See Chris Hill comments, Dayton History Seminar; Kerrick notes, November 11, 1995.
3. See Kerrick report to Lake, "Dayton SITREP #8, November 11–13, 10:30"; Shattuck, *Freedom on Fire*, p. 202; Holbrooke, *To End a War*, p. 267; Bildt, *Peace Journey*, p. 143.
4. See Neville-Jones, "Dayton, IFOR, and Alliance Relations in Bosnia," p. 48; Bildt interview.
5. Gallucci interview, October 2, 1996.
6. See memorandum to Holbrooke from Jack Zetkulic, "Euro-Handling: (1) OSCE Consultations; (2) Bildt's Pique," November 12, 1995; and "French Line on Bosnia: U.S. Wants the Credit But Not the Bill," Cable, The Hague 5952, November 8, 1995; Bildt, *Peace Journey*, p. 145.
7. See Holbrooke interview with author (notes), November 26, 1996; Kornblum/ Owen interview, June 18, 1996; Kornblum interview, July 26, 1996; Zetkulic interview, July 19, 1996; Gallucci interview; Bildt interview; Holbrooke, *To End a War*, p. 265; Bildt, *Peace Journey*, p. 147.
8. See "Basic Agreement on the Region of Eastern Slavonia, Baranja, and Western Sirmium," November 12, 1995; "Fact Sheet on Eastern Slavonia," no author, Pardew Dayton Notebook; and "GOC and Eastern Slavonian Serbs Sign Agreement on Eastern Slavonia," Cable, Zagreb 4509, November 12, 1995.
9. Memorandum for Christopher from Holbrooke, "Your Long Day in Dayton, November 14," November 14, 1995.
10. Holbrooke and Hill comments, Dayton History Seminar; Menzies interview; Holbrooke interview with author (notes), November 26, 1996; Holbrooke, *To End a War*, pp. 271–272.
11. See memorandum to Christopher from Holbrooke; and Kerrick report to Lake, "Dayton SITREP #9; November 14, 1995, 1:10am."
12. Kerrick SITREP#9; and Holbrooke, *To End a War*, pp. 272–273.
13. Memorandum for the Deputies Committee from Holbrooke, "Changes to the Military Annex to the Peace Plan," November 12, 1995; "Delegation of Bosnia and Herzegovina Proposed Changes to Annex I," November 10, 1995, 1:30 P.M.; and Holbrooke, *To End a War*, p. 258.
14. Clark, *Waging Modern War*, pp. 65–66.
15. Pardew interview, June 27, 1996; Holbrooke interview with author (notes), October 19, 1996; Slocombe interview; Holbrooke, *To End a War*, pp. 270–271.

16. See memorandum to Christopher from Holbrooke, "Your Long Day in Dayton, November 14," November 14, 1995; memorandum to Christopher from Holbrooke, "Briefing Materials for Your Visit to Dayton, November 14," November 14, 1995.
17. Memorandum for the President from Christopher, "Night Note en route to Osaka," November 15, 1995.
18. Ibid. For a similar assessment, also see Kerrick report to Lake, "Dayton SITREP #10; November 14, 1995, 11:10pm."
19. Christopher interview, October 30, 1996.
20. Christopher to Clinton, "Night Note."
21. Christopher to Clinton, "Night Note"; Christopher interview, October 22, 1996; Holbrooke, To End a War, pp. 274–275; Bildt interview.
22. Christopher to Clinton, "Night Note"; Kerrick report to Lake, "Dayton SITREP #11; November 15, 1995, 9:10pm."
23. See Christopher to Clinton, "Night Note."
24. Memorandum to Roberts Owen from Momcilo Krajisnik, "Remarks on Draft 'Constitution' of 12 November 1995," November 15, 1995.
25. See memorandum to Talbott from Richard E. Hecklinger (EUR), "Principals Committee Meeting, Wednesday, November 15, 1995," November 15, 1995; and NSC memorandum, "Bosnia Issues for Discussion at November 15 PC Meeting," November 15, 1995.
26. See "Summary of Conclusions, Principals Committee Meeting on Bosnia, November 16, 1995 (misdated: November 15, 1995)" NSC memorandum, November 18, 1995; Holbrooke, To End a War, p. 278.
27. See Gallucci interview.
28. Harris, The Survivor, p. 223.
29. Menzies interview; Holbrooke interview, November 18, 1996.
30. Holbrooke, To End a War, p. 279; Roger Cohen, "Bosnia Asks U.S. Arms Aid as Part of Any Peace Accord," New York Times, November 19, 1995; and "For Bosnia's President, An Agonizing Choice," New York Times, November 20, 1995.
31. See Holbrooke interview, November 18, 1996; Hill phone interview with author (notes), December 5, 1996; Holbrooke, To End a War, p. 280.
32. See Menzies interview; Holbrooke, Hill, Pauli comments, Dayton History Seminar; Holbrooke, To End a War, pp. 280–281.
33. See memorandum to Christopher from Holbrooke, "Closure or Close-down: The Situation as of 2 AM," November 17, 1995.
34. See Vershbow interview, July 23, 1996; Fuerth interview; "Sanctions Suspension Resolution," November 19,1995, 1:45 P.M. draft, COS files; Holbrooke, To End a War, p. 282.
35. See Kerrick report to Lake, "Dayton SITREP #12, November 17, 1995, 11:10am"; Holbrooke to Christopher, November 17, 1995; Holbrooke, To End a War, pp. 283–285.
36. Talbott memo to Berger, November 12, 1995; Talbott personal files.
37. See memorandum to Secretary Perry from James Pardew and Mark Sawoski, "Dayton Talks—Beginning the Third Week," November 16, 1995.
38. See Holbrooke to Christopher, November 17, 1995; Holbrooke interview with author (notes), December 20, 1996.
39. "Talking Points for SECDEF at Dayton," Pardew Dayton notebook; Kerrick report to Lake, "Dayton SITREP #13, November 17, 1995, 7pm"; Pardew memorandum to Slocombe, "SECDEF Visit to Dayton," November 16, 1995.

40. Perry interview with BBC, January 18, 1996, transcript; Holbrooke, *To End a War*, p. 286.
41. See Pardew report to Perry, November 16, 1995.
42. See "Status Report," November 17, 1995; Pardew to Perry, November 16, 1995; and memorandum to Holbrooke from Jack Zetkulic, "Elections: Endgame Tactics," November 16, 1995.
43. See "OSCE: OSCE Role in Bosnia Taking Shape," Cable, State 268884, November 17, 1995.
44. See Holbrooke to Christopher, November 17, 1995; Kerrick SITREP #13; and Holbrooke interview with author (notes), December 20, 1996.
45. See "Closing Scenario for Proximity Talks," November 18, 1995 draft, 7:00 P.M.; Holbrooke interview with author (notes), November 26, 1996; Holbrooke, *To End a War*, pp. 293–294.
46. Holbrooke, *To End a War*, pp. 294–295; Bildt, *Peace Journey*, p. 150.
47. See "Bosnia: Prime Minister's Conversation with President Izetbegovic," UK memorandum written by Roderic Lyne, Resident Clerk, Foreign and Commonwealth Office, 10 Downing Street, London; November 18, 1995; fax to Ambassador Marc Grossman, U.S. Embassy Ankara, from Jack Zetkulic, November 19, 1995; "Ankara to Play 'Active Role' to Establish Order in B-H," Cable, FBIS Tel Aviv 18573, November 11, 1995; Holbrooke, *To End a War*, p. 294.
48. See Holbrooke, Hill, Pardew, Owen comments, Dayton History Seminar; Menzies interview; Holbrooke interview with author (notes), November 26, 1996; Holbrooke, *To End a War*, p. 291; Christopher, *Chances of a Lifetime*, p. 263.
49. Holbrooke comment, Dayton History Seminar; Holbrooke, *To End a War*, p. 293.
50. Holbrooke, Pauli comments, Dayton History Seminar; Holbrooke, *To End a War*, pp. 293–294.
51. Holbrooke interview with author (notes) November 26, 1996; Menzies interview; Silber and Little, *Death of a Nation*, p. 374; and Holbrooke, *To End a War*, pp. 294–295.
52. Chris Hill phone interview with author (notes), December 5, 1996.
53. Chris Hill phone interview with author; Holbrooke, *To End a War*, p. 297.
54. See Tom Malinowski interview, October 30, 1996; and draft failure statement, no date (John Burley EUR/SCE files; Malinowski PA/S files; COS files); Holbrooke, *To End a War*, p. 298; Christopher, *In the Stream of History*, p. 356.
55. Holbrooke interview with author (notes), December 20, 1996; Christopher interview, October 22, 1996.
56. For details, see Holbrooke, Hill comments, Dayton History Seminar; Christopher interview, October 22, 1996; Hill interview, December 5, 1996; Holbrooke, *To End a War*, p. 300; Christopher, *Chances of a Lifetime*, p. 264.
57. Christopher interview, October 22, 1995; Bildt, *Peace Journey*, pp. 152–153.
58. See Christopher interview, October 22, 1995; Vershbow interview, December 17, 1996; Holbrooke interview with author (notes), December 20, 1996.
59. "Telephone Conversation with Croatian President Tudjman, November 20, 1995" NSC memorandum, December 4, 1995.
60. Holbrooke, *To End a War*, p. 303; Bildt, *Peace Journey*, p. 155.
61. See Rosemarie Pauli notes, Dayton notebook 3; Christopher interview, October 30, 1996; Vershbow interview, December 17, 1996; and Holbrooke, *To End a War*, p. 304.
62. Christopher interview, October 30, 1996; and Christopher, *Chances of a Lifetime*, p. 265.

63. See Christopher interviews, October 22 and 30, 1996; Holbrooke, *To End a War*, p. 305; Christopher, *Chances of a Lifetime*, p. 265.

64. Holbrooke interview with author (notes), December 20, 1996; Holbrooke, *To End a War*, p. 305.

65. See draft "failure" statement, PA Malinowski files; for interim agreement, see "Draft Closure Statement," Pardew Dayton notebook.

66. See Christopher interview, October 22, 1996; Holbrooke, Hill comments, Dayton History Seminar; and Holbrooke, *To End a War*, p. 305.

67. Vershbow interview, December 17, 1996; Holbrooke interview with author (notes), December 20, 1996; Clark, *Waging Modern War*, p. 67; Holbrooke, *To End a War*, p. 307; Talbott personal files.

68. Christopher interview, October 22, 1996; and Christopher, *Chances of a Lifetime*, p. 266.

69. Holbrooke comment, Dayton History Seminar; Christopher interview October 22, 1996; Holbrooke, *To End a War*, pp. 307–308.

70. Christopher interview, October 22, 1996; Holbrooke comment, Dayton History Seminar; and Kornblum/Owen interview.

71. Holbrooke interview with author (notes), December 20, 1996; Holbrooke, *To End a War*, pp. 308–309.

72. In 1999, Brcko was made into a special political district, with an appointed local government and an American supervisor with broad powers.

73. Holbrooke comment, Dayton History Seminar; Kornblum/Owen interview; Holbrooke, *To End a War*, pp. 308–309.

74. Holbrooke comment, Dayton History Seminar; Christopher interview, October 22, 1996.

75. See Statement by President Clinton, "Agreement Reached on Peace in the Balkans," U.S. Department of State *Dispatch*, December 1995, p. 18.

76. Christopher interview, October 22, 1995.

77. Pardew interview, June 27, 1996; Holbrooke, *To End a War*, p. 310.

78. Holbrooke and Christopher quotes from U.S. Department of State *Dispatch*, December 1995, pp. 14–17.

79. See Zimmermann, *Origins of a Catastrophe*, p. xii.

Epilogue

1. For example, Ivo Daalder gives his own five reasons for the Administration's decision to engage: the prospect of UNPROFOR's collapse; the threat to NATO; the possibility of U.S. troops entering Bosnia; congressional efforts to lift the arms embargo; and the political pressures around the upcoming 1996 presidential campaign. See Daalder, *Getting to Dayton*, pp. 162–166.

2. Quoted in James M. Goldgeier, *Not Whether But When: The U.S. Decision to Enlarge NATO* (Brookings, 1999), p. 98.

3. Daalder explains that the Croatian offensive, Milosevic's decision to speak for the Bosnian Serbs, and NATO's air campaign changed the "strategic landscape" to make Dayton possible, yet he underemphasizes the extent to which the Americans manipulated these factors to their advantage. See Daalder, *Getting to Dayton*, pp. 119–134.

4. Albright, *Madam Secretary*, p. 191.

5. Christopher, *In the Stream of History*, p. 350.

6. Clark, *Waging Modern War*, pp. 67–68.

7. See Daalder, *Getting to Dayton*, pp. 120–127.
8. Bildt interview; Tim Judah, *Kosovo: War and Revenge* (Yale University Press, 2000), pp. 120–126; Ivo Daalder and Michael O'Hanlon, *Winning Ugly: NATO's War to Save Kosovo* (Brookings, 2000), pp. 184–187.
9. Bildt, *Peace Journey*, p. 392; John Deutch, "Time to Pull Out. And Not Just From Iraq," *New York Times*, July 15, 2005.
10. Holbrooke, *To End a War*, p. 352; Holbrooke speech at the University of Sarajevo, October 27, 2000, available at <http://www.un.int.usa/00_152.htm>.
11. Holbrooke, *To End a War*, p. 363; Holbrooke speech before the Bosnian Parliament, Sarajevo, October 2, 2003, author's files; Bildt interview; Holbrooke interview with author, May 10, 2005.
12. Ibid.
13. See Sumantra Bose, *Bosnia After Dayton: Nationalist Partition and International Intervention* (Oxford University Press, 2002), p. 202; Thomas Friedman, "Not Happening," *New York Times*, January 23, 2001; and Shawcross, *Deliver Us From Evil*, p. 400.
14. Daalder, *Getting to Dayton*, p. 174.
15. See James Dobbins et al, *America's Role in Nation-Building: From Germany to Iraq* (RAND Corporation, 2003), p. 100; Bildt, *Peace Journey*, p. 109.
16. See Neville-Jones, "Dayton, IFOR, and Alliance Relations in Bosnia," pp. 51–52; Holbrooke, *To End a War*, p. 364; Clark, *Waging Modern War*, pp. 444–445; and Daalder, *Getting to Dayton*, pp. 153–159.
17. Berger interview, Halberstam, *War in a Time of Peace*, p. 359.
18. Holbrooke, *To End a War*, pp. 337–339; Albright, *Madam Secretary*, p. 265.
19. Holbrooke, *To End a War*, pp. 356–357; Albright, *Madam Secretary*, p. 271; Daalder, *Getting to Dayton*, pp. 174–178.
20. Edward Joseph, "Back to the Balkans," *Foreign Affairs* (January/February 2005), p. 115; Bildt, "Holbrooke's History," p. 189; Report of International Commission on the Balkans, *The Balkans in Europe's Future*, April 2005, p. 24.
21. See David Chandler, *Bosnia: Faking Democracy After Dayton* (Pluto Press, 1999); and Keith Brown, "Unraveling Europe's Raj," *Foreign Policy* (November/December 2003), pp. 84–85.
22. Pardew report, October 19, 1995; Belgrade 5122; and Belgrade 5030. For Holbrooke asking for the CIA document, see Holbrooke, *To End a War*, p. 212; and Bass, *Stay the Hand of Vengeance*, p. 236.
23. Pardew interview, June 27, 1996; Holbrooke, *To End a War*, p. 212; Bass, *Stay the Hand of Vengeance*, pp. 236–237.
24. Michael Ignatieff, *Virtual War: Kosovo and Beyond* (Metropolitan Books, 2000), p. 49; Shattuck, *Freedom on Fire*, p. 191.
25. See Daalder, *Getting to Dayton*, p. 181; and Paul R. Williams and Michael P. Scharf, *Peace with Justice? War Crimes and Accountability in the Former Yugoslavia* (Rowman and Littlefield, 2000).
26. Asmus, *Opening NATO's Door*, p. 124; Christopher, *In the Stream of History*, p. 358.
27. John Norris, *Collision Course: NATO, Russia, and Kosovo* (Praeger, 2005).
28. Daalder, *Getting to Dayton*, p. 188.
29. Holbrooke, *To End a War*, p. 361; Harris, *The Survivor*, p. 321; and Stephen Sestanovich, "American Maximalism," *The National Interest* (Spring 2005).
30. Bildt, *Peace Journey*, p. 387.

SOURCES

Unless otherwise specified, all of the U.S. government documents cited in this book were collected and organized in 1996 by a special State Department initiative to create an archive of records concerning the Bosnia peace process. This collection includes, for example, all cables from the State Department's central records management system concerning Bosnia and the Dayton negotiations; all relevant files from the State Department's European Bureau (including internal e-mail and computer databases); Operations Center "Watch Reports" and telephone logs; "out-of-system" documents; State Department intelligence (INR) reports; and personal notes and memoranda of numerous senior officials. It also includes any records from other government agencies, such as the National Security Council, Department of Defense, or CIA, that were sent to the State Department originally (for example, the NSC's "Summary of Conclusions" from Deputies or Principals Committee Meetings) or provided by individuals specifically for the archive (such as Jim Pardew's memoranda to Secretary of Defense William Perry, or Ambassador Peter Galbraith's daily "Diplomatic Diary"). While this archive regrettably remains unavailable to the public, the endnotes can be used to request documents through the Freedom of Information Act—a process that, working with Tom Blanton and Malcolm Byrne at the National Security Archive, I have initiated. And my hope is that the archive's entire contents will be available soon so that it can become an invaluable resource for all scholars of this critical period in U.S. diplomatic history.

In addition to this substantial documentary collection—which fills more than ten file-drawers—this book includes information and insights from nearly 60 hours of interviews with over 40 officials involved in the negotiations. Most of these original interviews have been transcribed and are stored in this special archive, and they too are cited in the endnotes. Such interviews—most of which were conducted less than a year after the Dayton peace process—enabled me to bring the documents to life, identifying ones of particular importance and placing them in the context with which they were used or read. Notable among these interviews is a day-long, video-taped "Dayton History Seminar" held at the Foreign Service Institute on June 26, 1996, in which the core shuttle team—Clark, Hill, Holbrooke, Kerrick, Owen, Pardew, and Rosemarie Pauli—joined several other State Department officials to discuss the events leading to Dayton.

These original records have been supplemented by my recent interviews with Sandy Berger, Carl Bildt, General George Joulwan (retired), Anthony Lake, and Walter Slocombe, as well as the many hours I have spent discussing these events and issues informally with several participants, including Warren Christopher, Richard Holbrooke, Strobe Talbott, Chris Hill, Jim O'Brien, Peter Bass, and Phil Goldberg. I have also relied upon many public sources, such as newspaper accounts, memoirs by many of the key American and European participants—especially Madeleine Albright, Carl Bildt, Warren Christopher, General Wesley Clark, President Bill Clinton, Richard Holbrooke, Anthony Lake, William Perry, and Strobe Talbott—and other histories and analyses of the events described here. What follows are those that I found particularly useful.

Albright, Madeleine with Bill Woodward. *Madam Secretary: A Memoir*. New York: Miramax Books, 2003.

Asmus, Ronald D. *Opening NATO's Door: How the Alliance Remade Itself for a New Era*. New York: Columbia University Press, 2002.

Baker, James A. III with Thomas M. DeFrank. *The Politics of Diplomacy: War, Revolution, and Peace, 1989–1992*. New York: G.P. Putnam's Sons, 1995.

Bass, Gary Jonathan. *Stay the Hand of Vengeance: The Politics of War Crimes Tribunals*. Princeton: Princeton University Press, 2000.

Bert, Wayne. *The Reluctant Superpower: United States' Policy in Bosnia, 1991–95*. New York: St. Martin's Press, 1997.

Bildt, Carl. *Peace Journey: The Struggle for Peace in Bosnia*. London: Weidenfeld and Nicolson, 1998.

Bose, Sumantra. *Bosnia after Dayton: Nationalist Partition and International Intervention*. New York: Oxford University Press, 2002.

Boutros-Ghali, Boutros. *Unvanquished: A U.S.-U.N. Saga*. New York: Random House, 1999.

Burg, Stephen L. and Paul S. Shoup. *The War in Bosnia-Herzegovina: Ethnic Conflict and International Intervention*. London: M.E. Sharpe, 1999.

Carter, Ashton B. and William J. Perry. *Preventive Defense: A New Strategy for America*. Washington: Brookings Institution Press, 1999.

Chandler, David. *Bosnia: Faking Democracy after Dayton*. London: Pluto Press, 1999.

Christopher, Warren. *Chances of a Lifetime*. New York: Scribner, 2001.

——. *In The Stream of History: Shaping Foreign Policy for a New Era*. Stanford: Stanford University Press, 1998.

Clark, Wesley, K. *Waging Modern War: Bosnia, Kosovo, and the Future of Combat*. New York: Public Affairs, 2001.

Clinton, Bill. *My Life*. New York: Knopf, 2004.

Cohen, Roger. *Hearts Grown Brutal: Sagas of Sarajevo*. New York: Random House, 1998.

Crnobrnja, Mihailo. *The Yugoslav Drama*. Montreal & Kingston: McGill-Queen's University Press, 1994.

Daalder, Ivo H. *Getting to Dayton: The Making of America's Bosnia Policy*. Washington: Brookings Institution Press, 2000.

—— and Michael E. O'Hanlon. *Winning Ugly: NATO's War to Save Kosovo*. Washington: Brookings Institution Press, 2000.

Dobbins, James, et al. *America's Role in Nation-Building: From Germany to Iraq*. Washington, DC: RAND Corporation, 2003.

Doder, Dusko and Louise Branson. *Milosevic: Portrait of a Tyrant*. New York: The Free Press, 1999.

Drew, Elizabeth. *Showdown: The Struggle Between the Gingrich Congress and the Clinton White House*. New York: Simon & Schuster, 1996.

Glenny, Misha. *The Fall of Yugoslavia: The Third Balkan War*. Third rev. ed. New York: Penguin, 1996.

Goldgeier, James M. *Not Whether But When: The U.S. Decision to Enlarge NATO*. Washington: Brookings Institution Press, 1999.

—— and Michael McFaul. *Power and Purpose: U.S. Policy Toward Russia after the Cold War*. Washington: Brookings Institution Press, 2003.

Gow, James. *Triumph of the Lack of Will*. New York: Columbia University Press, 1996.

Halberstam, David. *War in a Time of Peace: Bush, Clinton, and the Generals.* New York: Simon & Schuster, 2001.

Harris, John. *The Survivor: Bill Clinton in the White House.* New York: Random House, 2005.

Holbrooke, Richard. *To End a War.* New York: Random House, 1998.

Honig, Jan Willem and Norbert Both. *Srebrenica: Record of a War Crime.* New York: Penguin, 1997.

Ignatieff, Michael. *Virtual War: Kosovo and Beyond.* New York: Metropolitan Books, 2000.

International Commission on the Balkans. *Unfinished Peace: A Report.* Foreword by Leo Tindemans. Washington: Carnegie Endowment for International Peace, 1996.

———. *The Balkans in Europe's Future.* April 2005. Available at www.balkan-commission.org

Judah, Tim. *Kosovo: War and Revenge.* New Haven: Yale University Press, 2000.

Lake, Anthony. *Six Nightmares: Real Threats in a Dangerous World and How America Can Meet Them.* New York: Little, Brown and Company, 2000.

Le Bor, Adam. *Milosevic: A Biography.* New Haven: Yale University Press, 2004.

Mazower, Mark. *The Balkans: A Short History.* New York: The Modern Library, 2000.

Morris, Dick. *Behind the Oval Office: Getting Reelected against All Odds.* Los Angeles: Renaissance Books, 1999.

Murdock, Clark A. *Improving the Practice of National Security Strategy.* Washington: CSIS Press, 2004.

Norris, John. *Collision Course: NATO, Russia, and Kosovo.* London: Praeger, 2005.

Owen, David. *Balkan Odyssey.* New York: Harcourt Brace & Company, 1996.

Owen, Colonel Robert C., ed. *Deliberate Force: A Case Study in Effective Air Campaigning.* Maxwell Air Force Base, Alabama: Air University Press, 2000.

Power, Samantha. *"A Problem From Hell": America and the Age of Genocide.* New York: Basic Books, 2002.

Rathbun, Brian C. *Partisan Interventions: European Party Politics and Peace Enforcement in the Balkans.* Ithaca: Cornell University Press, 2004.

Rohde, David. *Endgame: The Betrayal and Fall of Srebrenica, Europe's Worst Massacre Since World War II.* New York: Farrar, Straus and Giroux, 1997.

Rosegrant, Susan. "Getting to Dayton: Negotiating an End to the War in Bosnia." A case study from the John F. Kennedy School of Government, Harvard University, 1996.

Rothkopf, David. *Running the World: The Inside Story of the National Security Council and the Architects of American Power.* New York: Public Affairs, 2005.

Sell, Louis. *Slobodan Milosevic and the Destruction of Yugoslavia.* Durham and London: Duke University Press, 2002.

Shattuck, John. *Freedom on Fire: Human Rights Wars and America's Response.* Cambridge: Harvard University Press, 2003.

Shawcross, William. *Deliver Us from Evil: Peacekeepers, Warlords, and a World of Endless Conflict.* New York: Simon & Schuster, 2000.

Silber, Laura and Allan Little. *Yugoslavia: Death of a Nation.* Rev. ed. London: Penguin Books/BBC Books, 1996.

Soderberg, Nancy. *The Superpower Myth: The Use and Misuse of American Might.* Hoboken: John Wiley & Sons, Inc., 2005.

Stephanopoulos, George. *All Too Human: A Political Education.* New York: Little, Brown and Company, 1999.

Talbott, Strobe. *The Russia Hand: A Memoir of Presidential Diplomacy*. New York: Random House, 2002.

Touval, Saadia. *Mediation in the Yugoslav Wars: The Critical Years, 1990–95*. New York: Palgrave, 2002.

Ullmann, Richard H., ed. *The World and Yugoslavia's Wars*. New York: Council on Foreign Relations, 1996.

Williams, Paul R. and Michael P. Scharf. *Peace with Justice? War Crimes and Accountability in the Former Yugoslavia*. Oxford: Rowman and Littlefield, 2002.

Woodward, Bob. *The Choice*. New York: Simon & Schuster, 1996.

Woodward, Susan L. *Balkan Tragedy*. Washington: Brookings Institution Press, 1995.

Zelikow, Philip and Condoleezza Rice. *Germany Unified and Europe Transformed: A Study in Statecraft*. Cambridge: Harvard University Press, 1995.

Zimmermann, Warren. *Origins of a Catastrophe: Yugoslavia and Its Destroyers*. New York: Times Books, 1996.

INDEX

73128018R00153

Made in the USA
San Bernardino, CA
01 April 2018